Yerba Mate

CALIFORNIA STUDIES IN FOOD AND CULTURE
Darra Goldstein, Editor

Yerba Mate

THE DRINK THAT SHAPED A NATION

Julia J. S. Sarreal

UNIVERSITY OF CALIFORNIA PRESS

University of California Press
Oakland, California

Library of Congress Cataloging-in-Publication Data

Names: Sarreal, Julia J. S., author.
Title: Yerba mate : the drink that shaped a nation / Julia J. S. Sarreal.
Other titles: California studies in food and culture ; 79.
Description: Oakland, California : University of California Press, [2022] |
    Series: California studies in food and culture ; 79 | Includes bibliographical
    references and index.
Identifiers: LCCN 2022022425 (print) | LCCN 2022022426 (ebook) |
    ISBN 9780520379275 (cloth) | ISBN 9780520379282 (paperback) | ISBN
    9780520976603 (ebook)
Subjects: LCSH: Mate (Tea)—Argentina—History. | Mate (Tea)—Social
    aspects—Argentina. | Mate (Tea) industry—Argentina—History.
Classification: LCC GT2920.M3 S37 2022 (print) | LCC GT2920.M3 (ebook) |
    DDC 394.1/5—dc23/eng/20220525
LC record available at https://lccn.loc.gov/2022022425
LC ebook record available at https://lccn.loc.gov/2022022426
ISBN 978-0-520-37927-5 (cloth)
ISBN 978-0-520-37928-2 (pbk.)
ISBN 978-0-520-97660-3 (ebook)

32   31   30   29   28   27   26   25   24   23
10   9   8   7   6   5   4   3   2   1

For my three boys—John, Félix, and Benicio

CONTENTS

ACKNOWLEDGMENTS

The roots of this project go back over twenty years to when my husband and I were Peace Corps volunteers in rural Paraguay. For more than two years, we spent hours building relationships while sharing tereré or mate with Paraguayans whose friendship we prize to this day. Tereré with *yuyos* (herbs) was especially refreshing on hot days, while mate warmed my body and soul on cold days and early mornings. Sometimes, I drank so much of the caffeinated beverage that I had trouble sleeping at night. Several years later, while living in Buenos Aires and conducting dissertation research, my intellectual interest in yerba mate was sparked. I was struck that almost every street corner had a café, and yet supermarket shelves were also filled with yerba mate. I wondered how coffee culture and yerba mate culture could both be so strong. And thus started an almost a decade-long intellectual exploration of yerba mate.

One of the most exhilarating aspects of this project has been the shared enthusiasm for yerba mate that I've encountered. Many Argentines and scholars of Argentina have been happy to share their thoughts and stories about mate, and a number have also generously shared useful information and documents. In this respect, I am especially grateful to Nicolás Sillitti, Diego Armus, Mariana Katz, Shawn Austin, Jeff Erbig, Billy Acree, Alex Borucki, Magdalena Candioti, Jennifer Adair, Patricia Aguirre, María Elsa Zapata, and Guillaume Candela. Another highlight was spending extended periods of time in Argentina. Pau Navajas spent hours conversing with me about yerba mate and provided helpful feedback on the entire manuscript. Jerónimo Lagier, Javier Ricci, and Rebekah Pite also shared their insights about yerba mate. Numerous friends, and especially other mothers from Colegio del Salvador, invited me to share mate and were willing participants in my yerba tastings. In Misiones and Corrientes, various yerba growers and processors taught me about how yerba mate is grown and processed. I will always remember the warm welcome and my many adventures in *la tierra colorada.*

I need to thank the staff members of the numerous archives and libraries that I consulted for this project, including the Biblioteca Nacional Argentina, Biblioteca Tornquist, Archivo General de la Nación, Archivo de Indias, John Carter Brown Library, and Huntington Library. When I was starting my research, Yovanna Pineda suggested libraries at an assortment of government ministries. Patricia León at Biblioteca Tornquist and Judith Gociol at the Biblioteca Nacional Argentina were especially helpful at tracking down documents. I am grateful to Fernando Rocchi and Pau Navajas for putting me in contact with Juan Trenado at the Archivo de Redacción at *La Nación* and to Diego Armus for introducing me to Sebastian Alonso at the Archivo de Redacción at *Clarín.* Both of those archives hold treasure troves of documents related to yerba mate. Florencia Levín, Elisa Pastoriza, Elisa Medrano, Juan Pablo Dobal, and Gabriel Di Meglio generously helped me get permission for various images for the book.

Grants and fellowships helped facilitate research and writing. At Arizona State University, the Institute for Humanities Research provided both a seed grant at the beginning of the project and a writing fellowship at the end, and Scholarship, Research, and Creative Activities grants funded summer research trips. A Helen Watson Buckner Memorial Fellowship enabled summer research at the John Carter Brown Library and an Andrew W. Mellon Foundation Fellowship facilitated summer research at the Huntington Library.

I am very grateful for feedback from everyone who generously agreed to read chapters of the manuscript. Kris Lane and Matt Karush provided important guidance at key stages of the project. Participants in the Río de la Plata Workshop (including Fabricio Prado, Alex Borucki, Lyman Johnson, Viviana Grieco, Brian Bockelman, Jeff Shumway, Ariel de la Fuente, Erika Edwards, Gabriel Di Meglio, Vitor Izecksohn, and Gustavo Paz) gave helpful feedback on several iterations of early chapters, along with cheerful encouragement and scholarly camaraderie. Ben Bryce, Natalia Milanesio, Ernesto Semán, Paula Halperin, Rebecca Stephanis, Shawn Austin, Brian Owensby, Kittiya Lee, James Woodard, and Marcy Norton provided valuable comments and suggestions on specific chapters. Kate Marshall at the University of California Press was enthusiastic about this project from early on, and I am grateful for her support and encouragement. Enrique Ochoa-Kaup made the publication process move forward smoothly. Chris Lura's edits made the arguments clearer and the text easier to read. I am immensely grateful to my writing group: Thomas Field, who read repeated drafts and gave insightful recommendations from the very beginning of the project, and Matt Casey-Pariseault, who later joined our group and provided another perspective. Our biweekly meetings not only led to a better book, but to friendship.

I could not have written this book without the support of my family. I first encountered yerba mate in Paraguay with my husband, John. He has unceasingly supported my intellectual passions and I look forward to many more years of sharing mate and tereré. My children, Félix and Benicio, have been my research companions throughout the project, spending protracted periods of time in Argentina, Spain, and Rhode Island. I treasure our many shared adventures and I look forward to sharing mate and tereré as both become adults.

Introduction

ONE SPRING DAY IN 2017, Cinthia Solange Dhers decided she'd had enough. She was tired of the noise her neighbors made at her weekend home in a resort-like housing development in Nordelta, a chic area just outside of Buenos Aires. Their dog barked and the kids yelled, and she abhorred their poor manners. But worst of all, said Dhers—who described herself as a fifty-three-year-old surgeon and average woman—when she looked out towards the big lake that bordered the property, she felt she couldn't visually relax. Her neighbors, she explained, were always out there, drinking mate and acting as though the housing development's waterfront space was just another lower-class beach like those at Bristol in Mar del Plata. In a voicemail message to her real estate agent, Dr. Dhers noted that, when she purchased the one-bedroom apartment for $200,000 US, she had thought the building had a cooler and more relaxed vibe. Instead, she found her neighbors to be "people of the lowest social category" ("*gente muy de cuarta y tiene modales de décima categoría*"). In the five-and-a-half-minute voicemail message, Dr. Dhers berated the neighbors at length. Now, she said angrily, she regretted her purchase and was ready to sell if things didn't improve.

Things, as it turned out, did not improve for Dr. Dhers, and her voicemail did not have the desired effect. Instead, it went viral, circulating widely on social media throughout Argentina. Stories about it even appeared in national and international news (including the *New York Times*). Actors impersonated Dr. Dhers, numerous memes made fun of the recording, and it became a provocative symbol of the deep class tensions in Argentina today. In her long message, Dr. Dhers was particularly focused on the way her neighbors sat around drinking mate (pronounced *mah-tey*). Both a drink and a social activity, mate is typically enjoyed by a small group of people leisurely conversing while a gourd filled with yerba mate (*Ilex paraguariensis*) and hot water is repeatedly passed around with each person drinking the liquid from the same metal straw (*bombilla*). As Dr. Dhers explained to her realtor, "The truth is that I cannot enjoy being in Nordelta, looking at the lake and seeing people who, with a lounge chair like at Bristol at Mar del Plata, go to the dock and drink mate."[1] Mate, she adamantly believed, should not be drunk publicly in a place like Nordelta. She called her neighbors "beasts without an education" who, with their constant mate drinking, were people of the lowest social standing. In response, Argentines rallied in defense of mate. Instead of drawing her realtor to her cause, the circulation of Dr. Dhers's diatribe against mate led to public outrage across the country, and she became the butt of many jokes.

The story of this viral voice message and the massive response to it are part of a bigger story about yerba mate and class tensions in Argentina, and this is a story that is very, very old. Yerba mate has been a part of the culture in Argentina and neighboring countries in South America since before "Argentina" or "South America" ever existed, and class tensions surrounding mate date back to the arrival of the Europeans. Mate was originally a beverage that was woven into the cultural life of Indigenous peoples living in the region that now makes up Argentina, Brazil, and Paraguay, and which would later become incorporated to varying degrees into the cultures of those nation-states. In Argentina, mate has a distinctive history, and a central place in the country's cultural heritage. Hailed as a basic necessity, the precise form of its centrality within the cultural practices of Argentina has been in constant evolution, often shifting based on larger political and economic changes in the country. After independence from Spain, it became a custom practiced along class lines. Long associated with the working and rural classes, mate—as both a beverage and a social practice—remains symbolic of a history of class identity and class tensions in Argentina.

Despite the fact that today it is not considered politically correct to demean and insult mate drinkers as a degenerate class, as Dr. Dhers did, it is also true that mate continues to be viewed by some people in Argentine society as a backward cultural practice. In March 2020, for example, Fernando Iglesias, a conservative congressman from Buenos Aires, made clear his views about mate drinking on Twitter, noting that the coronavirus pandemic was "a good time to completely eradicate the horrible custom of mate, responsible for the country's decline." After receiving widespread criticism, the congressman quickly backtracked, calling his statement "a small and ironic tweet that clearly said something so absurd."[2] He further clarified that he didn't have anything against mate, but he didn't particularly like it himself. The congressman's quick effort to take back his comment pointed to the fact that mate remains a culturally and politically potent topic in Argentina.

There is also another story behind Iglesias and Dhers's comments about mate, which is that urban, middle-class Argentines feel their social status threatened by the cultural and economic power of the popular classes and their own declining socio-economic position. Although the present tension in Argentina's evolving social hierarchies is due to economic and cultural changes in recent decades, it is unsurprising that drinking mate would end up being discussed during debates surrounding that social tension. Indeed, as this book explains, yerba mate, whose importance as a cultural practice in Argentina easily rivals the cultural importance of tea in India or England, or coffee in France or Italy, has been frequently, and historically, highlighted during major political or cultural debates in Argentina. People of all social classes have, since before Argentina was even a nation, used mate as a rhetorical symbol to try to shape the organization of power and cultural identity in the region. In Argentina, its consumption and cultivation have also long been at the center of key debates about economic policy and the distribution of essential government resources. As the chapters in this book outline, the story of yerba mate in Argentina is interwoven with the full political, cultural, and economic evolution of the country. Indeed, it is not unreasonable to say that to understand the history of yerba mate in Argentina is to understand how and why Argentina became the nation that it is today.

THE IMPORTANCE OF YERBA MATE IN ARGENTINA

Argentina is the world's largest producer, consumer, and exporter of yerba mate. Almost all Argentines have the caffeinated drink and its specialized paraphernalia in their kitchens; market shelves are stocked with dozens of brands; and poems, songs, and websites eulogize it. In 2013, the Argentine government declared mate the official national infusion. Although yerba mate is grown in Argentina, Paraguay and southern Brazil, in 2016 the Argentine government sought to assert its primacy in international markets by making "*Yerba Mate Argentina*" an official geographic indication (*indicación geográfica*) like "French champagne" and "Mexican tequila." Despite such official support of the country's "national infusion" and the complex place of yerba mate in Argentine culture, very few Argentine cafés or restaurants even serve mate. This is because many Buenos Aires elite, until fairly recently, would not publicly drink it, nor even admit to drinking it. This historically-rooted rejection of mate by Argentina's upper and middle classes has also led scholars to overlook the importance of yerba mate in Argentina and nearby countries, or to treat it as an afterthought.[3]

Yerba mate's roots as a consumable beverage and cultural practice go back well before Argentina became an independent nation in 1816. Comparably to how tea is engrained in India's cultural practices, yerba mate is a beverage intricately woven into the development of Argentine culture. But tea, along with coffee, became a global commodity during the colonial era. The spread of capitalism and imperialism in the seventeenth, eighteenth, and nineteenth centuries further drove the spread of products like tea and coffee, as well as others like cotton, sugar—and in the twentieth century, Coca-Cola—turning them into commonplace, everyday items for people around the world.[4] Yerba mate is different. Although companies and entrepreneurs have repeatedly tried to find mass markets for yerba mate outside of southern South America—where, in striking contrast, it is ubiquitous and commonplace—those efforts, as this book discusses, have repeatedly ended in failure. There are a number of reasons why yerba mate, despite being poised for such global expansion during the Spanish empire in Latin America, didn't achieve global status, most notably the commercial policies of the Spanish Crown. But even as the world would largely be deprived of another hot caffeinated beverage to rival coffee and tea, Argentina, like Paraguay, Uruguay, and southern Brazil, has persisted in embracing the practice of consuming yerba mate. This is particularly true among Argentina's popular classes, where common people continue to consume it in traditional ways, repeatedly resisting elite efforts at changing these practices.

As this book documents, mate has been at the center of Argentina's economics, culture, and even politics from the colonial era all the way through the twentieth century. Long prior to the arrival of Europeans in South America, yerba mate was consumed in the region by Indigenous peoples. They harvested the leaves of yerba trees that grew naturally in the wild (*yerbales,* in Spanish), drying the leaves and then preparing the infusion in a gourd in much the same way that people still do today in Argentina. Because of its centrality in the region, Spanish authorities used yerba mate as a medium for managing empire, exploiting native peoples for their labor and turning yerba into a taxable commodity. After Argentina became an independent nation in the nineteenth century, mate remained a central feature of its culture, even as the consumption, production, and various ideas about this caffeinated beverage exposed the contradictions and challenges of Argentine identity. Looking back over this remarkable history, this book describes how yerba mate, once an Indigenous staple, has played a key role in shaping Argentina's history, helping unify diverse populations and define territorial boundaries to create Argentina while also exposing divisions and fissures as it remained a point of contention between socio-economic classes. As the history of mate in Argentina demonstrates, it is the everyday actions of common people—and not just state policies and elite discourse—that shape the nation.

In addition to Argentina, yerba mate has an important place in the cultures of countries throughout the Río de la Plata region of southern South America. Mate and tereré (yerba mate drunk with cold water) are consumed not only in Argentina, but also in Paraguay, Uruguay, and southern Brazil. Mate is deeply meaningful to the people throughout this region. This shared significance points to a regional identity that extends beyond national borders. As such, any study of yerba mate is necessarily transnational. And yet, yerba mate has had a unique trajectory in Argentina—unlike in other countries in the region, the consumption of yerba mate in Argentina has long been associated with class, marked as unsophisticated or backward, with elites looking down on the popular classes who consume it. Consequently, the evolution of yerba mate as a cultural practice in Argentina is also tightly tied to broader shifts in the country's national identity.

By merging economic and cultural history and applying a *longue durée* approach to commodity history, this book reveals both continuity and change from pre-Columbian times to the turn of the twenty-first century. The history of mate in Argentina is also connected to the historic suppression of indigeneity in Argentina. For example, the first people to consume yerba mate were the Kaingang or Guaraní, two neighboring peoples who lived in the region prior to the arrival of Spanish rule. Because of this deep history, yerba mate is frequently celebrated by Argentines as a marker of cultural authenticity and something truly autochthonous to southern South America. At the same time, in Argentine popular culture, mate is more frequently associated with the *gaucho* (cowboy) than with the native peoples who discovered it. This preference for associating mate with the gaucho in popular culture points to a broader "whitening" of the traditions of mate, something that intersects with a much larger "whitening" of Argentine identity that occurred over the course of the nineteenth and twentieth centuries.

For nearly as long as Argentina has existed, yerba mate has been a barometer of its social and demographic shifts, and the accompanying anxieties these shifts have engendered in the population. These shifts followed key social changes and cultural trends. During the colonial era, yerba mate evolved from an Indigenous staple to a commodity consumed by all races, classes, genders, and social groups. Over the nineteenth century, however, as a part of a broader suppression of Argentina's Indigenous heritage, it became known as the drink of the gaucho and of the countryside. Moreover, it transitioned into a clandestine beverage of the Buenos Aires elite, who publicly emulated European tea and coffee culture. In the early twentieth century, as part of an effort to increase the prestige and economic profits from the sale and production of yerba, businessmen and intellectuals unsuccessfully tried to reshape yerba mate consumption into a more hygienic form of tea or iced beverage. But the tradition of sharing mate—drinking from the same bombilla and gourd, among friends—remained strong, particularly as immigrants integrating into Argentina became the most fervent mate drinkers. Nevertheless, even as the traditional methods of drinking mate persisted, from the late 1940s to the 1980s, per capita consumption, partly due to the cultural and political movements associated with Peronism, went through a long period of decline as the popular associations with mate conflicted with ideas of modernity and a dignified middle-class lifestyle.

And yet, the practice still continued to be widespread and meaningful for many Argentines. And at the turn of the twenty-first century, mate's popularity came roaring back. It re-emerged as a trendy social activity associated with authentic *Argentinidad*. In contrast to *criollo* (Creole) cuisine of the Americas, mate did not blend global and local food traditions.[5] Rather, mate's widespread acceptance in the 1990s and 2000s as an authentic marker of *Argentinidad* emerged in the context of neoliberal reforms and globalization as a rejection of the foreign and a celebration of the autochthonous and social connectedness. These recent shifts in the way yerba mate is perceived among people in Argentina, which are described in detail later in this book, underscore the enduring role of yerba mate as a site for the negotiation of Argentine identity.

YERBA MATE AND THE ARGENTINE ECONOMY

In Argentina, yerba mate is produced in Misiones and northeast Corrientes, a region located approximately six hundred miles north of the industrial and

MAP I. Map of South America. Credit: Gabriel Moss.

pastoral core of Buenos Aires and the pampas. Misiones and northeast Corrientes are on the borderland region where the frontiers of Argentina meet Paraguay and Brazil. Most yerba mate consumers have never seen the tree or visited the far northeastern part of the country where it grows. Consequently, despite mate's immense popularity, the region where it is produced remains largely unknown to those who consume it. In contrast, the pampas are widely known for their production of beef and wheat, two products synonymous with Argentina's criollo identity. This ignorance about the country's northeastern borderlands has shaped the political economy surrounding yerba mate, as politicians and power brokers repeatedly enact policies that overlook or are detrimental to yerba mate, prioritizing instead other economic sectors that favor urban areas and the region between the Paraná and Uruguay Rivers. Policymaking in Argentina around yerba mate has also long been shaped by widely competing economic interests, and by the wild fluctuations in Argentina's economic strength. The debates in Argentina about the best ways to grow and stabilize the economy—whether to prioritize protectionism vs. free trade, industry vs. agriculture, efficient large-scale plantations vs. diversified small farms, consumers vs. producers, or labor vs. capital—are economic debates deeply interwoven with the politics and class debates surrounding the consumption of yerba mate.

Like chocolate and tobacco, yerba mate is a stimulant that originated in the Americas and had profound meaning for Indigenous peoples. After initially expressing distaste for all three substances and claiming that they had diabolical origins, European settlers in the regions of origin became avid consumers.[6] Benefiting from Spanish trade policies that prioritized Mesoamerica, both chocolate and tobacco traveled to Europe, but yerba mate did not become an important part of this early trade. Later, even as mate consumption in South America expanded, Spain's restrictive trade policies severely limited exchanges between the Río de la Plata region and Europe all the way until the second half of the eighteenth century. By that point, coffee and tea had already taken hold in Europe, and mate did not gain a foothold within those now established European drinking customs.

Although consumption remained relegated to the Río de la Plata region of South America, ever since the colonial period proponents have repeatedly praised yerba mate and lauded its potential as an inexpensive substitute for coffee and tea. This praise did not lead mate to catch on in European markets, but it did help it spread in other regions. For example, mate is widely popular in Syria and Lebanon, where immigrants returning from Argentina brought it home. In the early years of the twenty-first century, yerba mate consumption has also been growing in the United States and Europe as an energy drink consumed in the form of a high-priced iced tea or carbonated beverage. But yerba mate's broader failure to globalize reveals a story of continuity and change, resistance and amalgamation.

By exploring both the consumption and production of yerba mate, the book engages two methodologies that are difficult to combine: cultural studies and political economy. It is based on an innovative combination of diverse sources (such as Guaraní dictionaries, Council of Indies records, government documents, newspaper articles, statistics, travelers' accounts, advertising, cartoons, literature, and film) that yield a nuanced and complex understanding of yerba mate and Argentine history. Looking at Argentina's history from the pre-Columbian period through the twentieth century, this book reveals a number of important continuities and ruptures in the development of Argentine national identity and class-based consumption, while simultaneously illuminating mate's role as a transnational commodity and practice.

WHAT IS YERBA MATE?

Yerba mate is a mild caffeinated stimulant. About an hour after entering the body, caffeine reaches its peak level in the bloodstream and remains there for four to six hours. Caffeine energizes and improves mental alertness by stimulating the central nervous system. Sometimes, it has negative side effects such as anxiety, insomnia, increased urination, heartburn, heart palpitations, tremors, and high blood pressure. Abruptly discontinuing caffeine consumption can lead to withdrawal symptoms including headaches, muscle aches, temporary depression, and irritability.[7] Determining yerba mate's caffeine content is difficult because it varies based on growing conditions, processing, and brewing. By one measure, a cup of coffee has approximately 85 mg of caffeine while a round of mate (500 ml) has 260 mg or more.[8] As with coffee, tea and alcohol, most people do not initially like the flavor of yerba mate. It is bitter and earthy. Many people say it tastes like dirt and grass. It is an acquired taste.

Mate rituals distinguish it from other caffeinated beverages and have special meaning for consumers. Mate is most typically shared. One person is the *cebador* (server) who oversees the mate round: refilling the mate gourd with water, passing it to each person, making sure that the bombilla is set properly, and adding new yerba when the old yerba becomes *lavado* (flavorless). The round continues for at least thirty minutes, if not several hours. People build connection and intimacy with each other by passing around the mate and drinking from the same bombilla. Although mate is most typically shared, people who drink it by themselves frequently claim that it provides them companionship. Drinking mate requires more engagement than coffee or tea. Instead of simply raising a cup and drinking from it, mate consumers have to stop what they are doing in order to pour water from a thermos into a mate gourd, and then they raise the bombilla to their mouths. Drinking mate also lasts longer than other caffeinated beverages: cups of coffee and tea are generally finished in less than a half an hour, before they get cold. In contrast, the mate gourd is refilled with hot water from the thermos again and again, often for hours at a time.

Until recently, people from outside Latin America only experienced yerba mate if they visited southern South America or if they had friends from the region. But over the past decade or so, yerba mate has also become increasingly available in stores and upscale tea shops in Western Europe and the United States. Most Americans know it as an energy drink and its purported health benefits are widely promoted. Scientific studies claim that it lowers cholesterol, protects the liver, stimulates the central nervous system, acts as a diuretic and an antioxidant, benefits the cardiovascular system, etc.[9] Popular medicine and herbalists recommend yerba mate for fatigue, arthritis, headaches, obesity, fluid retention, slow digestion, constipation, hemorrhoids, rheumatism, hypertension, and hepatic disorders.[10] Some of the drink's health effects are undoubtedly exaggerated—but yerba mate and health are subjects frequently tied together in consumers' minds. A 2021 Google search of "yerba mate health benefits" yields over half a million results.

HISTORY IN A NAME

The history of naming yerba mate is complex, slightly messy, and politically charged. As such, understanding how yerba mate came to be named yerba mate exemplifies the goals and the scope of this book. It is a complicated history of conquest, imperialism, nationalism, Indigenous persistence, and reinvention. Yerba mate originated among the Indigenous peoples of South America who called it *caá* (Guaraní) and *côgôî* (Kaingang). When Spaniards encountered it, they called it "yerba." Changing the name from an Indigenous term to a Spanish term was a form of conquest, transforming an Indian good into a Spanish good. The use of "yerba" not only exposes the Spaniards' disrespect for native nomenclature, it also reveals their ignorance of the natural environment. "Yerba" is a misnomer. The English translation of "yerba" or

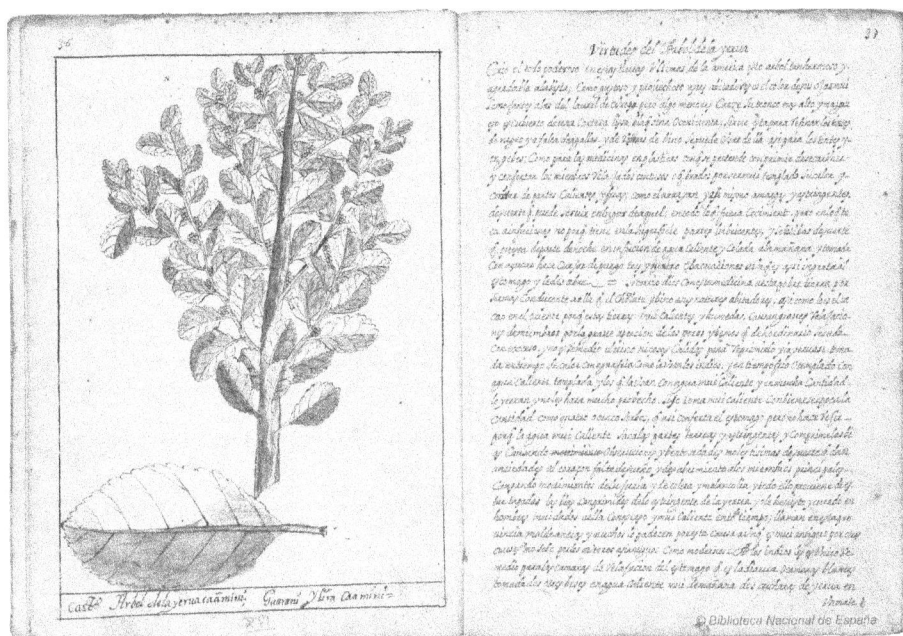

FIGURE 1. Drawing of a yerba tree. Pedro de Montenegro, "Libro primero de la propiedad y virtudes de los árboles y plantas de las Misiones y Provincia del Tucumán" (1711). Courtesy of the Biblioteca Nacional de España.

hierba is "herb," which is a plant with a soft stem. In contrast, yerba mate is a tree with a woody trunk.[11]

Early on, Spaniards also sometimes mistakenly called it "coca," conflating it with the Andean plant whose leaves native peoples have chewed since before European contact and which is the source of cocaine. For example, less than twenty years after the founding of Paraguay's capital city Asunción, a Spanish priest wrote that coca is the herb that Indians and Christians drink with water.[12] Such authors might have thought that coca and yerba were the same substance, or they might have purposely equated coca with yerba as a way to explain the latter. Europeans had greater exposure to the Andes than to Paraguay, and thus, calling yerba "coca" made it easier to understand as both were stimulants produced and regularly consumed by native peoples. Over the course of the seventeenth century, a striking difference emerged. Coca continued to be consumed almost exclusively by Indigenous peoples, while yerba mate became a colonial good consumed by people of all ethnicities and social classes, making it more amenable to criollo nationalist projects in the republican period.

As yerba mate's popularity spread beyond Indigenous communities, authors increasingly compared it with Chinese tea. In the 1630s, a Jesuit priest noted that yerba seemed to resemble "the Chinese herb called *cha*" in its ability to dispel drowsiness, and "even the name of the herb is not much different, being in the native language *caa*."[13] In the late colonial period, yerba was almost always compared to Chinese tea and generally deemed to be very similar. Such comparisons helped shape another colonial name for yerba: "Paraguayan tea." The reference to tea helped explain yerba mate to European audiences who were already familiar with Chinese tea, while the geographic reference to Paraguay made it clear that yerba was not completely synonymous with the Chinese substance. Calling it *"té del Paraguay"* was an act of erasure, classifying yerba mate as a subset of the Chinese beverage rather than a Guaraní or Kaingang beverage.

Most often, colonial sources called it "Paraguayan yerba" (*yerba del Paraguay*).[14] Yerba became practically synonymous with Paraguay. At the time, the region of Paraguay extended into parts of what are modern day Argentina and Brazil. Colonial texts about Paraguay almost always discussed *yerba del Paraguay*. Yerba's connection to Paraguay was so strong that a 1741 London newspaper advertisement omitted any reference to "yerba" or "tea." It simply mentioned the auction of six bags of "Paraguay."[15] In contrast to this close geographic association with Paraguay, mate's Indigenous roots were largely overlooked or forgotten. Into the early twentieth century, some authors even attributed its discovery to Spaniards rather than Indigenous peoples.[16]

While "yerba del Paraguay" was its most common name during the colonial period, it was also frequently called simply "yerba." Such terminology signaled yerba mate's pervasiveness. There were many other herbs, but there was no confusion about which herb was "yerba" in the Río de la Plata region. For example, in his early-eighteenth-century treatise about the medicinal plants of Paraguay, Pedro de Montenegro listed eight different types of yerbas that were not yerba mate, but he titled his entry for yerba mate simply "Virtues of the Yerba Tree" (see figure 1)[17] Conflating yerba mate into the generic term "herb" reveals the beverage's ubiquity and notoriety, similar to how "weed" means marijuana today.

The term "mate" was not initially associated with yerba. The first two Guaraní dictionaries, written in the 1630s, translated *caá* or *côgôî* into "yerba that is drunk." "Mate" is the gourd for drinking yerba, but in the period before European contact, Guaraní did not drink yerba exclusively from a gourd; they also used ceramic vessels. Both dictionaries included entries for "gourd," but its translation (*ĭá*) does not resemble anything like the word "mate."[18] Instead, mate likely comes from the Quechua term "*matí*." According to Garcilaso de la Vega (1609), the Incas produced many very good drinking vessels made of gourds, which they called *matí*.[19] Alternatively, the term might be of Nahuatl origin.[20] Francisco Saverio Clavigero, an eighteenth-century priest who collected information from Spanish and Indigenous sources, reported that the people of Mesoamerica made drinking vessels out of gourds, and they called the smaller and more cylindrical ones *tecomatl*.[21] Regardless of whether "mate" derived from Quechua or Nahuatl, the use of an Andean or Mesoamerican term instead of a Guaraní or Kaingang term highlights how yerba had moved beyond its region of origin to become a Spanish colonial good and a commodity. The use of "mate" reveals Indigenous influence, but in a foreign and reinvented form.

"Mate" became linked to "yerba" due to the gourd's centrality in the way the practice of its consumption developed. Gourds had long been used as drinking vessels by native peoples of the Americas. Growing naturally in the wild, they were accessible and inexpensive. To showcase their wealth, upper-class consumers purchased ornately decorated gourds that were expensive works of art. As a French traveler to Peru in 1712 described, "they put the herb into a cup, or bowl, made of a calabash, or gourd, tipp'd with silver, which they call *mate*. . . ."[22] The gourd's use in drinking yerba was so prevalent in the eighteenth century that European visitors now started to refer to the drink as "mate."[23] Juan Francisco Aguirre, a Spanish naval officer and diarist, noted this new naming style in his diary in 1791 when he wrote: "yerba for drinking mate" ("*hierba para tomar mate*").[24]

Today, yerba mate's official botanical name is *Ilex paraguariensis,* a name first given by the French botanist Auguste Saint-Hilaire in the nineteenth century. After spending six years studying flora and fauna in Brazil and the Río de la Plata region, Saint-Hilaire returned to Europe in 1821, and the following year he published an account of his travels where he described the "tree of mate or of *congonha*" found near Curitiba, Brazil. Saint-Hilaire identified the tree as "that which makes the famous Herb of Paraguay," and based on its flowers and fruit, he determined that it belonged to the genus *Ilex*. He named the species *paraguariensis*.[25] This name recognized, and documented for posterity, yerba's connection to Paraguay, but it almost wasn't so. Two years later, Saint-Hilaire published the same text using a different species name, "*mate*." But *paraguariensis* had already taken hold.[26]

For much of the nineteenth century, after the end of the Spanish empire in South America and the emergence of nation-states and national economies, and even into the early twentieth century, people debated what was and was not yerba mate. Saint-Hilaire entered into this debate, acknowledging that Spanish Americans believed Paraguayan yerba was far superior to Brazilian yerba, but he insisted that both came from the same plant and any difference was solely due to preparation.[27] Other botanists disagreed. Several decades later Aimé Bonpland and John Miers, two other scientists who made important contributions to the developing understanding of yerba mate, documented that yerba for mate was produced from other species of *Ilex,* in addition to *paraguariensis.*[28]

As the infusion drunk from a bombilla and gourd became increasingly recognized as mate, people started calling the substance "yerba mate." The Google Books Ngram Viewer, which charts the frequency of words or phrases in printed Spanish-language sources, does not record "yerba mate" until 1807, and its usage remained low until after 1850. In contrast, "yerba del Paraguay" regularly appears in the Ngram Viewer starting in 1762.[29] The shift to almost exclusively using the term "yerba mate" occurred in the first decades of the twentieth century, when Argentina became a major yerba-producing country. Argentina was already by far the largest consumer of yerba, but until the 1920s, it imported almost all yerba from Brazil and some from Paraguay. At this point the country began planting millions of yerba trees, and within two decades, Argentina overtook Brazil as the largest yerba-producing nation. The name "Paraguayan yerba" persisted for a while because yerba from Paraguay was considered superior quality, but it soon lost relevance and was replaced by the more geographically inclusive "yerba mate." This resolution is an important moment in the larger history of yerba mate in Argentina, as it resolved a longstanding complexity, and helped set the stage for the modern commercialization of yerba mate that would begin in the 1930s.

At the same time that the name "yerba mate" became prevalent, however, the acceptance of a single name also led to an explosion in the debates about what yerba mate actually was and was not. There are a number of species of *Ilex* that grow in southern Brazil, Paraguay, and northern Argentina, and native peoples who were the first to practice the consumption of yerba mate did not exclusively consume one kind.[30] Throughout the colonial period, authors described the different trees that produced yerba, and noted that some were more prized than others.[31] Being harvested largely from trees in the wild, it was difficult to restrict yerba to a single species of *Ilex*. This changed when Argentina exclusively cultivated *Ilex paraguariensis*. Brazil and Paraguay continued to harvest yerba from trees growing in the wild at that time, and Brazil was especially known for both selling other species of *Ilex* as yerba and adding leaves from other plants. Around the time when Argentina first began widespread cultivation of yerba mate in the first decades of the 1900s, nationalist sentiment led Argentina's yerba producers and consumers to claim that *Ilex paraguariensis* was the only true yerba mate. Magazines and newspapers in Argentina, eager to boost the country's status via this new agricultural venture, published editorials emphasizing that Brazilian yerba was adulterated because it was not exclusively *Ilex paraguariensis*. These opinions drew on a discourse that had been growing in the years surrounding Argentina's move to increase its own national production of yerba. Many came from prominent officials who voiced their concerns about Brazil's yerba, focusing on consumer safety and hygiene. For example, in 1911, Dr. Emilio Lahitte from the Argentine Ministry of Agriculture issued a report about the dangers of Brazilian yerba mate that circulated among top government officials (the ministries of agriculture, treasury, and customs) and received extensive press coverage. In one article, *La Prensa,* a prominent daily newspaper in Buenos Aires, highlighted that according to Lahitte, "the majority of the yerba imported from Brazil comes mixed with a weed (yuyo) similar in color . . . called 'congonilla' that can be detrimental to health."[32] In a front-page article the following day, *La Vanguardia* added, "the botanical section of the Ministry of Agriculture says that [congonilla] does not contain caffeine and lacks the properties that characterize yerba mate. . . . The morphological characteristics of 'congonilla' are quite similar to those of yerba mate, but its chemical constitution could possibly entail a true danger for the health of the consumer." The article concluded with the warning, "we must take caution, therefore, with the tasty Brazilian yerba (*cimarrón*)."[33]

This report clearly, though implicitly, promoted cultivated Argentine yerba. This promotion stemmed from more than just nationalist pride or health advice. Notably, this report about the health risks of Brazilian yerba was delivered by the Ministry of Agriculture, not the National Department of Hygiene. Just a few years before this report, Argentina had begun to invest huge amounts of money in domestic cultivation of yerba mate. It was a significant moment in the history of yerba mate in Argentina, and these investments would directly impact how Argentina's trade policies and economic ideologies developed in the coming years. When Lahitte issued this report, he had very specific monetary incentives. Nevertheless, Lahitte based his censure of Brazilian yerba exclusively on the assertion that yerba mate was *Ilex paraguariensis* (the plant species cultivated in Argentina) rather than on any scientific findings about the negative health effects of congonilla.[34] Lahitte's focus on the fact it was not "Argentine yerba" underscores how his argument was based on nationalism. His claims intersected somewhat confusingly with broader debates about the true substance of yerba mate. At the time, for example, it was not an established fact that "yerba mate" was or even should be considered exclusively *Ilex paraguariensis*. In fact, congonilla, described as a dangerous weed by Lahitte, had long been considered "yerba mate."[35] Congonilla was, in fact, the Spanish translation of *congonha*, the Brazilian name for the tree that Saint-Hilaire described as producing "the famous herb of Paraguay" and to which he gave the scientific name *Ilex paraguariensis*.[36] Later, Saint-Hilaire further clarified that congonha was synonymous for mate in São Paulo and Minas Gerais.[37]

Lahitte's report led to an uproar in Argentina and fueled the ongoing debates about what could and could not be considered yerba mate. In 1914, an agronomist published an academic article in Asunción that listed six species of *Ilex* consumed as yerba mate, in addition to *paraguariensis*.[38] In 1921, a professor of botany at the National University of Buenos Aires and La Plata conducted a serious study to determine if other species of *Ilex* should be considered yerba mate, concluding, "based on all [the study's] facets (scientific, commercial, industrial, and even popular) the official definition of yerba mate should be modified, not limiting the varieties and forms of *Ilex paraguariensis,* but also extending it to other species of *Ilex* and even to many other inoffensive plants, whose addition certain consumers demand as quality *sine qua non* for accepting the product."[39] While some scientists debated what qualified as yerba mate, Argentina was undergoing a wave of nationalist focus on its cultivation of yerba mate in these years. Consequently, Argentine officials and producers strongly argued that *Ilex paraguariensis* was the single legitimate form of yerba mate and that imported yerba was fake, adulterated, and dangerous to the nation's health. In 1924, complaints about congonilla became so intense that the Argentine government passed legislation prohibiting its importation.[40] Subsequent legislation defined yerba mate exclusively as *Ilex paraguariensis*.[41] Still, references to yerba mate as congonha continued. A 1930 article in *La Prensa* about yerba production in Misiones complained that imported yerba contained large portions of congonilla, known to be poisonous (*ser veneno*).[42] In 1935, the same newspaper reported that "Congoin Company of Los Angeles" was importing yerba mate into the United States.[43]

These debates about the true substance of "yerba mate," which frequently touched on economic and nationalist incentives, were not easily resolved. The ultimate irony is that congonha, the word which the Argentines asserted referred to an adulterated or falsified "yerba mate," was in fact the Portuguese translation of one of the two Indigenous names for yerba mate consumed by the Guaraní and Kaingang prior to the arrival of Europeans. Congonha is the Portuguese adaptation of *côgôî* (the Kaingang word for yerba mate).[44] Even today, the Kaingang continue to use variations of *côgôî* (*kógũnh/cóquín/kóngōin*) to refer to yerba mate.[45] While *côgôî* and congonilla disappeared from Spanish-language sources during the colonial period, the term continued to be widely used for yerba mate in southern Brazil through the early twentieth century.[46] In contrast, today few Brazilians associate congonha with yerba mate. Most Brazilians are familiar with the term through place names such as the town of Congonhas (a UNESCO World Heritage Site in Minas Gerais), and Congonhas Airport in São Paulo, but they do not associate it with yerba mate.

Yerba mate still has some traces of Guaraní influences in Argentina. The story of Ca'a Yari (the goddess of yerba mate) appears widely on the Internet and in children's books as an example of a Guaraní origin myth.[47] Its circulation does not so much reveal the persistence of Indigenous influence, but rather its recovery and hybridity. Colonial-era myths about yerba mate's discovery did not refer to Ca'a Yari, but rather the devil or Saint Thomas. The Ca'a Yari origin story emerged instead in the late nineteenth century when workers harvesting yerba trees asked for protection and good fortune from this goddess of yerba.[48] The story circulated more widely in the twentieth century as part of a growing interest in Indigenous culture.

Today, the Indigenous roots of mate are increasingly used in the marketing of yerba mate, especially in the United States, but also to a lesser degree in Argentina. This highlights the contested role of Indigenous culture in Argentina. For example, Guaraní words are sometimes used in branding yerba mate, although Spanish is most prevalent for mainstream brands. An exception is Taragüi, a popular brand that dates back to 1940. Organic and artisanal yerba, which have been growing in popularity in Argentina, also often highlight yerba's Indigenous past, using Guaraní terms such as *ca'a* or *ka'a*. The marketing of yerba mate in the United States especially emphasizes its Indigenous origins, but often in an idealized and distorted manner. For example, the most popular brand in the United States is Guayaki, the name of an Indigenous people in Paraguay who are neither Guaraní nor Kaingang and who prefer to call themselves Ache. In fact, Guayaki is a derogatory Guaraní term for the Ache.[49] Another brand that is popular in the United States is Yachack, the name of a Kichwa people from the Ecuadorian Amazon, a region where yerba mate neither grows nor is widely consumed.[50]

As this book documents, the history of yerba mate in Argentina is a history of conquest, imperialism, nationalism, erasure, re-creation, and persistence. The evolution of the name from *caá* and *côgôî* to "yerba mate" exemplifies this story. Replacing Indigenous terminology was an act of conquest that made an Indigenous good into a Spanish good. The use of "yerba of Paraguay" identified it with a specific geographic place within the Spanish empire, while "Paraguayan tea" placed it within a global context. The addition of "mate" added back a degree of indigeneity, albeit neither Guaraní nor Kaingang, while also obscuring connections to a single nation (Paraguay). More recently, Argentina's official designation of origin for yerba mate attempts to nationalize yerba mate and ignore its transnational presence and history.

It is important to also highlight that the history of yerba mate is a history of persistence in the face of globalization. Today, yerba mate remains ubiquitous in Argentina, and it continues to be consumed in the traditional manner, as a shared beverage that is drunk using unique Indigenous technologies. This persistence highlights not just the importance of yerba mate to the Argentine people, but also to its integration in Argentina's economic institutions, its national myths and memory, and its cultural narratives and national identity. Like other widespread beverages, yerba mate's modern history is intricately woven into a history of colonialism, capitalist economics, and custom. Although yerba mate did not gain the global stature that tea and coffee did, its unique history in Argentina nevertheless tells a very global story, even as it underscores how the Argentine people's historic and ongoing passion for mate helped shape the path of the nation.

CHAPTER SUMMARIES

This book is organized into nine chapters that follow the historical chronology. The first two chapters look at the pre-Columbian and the colonial eras. Chapter 1 explores how interracial mixing and ideas about religion and medicine helped yerba mate evolve from an Indigenous substance that Europeans didn't like into a colonial beverage widely consumed throughout much of South America.

Chapter 2 explores how various government officials and other actors turned yerba mate into an improvised and informal tool of empire that incorporated Paraguay's Indigenous inhabitants under Spanish rule, connected isolated frontier regions, and funded government activities from Paraguay to Buenos Aires, Santiago, Potosí, and Lima. Chapter 2 also looks at the enthusiasm about yerba mate's profit potential in Europe, a potential that was never realized due to Spanish trade policies and competition from British tea.

Chapters 3 and 4 focus on the long nineteenth century when Argentina struggled to become a nation-state and develop its northeast borderlands. Chapter 3 explains Argentina's inability to populate, develop, and incorporate its northeastern borderlands into the nation during the nineteenth century. While the onset of Argentina's rapid economic growth and national consolidation date to 1880, Misiones failed to attract many immigrants until after 1900, when people on the ground began cultivating yerba mate. Chapter 4 traces how, during the nineteenth century, mate became the drink of the gauchos and lower classes, and a clandestine beverage of the Buenos Aires elite. As the frontier disappeared and immigration surged, nativists praised mate as a national custom. Immigrants complicated this vision by becoming more fervent mate consumers—and retainers of Indigenous traditions—than native-born Argentines.

The last four chapters of the book center on the twentieth century, with the rise and fall of economic nationalism, working-class identity, and globalization. The chapters roughly alternate between yerba consumption and yerba production. Chapter 5 explores how yerba cultivation integrated Argentina's northeast borderlands into the nation-state. Predictions of high profits and anti-Brazilian rhetoric led capitalists and northern European immigrants to invest in domestic colonization projects, large-scale yerba plantations, and small- and medium-sized holdings that continue to shape Misiones into the twenty-first century. Chapter 6 uses yerba mate to explore the shift in political economy from free trade to protectionism starting in the 1880s. The process entailed a complex array of competing domestic and international interests that defied a stark divide between free-trade and protectionist ideology and practice. Although the creation of a regulatory board to oversee the yerba sector was ostensibly a protectionist measure to advance Argentine yerba, its creation was instead a political compromise that prioritized Argentine wheat as a national product.

Chapter 7 traces how Socialists, Communists, and Peronists portrayed yerba workers as the epitome of capitalist exploitation in Argentina. In doing so, they utilized works by muckraking journalists who described mixed-race Guaraní-speaking, Paraguayan and Brazilian yerba workers as "white slaves." Such terminology reveals an expansive and inclusive understanding of "white." Chapter 8 explores why mate was considered the drink of workers and yet per-capita yerba mate consumption declined from the late 1940s until the 1980s. The populist president, Juan Perón, empowered workers and actively incorporated them into a vision of Argentina as a modern nation of middle-class consumers. During this time, yerba mate's continued associations with poverty and backwardness would clash with ideas of modernity.

Chapter 9 studies the resurgence of mate and its evolution into a symbol of *Argentinidad* at the end of the twentieth century in response to the return to democracy, economic crisis, and globalization in the 1980s and 1990s. Mate's popularity grew due to its affordability, the feeling of social connectedness it created, and the sense that it was authentically Argentine.

An afterword concludes the book by bringing the study to the present day. Foreign companies (especially Guayakí in the US and Club-Mate in Germany) have popularized yerba mate outside South America as an energy drink. Mate is ubiquitous in Argentina, but per capita consumption has stagnated over the past two decades. Mate has become an idealized and romanticized symbol of Argentine identity that, as this book explains, continues to expose enduring underlying social tensions in the country.

ONE

From Indigenous Staple to Colonial Commodity

IN 1667, DIEGO DE ZEVALLOS, a lawyer living in Peru's capital city of Lima, published a treatise describing *yerba del Paraguay* as a wonder drug capable of curing a wide array of maladies. Based on a seventeenth-century understanding of "humors," de Zevallos explained that the consumption of yerba addressed a wide array of health problems.[1] Little is known about de Zevallos, or how it was he came to be writing a treatise about *yerba del Paraguay*. But his book became one of the first to directly discuss yerba mate, and it was widely cited by others in the years after its publication. One of those authors was the official Jesuit historian of Paraguay, who, a little less than a century later, recounted de Zevallos's claims and reiterated, "I believe that as virtues continue to be attributed to said yerba, it will soon be called in vulgar terms the cure-all (*sánalo todo*) and universal medicine for all types of ailments."[2]

At the time of publication, only the small portion of the Spanish-speaking population that was literate could read these works. For historians today, however, they provide important clues about colonial perceptions of yerba mate as it evolved from an Indigenous consumable that initially disgusted Europeans to a substance prized for its health benefits and a daily ritual for people throughout much of South America. Much as with chocolate and tobacco, during the seventeenth century Europeans in South America consumed yerba mate following Indigenous practices, but unlike those other stimulants native to the Americas, the custom spread primarily due to racial mixing, as Spaniards and their mixed-race offspring adopted native cultural practices including drinking yerba mate and speaking Guaraní.[3] Tracing yerba mate's evolution from an Indigenous good to a colonial beverage reveals the long-enduring influence of native practices and how such associations came to be obscured. Most Argentines today believe that their country is white or culturally Creole (mixed race) and has few Indigenous peoples (*pueblos originarios*). While military campaigns did decimate native peoples, especially during the "Conquest of the Desert" in the 1870s, pueblos originarios and native influences continue to exist in Argentina, as is shown here through yerba mate.

INDIGENOUS ORIGINS

Today, the Ca'a Yari origin story of yerba mate from Guaraní mythology has become part of popular folklore in Argentina. In his compilation of vignettes about the history of the Americas, the celebrated Uruguayan author Eduardo Galeano tells how one day the moon came down to earth. Twice an old peasant rescued her, and when the moon got hungry, he took her to the hut where he lived with his wife and daughter. The next night, the moon looked down from the sky at her friends' home and saw that the impoverished family had nothing to eat. They had given their last bread to her. In gratitude, the moon shone her brightest light and asked the clouds to shed a very special drizzle around the hut. In the morning, some unknown trees with dark green leaves and white flowers appeared. The daughter became the queen of yerba mate, offering it to others and never dying.[4]

While popular today, Guaraní origin stories only began to widely circulate in the twentieth century as a part of a growing interest in Indigenous culture. During the colonial era, yerba mate origin stories did not refer to the goddess of yerba. Instead, they attributed the discovery of yerba mate to either the devil or Saint Thomas. While the fact that yerba mate originated among the native peoples of the Americas seems obvious to us today, it was not always so. A number of people, even into the twentieth century, attributed its discovery to Spaniards, and especially to the Jesuits.[5]

Among scholars working today, yerba mate consumption is generally thought to have originated with the Guaraní, who descend from the Tupian linguistic family with origins in southern Amazonia. But there is also strong evidence that suggests it might have originated with the Kaingang of the Jê linguistic family, a people from the northeastern area of what is now Brazil. Some 2000 to 3000 years ago, Jê-speaking people moved south into what is today the triple frontier region of Argentina, Brazil, and Paraguay, and approximately 1,800 years ago the Guaraní split from the Tupi and migrated from Amazonia to the same region.[6] Both groups encountered the yerba tree growing there, and by the time the Spaniards arrived in the seventeenth century, they had integrated yerba into their cultural practices.

Jesuit missionaries intent on converting Indigenous peoples to Catholicism established missions among both groups in the first decades of the seventeenth century and wrote a number of ethnographic descriptions of both the Guaraní and the Kaingang. These Jesuit missionaries were struck by the common practice of consuming yerba mate among both peoples and they left many written accounts and descriptions of yerba mate. Although important information can be gleaned from these accounts about the presence and practice of mate consumption at the time, these accounts also reveal the authors' biases. For example, one of the first Jesuit missionaries to Paraguay, the Lima-born Antonio Ruíz de Montoya (1585–1652), wrote a lot on the subject, but he also acknowledged that he had never tried yerba and claimed that "it deserves condemnation" for a number of reasons, including "the abuses made of it," and "its superstitious employment in sorcery."[7] Ruíz de Montoya's bias against yerba was representative of the general viewpoint held by Catholic priests who encountered the substance early on.

Despite their views, the Jesuits did leave behind valuable written sources about yerba mate's role in native culture. Two of the most important are a Guaraní-Spanish dictionary and a Spanish-Guaraní dictionary. These reference works were compiled by Jesuits at the beginning of the seventeenth century and published by Antonio Ruíz de Montoya in Madrid in 1639 and 1640. Both provide important linguistic clues about the practices of yerba mate consumption among the Kaingang and Guaraní peoples. For example, both dictionaries include two words for "yerba that is drunk:" *caá* and *côgôî*.[8] The first is a Guaraní word. The second appears to be a Kaingang term. Not only does *côgôî* not follow Tupi Guaraní phonetic norms,[9] variations of the term appear widely in documents about the Kaingang.[10] As mentioned in the introduction, the Kaingang continue to use variations of *côgôî* for yerba mate. Spanish sources from the colonial period sometimes described *caá* as the Guarani word for yerba, but they never referred to *côgôî*. While *côgôî* disappeared entirely from Spanish colonial sources, *congonha* (the Portuguese form of *côgôî*) continued to be widely used in southern Brazil through the early twentieth century.[11]

It is plausible that the Kaingang people were the first to transform yerba mate into a consumable item. The fact that Ruíz de Montoya included this Kaingang word in the dictionaries when he was known to be very reluctant about incorporating any non-Tupi-Guaraní words speaks to the term's importance, as it suggests a wide usage of the Kaingang word for yerba mate even among the

Guaraní.[12] It also suggests a close association between the Kaingang and yerba. In the 1620s and 1630s, Ruíz de Montoya and other Jesuits drew attention to ceremonial uses of yerba in Kaingang religious practices. In a letter written in 1630, a missionary wrote that Kaingang shamans (*hechizeros*) "speak with the devil by way of yerba, and he tells them unknown things, like when Spaniards will come to rescue them, and they regularly say the yerba says this, etc."[13] Because the Jesuits associated such activity with the devil, they vehemently tried to stop it.

According to Ruíz de Montoya, the Kaingang did not have idols, but they used yerba to communicate with the supernatural.

> They have *hechizeros* whose science is nothing more than divining and telling lies. They consult the oracle with a gourd of yerba. They speak with them; they blow on it; they belch; they move their eyes around; they raise their head; they move it to one side and the other; they pay close attention; and do other ceremonies in this manner.[14]

A century later, the Jesuit historian and chronicler Pedro Lozano clarified that shaman drank the yerba. "*Hechiceros* have much esteem among this people, that they deceive them with their lies. To hear the false oracles of the father of lies, they use the Paraguayan yerba, which they drink ground in powders."[15] According to another source, Kaingang *hechiceros* used yerba powder as a narcotic. By inhaling the powder, they entered into a trance.[16] Notably, the Jesuits described about as many instances of yerba mate use by Kaingang shamans as by Guaraní shamans, even though they only established one mission among the Kaingang and many more among the Guaraní.

After asking Guaraní elders about the origin of yerba mate, Ruíz de Montoya concluded that the devil taught Guaraní shamans to use yerba in order to commune with him.

> I learned as a certain fact that in their youth the herb was not drunk or even known except by a great sorcerer or magician who trafficked with the devil. The devil showed him the herb and told him to drink it whenever he wanted to consult him. He did so, and under his tutelage, so did others whom we have known in our own days. The witchcraft they perform commonly derives from this herb.[17]

As with the Kaingang, yerba played an important role in Guaraní religious practices. Historian Shawn Austin describes how Juan Cuaraçí (a baptized

Guaraní shaman) combined Guaraní and Catholic religious symbols and practices to build an impressive following and undermine the missions in the 1620s. Curaçí's yerba-induced vision inspired him to call for native peoples to abandon the missions. After fasting, consuming large quantities of yerba mate, and vomiting, Curaçí picked the yerba-bile mixture off the ground and threw it into the air while saying, "yerba be calm." With another shaman, Curaçí repeated this process several times; then they had a vision of demons who told them that all Indians should leave the Spaniards. As Curaçí subsequently circulated in the region, he continued to employ yerba mate in ceremonies. In one ritual, Cuaraçí drew the sign of the cross into the dirt and poured yerba into the marks.[18] Catholic priests opposed such activities and did everything they could to disassociate yerba mate from Indigenous religion. Even so, they could not fully squash native religious practices. Over three decades after Crown officials condemned Curaçí to death, another Guaraní shaman (Rodrigo Yaguariguay) admitted to consuming yerba so that he could make prophecies and gain spiritual knowledge.[19]

Yerba mate not only facilitated communication with the divine, it also helped Guaraní and Kaingang shamans in their roles as healers. One Jesuit author described the Kaingang *hichizeros* who used yerba mate in their ceremonies as "*chupadores* (drunkards) and *curanderos* (healers)."[20] The Guaraní used yerba as a medicine. According to Pedro Montenegro, a Jesuit priest who wrote a treatise about Guaraní medicinal plants, yerba was their only remedy for stomach ailments and diarrhea.[21] Years later, a Jesuit chronicler and historian claimed that the Guaraní consumed it upon the outbreak of any pestilent illness.[22] The Guaraní understood yerba mate to have a variety of health benefits, including energizing properties. According to Ruíz de Montoya, "[Guaraní elders] claim that it has the following effects: it lightens work; it sustains them (we have daily experience that an Indian can row for a whole day with no sustenance beyond drinking the herb every three hours); it purges their stomach of phlegm; it makes the senses alert; it dispels drowsiness when one wants to stay up at night without sleepiness."[23]

Prior to European contact, yerba mate may have also served as a status symbol for shamans and *caciques* (native leaders). Most references to yerba consumption by non-acculturated Guaraní involved either a shaman or a cacique. For example, in two letters from 1628 and 1629, Ruíz de Montoya and Simón Masseta repeatedly wrote about "the great shaman" and "principal cacique" Pablo Guirabera, who "gave himself the name Creator of Heaven and earth." As Masseta described, Guirabara left his home once or twice each day with assorted plumage on his head, his face and legs painted, carrying different weapons, and always wearing new clothing. "With these various gestures and appearances, the Indians mainly fear him, speaking to them with superiority and arrogance, having all of them as his vassals and that he is the King of all and governor as some call him." Masseta also described Guirabara constantly drinking yerba. "I have never seen an Indian that was such a yerba-drinker (*tan yerbatero*) and friend of tobacco, as he is having yerba all day, drinking yerba and water. And I do not know how he does not burst."[24] In Masseta's description, Guirabara cultivated his image as a respected and powerful leader in part by drinking yerba all day long.

Guaraní leaders also used yerba mate to facilitate relationships and to mark special events. For example, a Jesuit recounted that when a cacique named TabacanVi learned that a missionary was nearby, he sent his nephew with "a good number of armed Indians and a large refreshing drink of yerba to receive the priest, telling him by invitation from the cacique, to stop for a while."[25] The Guaraní also used yerba in marriage ceremonies.

> The male and female that want to marry go in the early morning to the house of the cacique or main shaman who puts and mixes the yerba that they drink in a gourd with water, and he gives the two who are marrying the yerba to drink from the same gourd, and then the husband and the woman have to spit together the yerba in the same hole, and this is the public sign of marriage, or better said, concubinage.[26]

Native peoples consumed yerba in different ways. According to Pau Navajas, more than ten different ways of using yerba mate were recorded, including chewing fresh leaves, breathing its powder, burning it for smoke, and soaking oneself in a bath of macerated leaves.[27] Most early accounts describe native peoples drinking yerba mate.[28] As mentioned earlier, both *caá* and *côgôî* referred to "yerba that is drunk," and drinking it with water was the only method of consuming yerba mentioned in both the Guaraní-Spanish and the Spanish-Guaraní dictionaries.

The dictionaries make clear that drinking yerba was a part of daily life, especially before eating. Ruíz de Montoya translated various phrases about drinking yerba, many of which were listed under terms that initially seem unrelated to yerba, such as "head," "weaving," and "acidic." The fact that drinking yerba before eating was mentioned various times and was often associated with terms unrelated to yerba, eating, or drinking, emphasizes its importance in the daily life of the Guaraní. For example, the phrase "'I am going to make yerba,' which they also say it for politeness or modesty when they do their vital necessities" points to the centrality of yerba mate in daily life.[29]

Ruíz de Montoya included phrases that communicated feelings toward yerba: "I desire yerba" (*caa uheî*) and "I don't drink yerba" (*ndache caáguâri*). One could imagine a missionary declining an offer of yerba using the latter phrase. Ruíz de Montoya also included phrases that might have been relevant to the Jesuits' mission work. For example, a Jesuit who felt the need to drink yerba as a way to connect with and gain acceptance from Guaraní, but did not want to drink it, might ask his Guaraní host "to put very little yerba in the gourd to drink." A missionary also might use such a phrase to try to moderate yerba drinking. Two entries suggest that mission Guaraní sometimes spent extended periods of time drinking yerba. Under the heading "crazy," Ruíz de Montoya included "the yerba has made me crazy"—suggesting that the person had drunk so much yerba as to affect his or her behavior. And with phrases related to "morning," Ruíz de Montoya included "all this morning you have been drinking yerba."[30] One could easily imagine a priest making this accusation to a person who failed to attend the morning's religious activities or did not do something that the priest expected. Such phrases underscore Ruíz de Montoya's distaste for yerba.

While he did not like yerba mate, Ruíz de Montoya's repeated mention of caá in the dictionaries demonstrates that yerba permeated Guaraní life. *Caá* meant yerba, but it also meant *monte* (forest or wilderness in general) and all wild plants. Over a page and a half of the dictionary was dedicated exclusively to terms and phrases related to *caá*.[31] The Guaraní relied on the forests for food, medicines, and raw materials. Recent research suggests that the Guaraní actively managed forest resources and modified biodiversity.[32] Phrases related to *caá/monte* in the dictionaries support such a conclusion: for example, "clean below the forests so that it is clear" and "unused forest from which wood has not been taken."[33] It is probable that they actively tended to the yerbales.

One of the most interesting pieces of information in the early Jesuit dictionaries is that the methods for processing yerba mate were strikingly similar to what it is done today. Ruíz de Montoya included six different verbs about processing yerba. First, the Guaraní passed the yerba leaves over flames (without burning them) to remove humidity and stop the degradation process (*sapecar*), and then they dried the leaves for a longer period at lower temperatures before crushing them. These descriptions highlight not only

FIGURE 2. Nineteenth-century depiction of yerba production. Mary Hield, *Glimpses of South America; or, The Land of the Pampas* (London: Cassell & Company, Lmtd., 1883), 189.

different technologies used by the Guaraní, but also the complex and nuanced approaches which continue to be foundational to yerba processing today. Ruíz de Montoya even identified a tool specifically for chopping yerba.[34] Through the twentieth century, some rural producers also continued to use the *barbacuá* (an arched structure constructed of branches tied with vines that held the yerba over a subterranean fire) for drying the yerba (see figure 2). A few small-scale artisanal producers in southern Brazil still use the *barbacuá* and *carijo* (a flat structure similar to the *barbacuá* except that the fire is directly under the yerba).[35] Both of these structures are built entirely out of forest materials and are either Indigenous or hybrid technologies.

In addition to the similarities between the way that the Guaraní processed yerba and the way that it is produced today, the unique manner of consuming mate also appears to have a direct lineage to Guaraní tradition. The Guaraní appear to have used a variety of vessels (both ceramic and gourds) to drink yerba. In the Jesuit dictionaries, the phrase "With which yerba is drunk" was translated as *caguâba* and referred to the vessel (*vaso*) from which both yerba and alcohol were drunk. Guaraní archeological sites contain a number of small, semi-open ceramic vessels called *caguâba* (the same term that Ruíz de

Montoya translated both as "vessel for drinking wine" and "with which yerba is drunk") that were used for drinking the alcoholic beverage *cauim*.[36]

The dictionaries do not provide explicit evidence of the bombilla (the drinking straw with a sieve at the end to filter out the yerba) that is known to have been a key part of yerba consumption in South America during the colonial period. *Tacuapí* (the most common Guarani translation of bombilla) is not in either of Ruíz de Montoya's dictionaries and early documents about yerba mate do not mention anything like it. Scholars are torn about whether the bombilla was an Indigenous or hybrid technology.[37] While straws and straining tools were observed in ancient Egypt and among native peoples in Africa and the Arctic, they weren't commonly used in Europe until the twentieth century.[38] In terms of the use of the bombilla for drinking yerba mate, the first explicit reference is from an early eighteenth-century French traveler to Chile and Peru, who described:

> To avoid drinking the Herb which swims at the Top, they make use of a Silver Pipe, at the End wherof is a Bowl, full of little Holes; so that the Liquor suck'd in at the other End is clear from the Herb. They drink round with the same Pipe, pouring hot Water on the same Herb as it is drank off. Instead of a Pipe, which they call *Bombilla* some part the Herb with a Silver Separation, called *Apartador,* full of little Holes.[39]

Made of silver from Peru, such a bombilla was clearly a colonial utensil. Later sources describe Indians using bombillas made of *takuara* (bamboo).[40] Whether native peoples came up with the idea of a bombilla (made of bamboo) or modified a colonial invention (the silver bombilla), the development entailed significant technological innovation and entanglement.[41] Furthermore, only people with financial resources could afford to purchase bombillas made of silver. But for this to have happened, Spaniards and other non-native peoples had to have first found a way to overcome their aversion to yerba mate, something which had been particularly true of those in positions of power who often saw it as an abhorrent, degenerate activity.

EUROPEAN CONTACT WITH YERBA

While Jesuit missionaries in the early seventeenth century were among the first Europeans to record descriptions of yerba mate, the Spanish Crown had already begun a broader imperial conquest of that region of South America nearly a century before the publication of Ruíz de Montoya's dictionaries. From the records that have come down to us, all evidence suggests that many of the early Spaniards in the region considered the consumption of yerba mate to be a somewhat gross, even diabolical practice. Like with chocolate and tobacco, Spaniards were suspicious of the strange Indigenous substance and Church officials feared that it threatened Catholic piety. There were many efforts by local officials to prohibit its use altogether. These efforts were unsuccessful, however, and yerba consumption spread as Spanish people on the ground adopted Guaraní cultural practices, primarily as a result of the early unions between Spanish men and Guaraní women.

Europeans initially came to the New World in search of items that they could take back to the Old World for a good profit, and yerba mate did not fit this criterion. Mineral wealth, primarily from gold and silver, was the main target. But spices, furs, dyewood, and other trade goods were also sought.[42] New and foreign foodstuffs did not interest Spaniards, given that an Old World diet was integral to Spanish identity. They believed that Spanish food and drink made them Spanish and kept them healthy. The American foodstuffs (such as chocolate, tropical fruits, and chili peppers) that they did adopt were incorporated as supplements and not as a mainstay of the Spanish diet.[43] And early conquistadors were too concerned with their own survival in the region to pay much attention to a strange drink like yerba mate. The first written description of the region (Ulrich Schmidt's account of Pedro de Mendoza's 1535 expedition) repeatedly mentioned food but made no reference to yerba mate. It was an understandable omission. For most of the trip, Schmidt and his companions were on the verge of starvation. They focused on satiating their hunger, and yerba mate did not resemble a familiar foodstuff or a recognizable alcoholic beverage.[44]

Early Spaniards in the region had never encountered anything like yerba mate. Wine was their beverage of choice. It is highly unlikely that any of the conquistadors or early settlers had previously tried a caffeinated beverage. A small number of Spaniards had recently encountered chocolate in Mesoamerica, but European texts did not even mention coffee or tea until the second half of the sixteenth century.[45] When Europeans first tried caffeinated beverages, they almost never liked them. Caffeinated drinks were different and strange. Coffee, tea, chocolate, and yerba mate are naturally bitter, and thus, an acquired taste. Moreover, they are typically drunk hot and their color was unappealing to the European eye. Caffeinated beverages are learned habits. Chocolate, coffee, and tea were first consumed in Europe by elites who were attracted to the status, fashion, and exclusivity that these exotic beverages represented, in part because they were initially expensive luxury goods.[46] But yerba mate never caught on in this way. Not only did yerba mate consumption not spread in Europe, the many Europeans in South America who became avid yerba consumers considered it a cheap basic necessity rather than a luxury good or status symbol.

Early Spanish references to the drinking of yerba mate described it as a barbaric practice. The first known author to explicitly discuss yerba consumption, by both non-Indians and Indians, was Father Martín González in 1556, less than two decades after the founding of Asunción.[47] Over forty years later, the superior of the Jesuits in Paraguay, Juan Romero, alluded to his distaste for the substance when he described how the habit resulted in yerba mate consumers wasting half of their day.

> And also even Spaniards picked up the habit, and not a few, the custom of the barbarous Indians of drinking the juice of some roots many times a day, and a bunch mixed with a yerba called of Paraguay, and of which they drink the quantity of a medium-sized jug until they slurp and then they pass it around. And drinking and vomiting, they spend half of the day.[48]

In addition to highlighting the disdain that many Spanish elites felt for yerba at this time, these early mentions of the drinking practice also provide evidence that the Spanish did, as Romero explained, learn about how to consume yerba from native peoples. Two years later, Alonso de la Madrid (a member of the Asunción town council) similarly described the practice as learned from Indigenous people, but he also added that Spaniards distorted and abused it. He called yerba consumption, as practiced by Indians who contented themselves with drinking it once a day, a "vice and bad habit." In contrast, he claimed Spaniards had made yerba consumption "more barbarity than vice" by drinking it all day. De la Madrid was concerned that by consuming so much yerba, Asunción's Spanish population was becoming more Indian than the Indians. And he complained that the social order was under threat because native peoples had lost respect for Spaniards due to their excessive yerba consumption. "Lost is the pride and self-respect of the Spaniards and their sons; even the Indians hold them in low regard. Because of this it is advisable to extirpate this vice, even if it is for no more than the self-respect that the Spaniards should have."[49]

De la Madrid's opposition to yerba led him to lobby for a prohibition on its production. In addition to asserting that yerba consumption damaged people's reputations, de la Madrid also claimed that it was a threat to economic well-being, peaceful social relations, the Catholic faith, and personal health. In total, de la Madrid made five separate objections to yerba consumption, portraying it as a destructive and addictive practice. He concluded his letter with an appeal to the soon-to-be-governor of Río de la Plata and Paraguay, Hernando Arias de Saavedra (Hernandarias) "to take whatever means possible to put a permanent ban on the said yerba."[50]

Hernandarias agreed with de la Madrid, and in the same year of 1596, he took serious steps to end the production and consumption of yerba. He prohibited sending Indians to yerbales to produce yerba and ordered that any illicit yerba be burned in the public plaza; he ordered a fine of 100 pesos to be levied on anyone who either violated this mandate or who bought or sold yerba; and he mandated that, regardless of status, anyone found drinking yerba in public or private be charged a 10-peso fine and spend fifteen days in jail for the first violation, with more serious punishment for any further violations.[51] Despite these laws and fines, Hernandarias's efforts were ineffective in stopping the production and consumption yerba, and in 1603, he was forced to again issue prohibitions and burn yerba in the public plaza.[52]

Other Spanish elites concurred with Hernandarias and de la Madrid on the evils of yerba mate. For instance, Diego de Torres Bollo, the Jesuit provincial of Paraguay, supported Hernandarias's actions. In letters to the Jesuit hierarchy in Europe, Torres complained that the population of Paraguay learned the "vice" of consuming yerba in their youth and that it made them lazy, even though he also acknowledged that they got up before sunrise each morning. Torres bemoaned that they had corrupted this "old custom of the Indians" to such an extent that even the Indians now refused to do any work without receiving a daily ration of yerba and tobacco. On a more positive note, he reported that with the threat of excommunication, the Jesuits had effectively stopped anyone in their college in Asunción from possessing or consuming "that wicked yerba."[53]

Torres not only wanted to root out yerba consumption in Jesuit-run colleges and missions, in 1610 he also tried to get the Inquisition of Peru to prohibit all consumption and production of yerba. Like de la Madrid, Torres made a multifaceted argument about why yerba had to be stopped. One of his main points was that yerba threatened Catholicism in the region. On the one hand, the beverage had diabolical origins (the Indians learned about yerba through a pact with the devil who appeared to them in the form of a pig) and magical superstitions remained implicitly connected to yerba. On the other hand, yerba consumption negatively affected Catholic practices. As Torres described,

> ... the worst is that it keeps them from the Holy Sacrament because before sunrise they begin these vices, and it is very difficult for them to wait to take communion during the mass and not later vomit. And thus, it is very rare the person, male or female, who frequents the Holy Sacrament, and even fewer are those who attend the sermons or confessions and do not give an excuse why they cannot finish with it.[54]

Elsewhere in the Americas, church officials also made similar complaints about how tobacco and chocolate threatened Catholicism.[55]

In his appeal to the Inquisition in Peru, Torres described how yerba undermined society in general. Torres pointed out that Indians, Spaniards, and even priests used yerba, and that almost all consumers admit that it is a vice, but that truly, they cannot give it up. Torres alluded to health concerns that resulted from drinking yerba and the dangerous working conditions associated with producing it. He concluded his litany of complaints by asserting that yerba had degenerative effects on consumers. "[Yerba] makes them vagabonds and lazy. And those that come from Spain and the Spaniards born in the Americas are losing not only the use of reason, but also affection for things of the faith." After describing all of these negative outcomes, Torres declared that there was an easy remedy: attentive that many Indians had died in producing yerba, the King should prohibit the gathering of it and issue grave penalties for anyone who violated the prohibition.[56]

Despite these diatribes against yerba by a number of colonial officials, there is evidence that some Spaniards at this time did embrace a more positive view of yerba mate. In 1602, when Hernandarias was issuing prohibitions on yerba, the Asunción *cabildo* (town council) wrote a long and detailed appeal to the king in support of yerba production. They framed their appeal in financial terms. They began by reminding the king that he was already well acquainted with Asunción's poverty. They then stated that it was a known fact that within the confines of the city's territory there was a certain tree with leaves that produced yerba sold in Asunción and other regions. Anyone who wanted could go and harvest it. They proposed the creation of a government monopoly (*estanco*) whereby only people with government-issued licenses could produce and sell yerba. The sale of these licenses would generate revenue for the government. To further facilitate yerba production, the cabildo members also requested confirmation that all Indians could freely go to the yerbales to produce yerba and transport it.[57]

It would take Spain almost another two decades to issue a ruling about yerba production. But it was already clear, based on the ineffectiveness of Hernandarias's local prohibitions against it in Paraguay, that yerba consumption would be an unstoppable cultural practice. One notable reason for this was the exceptionally high rates of *mestizaje*. In general, there were far more Spanish men than women in Paraguay, and Spanish men actively took advantage of Guaraní marriage practices. The Guaraní used marriages to build political alliances, and they initially tried to use this practice to build alliances with Spaniards, whom they saw as potential allies against their enemies in the Chaco and as a source for iron tools and other useful items. Wanting to incorporate Spaniards into their society as kin, they offered Spaniards their women. The Spaniards had a different vision of this interaction. They did not see the relationships as building kinship connections among equals. Rather, they saw the women as laborers and concubines and they used Guaraní kinship networks to build their labor force, especially since according to Guaraní practices, women were the ones who did most of the agricultural work.[58] These relationships often entailed sex, and within a short time, mestizos outnumbered Spaniards. The Governor of Paraguay, Domingo Martínez de Irala, estimated that thirteen years after the founding of Asunción, there were three thousand mestizos while Spaniards numbered less than four hundred. Over time, the proportion of mestizos continued to grow.[59]

These intimate relationships between the Spanish and Guaraní facilitated the spread of yerba mate. Mestizo offspring learned to drink yerba from their Guaraní mothers. Mixed-race children spent more time, and generally developed closer relationships, with their Guaraní mothers than with their Spanish fathers. Such contact meant that they adopted more of their mothers' beliefs and cultural practices, as well.[60] As the bishop of Paraguay observed in 1608, the population of Asunción "was raised without many Christian customs and most [are] offspring of Spaniards and Indians whose customs are like those of the Indians."[61] Consuming yerba was one of these customs, and one that rendered Hernandarias's prohibitions ineffective. Indeed, in 1618, Hernandarias complained again to the king that he had punished merchants and others who trafficked in yerba, but to no avail. Moreover, the merchants protested and other Spanish officials (in this case, the Audiencia of la Plata) sided against him. Thus, Hernandarias appealed to the king to confirm his prohibition of yerba.[62]

The status of yerba mate was finally resolved later in 1618. The king and the Council of Indies (the administrative body that oversaw Spanish territory in the Americas and the Philippines) permitted Indian labor in the yerbales except during the times of the year that were dangerous and harmful to their health.[63] This ruling gave royal approval to yerba production. Two years later, in 1620, an anonymous Jesuit confirmed that efforts to prohibit yerba had failed and that great quantities were being produced.[64] Even though some still found yerba distasteful, there were no longer any proposals to prohibit it. Some Europeans remained skeptical, but people in southern South America realized that it could not be stopped. In 1628, the head of the Jesuit province of Paraguay claimed that people would do anything to get their fix. "And when they do not have anything with which to buy it, they give their undergarments and blankets, and there was a woman who removed the tiles from the roof for yerba."[65]

A century later, the Jesuit superior general, Francisco Retz, vehemently forbade any Jesuit to consume yerba mate (and also tobacco) at a time when the Jesuit missions produced hundreds of thousands of kilos of yerba and the Jesuits sold large quantities through their trade offices in Alto Peru.[66] In response, the head of the Jesuit province of Paraguay, Jaime Aguilar, obediently wrote, "*I will not overlook any possible way to root out the use [of yerba mate] in this province*" (emphasis in the original), but he also gave himself some leeway in enforcing the prohibition. Aguilar added the caveat that a Jesuit could get permission to drink yerba in an austere manner like a medicine: one time a day without adding any sugar or other condiment, and the Jesuit had to be alone and nobody could witness him drinking yerba.[67] Some five years after Aguilar's response, his successor, Antonio Machoni, wrote to his superiors in Europe that he could not restrict yerba mate to the degree they desired. In defense of yerba, Machoni compared it to the chocolate, tea, and coffee that many European priests who came to Paraguay were accustomed to drinking and he asserted that it was not something that should be stopped. In the end, Machoni did little to reverse Aguilar's order that no Jesuit would be allowed to use yerba without the provincial's consent, and he added that a doctor also had to conclude that the person needed yerba mate. Unlike Aguilar, however, Machoni did not specify that the person had to consume yerba mate alone and in secret.[68] Such repeated medical exceptions by Jesuit leaders on the ground confirmed that prohibitions from the highest levels of church hierarchy were ineffective.

Despite occasional attempts at prohibition, yerba mate consumption rapidly spread in the seventeenth century to become a southern Spanish American staple. While an undercurrent of opposition continued, it was eventually considered a foodstuff. In fact, proponents enumerated a long list of medicinal attributes and it became a basic necessity for people of both genders and all ethnic, social, and economic classes. Its consumption unified people from Paraguay to Buenos Aires, Santiago, Potosí, Lima, and Quito, with only minor social distinctions based on mate accoutrements and additives. Yerba consumption became a shared social practice and a marker of Creole identity.

Once it was determined that yerba could not be stopped, Church officials sanitized the drink by obfuscating the diabolic connections that they had initially complained about. Within two decades of the Crown's definitive ruling on yerba production, stories about how the devil had taught the Indians about yerba were transformed into the claim that Saint Thomas (one of Jesus's twelve apostles and a famous missionary to the ends of the earth) had introduced yerba to the Guaraní.[69] By reinterpreting the story through a positive Christian lens, yerba became an acceptable, and even estimable, substance. Moreover, claiming that yerba was a gift from one of Jesus's disciples created a sense of obligation to utilize that gift.

Well before Church officials turned to Saint Thomas to justify yerba, others rationalized its use medicinally. As Antonio Ruíz de Montoya wrote in the 1630s, "The Spaniards have found it a remedy against all ills and claim that it is a well-proven remedy against urinary illness, and for this reason they use it in those regions without any moderation or restraint."[70] Some thirty years later, Diego de Zevallos published "Treatise on the Correct Use of the Yerba from Paraguay," as mentioned at the beginning of this chapter. In this document, Zevallos elucidated numerous health benefits associated with yerba consumption, implying that the substance was a veritable wonder drug that cured almost every ailment.[71] Similarly, scholars have claimed that other caffeinated beverages were popularized in Europe because of purported medicinal benefits, especially an association with sobriety, health and respectability.[72]

Many of the earliest medicinal descriptions of yerba mate referred to how it caused vomiting, which possibly occurred due to mold or additives. While people today would generally avoid something that made them vomit, this was not the case in the seventeenth and eighteenth centuries. Purging was seen as healthful. As late as 1860, a British medical text informed readers that "emetics, or medicines given to produce vomiting, are among the most anciently, the most universally, and the most constantly employed of all remedial agents."[73]

Even as yerba consumption became more widespread and its purported health benefits multiplied, a negative undertone persisted due to the habit-forming characteristics associated with caffeine. The Jesuit Martin Dobrizhoffer wrote in the mid-eighteenth century, "the moderate use of this herb is wholesome and beneficial in many ways," and he described a number of these positive traits. But Dobrizhoffer's tone turned sober as he warned about "immoderate and almost hourly use" and claimed, "I have known many of the lower Spaniards who never spoke ten words without applying their lips to the gourd containing the ready-made tea. If many topers in Europe waste their substance by an immoderate use of wine and other intoxicating liquors, there are no fewer in America who drink away their fortunes in potations of the herb of Paraguay."[74] Others also warned that yerba's habit-forming characteristics could lead to an obsessive and destructive addiction, but also like Dobrhizhoffer, they tended to focus more on the positive effects.[75] Most found the stimulating characteristics associated with caffeine especially commendable because people could work longer and endure discomfort. As the Spaniard Juan Francisco Aguirre, who spent sixteen years in South America, observed in the 1790s, yerba's attributes "consist in alleviating insomnia and labor. And it even numbs hunger, and sometimes it is better suited than water for extinguishing thirst." In addition to such practical concerns, Aguirre was one of the few colonial-era authors to write explicitly about yerba's value as a shared social activity that provided comfort and a sense of well-being. "How [yerba mate] consoles during bad weather is only known by observing it," Aguirre wrote. "So, a huddle [of people] are seen entertained around the fireplace for hours and hours, exhausting one kettle after another and its aforementioned qualities are seen fulfilled."[76]

A dispute over a transit tax on yerba in the early 1680s underscores how important yerba had become for the laboring class throughout much of South America. At the time, Santa Fe, a port city on the Paraná River, was the transit center for yerba mate on its way to Buenos Aires and the Andes region. Everyone involved in the trade feared that taxes imposed in Santa Fe would increase the market price of yerba, and thus, demand would fall.[77] In opposition to the tax, Pedro del Casal, a Santa Fe cabildo member, recorded the testimony of eight individuals involved in the yerba trade. Each was asked about yerba's role in the labor market. All eight asserted that yerba was absolutely critical for obtaining labor from both native peoples and Spaniards, as nobody would work without it. Seven of the eight highlighted that workers valued yerba above beef, bread, or all sustenance combined (the one exception referred to both yerba and tobacco as the primary sustenance of laborers).[78] In a separate petition, the lieutenant governor of Santa Fe claimed, "nothing bothers laborers except not having yerba readily accessible" and he asserted that a high price that made yerba inaccessible to the poor would infringe on a natural right.[79] In sum, the petitions described yerba as a critical consumer good—both a foodstuff and a basic necessity.

Such descriptions resonated with the *fiscal* (attorney general) of the Audiencia in Peru. In his response regarding the proposed tax, the fiscal not only confirmed yerba's importance to the region's labor market, he also described it as a food item that was a central part of the common diet. "Said yerba is used as a foodstuff (*alimento*) by all classes of people, Spaniards as well as Indians. The lack of which is felt no less than that of bread and meat, and to such a degree that workers, day laborers, and service people are given it without making any deduction to their wage."[80] In a separate letter to the king written under different circumstances, the governor of Paraguay also claimed that yerba "has passed from a drink to a foodstuff."[81]

During the colonial era, drinking yerba became widely engrained in the workday. For example, mate punctuated the daily work schedule for the Río de la Plata wheat harvest. Regulations issued by the viceroy in 1777 specified that workers had six mate breaks over the course of the day.

> They are to get up at four in the morning to drink mate and enter immediately to work. And after an hour and a half there, give them another mate, and half an hour later [breakfast], and an hour after this another mate—and from then until they leave work, all the cold water that they want. At 11:30, they retire to the House, where they will rest for a half an hour. And at 12:00, give them Food so that they can sleep for the siesta until 2:00. To wake them, give them mate and return again without delay to work. There, with the same distribution of time, serve them another two Mates, and afterwards all cold water until all have stopped working, which will be an hour after sundown.[82]

Employers not only had to give their workers time to drink mate, they also had to supply yerba rations.[83] According to historian Eduardo Saguier in his study of cattle hide production in the Banda Oriental (Uruguay) during the late colonial period, supplying yerba and tobacco rations was "essential." The first thing that a rancher did to initiate a work project was to give rations of tobacco and yerba to his peons, because otherwise, "there would not be laborers."[84] Indeed, fearing a lack of yerba for its citizens in 1732, the cabildo of Buenos Aires recommended a prohibition on transporting any of this substance "reputed to be a necessary foodstuff for human life" out of the city.[85]

A number of commentators noted that even Spaniards in the region considered yerba a basic necessity. Like the fiscal described above, another Crown official commented in 1681, "even those who come from Spain find themselves within a short period of time obligated to use it."[86] And in the 1760s, a French traveler wrote,

> Custom renders the use of it necessary; and it is often with difficulty that people abstain from an immoderate use of it. . . . The Spaniards of Europe care very little for this drink, but the Creoles are passionately fond of it. They never travel without a supply of the Paraguay plant; and never omit taking it every day, preferring it to all other kind of food; and never eating any till after they have taken it.[87]

Many commentators felt compelled to highlight how yerba consumption crossed gender and ethnic and class divisions. As early as 1628, Jesuit Nicolas Mastrillo Duran pointed out, "the use of this yerba is by all Spaniards, men and women, and all Indians drink its powder in hot water."[88] And in 1637 an Augustinian priest who had spent some years in the region described to the king, "he who does not consume it is very singular. . . . The male and female, Indians, Blacks, Spanish Creoles from there, and most everyone who has gone there [consumes it] two times every day, others one and others less." The priest estimated that there were at least sixty thousand consumers in Paraguay, Tucumán, and Río de la Plata.[89] Throughout these areas, yerba became a marker of regional identity, adopted by both Spaniards born in South America (Creoles) and Spaniards born in Spain who integrated into the region and adopted local practices. Over a century later, the official chronicler and historian of the Jesuit order in Paraguay wrote, yerba "is so customary in these three governorates in the realm of Peru and in that of Chile that it is drunk with more frequency than chocolate in Spain, and more widely, because from the vilest and poorest Black or Indian to the highest standing and wealthiest señor drink it various times a day."[90]

Public yerba consumption also became part of high society, especially during *tertulias* (social gatherings, often with a literary or artistic focus). Describing Buenos Aires in the early 1800s, José Antonio Wilde, an

Argentine author and doctor, wrote that the most notable and well-off families and a number of decent families regularly hosted tertulias at least once a week. During the tertulia, they generally "danced until twelve at night, or later, until the early morning; in such a case, only mate was served; when the dance lasted until the day, chocolate was added."[91] Mate was not limited to tertulias in Buenos Aires. A short fictional account of late colonial Ayacucho, Peru described elite guests being served mate when they arrived at a tertulia.[92] And Claudio Gay's painting of a 1790 tertulia in Santiago shows the men drinking mate and servants getting ready to serve chocolate.[93]

While the practice of consuming yerba cut across all sectors of South American society, additives and accoutrements allowed for some social distinctions. Some people—especially those with more resources—added flavorings to their yerba. The Jesuit Martin Dobrizhoffer commented that due to the natural bitterness, wealthier people drank it with sugar, but "the Indians, however, and the lower orders amongst the Spaniards, drink it unmingled with any thing."[94] Similarly, the Jesuit José Cardiel wrote, "the people of some standing toss in sugar, and even bitter orange and aromatic pastes. Ordinary people [drink it] without these kind of things." In addition to adding flavorings, yerba paraphernalia signaled status. Cardiel noted that "the wealthy have [their mate cup] decorated with silver, and of *palo santo* (very medicinal wood)."[95] The elite often spent large sums of money on ornate and ostentatious silver gourds, bombillas, and water heaters with internal braziers—examples of which are now housed in museums and private collections (see figure 3).[96] Servants or slaves generally served the beverage, and according to historian Ricardo de Lafuente Machain, it was not uncommon for slaveholders to force African slaves in eighteenth century Buenos Aires to serve mate on bended knee.[97]

Even though the slave or servant served the master in wealthy households, the practice of consuming yerba often blurred social divisions. As a traveler to the region wrote in 1808, "the use of this plant [yerba mate] is universal, being confined to no class. The slave drinks it as well as his master, and usually out of the same vessel too."[98] Historian Juan Carlos Garavaglia describes colonial Latin American society as deeply hierarchical, with each ethnic and social group having its own distinct consumption habits; but yerba was different. It was a practice shared by people of all social, economic, and racial classes, setting it apart from tea, chocolate, and coca—substances to which yerba was frequently compared.[99]

FIGURE 3. Colonial era mates and bombillas. Courtesy of the Casa Histórica. Museo Nacional de la Independencia, Tucumán, Argentina.

Yerba consumption not only crossed racial, economic, and gender barriers, it also spread geographically. It was drunk extensively throughout the Río de la Plata region, and large quantities of yerba crossed the Andes mountains to Lima and mining centers like Potosí.[100] In 1647, Gaspar Escalona Agüero, a lawyer born in Bolivia who wrote a book about the finances of Peru, also described to the king how people in Potosi and other parts of the region gathered to drink yerba like they did with chocolate in New Spain.[101] Right around that same time, a French traveler named Acarate du Biscay traveled up the Rio de la Plata and by land to Peru, a voyage which he documented in a book where he provided a rather fantastic overview of the essential healing function of yerba mate in the daily life of people in Peru at the time:

... without that Herb (with which they make a refreshing Liquor with Water and Sugar, to be drank lukewarm) the Inhabitants of Peru, Savages and others, especially those that work in the Mines, could not subsist, for the Soil of the Country Being full of Mineral Veins, the Vapours that rise out of the Ground suffocate them, and nothing but that Liquor can recover them again, which revives and restores them to their former Vigour ... and for this they have no other remedy, than the Drink which is made with the Herb of Paraguay, of which they prepare a great quantity to refresh and moisten 'em, when they come out of the Mines at the times appointed for eating or sleeping.[102]

Despite praising mate as a necessary and nourishing stimulant, du Biscay had a more negative take on the chewing of coca leaves (a practice that continues today to be closely linked with Indigenous peoples in the Andes), suggesting that it was detrimental to the Indians. He claimed that chewing coca "heats and fuddles 'em" whereas drinking yerba "refresh[es] and moisten[es] 'em."[103] Du Biscay was part of a trend of Europeans traveling to the region and writing books about their experiences there, often describing yerba mate with praise. Like du Biscay, a number of these authors also claimed that the beverage was critical to maintaining health in the inhospitable conditions of the cold and arid altiplano.[104] Although claims about its importance for surviving the harsh living conditions are likely implausible, it is true that yerba was increasingly consumed across the southern region of South America, and that this consumption was not limited to workers and the lower classes. The elite, often drinking from their gourds covered in silver, preferred the higher priced yerba *caamini* (exclusively yerba leaves and powder), which was only produced by the Guaraní missions under the Jesuits, over yerba *de palos* (yerba leaves, powder, and small sticks), which was produced more broadly and that common people would have consumed.

In the seventeenth and eighteenth centuries, the consumption of yerba continued to spread, reaching across the Andes to Chile. One mid-eighteenth century British explorer to Chile described in a book published in 1768 how the consumption of yerba had become well integrated into the lives of the Chilean elites with whom he interacted there, and he described its elaborate practice in detail: "Paraguay tea," he wrote, "which they call matte ... is always drunk twice a day: this is brought upon a large silver salver, with four legs raised upon it, to receive a little cup made out of a small calabash, or gourd, and tipped with silver."[105] The consumption of yerba in Chile continued to grow, and by the late colonial period, the region was a major market for yerba.[106] As far away as Ecuador, people observed the prominence of mate in the daily routines of regular people. In Quito, the Spanish scientist Antonio de Ulloa described how it was the usual drink of Creoles, who consumed it more than chocolate and for whom "it is the highest enjoyment."[107] Yerba mate had become a staple of everyday life for people throughout Spanish South America.

LABOR AND THE PRODUCTION OF YERBA

Over the course of the seventeenth and eighteenth centuries, as yerba's popularity spread across the continent, larger and larger quantities had to be produced. Indigenous people did most of the labor. As in much of the Americas at this time, Indigenous peoples in Paraguay were becoming increasingly integrated into the market economy. But in this region, yerba production, which had a long tradition among Indigenous groups, was the key mechanism for such integration. The Guaraní continued to harvest yerba mate from trees in the wild yerbales, but doing so became more onerous. Greater demand for yerba increased production and Paraguay's native population was coerced into labor. Even in the Jesuit missions, where the Guaraní were ostensibly exempt from forced labor, yerba work intensified as they produced large quantities from both wild yerbales and cultivated plantations.

Yerba mate (both *Ilex paraguariensis* and other similar species used for the infusion) are trees in the holly family (*aquifoliaceae*) that grow in parts of present-day Paraguay, Argentina, and Brazil between twenty and thirty degrees latitude. *Ilex paraguariensis* grows best in alluvial soils with consistent moderate rainfall and average temperatures around seventy degrees Fahrenheit, although it can tolerate extremes as low as twenty-one degrees Fahrenheit. In the wild, this evergreen grows in the understory and can reach heights of sixty feet. Cultivated trees can remain productive for over fifty years and up to ninety-five percent of leaves and branches can be harvested, ideally every other year.[108]

With the exception of Guaraní mission plantations in the eighteenth century, yerba mate was harvested from wild yerbales until the early twentieth century. This was different from other stimulants from the Americas; Indigenous peoples cultivated chocolate, tobacco, and coca long before the arrival of Europeans. Although yerba grew in the wild, harvesting and processing it was a fairly complex procedure that mixed Indigenous technologies for producing yerba with European innovations such as cattle hide sacks and mules for transportation. Spaniards disdained manual labor like harvesting and processing yerba, and so they created labor systems to get the Indians to do such work for them. Achieving this goal was not straightforward since the Guaraní did not practice wage labor or taxation, or believe in wealth accumulation, prior to the arrival of Europeans.

From early on, colonial sources referred to Indians working in the yerbales as both voluntary and coerced. In 1611, the Crown dispatched Francisco de Alfaro (a judge from the Audiencia of Charcas) to inspect the state of Indian labor in Paraguay. Alfaro decreed a blanket prohibition: "Under no circumstances, even if it is their own desire can [Indians] be allowed to go to Maracayú (the location of the yerbales) to harvest yerba due to the many deaths and harm that results from this." Punishments for violating this decree varied based on race. An Indian received the humiliating and infantile punishment of 100 lashes, while a Spaniard was fined 100 pesos, and any official who knowingly permitted a violation was removed from office.[109] The punishment for Indians suggests that some chose to work in the yerbales on their own, but still, Alfaro did not believe they were capable of acting in their own best interest. Rather, he thought it was the duty of Spanish officials to protect the Indians like a father who protects and punishes his children when they make a bad decision. Royal officials continuously struggled to maintain a balance between protecting the King's Indian subjects and meeting demand for Indigenous labor. In 1618, the Council of Indies tried to strike such a balance when it modified Alfaro's orders. Indians were not allowed to work in yerbales, even if they wanted to do so, but this time the prohibition was limited to "the times of the year that are dangerous and harmful to their health" (that is, the hot summer months, from December to March).[110] The revised ruling continued to protect and infantilize the Indians. Given the king's obligation to protect the interests of the weakest members of society, defenders of the Indians repeatedly lobbied for official investigations of, and limitations on, yerba labor throughout the colonial period.

The Jesuits vociferously criticized the exploitation of Indian labor in the yerbales, and when Alfaro drafted the ordinances regarding yerba production, he relied principally on the advice and direction of Diego de Torres, the head of the Jesuit province of Paraguay, who had lobbied the Inquisition in Lima to prohibit yerba altogether.[111] In that appeal, Torres decried the abysmal working conditions and called for a prohibition on yerba harvesting.[112] The Jesuits were especially critical of Indian labor in the yerbales, not only because it was onerous and many Indians died, but also because they felt that it threatened their missionary project. Laboring in the yerbales took the Indians away from the missions where they were under the watchful care of the Jesuits who taught them Catholicism, policed their behavior, and kept out bad influences.[113]

While filtered through Jesuit paternalism, the 1630 response of Guaraní leaders from Mission San Ignacio to two royal provisions adopted by the Audiencia of La Plata provides a glimpse into how some Guaraní felt about work in the yerbales. The provision both limited Indian labor services to no more than two months and prohibited Indians from going to Maracayú to work in yerba during times of sickness, even of their own free will. The Jesuits translated the Guaraní response into Spanish and added their own affirmations and signatures. Although the priests shaped and filtered the text, it is the only existing document on the subject that claims Guaraní authorship. It begins with the Guaraní expressing their happiness to learn of these royal provisions, which make them believe that the King is finally paying attention to them and their needs. The tone then quickly shifts. The rest of the text is a multifaceted complaint about yerba labor in Maracayú. The authors claim that Indians are forced against their will to do such work and the king's prohibitions are disobeyed. They highlight that the deaths of Indians working in the yerbales are destructive to Catholic practices and to Guaraní society.

> Even though we have heard many times, like now, [orders] that we do not go to Maracayú against our will, but the Spaniards did not obey. Before and after his Majesty had ordered this, they take each day our brothers, sons, and vassals to Maracayú, a place where they die and all are finished because there, our vassals have all been consumed. And not only our vassals but the sons of principal caciques, and even many caciques the Spaniards took to Maracayú where they were consumed and finished, dying in this wilderness without confession nor communion, as if they were infidels or animals without reason, keeping those yerbales full of the bones of our children and vassals. . . . Because of this, we do not want to go any more to Maracayú nor send our vassals there, because those that remain will not stop being consumed there.

The Guaraní authors wanted a complete prohibition of yerba labor in Maracayú. "Oh, if we had the good fortune that this which we say were done when His Majesty was informed. That the door and path to Maracayú were closed so that no more of our vassals go there . . . !" Twice, they explicitly stated that they did not want to go anymore nor have any of their vassals sent to Maracayú.[114] Despite such appeals, the Guaraní did continue to labor in the Maracayú yerbales.

As yerba's popularity grew in the seventeenth century, *beneficios* (one-time allotments of Indian laborers to produce and transport yerba) became increasingly important. In this forced labor draft arrangement, the governor served as the intermediary who obligated Indian towns to provide a yerba producer with a set number of laborers. In return, the yerba producer paid the Crown a specific amount of yerba mate per laborer and the Indians a wage.[115] The beneficio resembled, and likely was modeled after, the *mita* labor draft of Peru. In fact, the beneficio was often referred to as a mita.[116] Complaints about abuses of Indian laborers in the yerbales continued throughout the seventeenth century. Beneficio labor drafts often extended beyond the legally permitted duration. And in 1684, the governor of Paraguay followed Alfaro's example, ordering punishment for both Indians and Spaniards who illegally worked in yerba. Any Indian from Villa Rica working in the yerbales without official permission was to receive twenty-five lashes and labor two months at the Itapua fort, while the Spaniard who violated the law received a 50-peso fine and six months of labor.[117]

Yerba labor was onerous and tended to be exploitative, but it should not forgotten that there was still some room for agency. Some Indigenous groups used violence to make outsiders wary of entering yerbales, thereby limiting their ability to produce yerba.[118] According to one source, a group of Kaingang who regularly avoided violent confrontation furtively burned yerba produced by outsiders and blocked pathways with piles of branches in an effort to keep the intruders out of those areas.[119] Other Indians chose not to work in yerba and simply fled. As the governor of Paraguay explained to the Audiencia of Charcas in 1698, the accepted custom was for Indians to work in the beneficio of yerba for sixty days, "and the same Indians are so well informed that if they are obliged to work after those sixty days they flee."[120]

In the eighteenth century, wage labor became increasingly common and native peoples, along with mestizos, mulattos, and poor Spaniards, worked in yerba. According to Juan Carlos Gavaglia's estimates, free peons made up 35 to 45 percent of the yerba mate labor force by the beginning of the eighteenth century.[121] Even though they labored for wages, exploitation continued to occur in the form of debt peonage. But just like yerba consumption, yerba labor was not static, and it was tightly connected to the expansion of the market economy. As the subsequent chapters in this book discuss, the dark side of the growing demand for yerba mate remained a constant, and the exploitation of yerba workers continued for centuries—with varying degrees of intervention by governing officials. In general, the degree and nature of the oversight of the yerba markets and labor was dictated according to larger political debates and opportunities. This was true later in nineteenth- and twentieth-century Argentina, just as it was true during the colonial centuries. The next chapter describes how yerba mate became an informal tool of empire that helped integrate territory and people under Spanish rule.

TWO

———

Tool of Empire

FOR A FEW MONTHS IN 1731, a 1-shilling political pamphlet circulated on the streets of London. The pamphlet was titled *A Proposal for Humbling Spain,* and the anonymous author informed readers that if the British could find a way to wrest control of Buenos Aires from the Spanish, and in the process gain control of the yerba mate trade in South America, it would open the door to immense profits. "No one Place or Country under Heaven," he claimed, "is so capable of increasing the Trade and Riches of *Great Britain.*" The author, described only as "a man of distinction," predicted that by taking Buenos Aires, the British would eventually gain control over all of South American trade because the city's port and resources would allow the British to sell European goods cheaply and dominate the region's markets for European merchandise. But then he added, "without trusting to that, we should have them in a manner at our mercy, by having the Herb of *Paragua* in our hands."[1] As the pamphleteer highlighted, yerba mate was more than just a drink; it was a critical commodity in southern South America.

By the early eighteenth century, yerba mate had gained an important place in the culture and economy of southern South America. During the early colonial period, Spain's trade policies were heavily restrictive, and this had the effect of limiting the opportunities for merchants to develop yerba mate markets outside that region. But by the late eighteenth century, people outside of Spain began to recognize yerba mate's commercial potential—not only scientific explorers and merchants, but also European adventurers who wanted to take South America from the Spanish, such as the anonymous author of *A Proposal for Humbling Spain.* Despite this growing recognition of yerba mate's trade potential, by that time other "exotic" drinks such as tea, coffee, and chocolate had already infiltrated European beverage markets. The

Latin American wars of independence at the start of the nineteenth century—independence movements that created today's nation-states in South America—further disrupted any commercial efforts to expand the yerba mate trade.

This chapter argues that although yerba mate did not expand beyond the Americas, the independent actions of priests, merchants, and Spanish officials at all levels of hierarchy nevertheless made yerba mate an improvised and informal tool of empire. Like chocolate and tobacco, yerba mate was widely consumed thousands of miles from where it was produced, but unlike the other two stimulants from the Americas, yerba mate grew in an isolated frontier region. As such, it incorporated Paraguay's Indigenous inhabitants under Spanish rule, connected an otherwise marginalized region into the Spanish empire, and funded empire-building projects throughout the Southern Cone. From the late sixteenth century all the way until the wars of independence in the nineteenth century, it was the glue that connected Paraguay with the rest of southern South America—not only economically, but also culturally and politically.

YERBA MATE AND INDIGENOUS PEOPLES

One of the earliest and most important examples of the way yerba mate helped serve Spain's larger empire project in South America was the Jesuits' provision of yerba mate to advance their missionary work among Indigenous peoples. Although missions were principally focused on effecting religious conversion, missionary work also played a fundamental role in the early development of Spain's larger empire across the continent. Yerba mate, which was widely consumed by Indigenous people throughout southern South America, became a key tool for the Jesuits in their efforts to encourage people to join their missions, and consequently in the growth of the Spanish empire.

Jesuit missionaries, whose writings in the Río de la Plata region date back to the early sixteenth century, were among the first Europeans to write about yerba mate. After initially opposing its consumption because they believed it was a tool of the devil, the Jesuits quickly changed their tune when they recognized that it was a useful tool for incorporating native peoples under Spanish rule. The Guaraní valued yerba mate, and over time, the Jesuits became convinced that the drink was essential for the success of the missions.[2] They realized that in order to make religious advances, a mission had to first provide for the Indians' material well-being—and since the Indians' lifestyle was woven around the daily consumption of yerba mate, it was impossible to overlook the importance of this material provision to their larger missionary work. In his description of the Jesuit missions in the eighteenth century, José Cardiel specified, "[the missionaries] join the temporal with the spiritual . . . because in these [Indigenous] people, the good of their souls is not obtained, nor the spiritual reached without the temporal. If the temporal is good, the spiritual moves ahead well; if bad, the spiritual advances very poorly."[3] Provisioning the Indians with ample yerba was critical in this respect. In 1667, the Jesuit provincial of Paraguay acknowledged in a letter to missionaries that yerba was necessary for the Indians.[4] Two decades later, another provincial highlighted only two items (cattle and yerba mate) when discussing the requisite goods for a mission.[5] Regularly providing mission Indians with these two items was essential and the Jesuits tried to make sure that each mission distributed yerba rations twice daily and beef rations daily or several times a week from communal supplies.[6]

Another way that the Jesuits used yerba mate to advance their missionary work and, in turn, further Spanish oversight of native people, was by encouraging its use as a substitute for alcohol, as the Jesuits were eager to restrict alcohol use among native peoples. As the Jesuit priest Florian Paucke recounted, an Indigenous leader from the Chaco named Cithaalin purportedly told him, "Well, if I had this [yerba] every day, I would not think much in our [alcoholic] drink. I like this and it does not give me a headache."[7] Of course Paucke responded by regularly giving yerba to Cithaalin. Elsewhere, Paucke wrote, " . . . I should be thankful nonetheless. An especially good *effect* that I have achieved by the introduction of this drink among my *Indians:* for the most part I have gotten them to stop drunkenness with *chicha.*"[8] Other missionaries also affirmed that they used yerba mate to keep native peoples from becoming intoxicated.[9]

The Jesuits also liked that drinking yerba mate invigorated Guaraní workers. As an earlier provincial had explained, all native peoples drank it before sunrise and then throughout the day. Every time they did so, the yerba gave them sustenance and rekindled their strength to work, even when they didn't eat.[10] Over a decade later, another Jesuit acknowledged that drinking yerba reinvigorated the Indians and pointed out that it was always in the background while the Guaraní worked, ready for when they took a break.[11]

The Jesuits valued yerba mate not only as a tool for mediating relationships with native peoples, but also for its economic value. As a leader of the order in Europe explained, yerba was a necessity for the Indians because it served both as nourishment and as money to buy what they needed to live.[12] Individual Guaraní directly engaged in some of this trade, but mostly it was overseen by the Jesuits.[13] As provincial Andrés de Rada instructed missionaries in 1667, yerba mate was the commodity best suited for generating revenue to pay tribute to the Crown. He proceeded to give explicit instructions about how the missionaries should send Indians to the wild yerbales to produce yerba mate.[14] Concerned about their lack of control over Indians in these distant locations, the Jesuits had found a way, by the end of the seventeenth century, to limit such absences by encouraging the Guaraní to cultivate yerba on plantations closer to the missions.[15] Yet, while this innovation helped the Jesuits maintain more oversight, cultivation required more labor than harvesting yerba from wild yerbales, and it did not eradicate the Guaraní practice of harvesting from the wild. Ultimately, the missions used both methods—harvesting yerba from cultivated plantations and from wild yerbales—to help raise the funds to pay tribute to the Spanish Crown.[16]

The selling of yerba mate was one of the key methods that Paraguayan missions used to maintain their financial well-being and fund mission operations. It also made the Guaraní-Jesuit missions into a major player in the yerba economy.[17] The missions sold yerba *de palos* (yerba leaves, powder, and small sticks), but they were also the exclusive producers of yerba *caamini* (yerba leaves and powder without small sticks), which was most popular in Cuzco and Lima where it sold at a much higher price.[18] Legally, the missions were limited to selling 12,000 arrobas (300,000 pounds) of yerba per year, and between 1731 and 1745, the missions' yerba sales earned almost 50,000 pesos yearly—far surpassing revenues from any other mission activity. This money enabled the Jesuits' thirty missions in Paraguay to sustain 140,000 Guaraní at their peak in the 1730s, thereby making them the most populated of all the Catholic missions in the Americas.[19]

The Jesuits also used yerba to attract new Indigenous converts. Recognizing that native peoples held yerba in high regard, the Jesuits gifted it to those who they targeted for conversion.[20] Many of these people did not live in areas where yerba mate grew naturally. In writing about his interactions with the Cloyá nation in the land of the Charrúas of northeastern Argentina and southern Brazil, Francisco Garcia told how he distributed tobacco and yerba mate—items of great esteem to the Cloyá nation—to help encourage people to participate in the missions.[21] In this way, the Jesuits used yerba and other items to manipulate native peoples and create a dependent relationship.

Missionary letters and other documents from this era attest to this. In a book called *An Account of the Abipones,* for example, the Jesuit Martin Dobrizhoffer described how a man named Ychoalay (an Abipon who helped the Jesuits) recognized what the priests were trying to do. Dobrizhoffer wrote that Ychoalay "drank [yerba] when it was offered him, but never requested it of us. He prudently feared, that if, by a too frequent use, he accustomed himself to this costly beverage, he should some time or other be obliged to either beg or buy it."[22] Father Florian Paucke also explained how Jesuits used yerba to influence Indians in the Chaco region, where it "was very avidly requested and drunk a lot by the Indians but none had the power or the opportunity to procure it for himself because it had to be brought from the Guaraní missions that plant it."[23] Recognizing how much the Indians liked yerba, the Jesuits used it to gain control over them, giving it as a reward for attending religious services, participating in work activities, and refraining from intoxicating drinks. The missionaries also used yerba to influence the native leadership structure and make native leaders more compliant and submissive. Paucke wrote that the Chaco leader Cithaalin, after introducing his followers and friends to the drink, frequently pestered the priests for large quantities of yerba. Displeased by Cithaalin's independence, the priests subsequently gave yerba to one of Cithaalin's competitors so that he could then use the distributions to cultivate followers.[24]

Not only did missionaries use yerba mate as a tool for manipulating the Indians, Crown officials also found yerba mate to be a powerful diplomatic tool for establishing relations with Indigenous peoples and making them into colonial subjects. The cabildo of Santa Fe explicitly budgeted allotments of yerba mate in the 1650s to pacify and buy the allegiance of the Colatastinés people and other native allies from the Calchaquí Valley.[25] Around 1720, José García Inclán communicated with Indian leaders near Montevideo and gave them "yerba del Paraguay and tobacco, which for them are the best gift." He believed that in this way the Indians "could be softened" such that, with time, they could be brought into settlements.[26] A little over a decade later, leaders of Montevideo celebrated the diplomatic negotiation of general peace with the Minuanes by gifting yerba, tobacco, knives and bridles to the caciques.[27] Native peoples often considered the provisioning of yerba mate and other items an exchange and not a gift. For example, some Charrúas agreed to settle near Santo Domingo Soriano on the condition that they be given a cow and, each day, four pounds of yerba mate. When they did not receive these items, they revolted.[28]

Another way that yerba mate helped serve the broader development of Spanish power in South America was the way non-Indian outsiders used it to gain access to resources under Indian control. In 1636, Baltasar de Pucheta testified that Martín de Ledesma Valderrama wanted to hunt wild cattle, but the territory was under the control of hostile Guaicuru who had already killed a Spaniard. Ledesma Valderrama conversed with the main cacique, his son, and some other Indians and gave them a lot of yerba and corn. As a result, Ledesma Valderrama reported that the Indians were content, and the Spaniards were subsequently able to hunt cattle in the region.[29] In another instance, a priest used yerba mate and tobacco to purchase the freedom of two Spanish women held captive by Charrúas.[30] On the eve of independence, yerba mate continued to be a useful tool for negotiating with native peoples. The leader of an expedition to salt flats in Patagonia reported to the viceroy that cacique Calepuqueo made it clear that "we had to pay to step on their lands, and tribute, to extract salt . . . the aguardiente, yerba, and tobacco that the Christians gave to them were not a gift."[31] Spaniards also gave yerba to native peoples in order to buy their labor. In the early years of Asunción, governor Martínez de Irala (1530s-1550s) gave rations of yerba to Indian workers.[32] Likewise, in 1609 the cabildo of Buenos Aires gave yerba, wheat, and beef to Indians who transported wood to construct the cabildo building, and in 1658, the cabildo of Santa Fe provided yerba and tobacco to Indians who worked in public buildings, churches, and the houses of impoverished inhabitants.[33]

By giving yerba to Indians, Spaniards expanded both its consumption and geographic reach. Some Indigenous peoples, like those in distant locations such as Patagonia and the pampas, had had little to no contact with yerba before European contact. Others were already consuming yerba, but the amounts grew as a result of their relations with Spaniards. Writing in the eighteenth century, the Jesuit Jose Cardiel claimed that Indians consumed relatively little yerba before European contact, but in contrast, almost all unconverted Indians (*infieles*) now consumed yerba mate due to contact with Spaniards.[34] This expansion of yerba consumption benefited the Spanish who exploited this new demand for their own economic and governing interests as the Indigenous peoples actively traded goods to obtain yerba. Lozano reported that the Yaro people, who were the sworn enemies of the Guaraní, would come to Jesuit missions whenever they were at peace to buy some goods that appealed to them, such as yerba and tobacco, in exchange for horses.[35] Similarly, Indigenous people of the pampas exchanged various articles that they made (such as the throwing weapon *bolas*, traps, hides, salt, ostrich feathers, blankets or clothing of leather, coarse cloth, and wool ponchos) for yerba, hats, knives, bits, spurs, and some dried fruit.[36] After independence, the Swiss doctor and scientist Johann Rengger attributed the spread of yerba solely to Spaniards. During his six-year residency in Paraguay (1819–1826), Rengger never encountered Indians using yerba who had not had frequent contact with non-Indians.[37] By developing these trading networks, and working to encourage its use and dependency among Indigenous populations, yerba mate became a useful tool in Spain's large empire building project in South America.

YERBA MATE: TRADE AND MONEY

In addition to serving as a key material for the Spanish to advance their missionary and trading networks with Indigenous peoples, and despite never becoming a major beverage among the rich European markets, yerba mate played a foundational role in Paraguay's participation in both interregional and transatlantic trade.[38] Because Spain had already worked to establish its presence in Paraguay and among the Guaraní, this had the long-term impact of advancing Spain's dominance in the region. While silver drove the Spanish American economy that linked the Americas with Europe and the rest of the world, yerba mate was central to regional trade. Deemed critical for subsistence in much of South America, yerba mate made places like the distant Andean mining center of Potosí dependent on Paraguay.

As a frontier periphery, Paraguay was distant and difficult to get to from the main outposts of Spanish rule in South America. The route that traders needed to travel from Asunción to Potosí is approximately the same number of miles (almost 1,600) as from Miami, Florida to Portland, Maine, plus it included climbing the Andes. High transportation costs made most Paraguayan trade goods uncompetitive.[39] The main exception was yerba mate. Paraguay was the sole producer of this consumer good considered to be a basic necessity throughout much of South America.[40] As one Spaniard who spent over a decade in the region wrote, Paraguay's poverty would have led to isolation but for a strange success. Commerce was the key for him, and yerba mate was "most essential."[41]

During the seventeenth century, Paraguay was a geographic region that bordered the Peruvian territories of Santa Cruz and Charcas to the west and extended to Portuguese territory in the northeast. To the south, the Iguazú and Paraná Rivers separated the province of Paraguay from the province of Buenos Aires. It comprised the regions that make up modern-day Paraguay and extended into what is now Argentine and Brazilian territory. Spanish settlement centered around Asunción, the capital, which was along the Paraguay River, while the wild yerbales were mostly toward the eastern part of the province.

During the first hundred years or so after Spanish contact, yerba quickly became Paraguay's main trade good. By the early 1630s (about two decades after the Crown confirmed that it was legal to produce yerba mate), the yerba trade reached 890 arrobas or roughly 22,250 pounds, as compared with 680 arrobas of sugar and less than 100 arrobas of wine. Thirty years later, yerba mate export revenues far surpassed those generated by any other trade good.[42] As a Frenchman waylaid in Buenos Aires in the 1660s observed, "there are a good number of Spanish inhabitants [in Paraguay] who harvest wheat, wine, sugar, excellent tobacco, and many types of fruits. And even though all these things are very good, there is an herb called *Yerba Santa* whose trade among all of them is the most important in the region."[43] According to account books, the yearly average quantity of yerba mate that arrived in the transit point of Santa Fe on its way to markets in the Andes and Buenos Aires jumped to over 25,000 arrobas (625,000 pounds) in 1675–1682 and almost twice that amount by the early 1700s.[44]

The yerba trade broke Paraguay out of isolation and connected the distant imperial backwater with other parts of Spanish South America. In 1658, a Frenchman who traveled from Buenos Aires to Potosí and Peru observed that the yerba mate trade "obliges the Merchants of *Chili* and *Peru,* to hold a Correspondence with those of *Paraguay.*"[45] A 1680s tax dispute provides further details about how the yerba mate trade connected the region with Spanish centers in South America. During the investigation, eight individuals involved in trade between Paraguay and the Andes provided testimony about the impact of a proposed tax on yerba passing through Santa Fe. All eight used strong wording to emphasize that the yerba mate trade was absolutely necessary for Paraguay's well-being, acknowledging that yerba was essentially the only reason that merchants went there.[46] Without it, they believed that Paraguay would be disconnected and the inhabitants left without any means for purchasing the basic necessities that they could not produce themselves. As Bernave Arias testified, "dealing in yerba is simply necessary for the conservation of this city, without it [the city] would be absolutely ruined because it is the only thing attractive to merchants to whom it gives some convenience. Removing this [would be] very damaging because shipping with Paraguay would not continue." Similarly, Rafael Vallesteros stated, "without a doubt, the principal foundation for the conservation of this city are the dealings in yerba. First because merchants come only for [yerba] and this results in the citizens acquiring the things that they need for their apparel." Such opinions were not limited to people involved in the yerba mate trade. Government officials and travelers also acknowledged that the yerba mate trade was critical to Paraguay's well-being, and that it connected the region to other parts of the Spanish empire.

The vital importance of the yerba mate trade was also repeatedly mentioned in a lengthy dispute about Indians laboring in yerbales that reached the Audiencia of Charcas (the appellate court with jurisdiction over Paraguay and the Río de la Plata region) and the Council of Indies in Spain. In 1696, the Audiencia of Charcas responded to a request from the king about the matter, confirming that yerba production was critical to Paraguay.

> [T]he production of Paraguayan yerba is necessary, in the opinion of everyone, for the conservation of that region. Since, if they lacked this, without any doubt the people would be jeopardized because the inhabitants maintain themselves with this, the only good that is produced, and because no other province produces this yerba (and its use being common and the healthful effects it creates, especially in these [regions] that have extremely dry climates, and the majority of them cold, [yerba] is part of the necessary sustenance). Merchants go and look for it, bringing trade goods that the inhabitants of the city of Asunción need, to exchange and trade for the yerba that they bring to these provinces. Thus, without [yerba] it would be impossible to conserve said city, being only [yerba] that has sustained that province.[47]

A decade later, the Audiencia of Charcas again described the yerba mate trade as Paraguay's lifeblood. "Yerba is the only product, and it qualifies as a foodstuff, hence the commerce, agreements, and contracts provide what is necessary for the political and social life [of the province]."[48]

At the same time as Spain worked to establish its administrative and military presence across the continent during the seventeenth and eighteenth centuries, yerba became an intricate part of Paraguay's status and position within that larger colonial and economic network. Its importance extended beyond its role as Paraguay's major trade good; it also served as money, which by definition has three main functions: a medium of exchange, deposit of value, and unit of account. Yerba was not unique in this respect. Alternate currencies coexisted with coinage throughout the early modern world. In the Americas, Europeans co-opted forms of money used by Indigenous peoples prior to conquest. Cacao beans in Mesoamerica and wampum in North America continued to be widely accepted as money throughout the colonial period.[49] Food items and stimulants also widely functioned as commodity money to facilitate trade and financial transactions in the seventeenth century: sugar in Barbados, tobacco in Britain's southern colonies, and tea in Central Asia.[50] Coins were widely used only along the more important trade routes and in large cities. Elsewhere *monedas de la tierra* (locally-produced goods) such as yerba mate were the norm. These alternate currencies persisted even though Spain had a formal system of coinage and Spanish America produced tons of silver coins. The Crown's mercantilist economic policies channeled silver to Spain, and from there, throughout Europe and Asia to pay for imperial debts and imports. Crown policies combined with voracious global demand for silver limited the amount of coinage that circulated in the Americas. The large denomination of Spanish coins used in the Americas further limited their circulation. The smallest coin was a quarter *real,* which was too valuable for small, everyday transactions. Even in the core area of New Spain, cacao was widely used throughout the colonial period, and shop tokens became prevalent in both New Spain and Buenos Aires in the eighteenth century.[51] The limited circulation of hard currency led some to prefer commodities over coinage for commercial transactions. In the early 1770s, a Spanish official observed that the common people of the Tucumán countryside did not know "a better gift than the yerba of Paraguay, and tobacco, sugar and aguardiente" and that they preferred to trade for these goods over silver coins.[52]

In Paraguay itself, yerba served as an essential currency. Very little silver made its way to this remote region, and from early on, the lack of hard currency was a problem. Only a year after Asunción's founding, the city's leaders complained that the lack of gold and silver made it difficult to conduct trade and pay taxes.[53] Various locally-produced goods took on the role of moneda de la tierra, and as yerba mate developed into Paraguay's main trade good, it became recognized as the "usual money between the people of Paraguay."[54] Even the king acknowledged in 1680 that yerba was Paraguay's *moneda corriente* (common currency) when he instituted the disputed tax on yerba passing through Santa Fe referred to earlier.[55] In 1717, citizens of the yerba-producing region of Curuguaty wrote to the governor that it was customary since time immemorial to use yerba as currency at the going rate of one peso per arroba, and that the king, by way of his royal treasury, regularly received tax payments in the form of yerba in lieu of currency.[56] In 1761, the bishop of Paraguay described, "here neither gold nor silver circulate. Paraguayans make hollow pesos of goods produced from the land: some are minted in the Philosopher's Stone of yerba."[57]

In accounting records, yerba mate quantities functioned as a unit of account that calculated value. An inventory of the assets and liabilities of a French doctor, Francisco Obet, after his sudden death in Asunción highlights yerba mate's role as both a trade good and a form of money.[58] Obet had amassed significant wealth by the time of his death in 1718. His extensive inventory included personal items, books, medicines, and tools related to his medical profession. The first item, however, was twenty-eight bags of yerba found in his home, and another fifteen bags were mentioned later. These forty-three bags of yerba weighed a total of 290 arrobas (7,250 pounds)— definitely much more than Obet could ever consume personally—and were worth the large sum of 580 pesos. The only other trade good in Obet's home was tobacco, with three small bags worth only twenty-nine pesos. As Obet's inventory shows, involvement in the yerba mate trade in Paraguay extended beyond producers and merchants.

Obet's estate shows how royal officials utilized the yerba mate trade to connect Paraguay to the larger Spanish empire. A decade after his death, the king of Spain formally asked the royal treasury in Asuncion for a report about the doctor's estate. The case attracted royal attention not only because Obet was a foreign citizen who had died in Spanish territory with significant wealth, but also because he had no known legitimate heirs in the region. In response, the royal treasury in Asunción sent a lengthy report, describing all of Obet's assets and liabilities. After taking possession of Obet's physical assets, the royal treasury sold the items at auction. It also collected debts owed to Obet and paid debts owed to other parties. In the early pages of the document, items were valued in pesos. In contrast, the final value of Obet's estate was not calculated in pesos, but in yerba mate. His assets totaled 4,365 arrobas 13 pounds (109,138 pounds) of yerba mate and his liabilities totaled 3,772 arrobas 3 pounds (94,303 pounds). The valuing of Obet's estate in arrobas of yerba mate rather than in pesos vividly illustrates that it was a standard measure of value that facilitated exchange.

Yerba mate was not just a recorder of value. Paraguayans regularly made monetary payments to the Spanish government in yerba mate. For example, Diego de los Reyes Balmaceda, a native of Spain whose business operations centered on transporting yerba between Asunción and Buenos Aires, made a *donativo* (donation) of a large quantity of yerba to the royal treasury so that he could become governor of Paraguay, a position that he held from 1717 to 1721.[59] Decades later, an observer commented that Paraguayan elite aspired to *regimientos* (military offices) valued at 4,000 arrobas of yerba.[60] During wartime in the 1790s, Paraguayans frequently donated yerba mate to the Crown.[61] As these examples demonstrate, the Crown recognized yerba mate as currency.

While the yerba mate trade was vital to Paraguay, many complained about inequalities and exploitation. The merchants of Buenos Aires were commonly portrayed as the root of the problem, but individuals at each level of the trade and production of yerba mate frequently manipulated unequal power relations to their advantage. One of the most descriptive complaints comes from Archbishop of Paraguay Manuel Antonio de la Torre in 1761. De la Torre perplexingly commented "all man is yerba; with this yerba, the Paraguayans stop being men when it makes others men; and from this point emerges the enigma of Paraguay."[62] The archbishop then spent several pages explaining what he meant, which he summarized, finally: "yerba has enriched and fattened many merchants" while it "enslaves and entirely destroys the Paraguayans." He went into detail, explaining that merchants bringing goods from Buenos Aires to sell in Paraguay marked them up by at least 300 percent, and when they were in short supply, 500 percent or more. In this exploitative system, de la Torre not only faulted the traveling merchants, he blamed Buenos Aires merchant houses for selling poor quality and high-priced goods on credit to the local merchants, often taking advantage of the situation to "dispose of the excrement in their store . . . covering it all with some stylish items."

According to de la Torre, the peons who produced yerba mate were the most exploited of all. Businessmen enticed peons to work in yerba by selling them trade goods on credit, adding a 30 to 50 percent premium to the price of the goods. To support his claim, de la Torre provided specific examples of price differences for textiles purchased in Buenos Aires and then sold to peons working in yerba mate: *pañete* cost 4 reales in Buenos Aires but 32 reales in Paraguay; *bayeta* cost 3 reales in Buenos Aires and 20 reales in Paraguay; *Bretañas* cost 4 pesos in Buenos Aires and 20 to 24 pesos in Paraguay, and if there was some need, 30 pesos. According to his calculations, peons paid five to eight times the price in Buenos Aires and had to work one year or more in yerba to pay for 200 pesos of clothing that were not worth 30 pesos. As a result, "with said exercise [the peons] wear out the clothing, and at the end of the assignment, they return poorly fed and poorly dressed." To solve the inequalities and injustices of the yerba trade, de la Torre told the king, "Señor, there is no other means than to curb the greed of the merchants, imposing on them by law that they cannot earn more than 100 percent [profit] on their merchandise." He also asked for a prohibition on the sale of unnecessary trinkets that the Buenos Aires merchant houses regularly forced onto the traders. De la Torre was not the only one to claim that Paraguayans were exploited in the yerba mate trade, but regardless, the Council of Indies decided not to act on his recommendations.[63] The *fiscal* (attorney) for the Council acknowledged that returns to trade are fickle. Merchants sometimes experienced high margins and other times losses. Thus, he deemed it too difficult to set a limit on profit margins.[64] The Crown did not take action against the unequitable and exploitative aspects of the yerba trade because it served a critical role in connecting the frontier region of Paraguay to the core areas of the Spanish empire and because of its key role in funding empire-building projects.

YERBA MATE AND TAXES

The deep integration of yerba mate into regional economies during the early centuries of the Spanish empire was made possible because of yerba mate's historically central role in the cultural practices of people living in southern South America—cultural practices that continue to influence life in Argentina, Paraguay, Uruguay, and southern Brazil today. Eager to exploit and profit from its centrality in local culture, government officials directly intervened in the yerba trade in the seventeenth and eighteenth centuries. This interference reveals the polycentric nature of the Spanish empire, showing how yerba mate was not just a tool of a central power, but was used by local officials across the region to fund empire-building projects that addressed local needs. As a number of scholars have pointed out, Spanish policy in the Americas developed as a complex interplay of actions, reactions, and non-actions by agents at all levels of the empire.[65] Even though Spanish rule in the Americas was formally organized under a monarch advised by the Council of Indies, yerba mate's role in local empire-building shows how it was held together by diffuse local officials who took initiative and found creative ways to respond to the pressing needs of their jurisdictions.

Because yerba mate was such a central activity culturally and economically for people in the region, Crown officials in the Americas turned to yerba mate when they had to scramble to generate funds. Spanish America received little money from Spain, and when the need for additional revenue arose, the Crown rarely provided emergency financial assistance. Taxing the yerba trade was an easy way to collect money for emergencies or to fund projects that addressed critical concerns. For some, it was also a tool for social engineering—an early example of a sin tax. The taxation of yerba mate at all levels of the local, regional, and vice-regal hierarchy is evidence of the devolution of fiscal decisions to local authorities. It also is an example of redistribution and the high rate of cross-subsidization between regions, as much of the tax revenue was used far from yerba mate's origins in Paraguay.[66]

Tapping into the yerba trade to fund empire-building projects was not a part of a coherent strategy; rather, each project was an isolated effort to generate money. Spanish officials were constantly worried about financial shortfalls. While mines in Spanish America accounted for about eighty percent of world production of silver (some 150,000 tons) between 1500 and 1800, the Spanish empire experienced constant fiscal shortages.[67] Not only did mercantilist economic practices channel most of the silver to Spain, wars and other expenditures consumed most of the Crown's budget. Spain was perennially squeezed for cash and had little to spend on empire-building projects in the Americas, leaving local officials to scramble for their own resources. As Regina Grafe and Alejandra Irigoin have shown, both the collection and re-allocation of Spanish imperial revenue were decentralized and locally managed, and a large share of the revenues was spent in a different region from its collection.[68] In emergency situations such as an attack by hostile Indigenous peoples or an environmental calamity, administrators often had to find creative ways to raise money. This often meant turning to the extremely popular and habit-forming yerba mate.

Because of the way it was produced, Spaniards approached yerba differently than other Indigenous American substances. With the exception of the Guaraní missions, native peoples did not cultivate yerba mate like they did tobacco, chocolate, and coca. Instead, they harvested it from trees that grew naturally in the wild. Spanish documents frequently refer to yerba as a mineral. For example, a Spanish official in Asunción explained in 1697 that yerba is "the mineral of this Province."[69] Two decades later, the governor of Paraguay described how "the goods of the land that produce the minerals of [the province]—which are yerba, tobacco and others—are given as money because silver does not circulate in this province."[70] While the governor also referred to tobacco and other products, most people meant yerba mate when they mentioned minerals in Paraguay.[71] In a similar vein, the wild yerbales that produced yerba were often called mines. In 1790, Juan Francisco de Aguirre wrote, "The yerbal is called mine and this reference makes me agree that there is a parallel with those of gold and silver." Elsewhere, Aguirre explained that yerba trees were found "in the dense mines of Caaguaqué, Mbaracayu, and other distant ones."[72] References to yerbales as mines continued throughout the colonial period, and even extended into the early twentieth century.

Yerbales were thought of as mines because wild trees produce yerba mate without human intervention. In the early modern era, people did not understand how metals were created. Many (both Indians and Europeans) believed that metals and minerals grew like plants beneath the ground and were capable of auto-regeneration.[73] Yerba trees, metals, and minerals occurred spontaneously without human intervention, as an act of nature. Hence, Spanish law treated yerbales as mines. As such, the Crown claimed exclusive ownership, which could only be utilized by private individuals through a licensing system.[74] The understanding of yerbales as mines had implications for their capacity to generate government revenue. Taking the association of yerbales with mines to an extreme, an early governor of Paraguay tried unsuccessfully to apply the royal fifth (the tax applied on the mining of all precious metals and minerals) to yerba extracted from wild yerbales.[75]

Although yerba mate was never actually assessed the royal fifth, it became burdened by countless levies as South American bureaucrats at all echelons saw yerba as an easy target for generating much needed revenue. In 1778, the governor of Paraguay complained to the king that yerba was taxed at a much higher rate than all the other goods produced in the Americas, including precious metals, and that the total of the taxes on yerba far surpassed its original price. He speculated that yerba produced revenue for the Royal Treasury ten times more than its value in Paraguay.[76]

Local Spanish officials repeatedly taxed yerba mate when they needed funds. As a widely-consumed and habit-forming substance, demand was inelastic (in other words, consumers still purchased yerba mate even when its price increased), and thus, taxes were guaranteed to generate revenue. Yerba mate was also an easy mark for taxation since it was the driver of the Paraguayan economy. Elsewhere in South America, such as Buenos Aires, Lima, Potosí, and Santiago, it was convenient to tax yerba because it was not produced locally and distant Paraguayan yerba mate producers had little clout in influencing such taxation decisions. The most vocal opponents of yerba mate taxes were merchants, but their complaints were frequently drowned out by claims that they were profiteers who had artificially inflated yerba prices.[77]

From the beginning, Spanish officials extracted revenue from yerba mate. In 1602, a member of the Asunción town council recommended to the king that no one be allowed to produce yerba or even bring it for sale in Asunción without a license costing 100 pesos. In introducing his appeal, the author reminded the king, "you knew very well the great necessity that this city has for income."[78] A year later, a citizen of Asunción obtained such a license for the significantly higher fee of 510 pesos.[79] At the same time, the government also taxed yerba mate sales.[80]

Interest in capturing government revenue from the yerba trade even reached Spain. In 1637, the Crown received a proposal for a royal monopoly (*estanco*) on yerba mate by the Augustinian priest Gonzalo del Valle and found it so attractive that a committee was formed to investigate its feasibility. Del Valle speculated that if Crown officials imposed a yerba mate monopoly, or if a monopoly were leased to one or more individuals, the price could be regulated at 4 reales, which would translate to gross revenues of 300,000 pesos. The committee charged with investigating Gonzalo del Valle's idea spent a great deal of time and effort on the task; they searched for everything that had been written about yerba mate and asked for information from people familiar with the region. Concluding that del Valle's estimates were inflated, the committee instead settled for the imposition of a levy and royal orders were issued to officials in South America to follow up on the matter.[81]

The failure to create a yerba mate monopoly did not prevent Spanish officials in South America from continuing to identify other ways to generate government revenues from the yerba mate trade. The most frequent justification was that Spanish territory was under threat and there was not enough money to pay for its defense. In seventeenth-century Paraguay, these levies generally took the form of *beneficios*, whereby the government provided yerba producers with Indian laborers in return for fees per laborer, often paid in yerba mate.[82] Cabildo members and the governor claimed that these beneficios were issued whenever the local government needed money and that it was the only way to collect the necessary funds for defense against attacks by Indians and/or Portuguese marauders.[83]

Beyond Paraguay, Spanish officials found taxing yerba in the port city of Santa Fe to be the most effective method of capturing revenues for distribution elsewhere in the Río de la Plata region. Given its location along the Paraná River, the gateway to Paraguay, Santa Fe was ideal for taxing Paraguayan trade.[84] Although such taxes applied to almost all Paraguayan trade goods, those on yerba mate generated both the most revenue and the fiercest complaints. The revenue was frequently earmarked for defense projects throughout the Río de la Plata region, often in places far from Paraguay. As discussed earlier, a major dispute arose in 1680 when yerba mate passing through Santa Fe was assessed a tax of one-half peso per arroba if destined for Santa Fe and Buenos Aires and one peso per arroba if destined for Tucumán, Chile, and the Andes. The king approved the tax based on a 1664 letter from the governor of Buenos Aires, Joseph Martínez de Salazar, who claimed the need for such a tax to cover necessary defense expenditures in Buenos Aires, specifically the port city's fortifications and salaries for additional troops.[85] Great uproar ensued in Santa Fe and all over Paraguay as numerous parties lobbied intensely for revocation of the tax. In 1685, the tax was discontinued so that Santa Fe and Asunción would not shoulder the expense of defending Buenos Aires.[86] The revocation was only temporary; yerba taxes were again instituted in Santa Fe to cover defense expenditures in Buenos Aires and also in Montevideo.[87] Santa Fe also lobbied for similar taxes to cover its own defense needs, as did almost every location where yerba mate passed.[88] As the Jesuit missionary Martin Dobrizhoffer wrote when describing commercial trade in Cordobá, "the tax laid on the herb of Paraguay . . . was the chief source of money for paying the soldiers."[89]

The opportunity to tax yerba mate caught the attention of Spanish officials even in distant Potosí, the center of Spain's silver wealth. In 1672, a Potosino proposal recommending a tax of 4 reales per arroba was sent to the king, claiming that such a tax would yield more than 50,000 pesos in revenue for the treasury of Potosí. Proponents asserted that the tax would not harm either the purchasers or sellers of yerba mate since it would only minimally impact the sales price. The going rate for yerba in Potosí at the time was at least ten pesos per arroba (which meant a tax rate of five percent), and at times the price was double or triple that amount. If the tax were to reduce the trade of yerba mate (which they did not believe it would), the authors claimed that it would not be a problem but rather a positive because yerba mate "is only a vice that does not provide sustenance nor is it medicinal, even though it was first introduced here in that way."[90] In other words, this was an early example of a sin tax.

Other tax initiatives aimed at yerba mate in the decades to come would continue to highlight both yerba mate's enduring role in local and regional cultures, and how it was frequently viewed by the authorities—at least for the purposes of justifying new tax levies—as a social vice. For example, in Chile, over a century after Potosí proposed its tax on yerba, Ambrosio O'Higgins (father of Chilean independence leader Bernardo O'Higgins) similarly recommended taxing yerba mate in Santiago. O'Higgins proposed the tax soon after being named captain general and governor of Chile, a post that also made him president of the Audiencia of Chile. O'Higgins's rationale was, first and foremost, the need to defend Santiago from the serious threat of natural disaster. The revenue was to be spent for the construction of dikes to protect the city from the immense havoc caused by the flooding of the Mapocho River, which had threatened the city ever since, five years earlier, a flood had destroyed previous dikes and many buildings. O'Higgins claimed that this was a pressing need: "All residents clamor incessantly for this project, which has only been delayed due to a lack of funds." After taking office, O'Higgins went through the accounts and found that the funds were insufficient. He thus recommended the imposition of a tax of one peso per bag of yerba from Paraguay and sugar from Lima, products widely consumed in Chile that played an important role in Santiago's broader commercial trade linkages.[91]

As occurred elsewhere, O'Higgins justified yerba mate taxes because they promised to generate revenues due to the beverage's habit-forming characteristics. Moreover, O'Higgins claimed that the tax was not onerous either in terms of its duration (limited to six years) or the amount (estimated to be 3 percent of the sales price). Echoing Potosí's proposal, O'Higgins rationalized the tax as a tool of social engineering, claiming that both yerba and sugar were associated with immoral behavior, and thereby suggesting positive outcomes if the tax happened to reduce consumption: "In no other article could [a tax] be assessed with such naturalness and justice since [these goods] insinuate vice and indulgence, and [are] so burdensome to this territory." O'Higgins also suggested that the tax could help Chileans and benefit the local economy, based on the idea that the large amounts of money spent on these imports held back the economy and kept the population impoverished. According to O'Higgins, imports of yerba mate and sugar "alone absorb almost all the stock and output of mining, agriculture, and industry in the territory; with the notable backwardness of the region's inland development and its commerce with Spain." Moreover, he argued that consumers spent all the value of their work on yerba, which kept them poor. O'Higgins concluded his appeal by stating that the cabildo of Santiago considered the tax "the only possible means for safeguarding this capital." Moving ahead to impose the tax as an interim measure, he hoped that the king would approve of the action and codify the tax.[92]

Taxing imports produced far from Chile seemed like an easy target. Those involved in commerce, however, thought otherwise. Along with merchants, the official in Santiago who was in charge of commerce, Manuel Peres Cotapos, strongly opposed the new taxes, claiming that they went against the king's desire. Reflecting late eighteenth-century reforms aimed at increasing trade and growing the Spanish economy, Peres Cotapos claimed, in his 1788 report about the proposed taxes, that the tax on sugar and yerba "seem to be little in agreement with the merciful intentions with which our sovereign has favored and favors with his new royal dispositions about commerce and its merchandise." Peres Cotapos explained that in favoring commerce, the king "judges everything that is an increase of taxes to be repugnant."[93]

Like O'Higgins, Peres Cotapos highlighted the importance of both yerba mate and sugar in Chilean commerce and as consumer goods. In contrast to O'Higgins, however, Peres Cotapos claimed that these were reasons to oppose the tax.

> [Yerba and sugar] are the main items of commerce, and the most useful and necessary for the maintenance and conservation of the haciendas in the countryside, the labor in the mines, and whatever other tasks because they are the common daily and indispensable sustenance of all the laborers, and even all the people who populate this capital, like all provinces of this land. This means that lacking these items, there is nobody to dedicate themselves nor subsist in any work.

While both Peres Cotapos and O'Higgins agreed that Chileans imported large amounts of yerba, Peres Cotapas was not immediately concerned with the outflow of money to purchase this import. Instead, he felt it critical to keep this highly valued consumer product accessible to the Chilean population.

As further evidence to support his arguments against the yerba tax, Peres Cotapos pointed to testimony from Santiago's principal merchants. Like Peres Cotapos, they emphasized the importance of yerba and sugar to Chileans. They claimed that the population, which was mostly poor, so valued yerba both as a daily consumption item and an indispensable foodstuff, that "the poorest would first give up eating bread than [give up] drinking mate.... [For these people] any shortage is almost unbearable." While the merchants acknowledged that both were vices, they discounted this complaint by asserting that they were the least harmful vices.[94]

It took the king nearly two years to respond to the arguments sent by Peres Cotapos and others against this tax on yerba mate in Santiago. During that time, 50,000 pesos for dike construction were collected from this interim tax, but in 1790, the king finally decided that the tax was illegal.[95] As the story shows, yerba mate's central role in the daily life and customs of Chile, like in Paraguay, became articulated in arguments over taxes as either beneficial or, on the other hand, as destructive, according to the larger interests of those involved in the debate. As is discussed in later chapters, the consumption of yerba mate would—from the seventeenth century until the twenty-first—continue to generate political and economic debates in ways that intersected with evolving ideas about nationalism, class, and vice. In Chile, at this time, these debates about yerba taxes were conducted among elites, and pitted government officials against the vocal opposition of merchants. Feeling their financial interests threatened, merchants often rallied to the defense of the consuming poor who shouldered the burden of these regressive taxes. Despite such complaints, government officials throughout South America continued to tax yerba mate out of necessity and because doing so did not threaten local producers. Meanwhile, any negative impact on consumption was rationalized as positive social engineering.

YERBA MATE IN EUROPE

While yerba mate was a wildly popular consumer good and an informal tool of empire, its importance did not extend beyond South America. Although information about yerba mate, and some of the product itself, did reach Europe, unlike Mesoamerican chocolate it never became widely consumed there. This failure was largely the result of Spain's economic policies, and it was a failure that would have immense impact on yerba mate's spread around the globe in the coming centuries. The Crown's trade restrictions, in effect until the late eighteenth century, allowed only small quantities of yerba mate to reach Europe. Subsequent trade reforms in the last decades of the eighteenth century stimulated interest in the potential of the yerba mate trade, but such changes came too late. The Napoleonic wars in Europe and the Latin American wars of independence would then further hold back development of the global yerba mate trade into the nineteenth century.

The limited information about yerba mate that did travel outside of southern South America was mostly carried abroad by Spanish officials, merchants, and sailors crossing borders and moving throughout the Spanish empire. In addition to bringing information about yerba mate, they sometimes brought samples of the substance. Tracing the way yerba mate became known through these channels elsewhere in the Spanish empire and in Europe reveals the interconnectedness and porousness of the Crown's expanded domain. One notable discussion of yerba mate reached Spain as early as 1636, when the prominent jurist Antonio de León Pinelo mentioned it in a report to the Council of Indies about whether or not the consumption of certain substances should be considered a violation of Catholic fasting. Including a basic description of yerba and how it was consumed, de León Pinelo concluded that drinking yerba did not break religious fasts because it was a drink that contained little yerba relative to water. Still, he believed it broke moral fasting because "for most, it is a vice, and something without necessity nor benefit."[96] Other references to yerba mate appear in subsequent decades. For example, a Jesuit missionary reported seeing people drinking yerba in Mexico prior to 1650.[97] And in 1698, an Italian sailor reported that in New Spain, "going to visit a Spaniard aboard the Man of War, he instead of Chocolate, treated me with the Herb of *Paraguay*."[98]

Even though news of yerba mate reached Spain relatively early, the Crown's trade policies restricted its circulation. From the onset of the Spanish empire until the late eighteenth century, the Crown's mercantilist trade policies severely limited transatlantic commerce from Buenos Aires and elsewhere along the Atlantic coast of South America, as Madrid sought to monopolize trade between its American territory and Europe based on the belief that there existed a fixed amount of wealth to be gained from trade. In the sixteenth century, the Crown created the fleet system: ships with trade goods traveled in escorted caravans between Seville, Veracruz, and Portobello. As a result, almost all legal trade from Río de la Plata took a convoluted, indirect, and costly path to get to Europe. After crossing the Andes to the port of Callao near Lima, goods were loaded onto a boat for sea travel to Panama, where they were again unloaded and transported by land across the isthmus to the Atlantic coast port of Portobello and then by ship to Havana to join the fleet on its way from New Spain to Spain. This epic and costly journey made it prohibitively expensive to send large quantities of yerba mate to Europe, relegating it to the status of an exotic and foreign substance while other caffeinated beverages (chocolate, tea, and coffee) gained inroads in Europe.

Although Spanish laws had a heavy impact on the long-term transatlantic influence of yerba mate, the Spanish were not the only transporters of yerba mate to Europe, and in the relatively limited transatlantic yerba trade that did develop during the eighteenth century, British merchants played a significant role. Between 1715 and 1739, yerba went to England, sometimes in significant quantities, under the official *asiento* license to transport and sell African slaves in Spanish territory. Between 1714 and 1718, each of the eight British *asiento* ships that departed from Buenos Aires for which Victoria Gardner Sorsby has found data transported yerba mate, with quantities ranging from 948 pounds to 1,508 pounds.[99] Several decades later, in January 1741, the broker Samuel Torin placed three advertisements in the *Daily Post* of London announcing the public auction of six bags of "Paraguay," along with various other exotic goods from around the world.[100] Despite limited availability of yerba mate itself, learned audiences in Europe were aware of it. For example, the *Encyclopédie* edited by Denis Diderot and Jean le Rond d'Alembert and published in France between 1751 and 1772 included a two-page entry about "herbe du Paraguay."[101] Similarly, the English poet Robert Southey described "matté, or herb of Paraguay" to readers of his three-volume *History of Brazil*.[102]

The economic opportunities that yerba mate might offer European merchants if Spain's restrictive trade policies were not in place was not lost on elites elsewhere in Europe. Over the years, writers and officials from other European countries highlighted the profit potential of yerba mate as an important consideration in proposals for their homelands to challenge Spanish hegemony in the region by taking Buenos Aires. One such proposal came from a French military engineer named Barthélemy de Massiac who was engaged in the trade of slaves and merchandise between Luanda and Lisbon. Between 1660 and 1662, de Massiac had become waylaid in Buenos Aires where, to avoid trouble, he disguised himself as a Catalan. During his stay, he became convinced that France should rule the Río de la Plata region. Later, in 1664, upon his return to Europe, he argued to king Louis XIV that France should invade and conquer the region. Pointing to the economic potential of yerba mate, de Massiac wrote: "There is an herb that they call *Yerba Santa* whose commerce among [all trade goods] is the most important in the region." De Massiac noted how widely yerba was consumed: "its use is common among Spaniards and Indians such that they would rather be deprived of eating than of drinking, and at all hours, this yerba in hot water, like chocolate." He then concluded that its high price had the potential to garner great profits, as "they buy it at one peso of gold in places where there is a shortage."[103]

Similarly, in the pamphlet that circulated in London a half a century later, described at the beginning of this chapter, the anonymous English author wrote about the profit potential from yerba mate as a key opportunity for why Britain should declare war on Spain and seize Buenos Aires. After describing the port city's trade with Potosí and Peru, the author drew attention to the centrality of yerba mate:

> [B]ut what is yet of more Importance than all the aforemention'd Commodities, is the Herb of *Paragua,* that is only to be found in the Country adjacent, and depending upon the Government of *Buenos Ayres;* a thing of that mighty Consequence to *Peru* and *Chily,* that without it they would find it impossible to dig any silver Ore out of the Mines.

The author asserted that Britain could use yerba mate to force Spaniards to trade on England's terms, which would be an even more effective tactic than selling British goods at predatory prices; "we should have them in a manner at our mercy, by having the Herb of *Paragua* in our hands." Lastly, he emphasized how a high tax on yerba mate (and smaller taxes on hides and African slaves) would defray all of the governing costs and make Buenos Aires "one of the most important Colonies the Crown of *Great Britain* ever had."[104]

Calls for Britain to take Buenos Aires in the eighteenth century continued to highlight the value of the yerba trade. In 1762, William Temple explained the importance of yerba mate in a letter to the editor of *Lloyd's Evening Post and British Chronicle.* Temple expressed his support for the British taking Buenos Aires from the Spanish, arguing that conquering Havana was not worthwhile without also taking Buenos Aires and that the silver and gold mines could not be worked without the "herb Paraguay."[105] Although it is unlikely the English government relied much on these arguments about yerba mate in its decision-making, British troops did in fact invade Buenos Aires in 1806 and 1807 in an attempt to take the region, although they were repelled both times. In the years prior to that invasion, the promise of controlling the yerba mate trade had been of pressing interest to many. Another anonymous author who lobbied for just such an action by the British had, like the author of the London pamphlet, also highlighted the importance of the yerba trade, estimating that exports to Chile and Peru amounted yearly to 100,000 to 120,000 pounds sterling.[106]

While France and England were never successfully able to capitalize on yerba mate's trade potential, Spain's late-eighteenth-century trade reforms created further opportunities for exporting the beverage to Europe. Upon assuming a Spanish Crown rife with financial problems in 1713, the House of Bourbon started implementing a series of reforms to increase revenues and improve governance. The British capture of Havana and Manila in 1762 emphasized the fragility of the empire and the vulnerability of Spanish territory in the Americas, and the Crown thus intensified its reforms. A major component entailed the loosening of trade restrictions and tariffs. Instead of believing that there was a fixed amount of wealth, and that the Crown should monopolize trade in order to best benefit from it, reformers now endeavored to reduce commercial restrictions, expand trade between the Americas and Spain, and thereby increase overall wealth. From 1778 on, policies known as *Comercio Libre* (Free Trade) allowed direct trade between thirteen ports in Spain and twenty-four in the Americas. As a result, Río de la Plata trade goods could now be legally shipped directly across the Atlantic Ocean to Spain, instead of taking the convoluted mercantile route across the Andes and the isthmus of Panama. The more direct route stimulated transatlantic trade and made the viceroyalty of Río de la Plata one of the most dynamic regions of the Spanish empire during the last quarter of the eighteenth century.

The loosening of trade restrictions stimulated a growing interest in identifying heretofore undervalued items from the Americas that could be profitably sold in Europe. In addition to the Europeans who frequently highlighted the economic potential of yerba in their travel writings,[107] yerba mate also attracted the attention of a number of prominent scientists on expeditions to South America, including many of whom never reached Paraguay. For example, Antonio de Ulloa, a Spanish naval officer and scientist who traveled to South America in the 1730s, noted yerba's commercial value in a book he wrote about his voyage, describing "The herb called Paraguay, which alone would be sufficient to form a flourishing commerce in this province, it being the only one which produces it; and from hence it is sent all over Peru, and Chili, where its use is universal."[108] In 1777, José Pavón, who traveled to South America as part of the royal botanical expedition to Chile and Peru, investigated a possible substitute for Paraguayan yerba in the mountains of Huanuco, Peru, under the belief that yerba mate's high potential value would "advance commerce and be of particular benefit for this poor city."[109] While Pavón searched for a substitute for Paraguayan yerba, most parties were interested in advancing access to the genuine article itself.

In addition to specialists who had traveled to South America, Spanish newspapers even began to tout yerba mate's profit potential for Spain. Three years after its founding in 1758, Spain's first newspaper (*Diario Noticioso,*

Curioso, Erudito y Comercial Público y Económico) published a series of three articles that underscored the economic potential of yerba mate. The first emphasized the critical importance of yerba mate in Buenos Aires's trade with Peru and Chile.[110] A month later, a second write-up focused exclusively on yerba mate, claiming it was equal or superior to the best tea in Europe in terms of both quality and medicinal traits. The article also described the large market for yerba in South America, where it was widely consumed by rich and poor, and it hinted at yerba's potential in Europe.[111] The third article, a month later, highlighted the importance of yerba mate to Andean mining, asserting that if the miners of Potosí no longer had access to yerba mate (which they consumed in large quantities), they would be obliged to abandon the mine.[112] Each article focused on a different issue, but they all informed a broad Spanish audience about yerba mate's prominence in South American trade and its potential in Europe.

The voices advocating for a stronger incorporation of yerba mate into European trade— particularly those who had spent time in South America— only grew as the decades passed. Martin Dobrizhoffer, for example, the Jesuit priest from Bohemia who spent almost two decades as a missionary in Paraguay (1749–1767), observed, Europeans, "having never so much as tasted the herb, have no desire to fetch it from America, which they would certainly do, if acquainted with its virtue."[113] Similarly, Félix de Azara, an engineer and military officer who spent two decades in the Río de la Plata region as part of the Spanish delegation to fix the border between Spanish and Portuguese territory, assessed, "If the government was to find a way to introduce its use in Cadiz and other ports, maybe in less than a century it would replace tea and coffee in Europe with great benefits for this Province, and for the Metropolis, and new delights for humankind."[114] Even people who never traveled to South America recognized yerba's potential in Europe. The Portuguese diplomat Luis da Cunha, for example, questioned why yerba mate had not been promoted in Europe after he tried it in London with a well-known doctor who informed him that it was more wholesome than both tea and coffee.[115]

In addition to Spain's restrictive trade policies, competing markets in Britain put downward pressure on the yerba mate trade, and British tea interests had reason to obstruct the widescale introduction of yerba in Europe. In the late seventeenth century, the British East India Company (EIC) entered the tea trade in an effort to boost sugar sales. At the time, Britain consumed approximately ten times more coffee than tea, but by the 1730s, tea consumption had surpassed coffee. Evidence suggests that the EIC, together with the West Indian sugar lobby, applied political pressure to create market conditions in Britain that favored tea over coffee. British fiscal policies helped drive this shift in consumption. In the first decade of the eighteenth century, taxes on coffee and tea were roughly equal, but thereafter the taxes on tea were lower. British coffee planters complained about these tax policies, but to little effect. By midcentury, tea prices were low enough that common people could regularly drink tea, and by the end of the eighteenth century, tea was consumed in both urban and rural settings throughout the British territories. The EIC's tea sales in London grew exponentially, from 142 thousand pounds in 1711 to 15 million pounds in 1791.[116]

Eighteenth-century authors frequently claimed that British tea interests took much more forceful measures to prevent potential competition by yerba mate. For example, as Juan Francisco Aguirre reported in the 1780s, "It is also said that the English found [yerba] superior to tea . . . so they prohibited its introduction."[117] Similarly, Dobrizhoffer (who claimed that Europeans would want to "fetch" yerba from America if acquainted with its virtue) described how British tea merchants promoted false information so as to discourage the use of yerba mate.

> Paraguayan yerba had just arrived in England, and the high-class and humble people of both sexes preferred it to all others. When the merchants of London saw that Asian tea was being spurned and their trade in tea, generally so profitable, was languishing, they did everything possible to banish Paraguayan yerba as soon as possible from all of Great Britain. And to do this, they made seductive promises to whoever could achieve this. There was not lacking a venal doctor who, with a strong gesture and booming voice, protested against the innocent yerba; who proclaimed it extremely dangerous to the beauty and fertility of women, warning all against it like a poison. This salaried writer must have made such a great impression on the spirits of the English that immediately in all of London Paraguayan yerba was rejected, outlawed, and forgotten.[118]

By claiming that yerba mate threatened feminine beauty and fertility, the negative propaganda purposefully targeted women because eighteenth century British society considered tea drinking a feminine activity.[119] Decades later Alexander Gillespie, who came to Buenos Aires as part of the British invasions of 1806–1807, also blamed British tea interests for blocking yerba mate. According to Gillespie, "If East India monopoly would allow of [yerba mate's] importation, it would soon obtain general consumption amongst the lower orders, as a healthful nourishing substitute for tea, and I doubt not but the apothecary might be much indebted to its virtues."[120]

Even though there was interest in yerba mate's potential, little opportunity existed to act on such optimism. By the late eighteenth century, tea, coffee and Mesoamerican chocolate had established a strong foothold in Europe. Furthermore, after the Crown loosened trade restrictions between Buenos Aires and other Spanish ports, the Napoleonic Wars broke out in Europe, disrupting trade patterns and pushing Spanish America towards independence. During the subsequent decades of instability, yerba remained a regional good as the Río de la Plata region struggled to define itself into nation-states and establish a balance of power between the central governments and the provinces. Serious efforts to break into the European market would not begin again until the twentieth century.

THREE

Borderland Production and the Struggle to Form an Argentine Nation

AIMÉ BONPLAND WAS ONE of the most important French botanists of the nineteenth century. Fastidious in his research and a favorite of Napoleon's wife Josephine, Bonpland was one of the leading European experts on the flora of the Americas. Born in 1773, he gained fame for the major scientific undertaking he conducted as the assistant of Alexander von Humboldt, a prominent German scientist and polymath, in equatorial America from 1799 to 1804. Together, Bonpland and Humboldt published several books on South American botany that became foundational scientific works. In the years following that research with von Humboldt, a period of political instability in Europe, Bonpland began to look again to Hispanic America as a place to seek his fortune. And for this, he would turn to yerba mate.

In 1816, after living in France for more than a decade, Bonpland left for Buenos Aires at the behest of several representatives from Río de la Plata, including Bernardino Rivadavia, the future first president of the United Provinces of Río de la Plata. Rivadavia and other officials in Buenos Aires were eager to develop key areas of science and public research in the city, and they wanted Bonpland to found and direct a botanical garden there. Bonpland accepted Rivadavia's invitation. Even though political instability prevented the garden's realization, this did not stop Bonpland's botanical research. Yerba mate quickly attracted his attention, especially after he heard about some trees growing close to Buenos Aires. After researching the plant, he realized that the best quality yerba mate grew in the tri-border region of Paraguay, northern Argentina and southern Brazil. For the remainder of Bonpland's life, yerba mate cultivation was one of his greatest passions. Bonpland dreamed of creating his own yerba mate plantation and he invested a significant amount of time and money into this enterprise. He referred to the wild yerbales as an "inexhaustible mine" and, throughout his writings, he expressed great optimism about the potential for profit from yerba production, hoping that these plantations would make him a wealthy man.[1]

Unfortunately for Bonpland, his dream ran up against the turbulent political and economic realities of the nineteenth century, a period when the power structures of the former Spanish Empire were disintegrating and independence movements across the continent were leading to new alliances, borders, and conflict. When Bonpland did try to undertake his agricultural experiment in the northeast borderlands of Argentina, he was imprisoned as an interloper by the Paraguayan government, who sought to claim that region (and the rich yerba forests there) for the new nation.

At the start of the nineteenth century, the geopolitics of South America were in enormous flux. In 1808, Napoleon had forced the ouster of the king of Spain and installed his own brother on the Spanish thrown, creating widespread political instability in the Spanish colonies. As the Spanish empire began to crumble, states across the Americas claimed autonomy. The Wars of Independence in South America led to the nation-states that are recognized today across the continent. Colombia and Paraguay both declared independence from Spain in 1811; Argentina in 1816, Chile in 1818, Peru in 1821, and Bolivia in 1825. Brazil achieved independence from Portugal in 1822. It was a steady succession of boundaries being erased, drawn, and debated, while the power structures and economic policies that had been in force shifted as new alliances and trade rules came into place.

Out of the nation-states rapidly being drawn at this time, Paraguay, Brazil and the United Provinces of the Río de la Plata (what would later become Argentina) were well suited for the production and cultivation of yerba. However, just as Bonpland failed to create a profitable yerba enterprise, Argentina also failed to develop its own yerba mate enterprise for nearly one hundred years after independence.[2] Even though yerba mate grew naturally in its northeastern borderland regions, Argentina relied primarily on Brazilian and Paraguayan yerba to meet its domestic consumer demand. There were several factors behind this development. One was the fact that, for decades, Paraguay's leaders contested Buenos Aires's authority over this northeastern borderland territory. Indigenous peoples also occupied much of the region and sometimes violently reacted to people who they considered intruders. Such conflict, along with the region's remoteness and isolation, encouraged Argentina's policymakers to devote their time and agricultural investment to crops in other parts of the country. As a result, Argentina struggled to populate, develop, and incorporate this northeastern area, leaving its commercial possibilities for yerba untapped. Consequently, while national consolidation, largescale European immigration, and the onset of rapid economic growth date to 1880 for the country as a whole, Argentina's yerba-producing region in the northeast failed to attract European immigrants and agricultural colonies until after 1900. Prior to that time, Misiones and northeastern Corrientes were widely looked down on as a poor region for agriculture, as they were ill-suited for Argentina's traditional crops. Meanwhile, entrepreneurial individuals worked on their own to capitalize on the northeast's rich natural yerba forests, and these unregulated enterprises oversaw the harvesting of wild yerbales in the tri-border region, depleting the forests and exploiting contract laborers. The riches of the Belle Epoque bypassed northeastern Argentina until after 1900, when people on the ground finally started cultivating yerba. As a result, for the whole nineteenth century, Argentina, whose population made up by far the largest consumer base of yerba mate, needed to rely on yerba imports from neighboring countries, so that it was Paraguay and Brazil who first emerged as the major players in the yerba trade.

PARAGUAYAN AND BRAZILIAN YERBA

With Argentina making no significant effort to cultivate yerba in the years after Spanish rule ended, post-independence Paraguay was poised to continue dominating the yerba trade as it had during the colonial period. John Parish Robertson, a young Scotsman who first arrived in Buenos Aires in 1809 looking for business opportunities, was one of the people who recognized such potential. In 1811, Robertson undertook a mercantile trip to Paraguay where he contracted a boat large enough to carry fifteen hundred bales of yerba that he then sold downriver for "a little fortune."[3] Later, Robertson described yerba as the "most prominent and most important among the exports of the Republic."[4] Despite such optimism, Paraguay's role declined over the nineteenth century due to conflict with Buenos Aires over autonomy and access to trade. Instead, Brazil rose to dominate the yerba trade.

Although tensions between Buenos Aires and Paraguay had long existed, problems came to a head with the independence wars. When a *cabildo abierto* (open town hall) of white males in Buenos Aires renounced the Spanish regency and declared that a junta would rule the region until Ferdinand VII returned to power, Asunción disagreed. Not wanting to be subservient to

Buenos Aires, citizens of Paraguay convened their own *cabildo abierto* that rejected the junta's authority. Over the following decades, Paraguay continued to assert its independence while Buenos Aires repeatedly tried futilely to bring back the wayward province. When military efforts failed, Buenos Aires turned to economic measures.[5]

Authorities, both in Buenos Aires and in cities along the Paraná River, taxed Paraguayan trade goods (including yerba) at high rates. They did so to raise much needed revenue, but also to force Paraguay into submission. Following a period of instability and political maneuvering in Paraguay, José Gaspar Rodríguez de Francia gained power as a staunch defender of Paraguayan independence. In 1814, the Paraguayan Congress declared Francia dictator (a compliment at that time), a position he held until his death in 1840. While Paraguay maintained its independence, Paraguayan trade suffered. Not only did Buenos Aires institute trade restrictions in an effort to subordinate Paraguay, Francia enacted high taxes in order to generate government revenue and instituted licenses to control economic activity and consolidate power.[6] After Francia's death, Carlos Antonio López (president of Paraguay from 1844 to 1862) tried to open the Paraguayan economy but strongman Juan Manuel de Rosas, who ruled Buenos Aires from 1829 to 1852, continued to oppose Paraguayan independence and restricted river trade as a means for manipulating and controlling the upper provinces.[7]

Paraguay's yerba exports suffered dearly from these trade restrictions. In 1816, Paraguay exported a record amount of yerba mate: about 250,000 arrobas (6,250,000 pounds). Thereafter, exports plummeted to below 100,000 arrobas in 1820 and remained at such levels for three decades.[8] Paraguayans felt the blow. A Swiss naturalist held captive in Paraguay between 1819 and 1825 by Francia observed that villages formerly flourishing from the yerba trade had become ghost towns, and people who used to enjoy high standards of living from yerba sales now resorted to making their own clothes.[9] After Rosas lost power in 1852, Buenos Aires finally allowed free navigation of the rivers. Paraguay's exports increased substantially (generally surpassing 100,000 arrobas per year), but never reached their pre-independence levels.[10]

Even though the volume of Paraguayan exports declined, yerba sales continued to be critical for government revenues, much like in the colonial period. Francia and his successors recognized the value of yerba exports and used the revenue to fund government expenditures. Woodbine Parish, the British consul general in Buenos Aires, commented that whenever Francia desired some foreign goods, he sent someone with a trade permit to Corrientes in the incipient nation of Argentina, and after selecting what he wanted, the Paraguayan leader sent the ship back with the amount of yerba he thought was appropriate. According to Parish, yerba was in such high demand "that the people of Corrientes are glad to get it upon [Francia's] own terms."[11] Francia's successor, Carlos Antonio López, made yerba a government monopoly to further capture revenue. Yerba remained the country's most valuable export, accounting for almost half of all export earnings well into the 1850s.[12]

Until Brazil ramped up its own yerba production, mate consumers throughout South America suffered shortages and high prices as a result of Paraguay's declining exports. Into the 1820s, travelers repeatedly commented on the scarcity and high price of yerba mate throughout South America. They regularly carried supplies of this prized good to give as a payment or a gift, and upon receiving yerba mate, the local people showed great pleasure.[13] Such shortages meant that in some areas of Peru and Chile, yerba was suddenly unavailable at any price.[14] This contrasted sharply with the colonial period, when yerba mate was widely available and accessibly priced. In 1844, a United States government official in Lima assessed that the price of yerba was nearly as high as the price of tea from China and that imports had "greatly fallen off."[15] Even so, many consumers remained avid yerba mate drinkers. As the British businessman and traveler Alexander Caldcleugh concluded, "Such is the predilection for it that it must be procured at any price."[16]

Merchants soon realized that they could make hefty profits off of yerba if they could just get Francia's permission to take it out of the country. The prospects were so good that, in 1813, John Parish Robertson returned to Paraguay with his brother to pursue his business there. While the potential payout was high, so were the risks. Francia might not grant a license, and some businessmen were expelled from the country. Having lost Francia's trust, the Robertson brothers had to leave in 1815. Other foreign merchants tried to take advantage of the opportunity to make money off of the yerba trade. British consul general Parish described how British watchmaker Luke Cresser found himself making little money in Buenos Aires, so he went north to Salta to try his hand at tobacco. When Cresser's shipment reached the Paraguay River, he was detained upon Francia's orders and stripped of all he possessed. According to Parish, although Cresser was left in Paraguay without any money, he collected yerba and by the time he was allowed to leave five years later, "he found himself in comparative affluence; and, though only permitted by the dictator to carry out of the country a portion of the yerba he had by his industry collected, he had still enough left when he sailed for Buenos Ayres to compensate him for the loss of all the tobacco."[17] Not surprisingly, with so much profit to be made, contraband yerba also generated high returns.[18]

With the Paraguayan yerba trade obstructed by both Francia and the government of Argentina, Brazil became the region's principal supplier. In the book he wrote about his travels in the region between 1819 and 1821, Caldcleugh noted that "the Brazilians have found a great source of wealth in the preparation of this article. They supply the Buenos Ayrian states and Chile. . . . The Brazilians consume little themselves."[19] By the middle of the nineteenth century, Brazil had replaced Paraguay as the dominant yerba producer.[20] In 1860, for example, Paraguay exported less than 2 million kilos of yerba while the Brazilian province of Paraná alone exported 5 million kilos.[21] Although Paraguay never recovered its role as the largest producer, its yerba maintained a reputation in Argentina as being of the highest quality. Brazil overwhelmingly produced the largest quantities, but its yerba was considered lower quality.[22]

Most of the yerba produced by both Paraguay and Brazil went to Argentina.[23] Importing so much yerba mate had consequences for the fledgling nation: it cost so much money that it affected Argentina's balance of trade with its neighbors. According to Argentina's Treasury records, the country spent 1.1 million *pesos fuertes* (currency convertible into gold) in 1863 to legally import 7.2 million pounds from Brazil and 3.3 million pounds from Paraguay. In terms of revenue, yerba was Brazil's second most important export to Argentina, behind sugar and significantly greater than both coffee and tobacco.[24]

ARGENTINE YERBA AND THE INCIPIENT
NATION STATE

Northeastern Argentina is a verdant, subtropical region most known for its red dirt (*tierra colorada*). It has rolling hills and two major rivers, the Paraguay and Uruguay, border it on either side. The climate is one of the warmest in Argentina, with highs often surpassing ninety degrees from December to February. Temperatures drop during the winter months (May through August), and occasionally there is frost. There is abundant rainfall and high humidity throughout the year.

Like Paraguay and southern Brazil, northeast Argentina is well suited for growing yerba, and yet, for much of the first century after independence, political instability and border disputes disrupted efforts to take advantage of such opportunities.[25] Although Argentina failed to take advantage of this resource, there had been an example of successful yerba cultivation in the not so distant past—in the eighteenth century, the Jesuits together with the Guaraní created large plantations of cultivated yerba near their missions. Although smaller than some of the large-scale cultivation that would eventually become the norm in the twentieth century, the Jesuit-Guaraní plantations produced huge quantities of yerba and large profits. After the Crown expelled the Jesuits from Spanish territory in 1767, those plantations deteriorated due to lack of maintenance, in part because harvesting yerba from wild yerbales was more cost-effective and less labor-intensive. Still, the remnants of the earlier cultivated plantations remained alongside wild yerbales.

Despite Argentina not acting on opportunities for cultivation in the years after independence, there were many people who were eager to do so. Aimé Bonpland, the French botanist who was invited to create a botanical garden in Buenos Aires, was a good example of a prominent, well-connected individual who clearly saw the potential for Argentina to profit from yerba. When he first arrived in Buenos Aires, Bonpland was highly regarded in the scientific community for the collection and classification of some six thousand plants and for having authored several scientific volumes with Alexander von Humboldt. Bonpland had intended to spend a few years in the Americas in order to achieve financial independence and make further botanical discoveries for the advancement of science. As the historian Stephen Bell recounts, "No plant caught his attention more than yerba maté."[26] But in addition to his own dreams of gaining personal wealth, Bonpland also saw in the cultivation of yerba an extraordinary opportunity for the nation itself. After observing a small stand of yerba mate on the island of Martín García near Buenos Aires in 1818, Bonpland communicated with Juan Martín de Pueyrredón (the head of the incipient Argentine nation) about the idea of planting yerba. Pueyrredón expressed interest and asked Bonpland to present his plan in writing. But nothing came of the proposal.[27] Nevertheless, decades later, Bonpland continued to enthusiastically promote Argentine yerba. In 1852 he wrote, "The Province of Corrientes [including Misiones] is no less rich in yerbales than Brazil and Paraguay. It has in them an inexhaustible mine."[28] Up to his death in 1858, Bonpland repeatedly tried to establish a yerba enterprise and continuously lobbied for the rejuvenation of the abandoned Jesuit yerba plantations, the cultivation of yerba, and the rational exploitation of wild yerbales.[29] Despite so much opportunity, all of these efforts came to naught. Why did his attempts fail?

Ongoing struggles to unify the incipient nation-state caused Argentina to overlook yerba production for much of the nineteenth century. As in most of Spanish-speaking America after independence, conflicts over the form of the government led to civil wars that brought bloodshed, consumed resources, and hindered provincial development for decades. The major issue in the Río de la Plata region was the role of Buenos Aires: whether to pursue a Unitarist government with power centralized at the national level (advocated by Buenos Aires) or a Federalist government with power decentralized at the provincial level (advocated by the provinces). At the provincial level, local strongmen called *caudillos*, personalist and paternalistic leaders whose political power was based on both violence and patronage, competed for dominance.[30] Except for two decades, civil war was almost endemic in Corrientes from 1810 until 1852, and during this period, the rich yerba forests of Misiones were part of Corrientes.[31] At the same time, border disputes created instability as Argentina, Brazil, Paraguay, and Indigenous peoples claimed ownership of the yerba-producing region. All of the conflict disrupted river trade and complicated Argentine yerba production.

Bonpland's great plan to cultivate yerba was one of the casualties of these regional conflicts. In 1821, after years of planning, Bonpland finally set out for Misiones to establish a yerba enterprise. His goal during this trip was to restore and expand the deteriorated yerbales of the former missions. Before departing, Bonpland contacted General Francisco Ramírez (Supreme Director of the short-lived Republic of Entre Ríos) about his plans. Ramírez gave Bonpland practical support and explicitly instructed him to study the yerbales, along with the Indigenous peoples of Misiones.[32] With the assistance of the Indigenous leader Nicolás Aripí, Bonpland established a base at the Santa Ana mission, a borderlands territory on the eastern side of the Paraná River claimed by both Entre Ríos and Paraguay. Francia, however, felt threatened by this move, and claiming that Bonpland and Arapí were working Paraguayan resources without his permission, he sent troops to destroy the Santa Ana outpost, capture or kill Arapí, and take Bonpland prisoner. For the next decade (1821–1831), Francia held Bonpland as a hostage in Paraguay, where he could do little to advance Argentine yerba.[33]

The fight for dominance in the tri-border region led to the general destruction of the former missions. The violence not only depopulated and destroyed towns, it also contributed to the ruin and neglect of the yerbales. Looking back on the period, the Robertson brothers explained, "the wars of Artigas desolated [the missions]; the policy of Paraguay has nearly annihilated them. From a hundred thousand inhabitants, the population has dwindled down to eight thousand ... every vestige of property and of cultivation has been swept away."[34]

The prolonged battles consumed resources as local caudillos fought for power. The caudillos also competed over yerba production and access to yerbales, as shown by the actions of General Ramírez, the Supreme Dictator of the Republic of Entre Ríos. As mentioned above, Ramírez had backed Bonpland's plan to rejuvenate yerba production in the region. But Ramírez failed to realize his goals for developing yerba production, in part because his efforts to monopolize the trade conflicted with the interests of native peoples. In a letter to a Brazilian military commander in the region, Ramírez asserted, "with my permission [Indians] have entered to work in the yerbales."[35] Building on this claim, a military commander under his charge issued the following directive: "based on higher orders, I mandate and command that no individual can go to produce yerba without first appearing to this command under my charge, having permission from the Excellent Señor Supreme Director of the Republic, under the pain of having whatever is transported embargoed and his/her person imprisoned."[36]

Native peoples refused to obey such requirements. They did not believe Ramírez had control over the yerbales. Rather, they asserted their own ownership rights over said yerbales. The Guaraní military leader Francisco Javier Sití, who was briefly recognized as governor of Misiones by Ramírez, claimed that the native peoples "are legitimate owners of their land and its fruits." Sití explained that he had sent troops to imprison and embargo the yerba of people who were producing it in Misiones "without my permission. Being me, the boss and owner of my land."[37] While Sití was soon defeated by Ramírez's troops, native peoples did not give up their claims to yerbales, and for decades, outsiders wanting to produce yerba in Misiones continued to fear Indian attacks.[38]

At the same time, Buenos Aires did not promote domestic yerba production. Under the extended rule of Juan Manuel de Rosas, Buenos Aires took steps that discouraged Argentine yerba production. Rosas, a caudillo and governor of Buenos Aires province, abhorred progressive Buenos Aires city liberals. He used strong-arm tactics to consolidate power and promote the interests of Buenos Aires province. An *estanciero* (rancher) with immense landholdings, Rosas enacted policies that favored the export of pastoral goods (hides, jerked beef, and wool). Such policies worked against other economic sectors such as yerba mate, and from early on, Corrientes officials conflicted with him over economic policy. Pedro Ferré (the governor of Corrientes who was also in charge of Misiones) lobbied for free river trade and increased import duties to protect domestic products from foreign competition, but Rosas refused, based on the belief that doing so would hurt consumers and pastoral exports by increasing expenses. As the leader of the port city of Buenos Aires, Rosas held the balance of power because he controlled the duties charged on both river and oceanic trade. Since yerba was not central to Rosas's economic model, it was negatively affected by his policies.

One example was the Customs Law of 1835, which Rosas enacted to help industry and farming while still favoring livestock exports.[39] The law instituted tariffs ranging from 5 to 50 percent, with the lowest rates on vital imports (such as steel, tin, coal, and agricultural tools) and the highest rates on products that the government wanted to protect from foreign competition (such as beer and pastas). Unlike tariffs on other goods that competed with domestic products, however, yerba tariffs were not designed to stimulate Argentine production. Yerba mate that arrived in Buenos Aires by land incurred a 10 percent duty regardless of whether or not it originated in Paraguay or Corrientes/Misiones. Yerba mate that arrived by sea (in other words, Brazilian yerba) incurred a higher, but still moderate rate of 24 percent.[40] When the governor of Corrientes complained that Argentine yerba incurred the same tax rate as Paraguayan yerba, Rosas refused to give Argentine yerba a preferential rate. Rosas justified his decision by claiming that customs officials would not be able to distinguish Argentine yerba from Paraguayan yerba. And yet, Rosas also claimed that consumers preferred Paraguayan yerba and would be willing to pay more for it. Lastly, Rosas feared that if consumers did decide to switch to Argentine yerba as a result of a lower tax, Brazilian yerba would suffer, which could then lead Brazil to retaliate by threatening what Rosas considered to be more valuable Argentine commerce along the Uruguay River.[41] Clearly, Rosas did not prioritize Argentine yerba.

Despite the lack of support from Rosas, people in Corrientes were enthusiastic about Bonpland's earlier ideas for Argentine yerba production. When publishing some of the botanist's letters in 1850, the Corrientes newspaper, *El Comercio,* questioned why his plan had not yet been pursued in earnest: "The unheard-of consumption of yerba in our States, and the opinion expressed by such a competent guide, ought to have stimulated some of our influential men to introduce to us this new branch of agriculture."[42]

Eventually, a series of events would turn the tide more favorably towards yerba. In 1852, Rosas was overthrown, and a new, strong, centralized government called the Argentine Confederation (which united all of the provinces other than Buenos Aires) seemed auspicious for Argentine yerba. Encouraged by a conversation with Bonpland, the president of the Argentine Confederation called for the governor of Corrientes, Juan Pujol, to take steps to advance yerba production. In 1854, General Justo José de Urquiza wrote to Pujol, "The respective ministry is now occupied with the wealth of the yerbales of Misiones, and of dictating the steps that, upon accomplishing them, deliver to that Province the rich returns that this industry should yield."[43] Bonpland also weighed in with Pujol, convincing him of yerba's potential and obtaining from him a promise to execute the plan.[44] Although Pujol and Bonpland met in person and exchanged a number of letters about yerba and many other ideas for regional development, the plan never came to fruition. The governor instead focused his efforts on advancing ranching.[45]

Even though government officials paid scant attention to yerba mate, their attention was increasingly drawn to the region where it grew. The Confederacy recognized that it needed to attend to its northeast border region (where yerba grew naturally) not only for economic development, but also to secure the territory from foreign powers. In 1863, the Interior Minister wrote to the governor of Corrientes, who was in charge of Misiones, "So important is the portion of land bordering the Republic of Paraguay and the Brazilian Empire that it needs special and legal attention on the part of the national government, not only to avoid gradual usurpations that would lead to abandonment, but also in order to utilize for the industry and wealth of the Republic, that vast region so distinguished with the blessings of nature."[46]

The following year, Argentina, Brazil, and Uruguay went to war against Paraguay. The Triple Alliance War (1864–1870) especially devastated Paraguay, which lost about half of its population. This war, however, did lead to greater political stability in the border region, something that ultimately had a direct impact on Argentina's yerba production there.[47] Indeed, a naturalist sent by the Ministry of Agriculture to explore Misiones territory dated the beginning of Argentina's yerba industry to the year the war ended.[48] Formalizing borders took longer. An 1876 border treaty with Paraguay gave Argentina sovereignty over contested territory in Misiones. A little more than two decades later, American president Grover Cleveland resolved disputes with Brazil over upper Misiones (territory between the Uruguay and Paraná Rivers) by awarding what would become about half of the present-day Santa Catarina province to Brazil.

Pacifying the yerba-producing region required not only the resolution of international border disputes, but also on-the-ground agreements with Indigenous peoples. Prior to 1870, about half of present-day Argentina's land-mass, an area which included Misiones, was under Indigenous control. The first Argentine census in 1869 recorded Misiones's entire population as Indigenous, although this was clearly an exaggeration; among the missing were several hundred Brazilian residents.[49] Until the 1870s, groups of Kaingang made it difficult for outsiders to produce yerba in the upper Paraná region of Misiones. According to one account, yerba producers had abused Kaingang women in the 1840s, and in retaliation, a cacique named Prakan took revenge and kept them out of the region. In the mid-1870s, private citizens wanting access to the yerbales funded an armed expedition headed by a Brazilian yerba producer. This expedition was intended to force the new Kaingang leader, Bonifacio Maidana (Prakan's successor and a former child captive of the Kaingang) to open the region to production by outsiders. Ultimately, this expedition led to an agreement between the cacique and the province of Corrientes that conferred the title of captain of the Argentine army upon Maidana and promised land for him and his people in return for opening the region's forests to yerba production.[50] Thereafter, the Kaingang became actively involved in yerba production as a way to obtain prized goods. Still, employers continued to exploit Kaingang workers.[51] Gaining the upper hand in Misiones, yerba producers were able to marginalize and discriminate against native peoples. Throughout Argentina, native peoples faced acquiescence, displacement, or extermination.

In the last decades of the nineteenth century, Argentina not only made major steps toward settling border disputes with Paraguay and Brazil and conquering Indigenous peoples, it also came to a workable agreement between Buenos Aires and the other provinces. In 1880, Argentina finalized a power-sharing settlement that detached Buenos Aires city from the province and federalized it, making the city into the capital of the republic and La Plata into the capital of Buenos Aires province. This deal finally brought all of Argentina together under a single national government. With debates over the form of the nation-state seemingly resolved, the national government paid more attention to developing and incorporating frontier regions such as Misiones that had heretofore been neglected.[52] As the 1869 census reported,

Misiones had a population of 3,000, which was a small fraction of the estimated number of inhabitants prior to independence (27,000 people in 1797).[53] To many Argentines, Misiones was a stagnant and underdeveloped backwater.

Between 1880 and 1914, Argentina underwent rapid economic growth. Large flows of immigrant workers provided much of the labor force that fueled this expansion. For decades, Argentine leaders had called for European immigration. They even enshrined the idea in the country's 1853 constitution. Article twenty-five, which remains in place today, made the promotion of European immigration a cornerstone of the country and national policy. It reads: "The federal government will promote European immigration; and cannot restrict, limit, nor levy any tax on foreigners entering Argentine territory with the goal of working the land, improving industries, and introducing and teaching the sciences and arts." Argentine leaders envisioned agricultural colonies, primarily inhabited by European immigrants, as the means for advancing rural areas. They believed that European immigrants would develop the country's resources and serve as hard-working, industrious role models for the mixed-race population of the countryside who they saw as lazy and incapable. Argentine leaders tried to apply such logic to Misiones, but few European immigrants moved to the region to engage in traditional agriculture.

President Julio A. Roca (1880–1886 and 1898–1904) targeted Misiones, recognizing its potential and critical location bordering both Brazil and Paraguay. Before Congress in 1881, Roca claimed, "the most favorable calculations that are made about its future will not be exaggerated." His reasoning points to both the optimism and racism of the Belle Epoque period. "The most distant lands, of inferior conditions that have just been abandoned by the savages, incessantly increase in value and begin to be the seat of a growing and hard-working population."[54] According to Roca, such a vision for Misiones would become a reality if the government provided security to attract laborers and capital. To further strengthen his appeal for the national government to act, Roca emphasized Misiones's critical location as a borderland.[55]

Based on such rationales, the province of Corrientes, within which lay the yerba-growing Misiones region, passed legislation in 1875 promoting agricultural settlements. Two years later, the province set aside land for agricultural colonies and towns in Misiones. Several colonies were founded, but they failed to attract many immigrants.[56] In contrast, such efforts did attract immigrants to Santa Fe, Córdoba, and Entre Rios. By 1880, the three provinces had almost seven hundred colonies, with about 53,000 farms producing a large portion of the country's wheat supply.[57] The lack of "even the smallest nucleus of a stable population with the ability to establish themselves and multiply over the land" in Misiones led president Roca to conclude that Corrientes had failed to develop and populate the region, and thus, the province should turn it over to the national government.[58] Such action was not unique to Misiones; it was part of the larger process to extend and formalize the national government's authority. The province of Buenos Aires had already conceded the city of Buenos Aires and the province of Salta had already conceded the Chaco, Roca pointed out, so Corrientes should do likewise. After a contentious dispute between Corrientes and the national government, Misiones became a national territory on December 22, 1881.[59] One month later, president Roca's brother, Rudecindo Roca, became the territory's first governor. Recognizing the importance of incorporating frontier regions like Misiones into the nation, the national government passed legislation in 1884 that formally created governorships in national territories and established guidelines for transforming them into self-governing provinces. At this point, Misiones and eight other national territories encompassed almost half of Argentina's total landmass.

Realizing that it would have to relinquish control over the region, Corrientes authorized the sale of all public land in large plots, rather than small plots suitable for agricultural colonies. As was to be expected, this action created controversy and complaints that continued for years.[60] In addition to the questionable legality of selling land on the cusp of nationalization, many blamed the sale for creating inequities associated with latifundia.[61] Within six months, Corrientes sold 2,101,936 hectares (equating to over two-thirds of Misiones's landmass) to a mere twenty-nine purchasers. The average allotment was 70,000 hectares, but many were significantly larger (the largest was over 600,000 hectares). Only a calculation error on the part of Corrientes left some 800,000 hectares to the national government.[62] Within a matter of months, most of Misiones's land went from being government-owned to being privately owned by a few people. Over a decade later, the governor of Misiones claimed that the territory had the largest latifundia system in all of Argentina, and blamed Corrientes's land sale for this problem.[63]

In spite of this, the national government quickly took measures to move ahead with colonization for the limited amount of public land remaining in Misiones. This was part of a larger government policy regarding frontier regions. The Immigration and Colonization Law of 1876 created policies and earmarked financial resources to attract immigrants to Argentina. Immigrants deemed willing to work in useful industries, arts, or trades and who were judged as having good conduct received free accommodation for a fixed period of time and transportation within Argentina to the place of settlement.[64] In 1882, the federal government passed additional legislation formalizing the sale of public lands for colonization, not only in Misiones but also in the Chaco, La Pampa, and Patagonia.[65] The law declared land in Misiones to be *tierras de panllevar* (land for agriculture), meaning it could only be purchased for this purpose. The land was priced at two pesos per hectare, and to make the acquisition accessible to those with fewer resources, 20 percent was due upon purchase with the balance paid over four years. The legislation also took steps to prevent both minifundia and further latifundia by limiting sales in a single section to between 25 and 400 hectares per person or society.[66]

Even though yerba mate grew well in the region, it was not part of the colonization effort. Since colonial times, the government, and not private individuals, had owned the wild yerbales. Legally, as an abundant resource that grew naturally without human labor, yerbales were treated as mines and defined as government property. In 1832, 1864, and 1876, Corrientes enacted legislation to protect yerbales and reinforce government ownership. Those wanting to produce yerba had to obtain government licenses and comply with explicit rules when harvesting.[67] After the federalization of Misiones, the governor again confirmed in 1894 that yerbales were government property, calling them a "true vegetal mine (*mina vegetal*), that constitutes an immense fortune for the territory" and describing them as "valuable national assets."[68] Such status barred yerbales from colonization projects.

Even though large numbers of European immigrants came to Argentina (the country was the second largest recipient of European immigration between 1856 and 1930), few settled in Misiones when the focus was traditional agriculture.[69] By 1900 only ten agricultural colonies had been founded on public lands, half of which had been created prior to Misiones becoming a national territory.[70] European immigrants considered the humid subtropical climate of Misiones foreign and unwelcoming. Illnesses, dangerous animals, and exotic vegetation thrived in this environment. Clearing the forest, planting crops, and building a homestead required an immense amount of investment, and in return, a settler could not expect much profit. Grains and other marketable crops of European origin did not flourish as they did in the Argentine pampas. Misiones was better suited for crops like mandioca, corn, tobacco, peanuts, and beans. Most farmers in Misiones lived at subsistence level, producing enough to meet their own needs and little more. Settlers who did produce a surplus found it difficult and costly to get their goods to market. Not only was Misiones distant from Argentina's large cities, it also lacked transportation infrastructure. Rain often made the few roads impassable; there were no railroads until 1911; and agricultural colonies were often distant from fluvial transportation on the Paraná or Uruguay Rivers.[71] Difficulties associated with formalizing legal ownership of the land further deterred potential settlers. In order to obtain land title, settlers had to pay for the land, meet deadlines for cultivating it, and until 1894, they had to do all of the bureaucratic paperwork in distant Buenos Aires.[72] As a result, potential settlers generally avoided Misiones. Even into the second decade of the twentieth century, government reports highlighted the lack of agricultural development in Misiones.[73]

One of the first groups of European immigrants that did settle in Misiones's agricultural colonies was a small group of Polish-Ukrainian immigrants who arrived in 1897. Misiones was not their original destination. They initially planned to go to the United States but many in the group were rejected due to poor health, and so they decided on Argentina as an alternative. The immigrants wanted to settle in the province of Buenos Aires, but the land prices were beyond their limited means. Then they looked into Patagonia, but found the environment too inhospitable. After numerous unsuccessful attempts at finding a place to settle, an earlier Polish immigrant to Argentina took pity on them and wrote, as a last resort, to his friend Juan José Lanusse, the governor of Misiones. Lanusse invited the Polish-Ukrainian pioneers to Misiones and paid for their travel. In 1897, 14 families (69 individuals) arrived in Apóstoles, and an agricultural colony was officially founded the following year. The government provided generous financial assistance to help these first immigrants settle in Misiones; they received land free of charge and many of their start-up expenses were covered.[74] While life was not easy in the new agricultural colony, the immigrants sent letters encouraging their countrymen to come to Apóstoles, and by the end of 1903, the colony listed 497 European families (2,449 people), 25 Argentine families (125 people), 16 Brazilian families (85 people), and 1 Paraguayan family (8 people).[75]

While Misiones failed to attract large numbers of European immigrants until the twentieth century, the population increased significantly between 1888 and 1895. In 1888, the territory had only 10,736 inhabitants (of which only 294 were European immigrants).[76] As of 1895, the population had almost tripled to 33,163 (of which only 942 were European immigrants). Forty-nine percent of the population was born in Argentina, followed closely by people born in other South American countries (forty-eight percent). Ironically, no Indians were mentioned. Much of the increase was due to Brazilians and Paraguayans who came to Misiones to escape political and economic upheaval.[77]

Most of the immigrants to Misiones before the twentieth century were mestizo squatters who cleared small plots of land, engaged in subsistence agriculture, and exploited the natural environment without owning the land. This reality did not fit with the official vision of economic development and progress. As Pedro Yssouribehere assessed in his 1904 study of agriculture in Misiones,

> Brazilians and Paraguayans, especially the former, always counted on this territory as a place where they could live a tranquil life without being bothered by anyone. [A place] with all the land within sight for grazing their few animals, and with valuable resources within hand's reach, [all of which] easily made life tolerable without having to tire one's muscles.[78]

For the most part, the inhabitants of Misiones minimally engaged in trade; instead, they mostly subsisted on what they (or the natural environment) produced.[79] They also found work producing yerba mate in the region's yerbales.

WILD YERBALES

While yerba production fell outside of the government's formal development plans, frontier impresarios saw opportunity.[80] They lived on the edge of the law, exploiting wild yerbales and the *mensús* (yerba laborers) who worked for them until cultivated yerba replaced wild yerbales in the first decades of the twentieth century. An estimated 2,500 to 3,000 peons worked in the wild yerbales of Misiones during the last decades of the nineteenth century—a sizable number given that the 1895 census estimated the total male population between the ages of fifteen and seventy in Misiones to be 10,729.[81]

Accordingly, Misiones's main trade goods were yerba harvested from wild yerbales and hardwoods from the region's forests.[82] Even so, Argentine yerba received little recognition. Indeed, an 1869 handbook about the Río de la Plata cited yerba mate from Brazil as an example of the "sad contrast between what La Plata [Argentina] might be, and what it actually is."[83] Studies noted that Argentina imported all, or almost all, of its yerba at the end of the nineteenth century.[84] Indeed, after the end of the Triple Alliance War in 1870, yerba production became a transnational affair. The largest companies, Matte Larangeira and La Industrial Paraguaya, dominated production in Brazil and Paraguay respectively, but they also operated in all three border countries.

During the Triple Alliance War, Tomás Larangeira was a supplier for Brazilian troops, and after the war, he used his knowledge about the region and political connections to obtain the exclusive right to lease lands from the Brazilian government for the purpose of harvesting yerba from wild yerbales.[85] Dominating yerba production in Matto Grosso, Larangeira then sought to strengthen the company's position in Argentina, the destination of most of the yerba. To do so, Larangeira capitalized on his relationship with Ricardo Antonio Mendes, who had also provisioned Brazilian troops during the Triple Alliance War. After the war, Mendes stayed in Asunción and both he and Larangeira sent their yerba to Ricardo's brother, Francisco, in Buenos Aires. Francisco then processed, marketed, and sold the yerba in Argentina. In 1902, Francisco's company purchased Matte Larangeira and the combined company took on the name Compañía Larangeira Mendes y Cia. Thereafter, it was an Argentine company based in Buenos Aires with operations in all three countries. It continued to be one of Argentina's largest yerba mate companies until the end of the twentieth century, and its Cruz de Malta brand of yerba mate is widely consumed to this day in Argentina and abroad.[86]

The other main yerba-producing company in the region at the turn of the twentieth century also originated in the aftermath of the Triple Alliance War. Paraguay was in ruins at the conclusion of the war. Instead of a state-run monopoly of yerba mate production like before the war, Paraguay's provisional government resorted to selling large plots of public lands rich with wild yerbales in an attempt to generate revenue and pay off debts. Argentine and Brazilian entrepreneurs, along with Paraguay's political elite, took advantage of this opportunity. Founded in 1886 with a significant portion of the capital contributed by the Argentine company Uribe S.A., La Industrial

Paraguaya gained exclusive control over extensive wild yerbales and massive amounts of Paraguayan land (approximately 2.1 million hectares). Its processing facilities were located in both Paraguay and Argentina, and its brand of yerba mate (Flor de Lis) also became one of the most popular in Argentina.[87]

Other yerba entrepreneurs also operated in the tri-border region. For example, Domingo Barthe (originally from France) founded a business in Paraguay after the Triple Alliance War. Barthe became an important yerba producer, in part because of a lease agreement to produce yerba in territory owned by La Industrial Paraguaya. He also had yerba operations in Brazil and became the most important yerba entrepreneur in Argentina prior to widescale yerba cultivation. Barthe and others contracted much of the yerba labor for the tri-border region from Posadas, Argentina and across the Paraná River at Encarnación, Paraguay.[88]

For laborers, work in the wild yerbales was notoriously exploitative (see figures 12 and 13). Labor contractors used advances to entice potential workers to sign up to work in distant yerbales. Once there, managers and overseers used debt peonage and violence to keep people working during long hours in poor conditions for low wages. As explored in chapter 7, early twentieth century labor reformers decried the exploitation of yerba workers. For example, on April 10, 1908, the newspaper *A Noticia* in Curitiba, Brazil, published a letter from Julian Bouvier who described the "system of slavery imposed by Domingo Barthe" as leaving the yerba worker "robbed, exploited, defeated, used up, wasted, and gasping for breath."[89] As a result of numerous articles by Bouvier and others, the yerba worker (*mensú*) became a prime symbol of capitalist exploitation for decades into the future.

Just as labor was susceptible to abuse in this isolated frontier region, so were the forests. The wild yerbales were prone to overexploitation. Ever since Misiones became a national territory, concern over this disappearing resource circulated in Argentina. In 1887, one of the land surveyors sent to Misiones after the federalization of the territory shared this worry with readers of the newspaper, *La Tribuna Nacional:* "the Argentine yerbateros dreadfully work and destroy the yerbales. You must believe me because I say the truth: and if it is not remedied soon, the harm will be enormous. There are various reasons for this, one is that there does not exist any official surveillance, [the yerba producers] work in land that does not belong to them, and its conservation is not at all important to them."[90] Such concerns intensified over time. In the 1890s, many lamented that much of Misiones' yerbales had already disappeared, and they feared that those remaining would also soon be gone. Even an 1892 United States government report on yerba mate mentioned the problem.

> As the Argentine Government makes no proprietary claim to the product, the yerbales of western Misiones are all worked by individuals, who have no further concern for them than to make all they can out of their labor. Were the forests better protected from spoliation by the Government, the industry, now that Misiones has been organized under a territorial government, might acquire a great development.[91]

Looking back at this period, the Ministry of Agriculture observed in 1915 that the yerbales of Misiones monopolized the Argentine government's discussions about national forests.[92] The national government debated what should be done, ultimately opting to reinforce government ownership of the yerbales. Accordingly, the sale of land with natural yerbales was expressly prohibited.[93] To legally produce yerba, an individual had to get official permission, follow specific guidelines, and pay taxes.[94] The measure was largely ineffective. Two years later, a representative from Corrientes pointed out, "the yerbales of Misiones today already are not extensive, due to the irregular harvests that have been done in them; they are almost completely destroyed, and those that are not destroyed are found in places very distant from the centers where there are transportation routes."[95]

Legislation to prevent the destruction of the yerbales was largely ineffective because a "tragedy of the commons" scenario unfolded. Due to insufficient policing of public lands, individuals pursued their self-interest regardless of the law, which led to the overuse and destruction of a shared limited resource. The most well-known tragedy of the commons story is the overgrazing of common lands in Britain, but the same also happened in colonial Río de la Plata with the slaughter of wild cattle for their hides.[96] The government was similarly unable to dedicate enough law enforcement resources to prevent overexploitation of the yerbales.[97] It tried to limit the number of yerba producers and vet them by requiring that they apply for official permission to harvest wild yerbales; it tried to prevent tree damage by issuing fines for excessive pruning and by only permitting a tree to be harvested once every four years and only between the months of March and July; and it attempted to enforce these rules by paying an inspector to police yerba operations.[98]

These and other laws failed because yerba producers had little incentive to restrain their harvest of wild yerbales and the government could not effectively police its rigorous regulations.[99] Furthermore, producers had no reason to consider the yerbales' long-term well-being, as they did not own them and their harvesting concessions were short in duration and subject to revocation. Since they did not know if they would be able to harvest the yerbales in the future, they sought to minimize their costs and maximize their profit in the short run by harvesting as much yerba as possible from each tree.[100] Removing most of the foliage damaged, and could kill, the trees.[101] Yerba workers were also accused of cutting down entire trees in order to avoid having to climb them to harvest high branches.[102]

Looking back on the situation in 1919, the governor of Misiones assessed that "clandestine operations, done in a brutal form to yerbales in government lands, have in large part brought about their destruction." Little could be done to remedy the situation, however, because it was impossible to police the region given its large expanse, proximity to the Brazilian border, and lack of transportation and communication infrastructure.[103] Some years earlier, another governor of Misiones had come to a similar conclusion. In an effort to emphasize the futility of policing wild yerbales, the governor asserted that effective law enforcement would require an inspector to follow each yerba worker to make sure he properly harvested every tree and did not damage it —clearly something that was impossible to do.[104]

Some realized the futility of protecting yerbales and recommended cultivation as a solution.[105] Calls for yerba cultivation intensified in the last years of the nineteenth century. In an 1894 letter published in *La Prensa,* a visitor to Misiones appealed to the scientific community of Buenos Aires to study the cultivation of yerba. Seeing wild yerbales disappear due to overexploitation, the author was taken aback that nobody knew how to cultivate yerba mate. He was even more concerned that "here in this bustling city [of Buenos Aires] where everything is studied and analyzed, nobody tries to understand more than savoring it [yerba mate], sucking on the bombilla; nobody dedicates, say, a couple of hours to develop and enrich such a valuable product." The letter concluded with an expression of hope that someone in the Department of Agriculture would study yerba cultivation.[106]

After the germination of yerba mate from seed was finally achieved at the turn of the century, calls to expand cultivation largely supplanted appeals to protect wild yerbales. As the governor of Misiones explained in a 1907 report to the Ministry of the Interior, "the only means of preserving this natural treasure that is disappearing: [is] the substitution of the virgin tree by the cultivated plant, thereby even energizing and improving that national industry of such importance."[107] Emphasis on yerba cultivation led to calls for privatizing government-owned yerbales. In an 1896 book about Misiones, Juan Queirel, who had worked as a land surveyor in Misiones for eleven years, described some advances in yerba cultivation and then speculated that maybe the time had come for the Argentine government to sell its yerbales in small parcels to private individuals or partnerships. Queirel claimed that distribution to a large number of small landowners "would not only conserve the yerbales, but would also see them unceasingly increase for the greater wealth of the Territory of the Nation."[108] Like most others who came to the same conclusion, Quierel strongly believed that private ownership was preferable for two basic reasons. First, private owners would be more effective in protecting their yerba trees than government employees paid to police large tracts of government-owned yerbales. Second, private owners would be more motivated to develop their yerba trees than people who only had temporary permission to produce yerba from government-owned trees. These reasons led Quierel to speculate that private ownership would result in the yerbales flourishing (instead of being overexploited and destroyed), which would mean that Argentine yerba production would increase.[109]

The growing interest in yerba cultivation and the privatization of wild yerbales resulted in calls for linking yerba production to colonization. Up to this point, the Argentine government had had little success attracting Europeans to settle in agricultural colonies in Misiones. Some began to propose private ownership of yerbales as an incentive. As the land surveyor Francisco Foulliand optimistically asserted, allowing yerba producers to own yerbales would lead to "the national colonization of all of the Territory of Misiones."[110] In 1903, the national government tried to balance both the call for privatizing yerbales and the longstanding belief that the yerbales were a national resource by issuing legislation that set aside land with yerbales for yerba colonies and also specifying procedures for issuing permission to produce yerba from government-owned yerbales.[111]

Calls for turning over government-owned yerbales for colonization projects continued. As Pedro Yssouribehere wrote in his 1904 report to the Ministry of Agriculture, "the colonization of the yerbal not only compels, rather it is the only truly effective means for achieving the desired objective" of "saving the yerbales, and with them, the enormous wealth they represent."[112] Less than a decade later, a traveler to Alto Paraná optimistically described the sale of Yerbal Viejo in 50-hectare lots. "The new owners could dedicate themselves to caring for [the yerba mate trees] and crops with the interest that one cares for his own things." Furthermore, the author predicted that the sale would lead to a reduction in government expenditure for enforcement, an increase in future tax revenue, and population growth in "that deserted region."[113]

Despite the growing calls for privatization, government ownership of wild yerbales persisted. A 1915 national law about forests and yerbales confirmed that the national government owned yerbales in Misiones, and private parties continued to get permission to harvest them through the 1920s.[114] Even so, the idea of the government owning yerbales was becoming antiquated. As discussed in chapter 5, yerba trees began to be cultivated in Argentina in the first years of the twentieth century and turned into green gold. By 1919, the amount of yerba harvested from cultivated trees surpassed the amount harvested from wild yerbales.[115] With cultivation booming, legislation in 1930 made it illegal to harvest yerba from wild yerbales.[116]

FOUR

Gaucho Mythology and the Drink of the New Argentines

IN 1916, MARIO BRANT, a Brazilian journalist and government official, visited Buenos Aires on behalf of *El Imparcial*. The Brazilian newspaper had sent Brant to accompany the Brazilian delegation to the centennial celebrations of Argentina's proclamation of independence. The delegation stayed at the opulent Plaza Hotel, which Brant described as a luxurious establishment on par with first-class hotels in Europe and the United States. From there, Brant explored the city and wrote a series of essays about his observations that were published as a book the following year. He observed Buenos Aires from the perspective of an upper-class foreigner, visiting elite neighborhoods without ever venturing into poorer areas or considering the common person's point-of-view. Brant's stories gushed over the city's wealth, modernity, and cosmopolitanism and portrayed its citizenry as refined, cultured, and fashionable.

After describing the cafés of Buenos Aires as just like those in Europe, he commented on the striking absence of mate.

> In the cafes, all types of liquids—fermented and distilled drinks, tea, chocolate, milk and other beverage, excluding mate—are found. The same is true in the hotels, in restaurants and in family homes, where mate is not seen. The hotels, especially, are emphatic. They offer the guest all types of drinks imaginable.

> —Do you have champagne?
> —Yes, sir!
> —Whisky?
> —Yes, sir!
> —Vodka?
> —Yes, sir!

—Cauim? [an Indigenous Brazilian alcoholic beverage made from yucca]

—Yes, sir!

—Posca [ancient Roman beverage of vinegar and water], mead, capilé [popular sweet drink], julep, beer, grog, vinegar, kéfir, nectar?

—Yes, sir!

—Absinth, rum, kerosene, vitriol?

—Yes, sir! Of course!

—And mate?

—Mate, not yet, we do not have it!

Just after this passage, Brant pointed out that Argentina imported huge quantities of yerba mate from Brazil—three times more than coffee. The Brazilian journalist and diplomat was puzzled. What happened to all of the imported yerba?[1] The answer to this question—which is that the yerba mate was in fact being drunk, but often out of public view—points to one of the key ways that yerba consumption had evolved in Argentina since independence, and the way the drink itself had increasingly become a stratifying social marker within the country.

At the time of this journalist's visit to Buenos Aires in 1916, mate was still widely drunk in the traditional manner—that is, from a bombilla and a gourd—across Argentina. But instead of being consumed by people of all social, ethnic, and economic standings, as it had been for most of the nineteenth century, it had now become the drink of the *gauchos* (cowboys), the rural countryside, and the lower classes. Similar to how wealthy Mexicans publicly rejected the corn tortilla and other Indigenous foodstuffs in favor of European cuisine, the urban elite of Buenos Aires, in an effort to modernize and emulate European culture, began to consume mate as a clandestine beverage, and they replaced it in public settings with tea and coffee.[2] At the same time, with strong pro-immigration policies and large flows of Europeans to the Americas, new immigrants flooded the country during these years, and nativists praised mate as a national custom and symbol of true Argentine identity, even though drinking mate was a regional custom, and hardly exclusive to Argentina. But these immigrants, who became more fervent mate drinkers than native-born Argentines, helped propel a new vision of mate's place in Argentine national heritage, and in the process revealed how, a hundred years after Argentina first became a nation-state, mate consumption had become tightly wound up in deeper debates about the nature of Argentine identity.

Argentina first started on the path to independence from Spain in 1810. The period immediately following that independence was a politically turbulent one, filled with military and economic conflict with its new neighboring countries, particularly Paraguay. By that point, the Spanish Empire had been in place as the major governing force in South America for more than two centuries, and during the first decades of Argentina's existence, as it sought to define itself as a nation, many key questions and debates about the culture and political identity of the country quickly began to take shape—many of which still continue to this day.

During these first decades after independence, mate played a prominent role in daily life throughout the Río de la Plata region. Europeans who visited the region regularly commented on how almost everyone in the cities and the countryside consumed the drink. Seemingly, little had changed from the colonial period.[3] The Englishman George Thomas Love, who resided in Buenos Aires for five years in the early 1820s, recorded the daily ritual of mate when describing the typical meal schedule in the city. "They have *matté* the first thing, which they often take in bed," and again "*matté* at six and seven, followed often by a supper."[4] A decade later, the French naturalist Arsène Isabelle described mate as the hot drink of choice, taking the place of tea or coffee as in Europe. "Mate is drunk at any hour and when a visitor arrives, *una negrita* (a black woman) immediately brings it to her master who offers it, one after the other, to the people present. The inhabitants could not live without this drink, quite pleasant, even though it is repugnant at first." Isabelle also commented on how the women of Buenos Aires found it amusing to serve mate during social gatherings to foreigners who were unaccustomed to drinking it.[5] Although in the twentieth century, Argentina's elite would eschew mate and reframe it as a drink for lower classes, in the decades after independence mate remained important in the social and cultural life of the Buenos Aires elite. This is made visible, for example, in several artworks from this time.[6] Carlos Enrique Pellegrini, for instance, the French-born engineer/artist and father of Argentine president Carlos Pellegrini, made a series of images in the 1830s that show Buenos Aires elite drinking mate at *tertulias* (elite social gatherings in a private home) (see figure 4).[7] As the Englishman Love from the 1820s described, the fashionable London practice of afternoon tea had "not travelled to this quarter of the globe yet."[8]

FIGURE 4. Buenos Aires elite and woman of African ancestry drinking mate. Carlos Enrique Pellegrini, "Minuete," in *Recuerdos del Rio de la Plata* (1841).

In the Río de la Plata region, the nineteenth century picked up where the colonial period ended. The late imperial relaxation of trade restrictions begun by Spain in the 1770s accelerated after independence, making the region one of the most open economies in the world. The ensuing growth of trade reoriented Río de la Plata's economy away from the Andean mining region and toward Europe. Exports increased, driven largely by pastoral products (hides, tallow, wool, and salted meat), and the shift away from the interior and toward the littoral (the provinces of Buenos Aires, Entre Ríos, Corrientes, and Santa Fé) continued. Although the first fifty years after independence are typically portrayed as lost years during which the region experienced political turmoil and economic stagnation, the city and countryside around Buenos Aires experienced economic growth. The port city was an important transit hub for both transatlantic and interior trade and the nearby pampas were well suited for pastoralism and agriculture. Migration followed economic opportunity.

While the majority of the population lived in the interior at the beginning of the century, the balance shifted as people moved to the littoral. Some moved to cities, but most relocated to rural areas during the first half of the century due to the relative importance of pastoralism in the Argentine economy. Foreign immigrants began joining the mix in the mid-1840s, a trend that rapidly accelerated in subsequent decades.

In the post-independence period, mate became increasingly associated with the Argentine countryside. Visual representations indicate such an association. In addition to the works of Carlos Enrique Pellegrini described above, other well-respected artists such as, León Palliere, and Prilidiano Pueyrredón also created various images of the Río de la Plata countryside, and mate was visible virtually every time when people were not riding horses. Artwork showed people drinking mate by a fire while preparing meat and relaxing outdoors or inside a rural home;[9] at social gatherings with dancing, guitar music, conversation, and alcohol;[10] and during breaks in a journey.[11] Like artists, travel writers to Argentina also consistently depicted mate being drunk in rural settings, describing it as an integral part of daily life, and thus reinforcing the association of mate with the Río de la Plata countryside.[12] Almost all foreigners who wrote about mate in Argentina commented on its consumption in the countryside. While foreign observers generally wrote for non-Argentine audiences, elite Argentines also read these accounts, and this influenced how they saw themselves and their country.[13]

More or less simultaneously, the image of the gaucho emerged as a prominent cultural figure in Argentina. The term gaucho, at its essence, signifies a rural horseman of the Río de la Plata countryside, but otherwise its meaning varies across time and space (see figure 5). Scholars have used the gaucho as one of the main vehicles for exploring Argentine identity in the nineteenth and early twentieth century. In many ways, the gaucho is at least as important in Argentine historical memory as the cowboy or frontier settler in the United States.[14] Since colonial times, horsemen had played a major role in the region in and around Argentina. But the myth of the gaucho is drawn primarily from the nineteenth century, and this romantic figure is central to Argentina's national imaginary to this day. Over the decades, the gaucho became a symbolic figure who generalized the experiences of marginalized sectors of society in an exaggeratedly negative or positive manner. The figure had an enduring and somewhat flexible appeal to people throughout the country. Some writers tried to shape the image of the gaucho to serve their political interests and promote their interpretation of Argentine history and society, while others

FIGURE 5. Esteban Gonnet, "Tomando mate," ca. 1866. Miriam and Ira D. Wallach Division of Arts, Prints, and Photographs: Photography Collection, The New York Public Library.

eulogized the gaucho in popular books and stories because this mythic figure helped generate sales, particularly among the rural and urban popular classes.[15] While many of these books and stories about life as a gaucho were written by educated urbanites posing as rural gauchos, this did not mean Argentine intellectuals controlled the message or content, The lower classes also played a significant role in shaping how the gaucho myth took shape at this time.[16]

As stories of the gaucho as an appealing rural figure gained popularity, the image of mate as a drink associated with the countryside also became increasingly part of popular culture. Bartolomé Hidalgo, the first major *gauchesque* author, often referred to mate in his writings. It was part of daily life for country folk, and in Hidalgo's stories, dialogue between gauchos generally occurred while they were sharing mate. Later, other gauchesque authors followed the same formula.[17] In these stories, mate was also used to distinguish country folk from outsiders. In a patriotic song from 1820, Hidalgo used mate to highlight the virility and braveness of gaucho soldiers as compared to Spaniards who drank chocolate. As the narrator explained: "Keep your chocolate, we're all pure Indians here, and we only drink mate."[18]

Relatedly, as the nineteenth century progressed, and Argentine identity and class stratification evolved, the liberal elite of Buenos Aires also increasingly associated yerba mate with rural customs. One of the most highly regarded works of nineteenth century Latin American literature, Domingo Sarmiento's *Facundo: Or, Civilization and Barbarism,* describes a stark divide between the city (civilization) and the countryside (barbarism). Sarmiento was a prominent political figure in Argentina; he later became President in 1868. Published in installments in 1845 by a Chilean newspaper while the author was in exile, *Facundo* expressed the longstanding belief of Buenos Aires liberal elite about their superiority relative to the rest of the Río de la Plata region.[19] This belief underlay ongoing Unitarian calls for a strong central government directed from Buenos Aires. In contrast, Federalists continued their calls for the provinces to have more power and autonomy. Conflict over the form of government persisted until the second half of the nineteenth century. Representing the worldview of the Buenos Aires elite, Sarmiento argued that forces of civilization (based in cities and modeled after western Europe) and barbarism (encompassing rural Argentina and embodied by its mixed-race inhabitants) competed for dominance in Argentina. Sarmiento and his peers thought native peoples, Africans, and Spaniards were backward, lazy, and inferior as compared to western Europeans.

He especially targeted the gauchos who he claimed freely roamed the Argentine countryside. In 1861, Sarmiento advised General Bartolomé Mitre (who would become Argentina's president the following year), "Do not try to save the blood of gauchos. It is a contribution that the country needs. Blood is the only thing they have in common with human beings."[20] Sarmiento believed the gauchos were both uninterested in and incapable of exploiting the vast and underutilized natural resources of their territory for Argentina's advancement. Despite the idealized narrative depictions that appealed to popular classes, for nineteenth century liberals, the gaucho embodied barbarism and everything that was wrong with Argentina; he was poor, lazy, unreliable, uneducated, quick to anger, violent, and lawless. They believed that the natural abundance of resources in the countryside intensified the gauchos' inherent laziness, as they could work very little and still have enough to eat. The liberal elite contrasted such behavior with the purported industriousness of northern Europeans, who they believed would advance the country by building upon whatever nature had to offer. Accordingly, Sarmiento argued that Argentina's progress required mass European immigration and the eradication of the gauchos, either through forced change and education or by extermination.[21]

Negative ideas about gauchos carried over to the iconic gaucho beverage—mate. Those who believed the people of the countryside were backward and lazy also often described mate as a waste of time and a vice. For example, William MacCann, a British businessman who spent most of the 1840s in Argentina and traveled more than two thousand miles within its provinces, understood the rural population of Argentina much like Sarmiento, and such thinking carried over to his opinions about mate. He described the country people as "generally unwilling to occupy themselves in any way except in the ordinary duties of an estancia. They live in ranchos or huts, without the smallest spot of ground either to plant a flower or raise a vegetable. The land, though very fertile, is never tilled by them. . . . The resources of the country are altogether neglected for want of an industrious population." Instead of staying on task, "they usually take maté early in the morning; indeed they are drinking it throughout the entire day." Elsewhere, he also mentioned that "when idle, [the native peasant] is either sipping maté or smoking cigars."[22]

While the liberal elite of Buenos Aires considered the gaucho backward and an impediment to the nation's advancement, their enemy Juan Manuel de Rosas and his followers praised the gaucho. The caudillo Rosas ruled Buenos Aires province for over two decades (1829–1852) and dominated the Argentine confederacy through repression and a cult of personality. As a man of the countryside, Rosas was an avid mate drinker and he used this practice to build relationships with his followers. The gauchesque author Eduardo Gutiérrez explained that Rosas cultivated support among rural folk by exhibiting all of the traits of the gauchos and by "sharing with them the roughest work, even mate around the fire."[23] Contemporary images, again, show that Rosas's followers were closely associated with mate. One of the most famous paintings from the era is Cayetano Descalzi's *Boudoir Federal* (c. 1845), which shows a woman fixing her hair in an intimate setting. The woman is wearing the mandatory red scarf representing Rosas and there is a picture of Rosas on the wall; a mate with a bombilla are on the mantle.[24] Likewise, *Soldado de la guardia de Rosas* (1842) by Raymond Monvoisin shows a gaucho soldier dressed in the red of Rosas's followers who is relaxing while drinking mate (see figure 6).[25]

To liberals like Sarmiento, Rosas was the antithesis of everything they believed and valued. In demonizing Rosas, they disparaged his enthusiasm

FIGURE 6. Raymond Monvoisin, *Soldado de la guardia de Rosas* (1842).

for mate. As one author described, Rosas was accustomed to drinking one hundred bitter mates per day and his poor servants often waited an hour for him to take the mate that they served him.[26] In his criticism, Sarmiento connected Rosas's authoritarianism and violence with his mate consumption: "from deep within his office where he drinks his mate, [Rosas] sends the *Mazorca* (paramilitary) the orders they must carry out."[27] Even after losing power and going into exile in England, Rosas still valued and prioritized mate. Twelve years after being overthrown, Rosas wrote to a friend that his lack of funds forced him to economize to the point that "my food is a piece of grilled meat, and my yerba mate. Nothing more."[28]

Even though the liberal elite of Buenos Aires disparaged Rosas's mate consumption, people still widely consumed it in the city. Looking back from the 1880s, the intellectual elite of Buenos Aires associated mate with this period. In "Scenes from Past Times," the diplomat and director of the national library, Vicente Quesada, wrote, "tea wasn't consumed and few drank coffee. Mate—in the morning, at noon, in the afternoon, and at night—was the usual drink, both popular and of good society . . . mate and snuff helped pass the long hours of those sad days."[29] Another of Quesada's stories about the past revealed that mate was more than just a drink. It was a social practice that was central to illicit gatherings otherwise prohibited under Rosas. Students and young people could not gather in clubs or cafés to converse, so they met in a church's sacristy and talked (but not about political matters) while the priest served them mate.[30] Quesada wrote disparagingly about Buenos Aires during this period and praised the advancement of the 1880s. In doing so, he made clear that mate was antiquated. When describing his uncle, a man who was stuck in the past with outdated practices, Quesada simply stated, "in sum, he drinks mate."[31]

Like Quesada, the prominent doctor and intellectual José Antonio Wilde also wrote in the 1880s about how Buenos Aires had changed over the nineteenth century and how mate no longer fit with the times. Although Wilde did not overtly condemn mate, he thought that it held back progress. In several instances, Wilde described how lazy and unproductive people were, and connected this shortcoming to mate. "In those times, in which life was easy for all, and there was little to toil for, there was never lacking someone who said, 'yesterday I laid down to take my little siesta, and I slept until the [evening] prayers; I remembered them, drank my mate, and I returned to sleep until today, when the sun was high.' What times and what a life!" Wilde described how in the past, mate was often served in bed before breakfast, between breakfast and lunch, and again from 6:00 to 7:00 before dinner. For him, mate was a thing of the past, when "there had been enough servants and less need to economize time."[32]

Changing perceptions about mate were not limited to Buenos Aires elites, and other regions across South America saw similar developments. In Santa

Fe, for example, in Argentina's northeast, Lina Beck-Bernard, a French woman who moved there with her husband in 1857 to found a Swiss agricultural colony, wrote about how, at a dance she attended, only older women drank mate.[33] Similarly, in Chile, the elite now preferred tea and coffee over mate, even though mate had previously been the most widely consumed infusion and all social classes had drunk it at the time of independence. Many people who traveled to South America described this shift. Claudio Gay, a prominent French botanist contracted by the Chilean government to survey the country, visually portrayed this change in his 1854 atlas of Chile. In the book, Gay included an image of a 1790 *tertulia* in Santiago that showed the elite consuming mate, but his 1840 image of the same setting omitted mate.[34] It wasn't only the Chilean elite who began to consume more coffee and tea at mate's expense; mate's consumption also began to decrease among all sectors of the urban population as the other beverages became more pervasive. Still, mate consumption did not disappear in Chile. The country continued to import significant quantities of yerba, and mate consumption remained strong throughout the twentieth century, especially in the south of the country.[35] In Chile, however, the consumption of mate never became as tightly connected to ideas of class and national identity as it did in Argentina.

By the late nineteenth century, the elite of Buenos Aires no longer publicly consumed mate. Many visitors to the region commented on this observation. In a 1911 essay published in *La Prensa,* Georges Clemenceau (a former Prime Minister of France) described how "in all parts, in the city as in the countryside, the universal rite of mate is done in plain sight. Men and women gravely pass the small gourd, into which is introduced the tube of the 'bombilla,' which passes from mouth to mouth, giving the utmost pleasure to the enthusiast." In contrast, Clemenceau pointed out that "mate has been relegated as a drink of the masses while the aristocratic and bourgeois class, without ever speaking disparagingly of it, prefer, like all good Europeans, the tea of China and the coffee of Santos [Brazil]."[36]

Publicly, the Buenos Aires elite had replaced mate with both tea and coffee. In many ways, cafés replaced rounds of mate as a public venue for conversations and socializing. Reminiscing about Argentine customs of the nineteenth century in his memoirs, Pastor S. Obligado, a lawyer, author, and son of the first governor of the secessionist state of Buenos Aires, described the significant role of cafés for urban culture in Buenos Aires during the second half of the nineteenth century, and explicitly traced their origin to the sharing of mate by trusted companions at *tertulias*. He described in detail the most popular café—Café de Amistad. From its founding in 1842 until its closure in 1892 after a fire, Café de Amistad was open every day from 7:00 a.m. until 10:00 p.m. so patrons could have coffee throughout the day (just as they had done with mate). And like with rounds of mate, the conversations and social interactions were an important part of café culture. As Obligado described, all sorts of people frequented Café de Amistad and it was a center for debate and discussion about news and the state of the nation. Obligado remarked that by the time it closed, every street corner in the city had at least one café.[37]

By the late nineteenth century, Buenos Aires had changed and many in the upper classes thought that mate did not fit with modernity or an urban lifestyle. Sharing mate was a time-consuming activity—time that many believed should be used more productively. An article about official abuses in the major newspaper, *La Prensa,* explicitly condemned mate consumption by government officials.

> In the public offices, the official only attends the public from 2 to 3 o'clock or from 3 to 4, in order that nobody may interrupt him at the hour of taking mate. When mate is suppressed in the public offices, the Government will lose the aspect of town grogshops (*despachos de aldea*), and the administration of business will gain much in promptitude and regularity. Messieurs ministers and chiefs of bureaus, we denounce mate as a grand conspirator against the public interests, and especially against labor in the public offices.[38]

Two decades later, a British observer reported that it was his understanding that government employees in Buenos Aires were forbidden to drink yerba mate during office hours.[39] Criticism that mate wasted time was not limited to government officials. Carlos Enrique Pellegrini (the artist who made various images of people drinking mate in the countryside) expressed concern that mate did not fit with urban life when he questioned, "Who does not see that such a slow practice of absorbing a small amount of hot water [through a shared bombilla] is completely incompatible with the good use of time in any well-organized factory?"[40] Even Carlos Girola, a renowned agronomist and author of over twenty-five essays promoting yerba mate, recommended restricting mate consumption because it "presented the inconvenience of causing a great loss of time."[41]

But it was the awareness of mate consumption as anti-hygienic that most captivated the Buenos Aires elite. Sharing a bombilla spread germs, and this disgusted them. In 1854, the Buenos Aires socialite Mariquita Sánchez described the custom of drinking mate from the same straw as "piggish."[42] Such criticisms intensified in the late nineteenth and early twentieth centuries with growing concern about the spread of germs. Between the 1850s and 1870s, yellow fever killed thousands and reshaped Buenos Aires as the wealthy fled north to new neighborhoods in Barrio Norte, Palermo, and Belgrano. Disease continued to plague urban areas in later decades, and discoveries about the transmission of illnesses convinced many that mate was part of the problem. Prior to then, miasma or "bad air" was thought to spread diseases, but the linking of cholera to contaminated water exposed how germs spread disease. Hygiene became a major preoccupation. While mate, which used boiled water, was an inexpensive way for people to drink sterilized water, concern over the shared bombilla overshadowed this attribute.[43] Sharing a bombilla meant exchanging saliva, something that easily could lead to the transmission of disease. As an advertisement for yerba mate extract highlighted, the major conductor of tuberculosis (which killed large numbers of people in Buenos Aires between the 1870s and 1950s) was "the bombilla, with which people drink mate not only with members of their family but also with friends and even with strangers."[44] When the powerful *Sociedad Rural* published "Yerba Mate as a Hygienic Drink" in its journal, the author raved about yerba mate consumed in the form of a tea and its superiority over both Chinese tea and coffee, while also concluding that "the use of mate with a bombilla is the most anti-hygienic way it could be used, for reasons that it would be a waste of time to repeat and that are already in the consciousness of everyone."[45]

Sharing mate was considered unhygienic not only because of the potential for spreading illness but also because of the intimate contact it entailed between people of different social and economic classes, ethnicities, and genders. When drinking mate, everyone (men and women, young and old, healthy and sick, blacks and whites) put the shared bombilla to their lips, while the same people would not think of drinking from a cup that had been used by someone else.[46] In a particularly vivid description, Afredo Ebelot, a French engineer and journalist who authored a book about the customs of Argentina, explained that one person after another sucked from the same bombilla, and frequently, the *cebador* (server) who drank the first sips of mate was an old female gaucho (*china*) with only a few bad teeth and lips that looked like an old wineskin because of the profusion of wrinkles. Ebelot astutely pointed out that one would be more inclined toward mate if served by a young girl of an affluent family with a good complexion, pretty eyes, and a playful laugh.[47] Sharing mate was dangerous not only because it had the potential to spread germs, but also because it challenged class and social divisions.

Such concerns led a number of Argentines to call for an end to mate consumption. Others simply ignored or sidelined the practice. The abundant literature to educate children and immigrants about proper behavior took the latter approach. Concerned about large-scale immigration and urbanization in the late nineteenth and early twentieth centuries, the Argentine government and other interested parties published a number of books and manuals to educate the populace on topics such as finances, household administration, time management, etiquette, and hygiene.[48] By omitting mate, which was a central part of culture and daily life for much of the population and especially for the working and lower classes, many of these publications indirectly communicated disdain for the beverage. Guides for housewives provided detailed advice touching on various topics but rarely mentioned mate. For example, in consultation with his wife, Cipriano Torrejón published at least seven editions of his *Lecture on Home Economics* that provided housewives with detailed information including daily work schedules and home remedies, but without ever mentioning yerba mate.[49] A similar publication provided detailed guidance about home finances; this included a sample list of monthly groceries, but it did not contain yerba mate even though the government considered it a basic necessity. It also had instructions for entertaining that referred to the offering of tea to visitors but not mate, even though this had long been considered a basic courtesy for guests.[50]

When educational texts did mention mate, it was clear that their authors did not value it. A book about educating girls to be good housewives acknowledged that yerba mate, coffee, tea, and chocolate had positive characteristics (yerba mate was refreshing; coffee and tea stimulated digestion; and chocolate was nutritious), but the praise for yerba mate was tempered. "Yerba mate, when one does not abuse the infusion that is made with it, is refreshing, but drunk with excess produces languor of the stomach and dyspepsia."[51] Another book of short stories designed to educate young girls included a story about tea, chocolate, mate, and coffee, but it downplayed mate relative to other caffeinated drinks. The grandmother drank mate while the young girl drank chocolate, the mother drank tea, and the father drank coffee. By assigning mate to the grandmother, who refused to ever give it up, the author made it seem antiquated. Tea was clearly the preferred drink—five paragraphs were dedicated to tea while mate and coffee had two paragraphs and chocolate had only one. Nothing was said about how to consume mate.[52] In contrast, an instructional guide to civility and courtesy made clear that mate should never be shared. "To nobody should we offer food or drink that has touched our lips and [this should] not [be done] even [for] the most long-standing customs—such as the case of the bombillas of mate."[53] Whether didactic authors ignored or condemned mate, they all looked down upon the practice and did not see a future for it in Argentina.

In the face of such opposition, some attempted to find more hygienic ways to drink mate without abandoning the bombilla. Someone invented a small tube attachment for the bombilla that was removed after each person's turn. The innovation allowed people to share mate without everyone putting their lips directly on the bombilla.[54] Some legislators purportedly used such attachments during sessions of Congress as a way to drink mate while maintaining a dignified appearance and remaining within protocol.[55] In a 1923 article, "Our Old Traditions: Mate," the military magazine *El Soldado Argentina* praised mate but recommended using the same number of bombillas as people drinking the mate in order to reduce the spread of contagious illnesses.[56] In the same decade, the Confitería de Mayo (a café/teashop in Buenos Aires) experimented with selling mate with interchangeable straws, but its attempt at promoting a "hygienic" form of drinking mate failed to attract much interest.[57] As discussed more in the following chapter, others also tried, and largely failed, to replace mate with yerba mate tea. As a 1916 article in the popular magazine, *Caras y Caretas,* explained, "Mate is a custom so engrained that even though, under the pretext of hygiene, its replacement with tea was tried, [mate] has triumphed to such a degree that even in the trenches, according to photographs that have been published, the infusion is drunk, with mate and bombilla, in the criollo manner."[58] Criollo is a flexible term implying deep Argentine roots and it refers broadly to the country's rural past.

While most anti-mate efforts focused on the cities, some opponents also tried to discourage its use in rural areas. Godofredo Daireaux's guide for the modern livestock ranch, first published in 1887 and reprinted numerous times in the first half of the twentieth century, explicitly advocated an end to mate consumption.

> This custom of drinking mate, even though it is a national custom, has to be modified some day in the countryside, the same as it is disappearing in the city. It is the hope that this will happen soon and ranchers should work to accelerate the arrival of this happy day. Mate, as they drink it, results in an

incalculable loss of time. It weakens, even though the former is said. It cannot be denied that this quantity of hot water, that takes away the desire to eat, could replace a robust and heavy foodstuff.[59]

Although Daireaux wanted mate consumption to stop, he recognized that prohibition was not practical. Thus, he recommended that ranchers wake up at dawn like their ranch-hands "to prevent the damage caused by the custom of making mate last a long time." At least one modern rancher forbade the drinking of mate on his estancia, but overall, such advice had limited results.[60]

Some erroneously predicted that mate would disappear. For example, Ebelot, the French author and engineer who wrote about Argentine customs in the late nineteenth century, believed that mate did not have a place in the city. According to Ebelot, many servants spent three-quarters of their time just serving mate at estancias in the countryside, but this was no longer possible in the city as the high price of property led to smaller houses that did not accommodate "useless servants" who did little more than serve mate. Despite its waste of time and resources, Ebelot mourned the end of mate. "Mate is disappearing, and it is a shame. It was the symbol of the life out in the open; difficult, healthy, and free; of the life in the wilderness in which the only thing that one did not lack was space; of life full of deprivations and of attractions that those who have tried it will never forget."[61] Such nostalgia fit with the turn-of-the-century trend of eulogizing a mythical rural past.[62] While Ebelot was correct about changes in the Argentine countryside, he was wrong about mate. It did not disappear.

A NATIVIST AND GAUCHO DRINK

In the last decades of the nineteenth century, Argentina experienced great change, which was reflected in evolving perceptions about mate. Livestock and agriculture in the Argentine pampas drove rapid economic growth. Railways spread across the country, money was invested, and new technical practices were implemented. Fencing expanded rapidly in the 1880s, which helped secure property rights, prevented livestock from destroying crops, and made livestock-raising less labor intensive. The advent of refrigeration radically changed the livestock industry by allowing Argentina to export refrigerated meat starting in the 1880s.[63] All of these changes reshaped rural areas.

Livestock no longer roamed freely; estancias needed a reduced but permanent labor force; and foreign workers filled many of the new positions in agriculture, construction, and other jobs. The independent, free-spirited, and nomadic gauchos became obsolete.[64]

At the same time, large numbers of foreign immigrants arrived in the country. Between 1821 and 1932, Argentina ranked second worldwide in receiving the largest number of European immigrants. Over 6.5 million foreigners arrived in Argentina between 1856 and 1930. These immigrants had a huge impact on the composition of the Argentine population. By 1914, 30 percent were foreign-born; by way of contrast, the percentage of foreign-born never surpassed 15 percent in the United States.[65] Immigration helped spur economic growth, but its impact on society bothered the Argentine elite. They felt threatened by the emergence of an incipient middle class that blurred distinctions in the social hierarchy and demanded a more inclusive political system.

Opportunity created new wealth. In response, the old elite expressed concern about excessive materialism and the growing number of people who profited as middlemen. Speculation was rampant. Many blamed immigrants for being greedy and self-interested. Such anti-immigration sentiment led to attempts to differentiate "true" Argentines from immigrants, along with a newfound appreciation for Argentine traditions and culture. While many of the Buenos Aires liberal elite continued to disdain the gaucho, nativists, who themselves were often also elites, began to see the gauchos in a new light. Confronted with the advance of capitalism, urbanization and immigration, nativists romanticized Argentina's past and embraced the idealized gaucho as a noble figure who embodied genuine criollo identity. Instead of negatively portraying violence, lawlessness, laziness, and poverty, nativists understood gauchos as honorable, loyal, brave, and hospitable. For them, the gaucho was a positive marker of Argentine national identity, an idea made more palatable by the disappearance of real-life gauchos. Formerly criticized characteristics of the gaucho were refashioned: his nomadic lifestyle was romanticized and his lawless behavior was construed as independence. Literature and popular theater portrayed gauchos as persecuted and oppressed individuals who had trouble adapting to nineteenth century changes, and then as modest peons loyal to both their employers and homeland.[66]

A turning-point was José Hernández's 1872 publication of the epic poem *The Gaucho Martín Fierro*, followed by *The Return of Martín Fierro* in 1879. The poems cultivated understanding and appreciation for gaucho culture and exposed the hardships and abuses that they suffered. Hernández wrote the poem as a critique of Domingo Sarmiento's presidency and Sarmiento's portrayal of the gaucho and the countryside. In contrast to Sarmiento's *Facundo,* Hernández portrayed the city and "civilization" as corrupt, repressive, and oppressive, and he romanticized the gaucho as a brave, resilient, and rebellious free spirit. The poem is nostalgic about an idyllic past disrupted by capitalism and the state.[67] Mate played a central role in this idealized peaceful life.

> I've known this land where my fellow gaucho lived
> And had his little house and his children and woman. . . .
> It made you feel good to see how he spent his days. . . .
>
> And sitting next to the fire waiting for daylight,
> he sucked at his maté 'till he got warm,
> while his woman slept all snug in her poncho.[68]

In addition to mate's place in peaceful family life, Hernández also described its importance for the itinerant gaucho in passages describing how the gaucho traded goods to obtain mate and the deprivation he felt when not able to consume mate (imprisoned gauchos were not allowed to drink mate, talk, sing, or smoke).[69] Hernández alluded to mate's broader cultural significance for the gaucho by highlighting its consumption during social interactions; recounting how a husband killed his wife for serving him cold mate; describing a love-potion administered through mate; telling a joke about mate; and using mate as a simile.[70] To Hernandez's readers, mate was a nostalgic symbol that provided a sense of rootedness in the face of disorienting change.

Hernández's stories of Martín Fierro quickly gained a large following among rural folk and the lower classes, and their success inspired other authors to explore similar terrain. In 1879, for example, Eduardo Gutiérrez published *El gaucho Juan Moreira,* which became even more popular than *Martín Fierro* until the early 1900s. Again, mate played a central role in Moreira's story and the gaucho lifestyle. Gauchos drank it to begin their day and when they relaxed at the end of the day. They shared it with companions, friends, family, love interests, and strangers. In these stories, mate inspired conversation, and it also filled the void when the gaucho was overcome with sadness.[71] As Hernández described, "The other men respected [Moreira's] silence and did not speak even to each other as they passed the mate gourd from hand to hand. One heard only the slight slurping sound as each drinker drained the gourd before passing it to the next man."[72]

The adaptation of *Juan Moreira* for theater extended its reach and helped spur the widespread popularity of criollo theater in general. Like the book versions before them, these performances helped influence a perception among both urban and rural populations that the heritage of Argentine identity could be directly traced back to this frontier character and his cultural customs, including the consumption of mate. The popularity and elaborateness of these performances had an important impact in this regard. These shows weren't simply plays; they included acrobatics, music, and comedy. They often had live animals and accoutrements of rural life. Of course, mate played a central role.[73] In sum, criollo theater brought the countryside to the stage. By the 1890s popular audiences, along with urban elite, watched criollo dramas in mainstream theaters. Even though their popularity declined in later decades, the legacy of criollo dramas continued in film, radio theater, folk festivals, and especially in criollo social clubs.[74] This legacy would have a direct impact on the debates regarding cultural identity that were circulating at this time among elites, nativists, and immigrants.

Further influencing perceptions of Argentina's cultural heritage and identity as being tied to the gaucho, hundreds of criollo societies sprouted up throughout Argentina, Uruguay and southern Brazil between the 1890s and 1910s. The clubs were social spaces that drew people of diverse socioeconomic backgrounds together based on a shared vision that romanticized rural life. At the clubs, members escaped their daily lives for several hours by playing gaucho (dressing up and engaging in activities that celebrated rural traditions). Again, in this nostalgic vision of Argentina's cultural heritage, mate was omnipresent. Smaller clubs had, at the very least, a room for members to share mate and listen to guitar music.[75]

Criollo culture held wide appeal because it helped give meaning to the drastic changes of the late nineteenth and early twentieth century. It cultivated nostalgia for a simpler way of life, free of the obligations imposed by capitalism and the state. Scholars have identified four ways in which criollo culture appealed to diverse sectors of society. For people displaced from the countryside to urban spaces, criollo culture helped them cope with the changes by celebrating their rural roots. For immigrants, adopting criollo culture helped them assimilate, and often, rural culture also resonated with them. For the elite, criollo culture helped legitimate their position and status as native Argentines. For non-whites, criollo culture revealed the region's ethnic heterogeneity.[76]

Criollo culture had long fascinated foreign observers. Many fixated on the gaucho's diet, highlighting the centrality of mate. For sustenance, the

Gaucho Tomando Mate

FIGURE 7. Postcard by H. G. Olds, "Gaucho tomando mate" (early 1900s).

gauchos were supposed to have eaten only meat and only drank mate and booze. R. B. Cunninghame Graham, a Scottish politician and adventurer, admiringly wrote in 1896 that the gaucho "passed his life, living on meat and maté, without a drop of milk in the midst of herds of cattle, without a vegetable, without a luxury except tobacco and an occasional glass of *caña* (rum)."[77] Mate was portrayed as an integral part of daily life, not just sustenance. As a French traveler concluded, gauchos would rather not eat than be without mate.[78] It was also described as an important pastime for the gauchos. Whenever they were not working, they passed the time drinking mate.[79] After spending a year in the Río de la Plata region in the early twentieth century, John Alexander Hammerton summarized the gaucho. "He is essentially a child of nature, delighting to be in the saddle, roaming the plains, rounding up the cattle, living to the full his outdoor life, eating enormous quantities of beef and mutton, sipping his *mate* and strumming his guitar at eventide by the open door of his rudely furnished rancho."[80] Drinking mate was described as a shared social activity, where gauchos conversed, told stories, or sang. But they were also described as drinking mate for companionship when they were alone with their thoughts and on the open pampas.[81]

Visual imagery also associated mate with gauchos. Numerous postcards from the turn of the twentieth century depicted gauchos with mate.[82] The image of a rural woman handing mate to a man on horseback was especially popular, as demonstrated in a widely circulating postcard from around 1905 titled "Gaucho Drinking Mate" and identified as a "souvenir of the Republic of Argentina" (see figure 7).[83] Gauchos also appeared in film. Argentina's first box office hit, the 1915 silent film *Nobleza Gaucha,* had a title card stating, "A mate without sugar is a fine reward for a valiant gaucho." Following this, the gaucho's romantic interest and her mother serve him mate while he sits on his horse.[84] The film was so popular that it was remade in 1937 and a yerba distributor purchased the naming rights. Nobleza Gaucha continues to be a popular brand of yerba mate today.

Perceptions of close ties between gauchos and mate promoted the idea that gauchos were *the* authentic mate drinkers. For example, a contributor to one of the earliest cookbooks published in Argentina, in 1890, observed,

> among the populations of the Pampa, mate is almost a cult. Those bearded and serious men, drink it with a solemnity similar to adoration. And, strange thing, among the refined enthusiasts of mate, nobody knows how to make it like them. They give the yerba, in its infusion with boiling water, an exquisite perfume, that once tried, is yearned for.

Given such expertise, the contributor deferred to an "old gaucho" and transcribed his recipe instead of providing her own explanation about how to properly prepare mate.[85] In doing so, the cookbook recognized the gaucho as the mate expert and true mate drinker.

For many, the gaucho accompanied by mate symbolized Argentina. An Argentine traveling in Europe confirmed such a connection in a 1905 article for the newspaper *La Nación.*

> Argentine society is found represented, as a general rule, by the effigy of some Indian or gaucho with *chiripá* (pants) and *bota de potro* (riding boots), or by a lasso and a pair of *bolas* (weapon of stone balls attached to the ends of rope), or a mate with bombilla, so as to leave the public with the inerasable impression that is the most important and distinguishing characteristic that our country has.[86]

In this case, the author not only highlighted the gaucho, but also mate, clothing and other paraphernalia as representative of Argentine identity as perceived abroad. This description reflected key trends in the way mate and Argentina's identity were becoming defined through this rural heritage. It is also notable that the author brought up Argentina's native peoples in this description. However, despite this mention, the gaucho was increasingly becoming a central figure in the popular perception of Argentina's cultural heritage and identity and the Indigenous population—who continued to make up a significant percentage of the population in certain regions of the country and whose customs, including the consumption of mate, had been influential to Argentine culture—were increasingly overlooked.[87]

As the country's writers, artists, and other influential people increasingly highlighted the importance of criollo culture, and a broader population consumed this culture and embraced the vision of the gaucho as central to Argentine identity, the role of Indigenous people in Argentina's past and present culture was increasingly marginalized. This was particularly the case in the way mate's Indigenous ties were overlooked and forgotten. After the Conquest of the Desert (1870s–1884), which killed, displaced, and conquered the native peoples of the pampas and Patagonia, Argentina's Indigenous population was largely sidelined from national identity. They were primarily seen as vestiges of the past or subjects of study in museums and other scientific institutions.[88] Similarly, yerba mate's connection to Indigenous peoples was generally overlooked even though Indigenous peoples were the first to use the substance and even though mate continued to play an important role in Indigenous societies.[89] Just as native peoples receded from Argentine identity in general, mate was now not considered an Indian drink but rather a gaucho drink. As an article titled "Our Old Customs: Mate," in the military magazine *El Soldado* explained, the men of the countryside were the "true and intelligent drinkers of mate."[90] And while gauchos became reinvented and mythologized, mate persisted. Furthermore, despite the Buenos Aires elite's public disdain, Argentine consumption of mate increased.

A CLANDESTINE DRINK

Between 1875 and 1920, yerba mate consumption grew dramatically in Argentina, from less than 12 million kilos in 1875 to almost 30 million kilos in 1896, to 50 million kilos in 1910, and over 70 million kilos in 1920 (quintupling over less than fifty years). Argentines consumed large quantities of yerba mate—the equivalent of 7 to 8 kilos per person per year.[91] By comparison, the British, who were known for their widespread consumption of tea, consumed far less of this caffeinated beverage (2.7 kilos per person in 1900, with a saturation point of 4.4 kilos per capita in 1931).[92] A French traveler similarly concluded that an Argentine annually spent twice as much per year on yerba mate than a French person spent on coffee.[93]

Mate was so widely consumed in Argentina that it was considered a basic necessity by the state.[94] The Department of Labor repeatedly included yerba mate in its list of basic necessities.[95] It was so important that President Julio Roca expressed concern about what would happen if Argentines were unable to purchase yerba: "A grave situation would present itself if, for whatever circumstances, we found ourselves without this foodstuff for the consumption of the people, and I do not want to think about what an army in the countryside would suffer without yerba mate."[96] In addition to people in the countryside, people in the cities also continued to drink mate as part of their daily activities.[97] According to one source, working class families welcomed breadwinners home each day by sharing mate.[98] Another source remarked that the middle class continued to drink mate "with all the *ritual* inherited from our fathers."[99]

Despite the ongoing public rejection of mate by many of Argentina's elite, who claimed it was a drink for the lower classes, some praised mate and its contributions to the nation. In the 1870s, the writer and inspector general of Argentine schools, Marcos Sastre, wrote about his travels along the Paraná River and described his enthusiasm for mate: "How happily we participated beside his house in the aromatic mate, innocent vehicle of sociability among the towns of the great river! Pure and simple customs of the homeland!"[100] Several years later, one of Argentina's leading scientists, Pedro N. Arata, eulogized mate's role as a national custom in a lecture to the Argentine Scientific Society. Arata began by calling yerba mate a "gift to the human species" and describing the "savage" (*salvaje*) who first discovered it "a hero." Arata identified mate as superior to other drinks such as tea, coffee, and wine that are simply "served" (*servir*). Instead, the term *cebar* is used for mate, a word that expresses "the idea of sustaining, feeding, and nourishing something that is in a flourishing state." Arata highlighted how mate built community and well-being among people: "Mate is in effect a fountain of great pleasures for the sociable man, who lives with others and for others, contributing to the well-being, to the joy and contentment of the community."[101] A decade later, an Argentine anthropologist and archeologist who traveled extensively in Misiones, Juan Bautista Ambrosetti, went further in claiming that mate fostered democracy. "Mate has had a lot of influence on our customs, making us a genuine and sincerely democratic community of people."[102]

For the upper and middle classes who identified it publicly as uncouth or socially unseemly, mate became a guilty pleasure, to be consumed at home among the intimacy of family and close friends. Although the shifting discourse around the gaucho had helped promote mate across Argentina's rural areas and cities as quintessentially Argentine, the elite classes, who did not associate themselves with the gaucho image, no longer embraced mate as a public good shared at social gatherings or gave it to welcome visitors. Instead, for them, it was a private practice. In his address to the Argentine Scientific Society, Arata concluded that mate "will always be our *national drink*," but he also acknowledged that the social circles labeled "of good character" (*de bueno tono*) only consume it in private or at home with intimate friends.[103] They still treasured mate even though they no longer drank it publicly. The contributor to Juana Manuela Gorriti's 1890 Latin American cookbook nostalgically described, "even though the days of splendor have passed for this delicious drink, and it no longer traverses the salons of our high class in dozens of luxurious vessels of silver, always, mate is and will be the favorite in the retreats, dressing rooms and bedrooms."[104] Like Arata, most authors believed that "mate will always continue to be drunk" even though the upper and middle classes had publicly stopped consuming it.[105] This adherence to a custom decried as anti-hygienic and backward exposes the deep contradictions in identity among the Argentine elite. Outwardly they aspired for their country to be modern and European, but in private, they continued to appreciate and enjoy this criollo cultural practice.

Like Pedro Arata two decades earlier, the Argentine botanist Cristobal Hicken highlighted some of the tensions surrounding mate consumption in the conclusion of his presentation to the Argentine Scientific Society in 1900. He had chosen yerba mate for his presentation because it was related to his favorite topic of study—the national character.

In an imaginary exchange, Hicken described how gauchos benefited from drinking mate and questioned whether the same would be true for the elite of Buenos Aires.

—Perchance do we not see the gaucho, whose only food is the *asado,* look with contempt at the bread that we ask for every day?

—But drinking mate requires a lot of time and its consumption is unsanitary!

—Perchance does the gaucho not have time for everything and his hygiene is not precisely in mate?

—Yes . . . But for us?

—It is true. . . . For us, overworked by daily tasks; for us, who do not have the time for a proper meal; for us who see bacteria, bacillus, and microbes everywhere, would [mate] have any benefit? Could we dedicate ourselves to mate? I think not! And for this, I say also that our national drink, praised by the poets, and with its amorous language resembling that of flowers, increasingly tends to disappear from our society.

—But no! I am wrong! Mate has not disappeared at all! Perchance have we not found the necessary time to gather here and in the middle of the theatre have I not dared to serve you a mate?

—And now before concluding, do not answer my question, leave me in doubt. The mate that I have offered, would it be *cimarron* (without sugar)?

—Excuse me if I have not known to serve mate.[106]

Hicken's exchange reveals a sense of ambivalence and conflict regarding mate. It was thought to be unsanitary and a waste of time, but Hicken upended such claims, noting that the gaucho was healthy and had time for mate. The same could be said for the members of his audience, if they chose to drink mate as they had, in fact, made time to listen to his lecture on the subject. While Hicken pointed to mate as having a place in nationalism, he ended his talk without clarifying its future.

Observant foreigners also commented on the elite's habit of consuming mate in secret. As described at the beginning of the chapter, Mario Brant noted that Argentina imported three times more yerba mate than coffee from Brazil, and yet he could not find any place serving mate. Brant reconciled this contradiction by concluding that the upper class of Buenos Aires did not publicly consume mate, and thus, it was absent from places accessible to foreign visitors. In sum, "they judge it to be a clandestine drink; improper," similar to beans (*poroto*) in Brazil.[107] A number of other foreigners, like Brant, also noted that the Argentine elite continued to consume mate in private.[108]

IMMIGRANTS AND MATE

At the same time as the consumption of mate as an acceptable public practice became increasingly divided along class lines, mate also became woven into debates around immigration. At the beginning of the twentieth century, immigration to Argentina was booming as the country's pro-immigration policies helped encourage huge numbers of new immigrants from Europe to arrive in the country. This wave of immigration coincided with ongoing debates about Argentina's cultural identity—including the increasing suppression of the nation's rich Indigenous past in favor of a vision of Argentina as modernized and European. Many Argentine intellectuals employed mate in debates about nationality and what should and should not define

Argentinidad. In the 1910s, a group of conservative, anti-immigrant, nationalist writers known as the "Generation of the Centenary" began promoting criollo-based Argentine nationalism as a way to bring together the native-born Argentines and the country's large number of immigrants into a single nation. Many immigrants were enthusiastic about criollo culture, and by highlighting it as a central national narrative, the conservatives hoped to create cohesion among the new arrivals and the native-born Argentines who also readily identified with that vision of the country's identity.

In contrast, liberals preferred European culture and did not think that criollo culture should define Argentine identity.[109] They argued that describing mate as symbolic of Argentine identity was exclusionary. For example, in a 1925 article titled "Nationality and Mate" in *La Prensa,* the prominent lawyer and historian Juan Álvarez attacked mate on various fronts. These included the standard argument that it was anti-hygienic and a waste of time, but he primarily argued that mate was not a national custom.[110] Alvarez framed his long article as a response to those who believed that mate was an integral part of Argentine identity and nationality because of the connections of solidarity that developed when various people sucked from the same bombilla. Alvarez took a strong stance against such ideas, stating that history revealed "mate had no influence over the birth or development of the 'consciousness of nationality.' Maintaining [mate] or discontinuing it has not signified more for our internal cohesion than to prefer French bread over Creole bread." Furthermore, Alvarez claimed that such beliefs fostered divisions between Argentines, by distinguishing those "whose Argentinism is of better quality, more authentic" when instead, he believed that Argentines should promote unity and work to dismantle such distinctions. Álvarez opposed eulogizing the country's past and targeted mate for condemnation. "They exaggerate, those that believe that we are leaving behind traditional virtues to acquire only foreign, imported vices; instead, it is old Creole vices that they are not extinguishing."

Álvarez's essay attracted the attention of Julio Díaz Usandivaras, the founder of the literary journal *Nativa* that promoted criollismo and Argentine folklore. Two weeks after Álvarez's article, Díaz Usandivaras published a response—also titled "Nationality and Mate"—in *Nativa.* In contrast to Álvarez, Díaz Usandivaras called for a more exclusive definition of Argentinidad, shaped by the country's past and marked by customs like mate. Like Arata decades earlier, Díaz Usandivaras described mate's numerous attributes and strongly defended its place in Argentina. "It is a national custom, loved and respected in our homes, and because of its social characteristic, fits

¡Hermanos en la Gloria!

El triunfo de una raza

Argentinos y Uruguayos, al vencer, en varonil lucha deportiva, a todos los conjuntos mundiales que enfrentaron, han puesto de manifiesto, en forma elocuente, la potencialidad de la raza rioplatense, fuerte, sobria e inteligente, *tonificada desde su más tierna edad a base de mate*.

ÑANDUTY contribuyó poderosamente a cimentar esa extraordinaria vitalidad y resistencia que demostraron en Amsterdam los footballistas argentinos.

ÑANDUTY

LA MAS CARA DE LAS YERBAS

ha cumplido y demostrado, una vez más, sus grandes propiedades alimenticias y fortificantes.

FIGURE 8. Ñanduty brand yerba mate advertisement, *La Nación,* June 14, 1928.

perfectly under the designation 'nationality.'" Furthermore, Díaz Usandivaras argued that distinctive practices (such as mate) were essential to nationality. "The customs of each country are integral to its nationality. The peoples who lack them are the people without a solid base and without character. Thus mate, as a national custom, is an integral part of our familial and social idiosyncrasy, and because of that, it constitutes an integral part of our nationality, and that which cannot be separated without affecting said concept."[111]

Such debates about Argentine nationalist identity, however, overlooked mate's transnational importance. Mate was not just an Argentine custom; it was widely consumed throughout the southern cone. A 1928 advertisement for Ñanduty brand yerba mate in the newspaper *La Nación* celebrated the transnational nature of mate consumption (see figure 8). In recognition of Argentina's and Uruguay's soccer successes at the Summer Olympics

(Uruguay won first place and Argentina finished second), the advertisement pictured two male athletes shaking hands with a gaucha-styled woman embracing them from behind. Centered between them is a circular piece of Paraguayan ñanduty lace, superimposed with a mate gourd and bombilla. The phrases "Brothers in Glory!" and "the triumph of a race" are inscribed prominently above and below the image. Together, the phrases point to a regional identity that extended beyond national borders without threatening national identity. What brought them together was mate, to which the advertisement attributed commonality, and their athletic prowess. "The triumph of a race. Argentines and Uruguayans . . . have demonstrated in an eloquent form the potential of the Rio de la Plata race—strong, sober and intelligent, *toned since its most tender age based on mate.*"[112]

Similarly, the production of yerba mate was also transnational. It grew in Argentina, Brazil and Paraguay, and consumers recognized differences in yerba based on its provenance. A 1923 article in *El Soldado* (a magazine produced by the military and given free to conscripts) claimed that men preferred Paraguayan yerba while women preferred Argentine yerba because it was smoother and sweeter.[113] As these examples demonstrate, regardless of whether or not Argentine intellectuals supported preserving mate as a traditional criollo custom marking national identity, it escaped national boundaries. Mate was a transnational marker of national identity.

Immigrants' use of mate also redefined and extended criollo identity. Concerns that mate would disappear as immigrants introduced new customs and drank different beverages proved unfounded.[114] Even Juan Álvarez, who considered mate "an old criollo vice" and a personal preference rather than a national custom, acknowledged that "the consumption of this product increases rapidly in our country precisely because foreigners who settle here become fans of mate." But he downplayed this fact by highlighting that foreigners were generally not attracted to the shared bombilla, and thus, the popularity of mate cocido (yerba mate as a tea) was growing.[115] Álvarez was wrong. Many immigrants to Argentina, and especially their children, became fervent mate drinkers, thereby revealing the complexities of national and ethnic identity.

Immigrants and their children avidly consumed mate, so much so that many considered them more ardent fans than Argentine criollos.[116] In his 1925 essay about the integral role of mate in Argentine nationalism, Julio Díaz Usandivaras paradoxically wrote, "The foreigner is, in this land, the main consumer of yerba. Upon arriving and becoming familiar with our environment, the first thing that [the immigrant] does is drink mate. They, the foreigners, are more drinkers of mate than the criollos here."[117] Five years later, the Jewish immigrant and journalist Alberto Gerchunoff came to the same conclusion in his article "We drink mate," published in the widely circulating weekly magazine *Caras y Caretas*. "The curious thing is that it is not common for the Argentine of long ancestry to drink mate but rather the new Argentine progeny, the child of the immigrant, the recently settled, is the person who becomes attached to the marvelous gourd and does not let any free moment pass without warming it with his hand."[118] Indeed, criollo nationalism especially resonated with working-class children of immigrants who identified as Argentines.[119] According to an unnamed foreign traveler, immigrants became such fans of mate that

> the German colonists find it good, and it displaces beer in their daily habits; the Italian settler in the city or on the farm rapidly acquires the *mate* habit; the Spanish immigrant drops his high-priced wines and is as well satisfied with the nonalcoholic *yerba,* and even the north European peasant, beginning a strange life in this newest of new worlds, draws contentment and refreshment from this wonderful weed of South America.[120]

The daughter of Italian immigrants revealed her strong feelings toward mate in a 1912 postcard about her family's trip to Italy. Verónica Capurro de Demarchi wrote fondly about mate to her sister and expressed surprise that they had not drunk it since leaving Buenos Aires.[121]

While many immigrants did not initially like mate, and some never adopted the practice, writing from the period overwhelmingly emphasized immigrants becoming mate drinkers. As the English businessman W. H. Koebel described in his 1911 book, *Argentina Past and Present,*

> The comparative 'greenness' in the case of quite a newcomer may be tested by his behavior when confronted with the *maté* bowl—the gourd, with its *bombilla,* through which the Paraguayan herb tea is drawn up into the mouth. *Yerba maté,* the most healthful and invigorating of beverages, resembles oysters. The first tastings leave some doubts; but the later-day sippings destroy these one by one, until *yerba maté* becomes to the 'camp' man as longed for and as indispensable as are hen's eggs to the iguana.[122]

Inevitably, new immigrants to Argentina encountered mate soon after arriving in the country. Gerchunoff claimed that "before having left the *Hotel de Inmigrantes,* the man who came from far away adopts the custom."[123] Most immigrants were working class and quickly came into contact with mate. Laborers often received mate cocido in the workplace and many immigrants readily adopted mate, often as a substitute for coffee or tea. Yerba was especially attractive because it was readily available and cheaper than the other two caffeinated beverages. Some sources describe immigrants explicitly choosing mate over coffee.[124]

Consuming mate was not just the practice of drinking a hot caffeinated beverage; it also had symbolic meaning. By consuming mate, an immigrant overtly demonstrated that she was Argentine. Looking back from the 1980s, J. Puga, a Galician immigrant, remembered, "we had just arrived and Argentines told us that the foreigner who becomes accustomed to drinking mate no longer thinks in the return [to the homeland]."[125] In his 1935 essay "Nationalist Mission of Criollo Mate," the Peruvian writer, lawyer, and politician Manuel Seoane, who lived in Argentina from 1924 to 1930, recommended the promotion of mate as a way to acculturate foreigners and turn them into Argentines.

> [The] foreigner who drinks mate is the man who gives up his native pride, who prepares his soul to fully accept the life of the country that receives him.... The doors to becoming Argentine begin to open the day that the kettle sings the hymn of a boil before the immigrant who raises to his/her lips the banner of mate criollo, with the bombilla forming the coat of arms.[126]

Seoane urged his reader to think of and embrace mate as a tool for nationalizing and pacifying immigrants.

At the turn of the twentieth century, as waves of immigrants were arriving in Argentina to work and settle in the country, many immigrants found it important to publicly demonstrate Argentine identity. A number of Argentines, especially the less affluent and those in the countryside, distrusted foreigners and blamed them for their problems. Such anger sometimes exploded into violence and there were reports of armed discontents attacking, looting, and even killing foreigners.[127] Drinking mate was one way that immigrants could show that they had integrated and assimilated into Argentina. As the scholar Sidney Mintz and others have shown, cuisine is consistently understood as a marker of national and regional identity—and mate was a powerful example of "being Argentine."[128]

By consuming mate, immigrants were able to perform Argentine identity in a way that helped them break down barriers and seem less foreign. In stark contrast to the Buenos Aires elite, the people of the countryside understood mate to be a part of civilization. In an 1863 book about his travels in Brazil and the Río de la Plata region, a British author described how he was constantly obliged to drink mate even though he hated it, because someone who declined mate "would be considered something of a barbarian."[129] Another traveler similarly explained that rural people would respect an Englishman who drank mate and adopted other customs of the Argentine countryside. "He is a foreigner, it is true, but he is very civilized!"[130] Other examples abound for the way drinking mate was perceived as a means to mark one's assimilation into Argentine culture, and even demonstrate social status. For example, an Irish immigrant song from the pampas described the consumption of mate and cheap rum as signs of how immigrants adopted local practices.

> You thinking [sic] that immigrants
> don't knowing [sic] anything but
> tend sheep in countryside.
> But you are wrong
> because they also know how to
> drink mate and guzzle booze.[131]

In her study of Jewish Argentine identity, Molly Lewis Nouwen found repeated references to mate in the Yiddish memoirs, poems, and plays that taught Argentine cultural practices to new immigrants, and she concludes that Jewish immigrants used mate as one of the main markers for being a part of Argentine society.[132] Jews encountered mate in boarding houses with immigrants of other backgrounds and quickly adopted it as a pastime, drinking mate and reading Yiddish newspapers or conversing on outside patios during times of leisure, after work, or on Sunday mornings.[133] The symbolism associated with mate allowed immigrants to demonstrate integration into Argentina without having to abandon other cultural practices such as language, religion, attire, diet, and music. Mate was especially attractive for Jews because, unlike with many other comestibles, they did not have to worry about whether or not it was kosher. In Samuel Glusberg's aptly titled Jewish-Argentine short story from [1924] "Mate Amargo," the protagonist (uncle Petacóvsky) is a fervent consumer of mate, monotonously spending his days accompanied by mate and books while continuing to be "a good Jew."[134]

Some immigrants went a step further and incorporated mate into their ethnic identity. Syrian immigrants maintained their sense of community by gathering together regularly to drink mate (or anis), play cards, and smoke a hookah. Mate became such a part of Levantine-Argentine life that Christina Civantos used it to frame the questions addressed in her book about Argentine-Arab identity.[135] Some have suggested that familiarity with sharing a hookah (*arghileh*) made the custom of sharing mate less foreign to people from the Middle East.[136] Similarly, Jews from Eastern Europe replaced hot tea from a samovar with mate.[137] Sharing mate helped build relationships and advanced the business endeavors of the many immigrants who traveled in the Argentine countryside as itinerant merchants. It became so deeply engrained in the daily life that many Arab immigrants brought the practice with them when they returned to Syria and Lebanon.[138] By 1936, Syria had become an important importer of yerba mate, and as of 2020, Syria continued to be the second largest importer of yerba mate in the world (behind Uruguay).[139]

As these many examples show, mate remained a key means for foreigners to establish Argentine identity in the nineteenth and early twentieth centuries. Mate's role as a cultural marker of Argentine identity emerged directly out of the nationalist movements during that era when mate evolved from a drink shared by everyone in the Río de la Plata region to the symbolic drink of the mythologized gauchos, the poor, and the countryside. For the urban elite, mate was seen as backward and anti-hygienic. When they drank it, they did so privately at home. Publicly they drank coffee and tea instead, beverages they considered more civilized and cultured. However, outside of that population group, and in contrast with such modernizing trends, mate became a nostalgic symbol of criollo identity that crossed borders while simultaneously embodying Argentinidad. By adopting mate, immigrants turned concepts of national identity on their head. While mate was associated with gauchos and traditional criollo customs, foreigners used it as much or more than native Argentines. When drinking mate, immigrants showed their Argentine identity, and in doing so, they reshaped Argentinidad and made it more inclusive. For many, mate remained a daily beverage and a valued social activity, albeit enhanced with criollo symbolism. In this way, mate persisted as a national custom despite elite claims that it was an anti-hygienic and antiquated practice that did not fit with modern life. Indeed, mate's emergence and persistence as a national custom played a key role in the way Argentine policymakers were able to eventually spur European immigration to the country's yerba-producing region at the beginning of the twentieth century. As mate gained an ever more central place in sectors of Argentine society, and as the economy expanded in the late nineteenth century, more and more people began to describe the many profits that could be made from mate production due to this booming national consumption. The next chapter discusses how Argentine nationalism and Belle Epoque optimism turned yerba mate cultivation into "green gold," spurring heretofore elusive European immigration and development in Argentina's northeastern borderlands.

—————

FIVE

Profits and Nationalism

THE RISE OF GREEN GOLD IN ARGENTINA'S BELLE EPOQUE

UNLIKE COFFEE, TEA, AND CHOCOLATE, which had long been cultivated, it wasn't until the twentieth century that yerba mate was widely cultivated. Prior to that period, it had been harvested from the wild. But right
around the turn of the century, commercial, scientific, and political conditions coalesced into a boom in yerba cultivation that altered northeastern
Argentina's social and agricultural landscape.

In 1910, Pablo Allain, a Swiss agricultural engineer working in northeastern Argentina not far from the border with Paraguay, asserted that the cultivation of yerba mate was a business venture that could guarantee success like no
other. He also suggested that none could compare with the high profits that
such cultivation would yield, nor the guaranteed long-term durability of those
profits.[1] At the time, Allain was working as the director of Martín y Cía., the
first large-scale yerba mate plantation in Argentina.

Martín y Cía. was founded in 1895 in Paraguay by Julio Ulisis Martín (a
French-Swiss watchmaker who arrived in Buenos Aires in 1885) along with a
Swiss partner for the purpose of selling yerba.[2] The business immediately took
off. Hearing about this growing yerba-sales enterprise, the Argentine president at the time, Julio Roca, wrote to Martín and encouraged him to develop
a yerba cultivation business in Argentina. Martín's subsequent plantation was
the first large-scale yerba mate plantation. Founded less than a century after
Aimé Bonpland's stymied attempt in the years following Argentina's independence, it was a major event in the history of yerba mate in Argentina.

Much had changed since Bonpland's failed venture in the early 1800s.
Although the business prospects for yerba mate had long been seen as favorable, and yerba mate was still widely consumed across Argentina and in
neighboring countries, the Belle Epoque era in Argentina had stirred national

optimism about mate cultivation. Mate was, in the eyes of many, the national Argentine beverage—and it was a shame, as President Roca thought, not to mention a squandered opportunity, that Argentina itself was not actively investing in cultivating its own yerba mate. But there was another reason that mate cultivation in the northern borderlands of Misiones took off: immigration—specifically, European immigration—as policy makers and nationalists were eager to see the northeastern regions more fully developed and economically productive.

These events, as this point suggests, also show how national identity remained a central consideration in the larger drive to develop yerba in this region. At the turn of the century, after mate had become increasingly associated with national identity symbols like the gaucho and the countryside, influential Argentines increasingly called for policymakers to invest in its cultivation. These calls promised high profit margins and almost always employed nationalist rhetoric to justify and prioritize this enterprise. Just as Argentine nationalism spurred mate consumption, it also encouraged domestic yerba cultivation as a means to staunch the outflow of money for importing foreign yerba. Indeed, as Martín y Cía.'s director Allain pointed out in his own call for Argentina to increase domestic yerba production, "[it] will conserve in the country a part of the millions that yearly go to Brazil and Paraguay." He recounted that the national government had already lowered a tax on cultivated yerba so as to promote such an enterprise.[3]

After 1870 until about 1914, Argentina experienced a period of rapid economic growth and large-scale immigration. This period would come to be known as Argentina's Belle Epoque, and the productivity growth inspired an enthusiastic optimism surrounding yerba production that would ultimately turn out to be exaggerated. From the 1880s until 1913, the Argentine economy grew at one of the fastest rates in the world, and in 1913 it was one of the ten wealthiest countries in terms of GDP per capita.[4] Argentina's future looked bright. Livestock and wheat exports from the fertile pampas drove such prosperity, making it possible for the modern, urban elite of Buenos Aires to live luxurious lifestyles that rivaled, or even surpassed, those of affluent Europeans. In the 1920s other rural enterprises, such as sugar, cotton, and wine, flourished outside of the pampas, as did early industrialization projects. Numerous articles and essays promoting yerba cultivation both reflected and further stimulated the excessive optimism of the period. Guarantees of high profit margins for decades into the future led capitalists and immigrants alike to invest in colonization projects, large-scale plantations, and small- and medium-sized holdings. Furthermore, the call to domestically satisfy demand rather than depend on imports made it a national cause. European settlers—like the European settlers who had turned Brazil and Central America into important coffee-producing regions a half century earlier—would play a central role in transforming Argentina into a yerba-producing nation.[5] This rapid investment, however, did not lead to the enduring windfall that many had predicted. A short boom in the 1910s and 1920s was instead followed by bust. Nevertheless, even though the cultivation of yerba—"green gold" as it became known to some—would become an economic chimera for many, this period of investment and cultivation had long-term consequences for demographics and land ownership in Misiones, as well for trade and international relations at the national level.

The cultivation of yerba in Misiones first began when Julio Ulisis Martín and his Swiss partner followed up on Julio Roca's request to expand his yerba cultivation project in Argentina in 1895. It was further driven a little over a decade later, when their former employee, Allain, convinced the wealthy and important Argentine Jewish entrepreneur and founder of Quilmes beer, Otto Bemberg, to create what would become the largest yerba plantation in Misiones.[6] Government policy also tepidly encouraged cultivation in the region, and the boom in yerba production that occurred during these years led to large-scale European immigration to the region, at a level that would shape the region's ethnic composition and landownership patterns for years to come.

These developments were enabled by government policies that provided open borders and assistance upon arrival for European immigrants while immigrants from other parts of the world were given no such preferential treatment. The largest numbers of European immigrants to Argentina arrived between 1905 and 1913, but immigration to the yerba-producing region occurred mostly after 1910. Likewise, European immigration flows differed ethnically in Misiones from the rest of the country. Immigrants from central and eastern Europe topped the list for Misiones according to the 1920 census, while for the country as a whole, Spanish and Italian immigrants were most numerous.[7] Although Misiones is closely associated with its Paraguayan and Brazilian neighbors in the Argentine imaginary, the region became more ethnically diverse than most of the country, and to this day, German, Polish, Ukrainian, Swiss, Russian, and many other cultural identities remain strong.[8]

The boom in yerba cultivation and immigration also shaped land ownership patterns in the region in profound ways. Argentina is known for latifundia,[9] but during the yerba boom, colonists received small- and medium-sized plots. As a result, *colono* meant a landowning farmer in Misiones and southeast Corrientes, while elsewhere in Argentina the term generally became synonymous with "tenant farmer" because land was frequently too expensive for colonists after the 1880s.[10] To this day, many yerba producers in Misiones call themselves colonos, maintaining their colonist and eastern European identity, and they continue to be a powerful political force, often pitted against yerba laborers, industry, and large-scale producers. The quick social evolution in the Misiones region and investment in yerba cultivation thus had important consequences for how Argentine identity was worked out in this borderland region in the coming decades, as well as in larger contentious debates about economic policy over the course of the twentieth century.

PROMOTING CULTIVATION

Other than the cultivation of yerba mate by the Guaraní-Jesuit missions in the eighteenth century, yerba mate was almost exclusively harvested from wild yerbales prior to the twentieth century. This was true in both Argentina and in neighboring Paraguay and Brazil. A myriad of factors held back yerba cultivation. As discussed in chapter 3, although the northeastern borderlands had a prime climate where plentiful wild yerbales grew, limited property rights enforcement made investment in yerba cultivation irrational. Furthermore, growing yerba is difficult. The tree produces a small fruit the size of a pepper grain that contains four tiny seeds protected by a thick film of gelatin. A seed cannot germinate with this film, and in nature, birds that eat the fruit remove it during the digestive process.[11] Once removed from the gelatin, the seed takes a long time to germinate (two to four months or more).[12]

The idea that only nature could germinate the yerba seed was so pervasive at the turn of the twentieth century that an agronomist, looking back on the period, observed that people looked with shameless mockery or condescending smiles at anyone who attempted it.[13] Even as late as the 1890s, people continued to argue that trying to germinate yerba mate seeds was a fool's errand. As Luis Barbagelata humorously described in an 1894 essay for the popular newspaper *La Prensa,* "the attempts made to figure out its cultivation could be labeled ridiculous if it were not for the nobleness of the objective." People had tried "planting it next to a sweet orange [tree] and bitter orange [tree]; in humid and dry soil; in the sun and the shade; at night and at day; and finally, the same farmer has eaten the seed and scattered his own waste over the soil."[14]

Around this same time, however, scientists and agronomists were undertaking new efforts to germinate the yerba mate seed. And this time, things turned out differently. Around 1896, Federico Neumann, a German immigrant to Colonia Nueva Germania in Paraguay, successfully germinated yerba mate. He started selling seeds prepared for easy germination in 1901.[15] Several years later, when Martín y Cía. set up the first major yerba plantation in Misiones, the company used his seeds.[16] About the same time that Neumann began selling seeds in Paraguay, the director of the Buenos Aires Botanical Garden, Carlos Thays, also figured out how to germinate yerba mate seeds after over five years of work. Thays's instructions appeared almost immediately in various publications.[17] For years to come, Argentine newspapers continued to report about efforts to cultivate yerba, making it a matter of national interest.

From early on, calls for yerba cultivation employed nationalist rhetoric. Juan Queirel, for example, who wrote a popular book about Misiones in 1897, highlighted the financial opportunities for yerba cultivation by pointing out that Argentina wasn't producing enough for its own national consumption: "Yerba is a very important industry with future prospects assured as none other given that by only producing twenty times what is produced today in this country, it would be possible to cover the Republic's consumption of said article."[18] In another popular account of travels in Corrientes and Misiones, journalist Manuel Bernández made the nationalist case for yerba cultivation more explicitly. Bernández introduced his discussion of yerba mate by highlighting that Argentina imported more than four million pesos' worth of yerba per year even though "all of Misiones is especially suited for the cultivation of this precious vegetation."[19] Nationalist reasons for cultivating yerba centered not only on replacing imports with domestic yerba, but also on populating the region. In an 1899 report about Misiones Territory, the Sub-Secretary of Agriculture, Carlos Burmeister, wrote: "But that which above all needs to be done, and it cannot be emphasized enough, is the cultivation of yerba mate." As he explained, by transplanting seedlings from wild yerbales onto three hectares, "the colonist would assure himself revenues [estimated at 1,200 gold pesos per year], by no means negligible, to help assure his daily needs." Burmeister acknowledged that many immigrants had abandoned Misiones because they found making a living too difficult, and those who remained lived pretty much at subsistence level.[20] Burmeister hinted that if yerba cultivation meant a good living, this could advance the nation by making Misiones more attractive for settlement, a heretofore elusive goal for Argentina's policymakers.

Motivated by this desire for settlement in the northeastern borderlands, other political figures in Argentina also began to take concrete steps to spur development there through yerba cultivation. It was at this time that, just a few years after Burmeister published his report, Argentina's President Julio Roca wrote to Julio Ulisis Martín and encouraged him to expand his operation in Argentina. In his letter, Roca acknowledged that for a long time he himself had been thinking about yerba cultivation.[21] Martín met with the governor of Misiones who convinced him to acquire property in the region and hire the governor's son-in-law (the Swiss-born agronomist Pablo Allain) to manage the enterprise.[22] Like Martín, Allain thought yerba cultivation was a great business opportunity. A French consortium had initially sent him to investigate logging in Paraguay, but Allain decided instead on cultivating yerba mate.[23] According to Allain's own account, when he arrived in the region, Antonio de Llamas had successfully germinated yerba from seed but nobody was yet cultivating it. Martín invested a significant amount of money, allowing Allain to promptly build giant seedbeds and a nursery of more than 100,000 plants. In the following year, Allain established a plantation with thousands of yerba plants.[24]

As with the discovery of successful germination techniques, Martín y Cía.'s enterprise generated great interest. One year after Martín and Allain embarked on their project, agronomist Pedro Yssouribehere referenced it in his 1904 report to the Ministry of Agriculture about Misiones, advocating that "this cultivation should occupy first place in this Territory" and "the cultivation of yerba mate is that which most interests Misiones, because it constitutes its principal resource." Yssouribehere also hoped that Martín and Allian's success would inspire settlers.[25] Several years later, Yssouribehere reported to readers of La Nación, "this example of [Martín y Cía. in] San Ignacio, repeatedly cited, has been the great force propelling this movement [of cultivating yerba] that has awakened all from indifference and abandonment." As a result, he predicted, "within a few years, Misiones will be an agricultural zone of primary importance" dominated by yerba mate.[26]

The profit potential and nationalist implications stimulated enthusiasm. In 1906, the agronomist León Roger published an exuberant essay about yerba cultivation in the journal of the large landholders' association, Sociedad Rural. Roger asserted that "no [other cultivation] could pay so generously as the settler dedicated to [yerba mate]."[27] He made this claim even though yerba plants required four years' gestation before a harvest generated any revenue. Like many others, Roger tried to prove his point by including revenue projections based on concrete estimates—the cost of the initial investment and yearly expenses, the quantity harvested per hectare each year, and the sale price.[28] According to Roger's calculation, a yerba plantation would generate a good income within five or six years; the initial investment would be paid off after ten years; and annual revenues net of expenses would thereafter increase from 400 pesos to 720 pesos per hectare. Like others, Roger instilled a sense of urgency to this enterprise by referring to the large amount of money that left Argentina to purchase imported yerba.

> The republic of Argentina is thus at the point of seeing itself as entirely a tributary of the producing countries [that are] neighbors. At present, more than three-quarters of yerba consumed [in Argentina] comes from Paraguay, and above all Brazil. Thus, developing cultivated yerbales is absolutely necessary to save the Argentine political economy from such a sad situation![29]

A year later, the well-published agronomist Conrado Martín Uzal also complained about yerba imports from Brazil and Paraguay in the same journal, pointing out that Argentina consumed over 41.6 million kilos of yerba each year but produced less than 1.4 million kilos. Uzal then called for the promotion of cultivated yerba and reminded readers about how memorable it was when Argentina began to feed itself and export wheat for the first time.[30] Important newspapers such as *La Prensa* shared this concern with the general public. After reporting on the promise of an extraordinary harvest of Brazilian yerba and the large quantity of Paraguayan imports, a 1907 article noted, "it is remarkable that capitalists are not concerned with the nation's yerbales."[31]

Concern about imported yerba continued to propel nationalist calls for domestic production in the press. In 1909, *La Prensa* even hosted two conferences about yerba cultivation. At the first conference, the speaker asserted that settlers to Misiones could easily produce enough yerba to meet domestic demand, which would result in the retention of approximately forty million pesos currently spent on imports.[32] A year later, the same newspaper published a longer article that began with the claim that yerba mate accounted for sixty percent of Argentina's imports from Brazil.[33] Complaints about the large amounts of money lost to Brazil and the pressing need to develop domestic yerba intensified in the following years.[34]

As described in the introduction, nationalist concern about imported yerba exploded in 1911 when Emilio Lahitte, the head of the Division of Rural Economy and Statistics at the Ministry of Agriculture, warned that Brazilian yerba threatened the health of the Argentine population because it included a weed called *congonilla,* which he claimed could be detrimental to health and lacked the properties that characterize yerba mate. Lahitte's report quickly spread, circulating not only at the ministries of Agriculture, Treasury, and Customs, but also among the general public as *La Prensa, La Nación,* and *La Vanguardia* published seven articles about it over a period of twelve days.

Circulating in Argentine news, Lahitte's warning created a moral panic and indirectly promoted the consumption of domestic cultivated yerba. It built on widespread concern about adulterated food.[35] Decades earlier, similar concerns in Britain about tea adulteration played an important role in shifting British consumption from Chinese tea to Indian tea.[36] Notably, the Ministry of Agriculture and not the National Department of Hygiene drew attention to the health risks associated with foreign yerba. In doing so, Lahitte censured Brazilian yerba based on the assertion that only *Ilex paraguariensis* (the species of ilex cultivated in Argentina) was yerba mate, rather than on scientific findings about the negative health effects of congonilla.[37] At the time, it was not yet an established fact that yerba mate was exclusively *Ilex paraguariensis.* In fact, congonilla, described as a dangerous weed by Lahitte, had long been considered yerba mate. As discussed in the introduction, congonilla was the Hispanicized version of *côgôî,* one of the two Indigenous words for yerba mate recorded in the first Guaraní-Spanish dictionaries. Brazilian yerba was especially known to include a variety of different species of *Ilex,* as well as other additives. In the 1830s, Aimé Bonpland had observed that Brazilian producers labeled other plants "hierba legitima," and Brazilians also often added other plants to improve its taste.[38] Concern about adulterated yerba also extended to Paraguayan yerba. In 1916 and 1917, the Argentine yerba producer Domingo Barthe reassured consumers by publishing dozens of advertisements in the Socialist newspaper *La Vanguardia* that asserted that his product, "the best Paraguayan yerba," was not adulterated.

Debates about what was and was not yerba mate continued even after Lahitte's report. In 1914, an agronomist in Asunción found that seven species of *Ilex,* including paraguariensis, were consumed as yerba mate.[39] Then, in 1921, a professor of Botany at the National University of Buenos Aires and La Plata concluded,

> based on all facets (scientific, commercial, industrial, and even popular) the official definition of *yerba-mate* should be modified, not limiting the varieties and forms of *Ilex paraguariensis,* but also extending it to other species of *Ilex* and even to many other inoffensive plants, whose addition certain consumers demand as quality *sine qua non* for accepting the product.[40]

But Argentina's exclusive cultivation of *Ilex paraguariensis* overshadowed such debates, leading to the recognition of that single species as legitimate yerba mate and all others as fake, adulterated, and dangerous to the nation's health.

Interest in yerba mate spurred academics to study its composition and impacts on the body, and Argentine journals published a number of scientific (or pseudo-scientific) studies. For example, in a presentation published in 1908, Julio Lesage described how he confirmed many of mate's positive physiological effects by experimenting on animals. After giving both a dog and a cow an infusion of yerba mate, Lesage extracted gastric juices directly from the dog's stomach and pancreatic juices from the cow's pancreas. The results led Lesage to conclude that "a cup of mate at the end of a meal is excellent for a healthy stomach." Lesage also injected a horse's arteries with "massive doses of yerba mate, like it is drunk in the countryside. . . . Everything indicated suffocation. . . . As alarming as these symptoms are, nevertheless, [they are] fleeting. Within ten minutes of the injection, [the symptoms] slowly lessen and almost completely disappear in twenty minutes." Lesage downplayed these mixed results by reminding the reader that people drank yerba mate rather than injecting it.[41]

Unlike Lesage, most authors did not test yerba mate on animal or human subjects; instead, they relied on anecdotes. For example, in his presentation to the Faculty of Business Sciences, published by the *Anales de la Sociedad Científica Argentina* in 1913, Honorio Leguizamón asserted that the most important effect of yerba was that it "alleviates fatigue and stimulates work" and that no other aromatic beverage produces the same results. In support of such claims, Leguizamón fondly hearkened back to national myths about how mate drinkers achieved impressive feats: during the colonial period, Indians rowed a canoe all day without consuming any other foodstuff; during the independence wars, soldiers endured forced marches for prolonged periods without food or sleep; before the advent of wire fencing, gauchos tirelessly branded livestock from sunup to sundown; at the beginning of the twentieth century after drinking cocido (yerba mate tea), loggers and settlers returned from the forest or the threshing machine at 2:00 p.m. in the middle of the summer as fresh and relaxed as when they left for work in the morning; and Olegario Andreade wrote immortal lines of literature after his parliamentary work and first-class journalism.[42] For Leguizamón and many others, the ability to achieve such feats while consuming the unbalanced Argentine diet of meat with no vegetables proved that yerba supplied necessary vitamins and nutrients. Such associations mythologized mate and made it seem to have all sorts of positive health effects.

In line with the thinking of the time, proponents of yerba consumption often treated the body like a machine and described yerba mate as a tool for increasing productivity.[43] In 1915, the yerba company Mackinnon y Coelho highlighted such attributes in an advertisement published in *La Nación*. "The most renowned hygienists advocate the use of yerba mate as the best restorative tonic to remedy the wear and tear produced by neural activities or muscular work."[44] Also in 1915, an article in the same newspaper described yerba mate as a pseudo-nourishment and humans as machines: "[Yerba mate] extinguishes the sensation of hunger without the ingestion of other nourishment, permitting he who uses this substance to support fatigue and suffering without which, the human machine would resist."[45] Many scholars of the time wrote glowing summaries of yerba mate's attributes, always highlighting its stimulating and reinvigorating powers, primarily for physical but also mental activities.[46]

At the same time as mate cultivation was taking off, the ongoing intersection between mate consumption and broader negotiations of class and identity persisted. For example, the emphasis on yerba mate's energizing effects reinforced stereotypes associating mate with laborers. Indeed, a 1907 advertisement for Paraguayan yerba in the socialist newspaper, *La Vanguardia*, exclusively targeted workers.[47] About a decade earlier, the same newspaper published a letter complaining that families of underpaid peons, masons, carpenters, and cobblers subsisted on a diet of only grits and mate. From the letter-writer's point of view, yerba mate's invigorating and hunger-suppressing characteristics negatively impacted workers by enabling them to withstand malnourishment and extreme poverty.[48] In contrast, most authors praised these traits as making better laborers and better soldiers. In the conclusion of his address, Leguizamón urged the armed forces to substitute its rations of *caña* (rum), tea, and coffee exclusively with yerba mate.[49] In the following year, the Ministry of Agriculture published an article in support of Leguizamón's proposal, claiming that it would promote the health and morale of citizens serving in the army, while also reducing money spent on rations.[50] Some years earlier, a doctor's letter published in *La Prensa* suggested another benefit of yerba mate for the army: it was "an indirect means of getting the soldier to drink boiled water, in other words, sterilized."[51]

By 1919, nationalist fervor surrounding yerba became so intense that congressmen from three provinces distant from the yerba-growing region called its cultivation a "patriotic act" when discussing legislation to support such enterprises. "Argentine yerbales will enlarge our industries, mobilize capital, free the land of the uncivilized wilderness, and more than anything, will liberate us from foreign bondage, making our market independent by having production that meets our needs." The congressmen then pointed out that Argentina spent more than fifty million pesos each year to import yerba, "money that should stay in the country, paying for labor and contributing to public well-being with the growth and prosperity of the industry." And thus, "promoting the cultivation of yerba is of urgent, of vital need, and more than anything a secure business endeavor with copious returns."[52] Their claims encapsulate the inflated, euphoric hype that made yerba seem like green gold to Argentina's early-twentieth-century nation-builders. Argentine newspapers continued to regularly publish articles decrying adulterated Brazilian yerba into the 1920s, thereby further reinforcing the idea that yerba cultivation should be a national priority and that doing so would be good for both the country's finances and the health of its people.

It is notable that this push for yerba mate cultivation as a "patriotic act" continued to draw on a vision of Argentine identity centered on the gaucho and the rural classes. The nineteenth century movement to highlight the role of the gaucho as a central figure in Argentine identity, discussed in the previous chapter, helped pave the way for the nationalistic energy surrounding the cultivation of mate in the early twentieth century. It was a vision of Argentina that did not draw on mate's Indigenous roots, but rather on a nation of European inheritance, and this narrative, which emphasized the working class and rural lifestyle, allowed a wide variety of groups who espoused this ethnic and racial vision of Argentine identity to celebrate yerba cultivation as a part of nationalism.

YERBA IN THE WORLD

Enthusiasm surrounding yerba mate soon spread beyond South America, and foreign interest made Argentines even more optimistic about its future. This fervor extended across continents, and the many articles, studies, and exaggerations about yerba mate's health benefits, market opportunities, and overall potential helped propel public opinion in Argentina to support investing in the cultivation of yerba mate in its northeastern borderlands.

From the early years of the nineteenth century, yerba mate had caught the attention of European scientists. In the 1820s, the French botanist Auguste Saint-Hilaire published a detailed description of the plant, giving it its botanical name *Ilex paraguariensis A. St.-Hil.* In the following decades, German chemists researched its chemical composition, discovering an alkaloid that they identified as mate, which coincided with research about the composition of and potential medical uses of alkaloidal cocaine.[53] Other European scholars built on their work, and foreign literature about yerba mate became so extensive that Sprecher von Bernegg's 1936 bibliography referenced forty-seven pieces of scholarship written in a language other than Spanish or Portuguese and published outside of South America.[54] Argentine scholars frequently quoted and referred to such European scholarship as a foundation for, and often a confirmation of, their own yerba mate studies, thereby revealing that they still felt a need to justify their interest in this non-European substance associated with rural Argentina and the lower class.[55]

Proponents predicted that consumption would finally spread throughout the world and bring wealth to Argentina. In 1883, a land surveyor sent to Misiones proclaimed in a letter published in *La Tribuna,* "It is evident that when Europeans begin to use [yerba mate] . . . this product will be a fountain of wealth for the country."[56] Similar predictions followed.[57] A 1903 article in *The British Medical Journal* acknowledged that a previous attempt to introduce yerba mate into Britain had failed, but "a second attempt may be encouraged by an interesting account of the use and qualities of this herbal stimulant" made in answer to a published request for information.[58] This account caught a lot of attention in the English-language press. The *Journal of Tropical Medicine* published the original account in the same year; the American magazine *Public Opinion* summarized the *British Medical Journal*'s article several months later; and in the following year, the *British Medical Journal* published a response by a Uruguayan surgeon.[59] News of growing foreign interest in yerba mate reached Argentina. In 1914, *La Nación* published a long article titled "Letter from London: The Success of Mate," reporting that yerba mate "is attracting a lot of attention" and "people stop to curiously examine it" at an exposition about tropical products.[60] Four years later, another article in *La Nación* recounted that a new request for yerba mate "seems to demonstrate that the national product found immediate acceptance abroad."[61]

Yerba mate also attracted attention in the United States. Numerous letters requesting information about the substance led the American consul in Buenos Aires, Edward Lewis Baker, to prepare a report about yerba mate for the US State Department in 1882. Baker's report was published the following year and republished a decade later as part of the *Handbook of Paraguay.*[62] Both times, the report spurred articles in various regional newspapers about this stimulating South American beverage.[63] At the turn of the century, US consuls in Brazil and Paraguay again wrote reports about yerba mate. This time, they emphasized

"Hebe herself could serve no daintier cup"

Yerba Maté Tea

More delicious than tea or coffee. Used with or without milk and sugar. Invigorates body, brain and nerves. You will prefer it to all other breakfast, dinner or supper beverages. The national drink of South America.

The official analysis by the world-famous Philadelphia Commercial Museum says: "Yerba Maté Tea, a most valuable beverage. Especially beneficial for the stomach and nerves. It has great sustaining power, but does not irritate. Its effect is soothing and quieting, with no deleterious consequences. The almost total absence of essential oil in the results obtained from the analysis speaks volumes in this connection. Then let us look, also, at the tannic and gallotannic acid. This is a most serviceable astringent, when present in moderate quantities, as in Yerba Maté Tea, combined with a small percentage also of caffein alkaloid, which builds up the nerves and performs other good offices. It contains traces of manganese, which enriches the blood." — DR. ERNST FAHRIG, *Chief of Laboratories.*

Send ten cents for sample and illustrated booklet, containing the analysis in detail, or better yet, send one dollar and receive, postpaid, with the booklet, a month's supply of Yerba Maté for several persons.

THE YERBA MATÉ TEA COMPANY, Sole Importers
257 South Fourth St., Philadelphia. *Agents Wanted.*

FIGURE 9. Yerba Maté Tea Co. advertisement, *The Saturday Evening Post,* March 10, 1900, 829, and March 17, 1900, 850. *The Ladies Home Journal,* April 1900, 42.

that yerba cultivation, and its importation into the United States, promised to be profitable.[64] At the same time, Brazilian and Paraguayan government officials actively promoted yerba mate in the United States. For example, at the International Commercial Congress of 1900, both the Paraguayan and Brazilian delegates put a spotlight on yerba mate when summarizing their country's commercial opportunities.[65] Again, these reports generated press in regional newspapers, explaining yerba mate and its potential for profit.[66]

In 1900, the Yerba Maté Tea Company of Philadelphia tried to take advantage of this opportunity, spending thousands of dollars to introduce yerba mate to the American public (see figure 9).[67] Marketing it as an infusion like tea, the company published over a dozen advertisements in *The Saturday Evening Post, Ladies Home Journal,* and regional newspapers such as *The Seattle-Post Intelligencer* in 1900. The advertisements described yerba mate as more delicious than either tea or coffee; invigorating to the body, brain and nerves; and possessing a number of health benefits. Some also referred to the praise it received at the International Commercial Congress and by representatives of the US government. In the same year, the company published a booklet about the history of yerba mate that called it "the most healthful and nutritious beverage in the world" and recommended that men, women, and children in the United States and Canada drink it regularly.[68]

Americans continued to be curious about yerba mate, and in 1905, the *Monthly Consular and Trade Reports* published more laudatory reports from Argentina, Brazil, and Paraguay in response to the many calls for information regarding the beverage.[69] In subsequent years, the *Bulletin of the Pan American Union* (the precursor to the Organization of American States) also published several articles praising yerba mate and its potential abroad.[70] Despite all of this publicity, authors continued to remark about the public's limited knowledge of the beverage,[71] while also claiming that "inquiries in the trade and frequent references in scientific literature indicate an increasing interest in yerba mate."[72] Indeed, spurts of articles about yerba mate appeared in regional newspapers around the time of these reports.[73]

Many predicted that it could become a basic ration for soldiers. The agronomist Conrado Martín Uzal reported in essays published in 1906 and 1907 by the Faculty of Agronomy and Veterinary Science and the *Sociedad Rural* that both the Japanese and Italian armies had noticed significant hygiene and health benefits after introducing cocido to their soldiers. Uzal optimistically predicted that foreign militaries would substitute yerba mate for coffee once it was abundantly and regularly produced.[74] The possibility of yerba mate consumption spreading internationally through the military also circulated outside Argentina. In 1911, the *Bulletin of the Pan American Union* informed its English-language readers that troops in China and Africa had received yerba mate and that "soldiers in European armies, even if they have previously had no practical experience with the drink, take kindly to it as soon as they note its cheapness and healthfulness."[75] Argentines perceived World War I as an opportunity to advance this agenda. In 1915, *La Nación* published two articles assessing that fighting in Europe

> presents a very propitious opportunity to advance the appreciation of the excellent qualities of yerba. All of those who are interested in disseminating

the consumption of this product should take advantage [of the situation]. The millions of men subjected to the severe fatigue of war will find immeasurable benefits compared to those that tea and coffee can provide.[76]

Later that year, *La Nación* announced news from London that after some Anglo-Argentine volunteers introduced yerba mate, "it has become the favorite drink of some battalions," resulting in the English military administration being "preoccupied with the utility of yerba mate."[77] After the war, the agronomist Carlos Girola claimed that yerba consumption had increased in Italy, France and England, but it faced export challenges and difficulties associated with provisioning combatants and the civilian population.[78]

As early as the mid-nineteenth century, yerba mate was also promoted as a substitute for alcohol.[79] As Consul Eugene Seeger reported 1899, "it is preeminently a temperance drink, and the temperance societies in the United States could do a very useful work by helping to popularize it."[80] In a 1916 article titled, "Here's a New Morning Drink. Yerba Mate Furnishes Beverage That Rivals Coffee and Tea," the *Washington Post* reprinted the temperance advocate Dr. J. A. Zahm's assessment of yerba mate based on his participation in Theodore Roosevelt's South American scientific expedition. "I am greatly surprised that [yerba mate] has not yet been introduced into the United States. I am convinced it would, as soon as known, become immensely popular. . . . As a temperance drink it is nonpareil."[81] Other American authors repeated such assertions, calling yerba mate a harmless stimulant with beneficial effects and "a drink which 'cheers but does not inebriate.'"[82]

In their glowing descriptions of yerba mate, a number of proponents exaggeratedly claimed that it prevented alcohol from becoming a problem in South America. According to Seeger, "The great masses in Uruguay and Argentina, including the famous gauchos (cowboys) of the great prairies, who drink it constantly instead of water, tea, or coffee, hardly ever use alcoholic stimulants. Intoxication is a rare occurrence there."[83] Similarly, Dr. Zahm claimed that drinking yerba mate "has preserved a large part of South America from the debasing evils of alcoholism, and I can conceive of no more powerful aid to the cause of temperance in our country than the popularizing of a beverage that has proved so efficacious among millions of people in our sister continent."[84] Building on the idea that yerba mate reduced alcohol consumption, another author credited the beverage with making Paraguayans more peaceful and law-abiding: "It is fearful to contemplate what the crime and violence would be in a country like Paraguay, where strong rum can be bought for 6 cents a quart, if the people were deprived of this valuable plant."[85] Taking the idea to an extreme, a Yerba Maté Tea Company advertisement informed readers of *The Saturday Evening Post* in 1900 that in the "Argentine Republic and other parts of South America where Yerba Maté is the national drink," people "abstain entirely from alcoholic drinks, feeling no need of them and use tea or coffee but rarely."[86]

News about the potential for marketing yerba as a temperance drink spread. In 1919, *La Nación* informed Argentine readers that the director of the Pan American Union "has declared that it would be very convenient for the United States to substitute the use of alcohol, whose sale will stop next year, for that of yerba mate."[87] At the same time, American newspapers informed their readers that yerba mate was a superior replacement for alcohol.[88] For example, an importer of yerba mate published an article titled, "So. America Offers Drink for Wets" in the *Sun Times* of New York, promoting the drink as a substitute for alcohol and superior to tea and coffee. Among his ample praise, Tibbetts claimed, "the stimulation produced by mate is of much less nervous order and more lasting than tea or coffee. It has been observed by writers, lawyers and accountants that when they drink it regularly their brain efficiency is greatly increased and they are less liable to fatigue."[89] Given such praise, *The American Review of Reviews* published an article in 1921 that concluded by posing the question: "What enterprising firm will advertise and import maté, and thus give Americans a new and healthful drink?"[90]

Some entrepreneurs did try selling yerba mate as a temperance drink. In 1914, *The British Journal of Inebriety* publicized that the Mattè Non-Alcoholic Beverage Syndicate of London had introduced "Sparkling Matador," a new non-alcoholic beverage with yerba mate.[91] A year before prohibition, the *Great Falls Daily Tribune* published an advertisement by the Montana Brewing Company for the new beverage TAY, described as "the perfect substitute for beer" and containing yerba mate, "the popular South American beverage product which our government is endeavoring to introduce as a substitute for alcohol."[92] And the next year, Brazilla was marketed in Minnesota as a non-alcoholic carbonated drink with the "mysterious 'cheerfulness' ingredient" of yerba mate.[93] Over time, these yerba mate beverages disappeared.

Yerba mate experienced more success in Cuba and Germany as a carbonated beverage. In 1920, the Materva Soft Drink Company was founded in Matanzas, Cuba, and Materva became a popular soft drink. A 1950s advertisement in the popular cookbook *Cocina al minuto* marketed it to children and adults as a delicious, refreshing, healthy, energizing drink made with Cuban sugar.[94]

Under the Castro regime, Materva was nationalized and it stopped being produced in Cuba. In 1971, the Cawy Bottling Company of Miami began producing and selling Materva in south Florida, along with other popular Cuban soft drinks. Many Cuban Americans associated Materva with nostalgic memories of pre-Revolutionary Cuba.[95] Around the same time that Materva was first marketed, a German beverage company re-launched a carbonated yerba mate drink under the name Sekt-Bronte after the previous company went bankrupt due to yerba mate supply shortages during World War I. Yerba mate drinks had been sold in Germany since the beginning of the twentieth century, but this one continues to exist today. Although the name Sekt-Bronte associated the beverage with alcohol (sekt is the German word for sparkling wine and Bronte is a Sicilian city surrounded by a fertile wine-growing region), it was marketed as a non-alcoholic sparkling drink. In 1930, Sekt was removed from the name and the beverage was sold simply as Bronte. Production again stopped during World War II, but restarted in 1945. At some point, the name changed to Club-Mate.[96]

Most proponents of yerba mate did not focus on carbonated beverages, but rather they thought that it should be drunk as an infusion, like tea or coffee. Expectations about future demand optimistically implied that consumption would grow both in Argentina and abroad, but not using the shared bombilla. A 1910 *La Nación* article claimed,

> It is true that its use as an infusion to be absorbed by the bombilla is tending to disappear. In contrast, it has acquired great utilization in the form of an infusion prepared as coffee, constituting what is called mate cocido, whose use has been very propagated in the countryside.[97]

Such claims often revealed the authors' disdain for traditional mate. For example, an agronomist who published extensively about yerba cultivation wrote,

> The use of the product as infusion, absorbed by suction with the bombilla . . . is anti-hygienic, in addition to presenting the inconvenience of causing a great loss of time. And for these reasons, its use tends to be diminishing. In contrast, the use of it as an infusion prepared like coffee increases. The workers in the countryside use this infusion a lot.[98]

Proponents predicted a rapid growth in international consumption if yerba mate were marketed without the bombilla.

Yerba mate's low price made it an especially attractive substitute for tea and coffee. In an address to a Pan American scientific conference in Santiago, Chile, Alberto Corrado noted that yerba mate "continues to provide great utility to those who lack the resources to buy [tea and coffee]."[99] A German entrepreneur predicted, "if we apply the same efforts that Frederick the Great expended to introduce among the people the potato as a new food, I think that there is no reason to doubt the final success that would also crown the attempt to introduce yerba mate, and even more so if its cheap price is taken into account."[100] Such boosterish predictions about yerba mate's imminent worldwide spread made its potential for growth seem almost limitless. Given that northwest Argentina was well-suited to growing yerba, proponents called for the expansion of yerba production so that the country could capitalize on this golden opportunity.

EARLY STAGES OF CULTIVATION

Despite the growing push to cultivate yerba in Argentina as both an economic opportunity and an act of patriotism, the Argentine government initially only took tentative steps to promote its cultivation. In 1907, the national government spent the small amount of 5,000 pesos on seedlings for settlers interested in cultivation (equivalent to one percent of Pablo Allaín's estimate of the cost of planting 500 hectares with yerba mate).[101] The government made such limited investments in yerba despite optimistic predictions about future tax revenues to be derived from its cultivation. An inspector for the Office of Agronomy predicted in 1908, "even though it is true that developing said cultivation will require the spending of some sums of money, it is no less true that within a short time that money will return again in the government coffers in the form of taxes paid for each *arroba* (twenty-five pounds) of yerba that comes from our yerbales."[102] While the Ministry of Agriculture's purchase of 50,000 yerba seedlings for colonists in the region made national news, most early settlers received little or no government support.[103] The extension of a train line in 1912 from western Misiones (Posadas and Apóstoles) to Corrientes and markets further south provided more support because it reduced transportation costs by connecting the region to national markets.

Prior to the 1920s, the Argentine government did little to promote yerba cultivation other than publishing numerous informational articles and reports, primarily through the Ministry of Agriculture. These materials explicitly promoted yerba cultivation as a valuable endeavor for both the nation and farmers. Many encouraged government assistance in spreading technical information and facilitating access to land and financing; several even provided a concise checklist of action items.[104] Most frequently, the goal was to provide practical information for people interested in yerba cultivation. These documents often contained detailed instructions about how to begin and manage a plantation until the plants reached maturity, a budget, a checklist of action items, scientific information about the plant and its life-cycle, and often photographs and/or drawings.[105]

Of the materials published about yerba cultivation between 1910 and 1930, the series of more than twenty-five essays by Carlos D. Girola are especially noteworthy. A professor of agronomy and honorary director of the *Sociedad Rural*'s Agricultural Museum, Girola was an important public figure with close ties to the Argentine state. He was an active scholar and prolific author of numerous essays about agriculture. Girola's work reached academia, government officials, and elite agriculturalists, but also a broad audience as he published over five hundred articles in newspapers like *La Nación* and *La Razón*.[106] Girola studied various cultigens, but of the fifty-four articles Girola published between 1910 and 1929, 24 percent were about yerba mate.[107] The topic so interested Girola that he oversaw a series of five statistical censuses between 1919 and 1928 that counted the number of plantations and cultivated yerba trees in Misiones and Corrientes. In addition, Girola organized a widely publicized national competition with monetary awards for the cultivation, processing, machinery, and academic study of yerba mate.[108]

During World War I and into the 1920s, Argentine politicians designed projects to promote immigration and yerba cultivation, but yet again, the government was slow to act. In 1916, the national government issued a decree for a yerba colony in Misiones, but the project failed to attract sufficient funding. Three years later, the governor of Misiones, Héctor Barreyro, urged the national government to redouble its efforts by taxing wild yerba and using the proceeds to fund yerba colonies, extending the lot size to a maximum of two hundred hectares for settlers who agreed to plant half of the land in yerba, and making sure that there were enough yerba seedlings available to settlers at the lowest possible price.[109] In the same year, three national deputies went even further by introducing legislation for the distribution of fifty-hectare rural lots at no cost to settlers under the condition that, within three years, they plant half of the land with five hundred yerba plants per hectare. According to the legislators, such a plan would combat latifundia (something that they thought was a major

FIGURE 10. European planter with three-year-old yerba tree. Carlos Girola, *Monografía sobre la yerba mate* (Buenos Aires, 1926).

problem in Misiones), populate the region, advance the economy, and counteract problems associated with excessive urbanization in Argentine cities.[110] Three years later, national deputies again proposed the creation of yerba colonies. This time, a colonist would receive land title if half of the lot was planted with a minimum of five hundred yerba plants per hectare within three years; if not, rights to the land would be revoked.[111] These efforts culminated in 1921 with the establishment of two federally-supported colonies dedicated primarily to yerba cultivation—Aristóbulo del Valle and Manuel Belgrano.[112] In 1926, the government took even bolder steps by obligating colonists on national land in Misiones to plant 20 percent of their arable land in yerba within two years (an extended timeline of four years for one hundred hectares with 75 percent yerba).[113]

Capitalist investors also believed yerba cultivation enterprises would make colonization an attractive enterprise. In 1914, the German Adolfo Schwelm came to Argentina as the South American representative of the Rothschild banking house and made a series of investments throughout the country. After visiting Misiones as a tourist, Schwelm purchased large swaths of land and convinced important Argentine families (for example, the Tornquists and the Anchorenas) to invest in a limited liability company aimed at colonization. In 1919 the Compañía Eldorado Colonización y Explotación de Bosques Ltda. founded the colony of Eldorado, which targeted German immigrants, followed by Puerto Rico, Monte Carlo, San Alberto, and Victoria.[114] Similarly, in 1919 the Swiss businessman Eugenio Lagier settled in Misiones and convinced a prominent Argentine named Luciano Leiva to purchase lands in Santo Pipó for a colony aimed at Swiss immigrants.[115] In addition to promoting the development of yerba, these projects also drew on the pro-European immigration priorities that the Argentine government had set.

The vision for who should cultivate yerba exposed the racial hierarchy of the period. While Misiones had pre-existing Indigenous and mestizo populations, proponents of yerba cultivation expected outsiders to plant it, advocating either large-scale capitalist plantations or colonies where European immigrants would produce yerba on small- and medium-sized plots (see figure 10). Those native to the area only appeared as laborers working for capitalists or European settlers. Proponents of yerba cultivation did not explain how these laborers would profit from the enterprise. Rather, if anything, they pointed to the opposite: low wages benefited the employers. For example, in describing the profitability of yerba cultivation, Pablo Allain wrote,

> my personal experience in Misiones allows me to affirm that it is easy to recruit laborers to do the work, and I should add that it would be a happy occasion for a business venture to be able to benefit from the prevailing cheap cost of labor in Misiones ... and [the labor force] is extremely accommodating and easy to manage.[116]

Such a vision courted wealthy capitalists and European immigrants who would utilize Indigenous and mixed-race populations as an inexpensive, compliant, and accessible labor force. This vision was also one that was easily reconciled with the nationalist motivations of the political class at this time, and shows how yerba cultivation in the twentieth century intersected with a broader vision of marginalizing Indigenous peoples and suppressing the Indigenous history in the country. In general, early twentieth-century Argentine capitalism focused on efficiency and productivity, rather than on bettering the lives of the less privileged sectors of society.

GREEN GOLD

While the Argentine government was slow to actively promote yerba cultivation, the enthusiastic buzz about yerba's future led to what some called a "green gold rush." Rapidly growing consumer demand confirmed the likelihood that high prices, and thus, large profits, would continue indefinitely. Over the thirty-two years from 1896 to 1928, Argentine demand had increased by more than 200 percent, from over 29 million kilos (1896) to almost 93 million kilos (1928). Rapid population growth accounted for a large portion of the dramatic increase. Between 1896 and 1928, Argentina's population grew from 4 million to 10.9 million inhabitants (an increase of 169 percent), but yerba consumption increased even faster (over 200 percent). New immigrants accounted for much, but not all, of Argentina's growing yerba consumption. More people in Argentina consumed yerba, but also each person consumed more. Per capita consumption increased by 16 percent: from 7.3 kilos per person in 1896 to 8.3 kilos per person in 1928. Such quantities made Argentina the largest consuming country in the world, accounting for over 62 percent of total yerba consumption in 1928.[117]

The widely circulated, sanguine predictions about the future financial windfalls from yerba cultivation were largely based on the imagined durability of yerba prices. In recent years, consumer prices for yerba had increased. According to the government's cost of living statistics, which classified yerba mate as one of ten indispensable items, the average price paid by consumers in Buenos Aires for a kilo of yerba mate increased by 63 percent over roughly a decade, from 80 cents in 1915 to 1 peso 30 cents in 1926, and it remained high throughout the rest of the decade, averaging 1 peso 18 cents in the 1920s.[118] Similarly, in 1910, Pablo Allain based his claim that no other business or industry promised such high profits over the long term based on the belief that the price of yerba would not go below 40 cents per kilo. Eleven years later, in 1921, Allain's budget estimated the price to be 25 percent higher (50 cents per kilo).[119]

Rising yerba prices made already high profit estimates mushroom. In 1906, León Roger calculated that a plantation's annual net revenues would increase from 400 pesos to 720 pesos per hectare after ten years.[120] Pablo Allain's 1910 estimate was even higher: after the twelfth year, one hectare of yerba would generate almost 900 pesos in net revenues, with profits continuing to grow thereafter as the trees produced more leaves.[121] In 1912, *La Prensa* ebulliently estimated that a hectare of yerba would produce 5,000 kilos in the fifth year, and since "the costs of harvesting and processing the product will never surpass ten percent of its value," net revenues would total at least 2,000 pesos.[122]

Enthusiastic calls for cultivation combined with high prices and growing demand spurred planting in northeastern Argentina. According to the Ministry of Agriculture, as of 1912, sixteen plantations were harvesting and another forty-one had planted yerba. In total, over 770,000 yerba trees had been planted; the largest plantation (Martín y Cía.) had almost half of these trees, at 350,000.[123] Looking back, the governor of Misiones assessed that yerba mate's cultivation had entered a "period of truly feverish enthusiasm" by 1923.[124] By this point, pretty much all settlers in rural Misiones cultivated it. Even the Polish-Ukranian settlers who came to Apóstoles and Azara starting in 1897 and who initially resisted non-European crops had changed their strategy. In doing so, they made the region an important yerba-producing zone.[125]

By 1920, Misiones had over 3.3 million cultivated yerba mate trees and the number of hectares planted in yerba far surpassed any other crop. Most plants were in large plantations. Small producers accounted for only about 12 percent (400,000 plants) of cultivated yerba, while four producers accounted for almost 75 percent (over 2.4 million plants).[126] Yerba cultivation accelerated in the 1920s, especially after president Marcelo T. de Alvear signed a law in 1926 requiring colonists on national lands to plant yerba.[127] Argentina cultivated between 3.5 and 4.5 million yerba plants as of 1920 and about 20 million in 1928. By the end of 1933, the number had jumped to over 43.6 million plants. Likewise, the number of hectares planted in yerba quadrupled, from 5,000 or less hectares in 1920 to approximately 20,000 hectares in 1928, and then more than doubled again, to 45,051 hectares in 1933.[128] Massive yerba mate planting turned Misiones into a monoculture economy. In 1928, the governor of Misiones reported that 90 percent of cultivated land was planted in yerba mate.[129] For many years thereafter, rural inhabitants focused heavily on yerba cultivation as their primary source of income.[130]

European immigration to Misiones tracked with the yerba boom. While the largest number of European immigrants arrived in Argentina between 1905 and 1913, Misiones's increase came a few years later.[131] A census recorded just over 33,000 inhabitants in Misiones as of 1895, of which only 3 percent were European. By 1920, the number had almost doubled to just over 63,000 inhabitants, of which 11 percent were European.[132] But the census underestimated European immigration to the region by not including children born in Argentina to European parents and a number of German-speakers who had migrated to Misiones from Brazil. Both groups identified with their ethnic European heritage.[133] According to a 1937 census of Argentina's rural economy, over half of immigrant producers in Misiones reported arriving in the country over the previous fifteen years (1922–1937). In contrast, for the country as a whole, less than 18 percent of immigrant producers reported arriving during these years (80 percent reported having come to Argentina prior to 1922).[134]

Immigrants to Misiones came from all parts of Europe and they had long-term repercussions on the region's cultural identity.[135] In 1935, congressman Juan Simón Padrós of Tucumán judged that "if there is an Argentine zone that could be called a racial melting pot, it is Misiones."[136] According to Argentine historian Roberto Abínzano, no other region or province, except for the cities of Buenos Aires and Rosario, had such a diversity of ethnicities.[137] Foreigners had an especially strong impact because of the small size of the base population; the territory had just over 33,000 inhabitants in 1895. When immigrants started coming to Misiones, there simply were not enough native-born Argentines to assimilate them.[138] Furthermore, immigrants tended to cluster in colonies targeted at specific ethnicities.[139] Such divisions made it easier for diasporic communities to maintain their cultural practices, and as a result, European ethnic identities remain strong to this day. In recognition of the province's history, the government named Oberá, Misiones the official site for the National Festival of the Immigrant in 1992.

While most European immigrants did not choose Misiones solely because of yerba mate, it played an important role in populating the region. Carlos Girola assessed in 1923 that yerba cultivation was indisputably one of the most effective means for settling Misiones. Several years later, the immigrant Benito Zamboni confirmed in an Italian language newspaper, "if it weren't for yerba mate, [the territory] would be depopulated."[140] Settlers produced a wide variety of basic food crops, but they quickly recognized yerba's profit potential. As the governor of Misiones described in 1927, "after four or five years and when yerba begins to produce small harvests the colonist abandons those defensive cultivations [like corn, beans, manioc, tobacco, peanuts etc.], to dedicate himself to yerba."[141] By 1931, Adolfo Schwelm's Compañía Eldorado had attracted some six thousand people to its colonies in Misiones, in part by vigorously advertising them as prosperous European communities based on diversified agriculture.[142] Despite such advertising, a visitor to Eldorado in the same year reported in the *Buenos Aires Herald,* "one sees land hardly ready for sowing or planting, yet yerba trees are already being placed."[143]

Some European colonists came to Misiones specifically to cultivate yerba. Various Swiss immigrants said they came to Misiones to plant yerba because Professor Andreas Sprecher von Bernegg, a leading scientist in the study of tropical and subtropical agriculture, told his students in Zurich that they could go to Java-Indonesia to plant rubber or to Africa to plant oil palms, but it would be much better to plant yerba mate in South America.[144] At least two 1920s immigrants to Santo Pipó (Eugenio Lagier's colony targeted to Swiss immigrants) specifically listed *hierbatero* or *plantador* as their occupation on their arrival documents for Argentina.[145] To attract immigrants, Lagier personally sent letters to people he knew in Europe about the fertility of Misiones and the promise of yerba cultivation.[146]

Many learned about the enterprise from state- or privately-funded propaganda. Aiming for readership both within Argentina and abroad, the National Mortgage Bank published booklets in English and Italian with promotional information about yerba cultivation in Misiones.[147] Colonization companies also printed booklets and advertisements hawking the territory. Colonia Santo Pipó's advertisement in *The American Weekly* of Buenos Aires had the subtitle "Yerba Mate farming is a splendid investment with or without occupation" and estimated that after the third or fourth year, yerba cultivation would generate a yearly average return on investment of 20 to 30 percent (see figure 11).[148] In addition to its multilingual promotional brochures, the Compañía Eldorado Colonización y Explotación de Bosques Ltda. even offered a daily screening of a film about colonization.[149]

Despite the information circulating in Europe about yerba cultivation and the positive takes on its investment opportunities, most immigrants learned about yerba cultivation once in Argentina. The central role of mate in Argentine daily life and identity, as described in the previous chapter, likely convinced some immigrants that its cultivation was a worthwhile investment. The plethora of newspaper articles and academic essays about cultivating yerba further spread such ideas and the large quantity of available documents suggests that yerba cultivation was a topic of public discussion. Indeed, the

FIGURE 11. Colonia Santo Pipó advertisement in *The American Weekly of Buenos Aires,* September 25, 1926.

already-mentioned immigrant Benito Zamboni complained in letters to an Italo-Argentine newspaper that the Ministry of Agriculture profusely distributed official publications about yerba planting, which instead of serving as a guide, seemed to be made intentionally to mislead the farmer. And, Zamboni asserted, there were numerous settlers who were "tricked by these dazzling delusions of prosperity."[150]

Cultivating yerba required a significant outlay of money, labor, and time. Before earning any income, a planter had to purchase and clear the land; obtain and plant seedlings; and then care for the plants for several years before harvesting the yerba. According to the agronomist in charge of the section for developing yerba mate in the Ministry of Agriculture, Helevecio Antonini, yerba trees could not be harvested until their fifth year and thereafter every other year. Even after the second harvest, earnings would be completely offset by investment costs and all other expenses.[151] Getting into yerba cultivation entailed hard labor (deforestation) and significant expenditure (money to purchase land and cover both plantation costs and living expenses). Given the high start-up costs and the long lag before generating any income, a planter needed to have significant funds to invest in the enterprise and an alternate source of income until the trees matured. León Roger, a self-identified colonist and yerba planter, estimated that a medium-sized twenty-five-hectare plantation required an investment of 55,000 pesos and a ten-year wait before realizing a profit.[152] The historian Alfredo Bolsi suggested that the start-up expenses for a yerba plantation were so high that they exceeded even those of farming in the pampas.[153] Such high entry costs led some people like Julio Martín of Martín y Cía. to question, "thus how would a colono live with his family during the years of expansion? This cultivation is more for capitalists than colonos, and it is desirable that the government favor bringing capitalists."[154]

Some European immigrants, like many of the Swiss immigrants in colony Santo Pipó, did come with capital to invest. Accordingly, their plots of land were generally larger, with yerbales of fifty to two hundred hectares. Many of these colonists hired others to do the manual labor. Some even remained in Switzerland and sent representatives to manage their yerba investments.[155] For example, in 1926 Plantagen AG (a Swiss multinational that invested in plantations throughout the world) formed Yerba Mate AG, bringing together thirty investors who remained in Europe without ever traveling to Misiones.[156]

In contrast, the majority of European settlers arrived in Misiones with limited capital and limited access to credit. But this did not stop them from coming. They transitioned slowly to yerba cultivation, planting it on a small scale. First, they cleared the land and built a homestead. They planted food crops (maize, beans, peanuts, manioc, etc.) and raised animals (chickens, pigs, etc.) to both sustain themselves and generate a small income. Then, generally in the second year, they planted a few yerba seedlings and possibly tobacco. Benito Zamboni warned Italian readers that if they dreamt of riches, but didn't have capital, and didn't want to work hard, they shouldn't go to Misiones because the first years were very difficult. And yet, if they persevered, they could accumulate some capital through yerba cultivation so as to be secure in old age.[157] Despite such barriers to entry, many publicly lauded yerba cultivation as being well suited to farmers.[158] According to a 1910 article in *La Nación,* "the cultivation of yerba mate in Misiones can provide satisfactory results for a farmer. The wait [for income] of the first years is amply compensated for by the harvest of the following [years]."[159]

Purchasing small- and medium-sized plots of land, immigrants altered the preexisting landholding pattern of latifundia. Whereas large plantations dominated in 1920, by 1933 there were 4,169 growers and the average plantation size was only 10.8 hectares with 10,462 plants. While the majority of plantations were small (87 percent had less than 15,000 plants), small plantations accounted for only about one-third of the surface area cultivated in yerba (32 percent) and just over a quarter of the unprocessed yerba produced in Argentina. In other words, large plantations continued to produce most of the yerba. Three percent of plantations had more than 50,000 plants each, and together, they accounted for almost half of the total surface area cultivated in yerba (45 percent). The largest, the Bemberg plantation, had 1,300 hectares with 1.4 million yerba plants.[160] To this day, a majority of yerba producers in Misiones continue to have small plantations with roots in the early twentieth century. In 2011, 62 percent of growers had plantations of less than ten hectares, and they produced about a quarter of Argentine yerba.[161]

Immigrant ownership of small and medium-sized rural properties still dominates the life and culture of Misiones to this day. There, the term "colono" is still widely used in the media to refer to small farmers, who are understood generally to be of European descent. As Kenneth Lindsay observed of Eldorado in 1931, "all the landowners are white settlers and the great majority are Europeans, the natives being laborours who move from farm to farm, working on the roads and at special seasons such as the harvest."[162] This trend continued for decades. As late as 1970, Europeans or their immediate descendants accounted for a majority (over 76 percent) of colonos in Misiones. In contrast, very few people in this category (less than 4 percent) were agricultural laborers.

Meanwhile, 96 percent of all agricultural workers were either descendants of Argentine-born parents or Paraguayans/Brazilians.[163] Even today, small and medium landowners in Misiones are generally lighter-skinned people with a clear European ethnicity, while agricultural laborers are more frequently darker-skinned people, often with ties to Paraguay or Brazil.

These racial and class associations within the yerba producing region reflected broader trends within Argentine society. Although mate's associations as a beverage continued to appeal to broad populations in both urban and rural, immigrant and non-immigrant communities, the associations of class, race, and ethnic hierarchies also continued to organize yerba production and consumption. Immigration policies favoring European immigrants directly contributed to the way these issues took shape at this time within the yerba-producing region, and both the consumption of yerba mate and the economics of its cultivation would remain important sites for the negotiation of Argentina's class divisions and national character.

In addition to the ethnic and economic priorities that helped shape the yerba boom in the first three decades of the twentieth century, Argentine politics and combustible regulatory debates would directly collide with the industry's future. As national economies turned inward, implementing protectionist policies, Argentina's political factions began to take strongly opposing approaches to yerba cultivation, with significant long-term impact. The next chapter looks specifically at how these interests took shape around the yerba mate industry and the rest of the economy, and how the great vision of the yerba boom for Argentina would turn out to be very different from the reality.

SIX

Yerba Regulation, Nationalism, and the Fall of Laissez-Faire Ideology

ON SEPTEMBER 1, 1933, the prominent Argentine newspaper *La Prensa* reported that the Argentine Union of Yerba Growers had met with the nation's president to "inform him about the disastrous situation faced by Misiones's yerba sector and to ask that he adopt urgent measures in its defense."[1] At the time, Argentina's yerba sector was in crisis. While the twentieth century had begun with the boom of "green gold," by the early 1930s the country's Belle Epoque had ended.

When the Great Depression hit in the 1930s, there was a radical shift in economic thought and policies that prevailed for the next fifty years as countries around the world moved from free trade and export-led growth to protectionism and government intervention in the economy. Scholars have long argued that the economic crisis of the 1930s was the event that pushed Argentina to move from free trade to protectionism. However, a deeper examination of the politics and trade policies around the yerba sector during the first three decades of the twentieth century shows how this shift in political economy, from free trade to protectionism, started well before the 1930s. These moves towards protectionism and government assistance, moreover, were directly aimed at the yerba sector—first yerba processing, and then, in the 1920s, yerba cultivation. Despite being previously touted as a sector that would be filled with promise and "guaranteed profits," as the last chapter described, Argentina's yerba growers faced a chronic and destabilizing lack of competitiveness in the face of Brazil's thriving yerba production. Moreover, Argentina's policy makers were generally more worried about supporting urban industrialization, and the country's other trade and agricultural markets including wheat and livestock, leading them to prioritize tariff policies and other incentives towards those sectors in ways that were frequently at the expense of the country's rural yerba-growing sector.

Tracing Argentina's yerba policies from the early promotion of industrialization in the 1880s to 1935 when the government created the Comisión Reguladora de la Yerba Mate (CRYM), the regulatory board that would dramatically alter the way the yerba sector was managed and operated, this chapter brings into view the substantial growth and dilemmas that emerged in the sector during the first three decades of yerba cultivation in Argentina. It looks at the way the Argentine government created policies that prioritized yerba industrialization over cultivation, and shows how this favored big processing companies in urban centers over small- and medium-sized farmers in Misiones and northeastern Corrientes. The chapter also looks at the consequences of these policies, including the economic problems for yerba growers in Misiones and northeastern Corrientes; the growing political unrest in these regions; and the shift in national-level political debates in the 1930s towards protectionism.

Throughout this period in Argentina, these policy decisions were highly charged, bringing together a wide range of political and cultural interests. During congressional debates about whether or not to support yerba growers with tariffs or subsidies, nationalist rhetoric returned to the fore, as well as the rhetoric of class and cultural identity. Politicians framed yerba mate as a lower-class agricultural product as they tried to encourage policies geared towards urban populations and the country's wheat sector. Yerba mate's trajectory stands in sharp contrast to champagne in France, a regional product that grape growers and merchants successfully developed into a positive symbol of bourgeois society, and thus, the French government protected and promoted champagne as a national patrimony.[2] In the 1930s, faced with a broader economic slowdown and competing national interests, the Argentine government ultimately sought a way out of this political divide with the creation of the CRYM in 1935—a government entity that would oversee the yerba sector for the next fifty years. But the CRYM was in many ways a compromise settlement to placate the yerba sector while really favoring Argentine wheat and trade relations with Brazil. It was also the response to a largely unrealized dream: the cultivation of yerba mate, once the "green gold" fantasy of global capitalists, Argentine presidents, and agronomists, had become a sector that could not survive without government intervention.

INDUSTRIALIZATION OVER CULTIVATION

From its inception, nationalists promoted Argentine yerba cultivation as a patriotic and profitable enterprise that would prevent the outflow of money to Brazil and Paraguay by replacing imported with domestically produced yerba. Such rhetoric failed to account for competing domestic interests, foreign relations, and economic realities.

From the beginning of the twentieth century until 1930, two types of producers co-existed: those who harvested wild yerbales and growers who cultivated yerba. Both types of producers sold *hoja verde* (green leaf) or *canchada* (dried) yerba to processors who were typically industrial companies—far fewer in number than the producers—with the most important being in Buenos Aires or Rosario. These industrial companies would purchase the green leaf or dried leaves from producers, age it for nine months or more, and then turn it into processed *molida* (aged and ground), which they then packaged and sold to stores for consumers. While all the producers and processors in Argentina wanted domestic consumption and sales to increase, they frequently disagreed about where the yerba should be sourced and its price. Inevitably, producers wanted high prices for their raw or dried yerba, whereas the processers wanted to pay low prices. Moreover, processors cared little about whether the yerba they bought was wild or cultivated, or where it came from—what mattered most was the price.

The Argentine government further complicated these dynamics by implementing tax policies that favored some stakeholders over others. Up until the 1930s, the government primarily used tariffs (import duties) to generate revenues, but in 1882, two decades before people began cultivating yerba, the government instituted higher import tariff rates on processed yerba as compared to the raw material (dried yerba), in an effort to promote the development of Argentina's national processing industry.[3] As of 1888, the rates were 45 percent for molida and 25 percent for canchada.[4]

Since Argentina's yerba sector was relatively undeveloped, and the country imported mostly processed yerba at the time, the tariffs meant that consumers had to pay higher prices for their yerba. Most Argentines considered yerba a basic foodstuff and necessity for daily life, so they wanted to get it as cheaply as possible. Employers also favored accessibly-priced yerba because they worried that if yerba consumer prices went up, workers' finances and standard of living would be negatively impacted, and this would lead to pressure to raise wages. Plus, they felt, it delivered caffeine that raised workers' productivity. Urban politicians took such pressures into account. In 1891, Buenos Aires deputy Lucio Mansilla acknowledged the need to "put this article of first necessity, of national necessity, within the reach of the classes that preferentially consume it," while also highlighting that doing so should not prevent the protection of "a national industry." Thus, Congress reduced import tariffs on processed yerba (*molida*) (from 45 percent to 25 percent) as compared to the raw material (*canchada*) (from 25 percent to 10 percent).[5] Although these reductions helped drive down costs for consumers, the lower tariffs on imported raw material left Argentine producers at a disadvantage because domestic processors paid minimum duties when importing the raw material from Brazil or Paraguay.

The yerba tariffs helped urban industry, but they did much less to help rural cultivation. When yerba cultivation began to expand in the 1900s, the government provided minimal tax incentives. In 1903, the tax on yerba harvested from wild yerbales increased to five cents—but in what was framed as an incentive for cultivation, the government kept the rate for yerba from cultivated trees at three cents.[6] Such small steps, however, had limited impact when compared to support for industrial yerba processors. The tax differential for promoting yerba cultivation over harvesting from wild yerbales (67 percent) was significantly smaller than the differential for promoting yerba industrialization (a 168 percent difference for importing dried versus processed yerba). Moreover, the tax on unprocessed dried yerba produced domestically from wild yerbales (5.0 cents) was significantly higher than the import tariff on dried yerba (3.4 cents).

This discrepancy encouraged contraband. Yerba produced from wild yerbales in Argentina was smuggled out of the country and re-entered as imported dried yerba in order to take advantage of the lower tax rate.[7] Over the years, a few legislators introduced proposals to address this issue, but their efforts were generally ignored.[8] Remedying the problem required either raising the tariff on dried yerba, which would hurt Argentine processors, or lowering the tax on yerba harvested from wild yerbales, which would hurt Argentine growers, and the government prioritized both over the production of yerba from the country's wild yerbales. Furthermore, the issue gradually disappeared without governmental action as overharvesting depleted the yerbales.

Consumer preference played a role in the government's tepid efforts to use tax policy to promote domestic cultivation. Argentine consumers had long preferred Paraguayan yerba because it was considered high quality. Yerba advertisements reflected such preferences. For example, Martín y Cía. continued to market its brand as "Yerba Paraguaya La Hoja" as late as 1931 even though the company owned the first large-scale yerba plantation in Argentina.[9] Similarly, one of the largest Argentine yerba processing companies, Estévez & Cía., produced a silent film glorifying the company's operations as "La

Yerbatera Paraguaya," although its yerba came from Paraguay and the Brazilian state of Matto Grosso.[10]

Like Estévez & Cía., Argentine processors were ambivalent about promoting domestic cultivation. Large companies such as Larangeira, Mendes, & Cia. and La Industrial Paraguaya were transnational. They harvested much of their yerba in Brazil and Paraguay and processed it in or around the port cities of Buenos Aires and Rosario because of Argentine tax policies. For example, in 1891 Tomás Larangeira founded Companhia Matte Larangeia in Rio de Janeiro to produce yerba in the wild yerbales of Brazil and Paraguay and then export it to Argentina. When the company investigated where to process its yerba, it considered Puerto Murtinho, close to where its yerba was harvested, but instead opted to have an Argentine company process and market its yerba out of Buenos Aires because of the proximity to consumers, but more importantly, because Argentine duties on dried yerba were significantly less than those on processed yerba.[11]

As Argentina's yerba processing industry expanded, Brazil had the most to lose. Over the course of the nineteenth century, yerba had become an important Brazilian export. When Argentine yerba consumption increased rapidly from almost 12 million kilos in 1875 to 61 million kilos in 1915, Brazilian yerba exports boomed. Of the 61 million kilograms consumed in Argentina in 1915, almost 52 million were harvested from Brazilian yerba trees and over 6 million kilograms were harvested from Paraguayan sources. In sharp contrast, Argentina harvested less than 2 million kilograms from its own trees.[12]

While Brazil's yerba exports to Argentina grew rapidly, and would continue to do so until 1927, its exports of processed yerba declined as Argentine processors supplied more of the domestic market. An article in *La Prensa* assessed that prior to 1897 "the national [yerba] industry showed no signs of life," but by 1917 its twenty-three establishments employed 750 people and had factories valued at around 1.3 million pesos.[13] Indeed, between 1898 and 1928, Argentina's yerba industry grew from processing 38 percent to 82 percent of domestically consumed yerba.[14]

As Argentina's yerba processing sector expanded, concerns arose about potential retaliation by Brazil. As a 1916 article in *La Prensa* reported, "Without precedent in history, the legislatures of Brazil's yerba-producing states are intent on—and this is the act that we should prevent—agreeing to pass an export tax on dried yerba." By raising the cost of importing dried yerba into Argentina, Brazil would negate the protectionist effects of Argentina's higher tariffs on processed yerba. According to the newspaper, such action would mark "the ruin of Argentine yerba processors and the immediate and continual flourishing of Brazilian processors."[15] Other articles highlighted that such retaliatory action by Brazil would hurt Argentine consumers by making them pay significantly more for something that was "almost a good of first necessity."[16]

In the same year, the Brazilian states of Paraná and Santa Catarina took action to support their yerba processors by raising export duties on dried yerba. Argentine processors took this as a direct attack. A 1916 pamphlet titled "The Yerbatera Industry Petitions the Argentine Government" asserted that the legislation was designed so that Brazil would "monopolize the Argentine market, making it impossible for our yerba-processing industry."[17] According to one account, eight yerba-processing plants in Buenos Aires and Rosario had to close their doors due to Brazil's higher export taxes on dried yerba.[18] Conflict over yerba taxes temporarily subsided over the next few years as the price for dried yerba increased significantly—from 4.0 pesos per 10 kilos in 1915, to 6.4 pesos in 1920—and Argentina continued to import significant quantities of both dried and processed yerba from Brazil.[19]

Tensions re-emerged in 1923 after the Argentine government increased import duties by 31 percent on processed yerba and 24 percent on dried yerba as part of a larger package that raised customs tariffs overall by 60 percent. The higher yerba tariffs provoked an immediate reaction. Within four months, the Brazilian state of Paraná retaliated by reducing its yerba mate export duties by 30 percent, thereby negating the protectionist effect of the Argentine tariffs. On the same day in March 1924, the Argentine presidency lowered the newly instituted yerba mate import duties by 30 percent.[20] Concern that Brazil would take retaliatory action against Argentine wheat was central to President Marcelo T. Alvear's decision to lower the yerba tariff. And yet, the government publicly justified its backpedaling by calling attention to how reducing the tariff would help Argentine consumers. The government's official newsletter, *Boletín Oficial,* stressed that "the presidency, by all means within its reach, tries to reduce the costs of articles of first necessity" and "among those articles, yerba mate figures in first place, consumed by the majority of the country's population, especially among the working sector of the countryside."[21] Such rhetoric made sense. Yerba prices paid by consumers in Buenos Aires had risen considerably in recent years, from .8 pesos in 1915 to 1.2 pesos in 1921. Unfortunately for consumers, such high-minded intentions failed; the price in Buenos Aires for yerba remained high until 1932.[22]

The politics behind these tariffs against Brazil reveal important ways that Argentina's political establishment was evolving at this time, particularly around the yerba sector, and in ways that would set in motion key debates around protectionism and free trade in the coming decades. For example, in 1924, the Socialist Party supported the Radical Party President Marcelo T. Alvear's decision to lower yerba tariffs. Socialist Party deputies representing the city of Buenos Aires went so far as to propose completely ending import duties on all yerba (both dried and processed), along with other important consumer goods (coffee, rice, and manioc flour). Ironically, instead of emphasizing that lower import taxes would benefit workers by reducing the price of a basic necessity, the Socialists focused on free trade rhetoric and laissez-faire economic principles in order to garner support for their proposal. As deputy Alfredo Spinetto explained, "It is a demonstrated fact that one of the most efficient ways to maintain peace between civilized peoples is sustained commercial exchange." To emphasize this point, Spinetto referenced a misogynist and racist quote by the highly respected nineteenth-century Argentine intellectual and proponent of liberal economic principles, Juan Bautista Alberdi.

> Limiting or restricting the entrance of beautiful foreign products to create a higher price for inferior domestic products is like impeding the entrance of pretty foreign women into the country so that ugly women marry better; it is impeding the entrance of blonde and white males because the mulattoes who form the basis of the nation would be excluded by the women due to their inferiority.[23]

Ironically, mixed-race mate consumers made up a significant portion of the popular classes who Socialists like Spinetto claimed to defend. In future congressional debates over yerba, the Socialist Party paid more attention to mate consumers while continuing to draw on both laissez-faire economic principles and international relations.

On the opposing side, Argentine growers still pressed for protectionism. In 1924, a group of growers from Misiones sent a written request to Congress for continued tariffs on imported yerba. The growers praised their own efforts to carefully select "the seeds of the best *Ilex Paraguayensis* plants resulting in a perfection and purity that is impossible to obtain from wild yerbales." In contrast, they complained that Brazilian yerba was not only of inferior quality because it came from wild yerbales, it was also less expensive due to "abundant and extremely cheap labor" and lower transportation costs. The growers concluded their appeal by claiming that without tariff protection, Brazilian yerba would take over. And then, without competition, prices would rise and Argentine consumers would suffer.[24]

Not wanting to risk a tariff war, but pressed to take some action to protect Argentina yerba growers, the government found another way to limit Brazilian yerba imports. Six months after he rescinded the higher yerba tariff, President Alvear prohibited imports of congonilla, yerba produced from Brazil's wild yerbales that was widely portrayed in Argentina as fake yerba that posed a threat to consumers' health.[25] The government's yerba policies incurred an angry response from those concerned that such policies unnecessarily hurt Argentine yerba growers and helped big industry and Brazilian yerba interests. A few months after Alvear prohibited imports of congonilla, Lisandro de la Torre, a deputy from Santa Fe and founder of the Partido Demócrata Progresista, publicly requested an investigation of the government's yerba policies. Foreshadowing his vehement attack on alleged collusion between foreign meatpacking companies and the Argentine presidency a decade later, de la Torre argued before Congress in December 1924, "nobody will deny that the president of the republic, that the minister of finance, that the minister of agriculture, and also the minister of foreign relations have served the interests of the importers of processed Brazilian yerba in recent months."[26] Congress's lengthy inquiry into yerba imports, spearheaded by de la Torre, lasted until 11:30 p.m., and the sixty-two pages of the record include various complaints by fellow congressmen about fatigue resulting from the longwinded expositions. A month later, President Alvear confirmed the tariff reduction despite de la Torre's protests.[27] Tensions calmed for the next two years as revolutionary upheaval and climate problems reduced Brazilian yerba output.[28]

CONFLICT OVER YERBA INTENSIFIES

In the 1920s, the competition between Argentina's yerba growers and processors and Brazilian yerba interests became more and more intense, with greater profits and losses at stake. One of the most illuminating moments of this competition occurred in 1926–1927, when Brazilian output expanded and Argentina imported a record quantity of yerba. Argentina's domestic growers complained that the annual season for yerba growing in Brazil was defined by law, but during that year, Paraná and Santa Catarina had a second harvest after the legal end to the 1926 season. This resulted in an extra ten thousand tons of yerba being brought to market. Partly as a result of this second harvest, and also because of Argentina's own growing yerba production, the average price of dried yerba declined after 1926 and remained low all the way until

1938. Argentina's growers and proponents of domestic cultivation claimed that Brazil was engaging in an all-out trade war against Argentine yerba, "dumping" (selling large quantities at ruinously low prices) in order to purposefully destroy Argentine growers. Newspapers, economic journals, and the governor of Misiones reported that Dr. Lysimaco Ferreira da Costa (a Brazilian academic sent by the governor of Paraná to covertly study Argentina's yerba sector) had publicly called for such dumping after concluding that rising Argentine production threatened to shut Brazilian yerba out of its most important export market within several years.[29] On July 26, 1927, the Paraná newspaper, *O Dia,* published da Costa's inflammatory conclusions in a front-page article. "It is necessary to lower the price of mate from Paraná so that it can compete," da Costa claimed. "Our yerba needs, at the cost of some sacrifice, to be placed in the Argentine market with the goal that the product from Misiones, expensive by nature, cannot disrupt the Brazilian economy. For Argentine yerba, not having a market is fatal, the plantations will fall in total abandon."[30]

Paraná's government took da Costa's report to heart and named him Minister of Finance, Commerce and Industry in 1928.[31] Yerba's economic importance made it a priority in Paraná. Moreover, yerba's significance extended beyond just Brazil's yerba-producing states. According to the US consul in São Paulo, yerba consistently ranked among Brazil's top six generators of export income between 1924 and 1928.[32] Furthermore, Brazil produced far more yerba (116 million kilos) than it consumed (25 million kilos), and Argentina was its main customer, buying over 60 percent of all yerba produced worldwide.[33]

With da Costa as Paraná's Minister of Finance, Commerce and Industry, the Brazilian yerba threat galvanized Argentine yerba growers. In the last days of 1926—in an effort to organize a defense of their interests—large-scale growers from Misiones and Corrientes, a number of whom also owned rural yerba-processing mills, facilitated the formation of the Argentine Yerba Mate Growers Association.[34] By September 1927, membership had grown to more than 1,000 growers and 454 rural processors.[35] The association lobbied Congress and met with the president of Argentina to discuss yerba production, but to little avail.[36]

The association received a warmer reception, however, from the local governor of Misiones, Héctor Barreyro, one of its honorary presidents and the proprietor of fifty-five hectares of land with forty thousand yerba trees.[37] In a report to the Ministry of Agriculture dated January 19, 1928, which was later published in *Revista de Cicencias Económicas,* Barreyro called for the national government to act in support of the country's rural yerba sector, but without mentioning that he was also a yerba grower. Barreyro employed nationalist slogans, blaming Brazil for much of the local yerba problem, and he specifically mentioned da Costa's call to destroy Argentine yerba by flooding the market with large quantities of Brazilian yerba. Barreyro also complained that Brazilian yerba cost less than Argentine yerba because of unfair trade advantages: 1) lower taxes, 2) more additives, 3) lower expenses for harvesting from wild yerbales as compared to cultivating yerba, 4) lower labor costs, and 5) lower transportation costs, since most Brazilian yerba traveled by sea rather than the convoluted land and river route of Argentine yerba. Governor Barreyro called for the Argentine government to take action to protect the forty thousand people whose livelihood revolved around yerba mate production. To do so, he not only recommended the revocation of the 1924 law that had lowered the tariff on imported yerba by 30 percent, he also called for even higher import duties on both dried and processed yerba, in addition to several other protective measures.[38]

Although such pleas did not persuade President Alvear, the Argentine Yerba Mate Growers Association hoped for change when the populist Hipólito Yrigoyen was voted into the presidency for a second time in late 1928. The first issue of its monthly magazine, *Revista Yerbatera,* lamented the association's failure to convince Alvear's government to limit imports and decried the country's agrarian policy of "abandonment and carelessness," which "has systematically left the country's agricultural sector open to manipulation by all classes of foreign producers in their quest to conquer the Argentine market." In contrast, it anticipated that Yrigoyen would do more to promote the country's agricultural sector, including yerba mate.[39] The association expanded its lobbying effort by naming powerful and well-connected businessmen and politicians such as Otto Bemberg, Nicolás Avellaneda, Eduardo G. Bunge, and José Alfredo Martínez de Hoz as honorary members. The association also expanded outreach among small- and medium-sized yerba growers by establishing thirteen local commissions throughout the yerba-producing region of Misiones and Corrientes.[40]

The onset of the Argentine Yerba Mate Growers Association coincided with a shift in thinking in Argentina about Brazilian yerba. For years, the Argentine government had instituted protectionist measures to promote yerba processing, and as a result, Argentina imported relatively little processed yerba. By this point, domestic processing reigned supreme and so further protectionism for the industry no longer made sense.[41] At the same time, processors and important members of the Argentine elite had become involved in yerba cultivation. As a result, the national conversation shifted from protecting yerba processors to protecting yerba growers.

While the Argentine Yerba Mate Growers Association had varied goals related to advancing Argentine yerba, it increasingly focused on calls for government action for protection against cheap Brazilian imports.[42] In June 1929, *Revista Yerbatera*'s front-page article criticized Argentina's overall tariff structure as antiquated, benefiting foreign nations while "even the most free-trade countries have converted to protectionist and almost prohibitionist."[43] The lead article the following month applied such reasoning to yerba: "it is reasonable to expect, and [yerba growers] have the right to demand from the state," some form of protectionism to prevent "exposure to ploys and 'dumping' by foreign trusts." The article condemned imported yerba, which not only channeled millions of Argentine pesos to foreign economies, but also introduced "a perverted, impure foreign product subjected to thousands of fraudulent manipulations that threatens the health of the Argentine consumer."[44] By September, the magazine asserted that the yerba sector had entered a grave crisis unlike any other, blaming the Argentine government's "absolute lack of defense or protection" against large Brazilian yerba mate producers who "carry out the most extraordinary ploys to annul all possible competition from the Argentine product."[45]

Its last issue culminated with the publication of a long petition delivered in December 1929 to President Yrigoyen by six elite yerba growers representing the association. It was their third meeting with the national government.[46] Again asking for assistance, the growers' association pointed to the fact that the price of Argentine dried yerba had fallen precipitously from 7.40 pesos per ten kilos in 1924–1925 to 2.60 pesos in 1929 (independent sources recorded a less drastic decline of 4.5 pesos to 3.7 pesos).[47] The association asserted that the sharp drop in price could not have resulted from overproduction by Argentine growers, given that domestic production had increased less than domestic consumption. Instead, "the grave damage inflicted on [Argentine] yerbateros, and thus the national economy, has its origin in the tenacious persistence of Brazilian producers . . . in provoking the ruin of our [yerba] sector in order to avoid [their] loss of our market." The association avoided asking for higher tariffs, even though such action would be "amply justified in this case due to national interest and its application by all nations of the world." Instead, it asked for a quota to limit yerba imports to the difference between Argentine consumption and production.[48] Several weeks later, the president designated a commission of leading agronomists to study the situation and make a policy recommendation.[49]

The most likely reason that the Argentine yerbatera association chose to petition President Yrigoyen to impose a quota rather than a tariff increase was because tariff requests had heretofore failed.[50] Although the government had, in fact, increased tariffs significantly in 1923 under President Alvear, it negated those tariffs only four months later—and no action had been taken since then.[51] Also, increasing yerba tariffs threatened to both undermine Argentine-Brazilian trade relations and hurt Argentine consumers. An April 12, 1930 editorial in *La Prensa* vehemently denounced raising yerba tariffs, which "legally obligated [consumers] to pay a premium that [yerbateros] could not obtain by another manner."[52] Less than a week later, *La Prensa* published another editorial even more vociferously opposing higher taxes on imported yerba because they would "preserve unproductive enterprises whose disappearance should occur according to the well-known process of healthy economics, that at the same time as curing deficiencies of viable activities, eliminates those that aren't [viable]." Despite such adherence to laissez-faire policies, the editor equivocated in favor of nationalist measures such as sanitary and hygiene regulations, propaganda efforts to promote yerba consumption abroad, and the formation of cooperatives to help Argentine growers.[53]

Pressed by yerba growers to take action, on August 21, 1930, Yrigoyen ended the 30 percent tariff reduction on all imported yerba that had been in place since 1924. He also instituted several measures to ensure the purity of imported yerba mate (exclusively defining it as *Ilex paraguariensis*), and awarded some money for the construction of warehouses to store yerba mate until prices increased. In announcing the legislation, the government ignored the effect these measures would have on consumer prices, instead concentrating on yerba as "a product of first necessity whose qualities should be properly monitored in defense of the consumer and to safeguard public health."[54] Keeping yerba's market price low for consumers was less of a concern at the time, as prices for most basic necessities had plummeted in 1927 and still had not recovered.[55] Financial problems also made the additional tax revenues from higher yerba tariffs especially attractive; as of 1930, the Argentine government resorted to debt in order to finance some 40 percent of its budget.[56]

Yerba processors joined in this nationalist shift away from foreign yerba. Heretofore, Mackinnon y Coelho, one of Argentina's largest yerba industrial companies, had actively marketed its product as "yerba paraguaya" in order to give it more prestige. And in 1928, the company filed for trademark protection in the United States for "Yerba Paraguaya Legitima."[57] Now, in 1930, MacKinnon y Coelho took a dramatically different approach to marketing in Argentina. In advertisements, the company described its main brand, Yerba Salus, as "the first yerba that proclaimed its national origin," explaining that,

> against the popular and defeatist prejudice that only attributes merit to the exotic, Salus, conscious of its superiority, was the first brand of yerba that, proud to be Argentine, proclaimed its origin to the four winds. And the confident instinct of being a patriotic and expert mate drinker, gave it immediately all preference because with Salus arrived the moment of not being a tributary to the foreigner in order to have a good mate. . . . Be a Patriot also!!! Consume Salus. . .[58]

Less than a month after the tariff reduction in support of Argentine yerba, Yrigoyen fell from power, in large part due to the country's economic problems. A bloodless coup brought the armed forces to power and began the *década infame* (infamous decade) of military rule from 1930 to 1943, a period characterized by conservativism, electoral fraud, government corruption, growing nationalism, and the shift away from free market economic policies to protectionism and import substitution industrialization. The new economic paradigm extended beyond Argentina as countries throughout the world turned inward and experimented with policies to protect domestic production under the economic duress of the Great Depression.

THE RISE OF PROTECTIONISM AND THE PRIORITIZATION OF WHEAT OVER YERBA

During the first decade of the twentieth century, Brazil created a coffee valorization program that set an early precedent for market intervention to help domestic agricultural producers. In 1906, Brazilian states purchased domestically-produced coffee as a way to reduce worldwide supply and raise prices. They did not present this action as an attack on the free market, but rather as a corrective measure to strengthen the market by remedying unfair monopolistic blockages that impeded demand. Companies joining together to form buyers' trusts had long been thought to impede the free market, but government intervention was beginning to be seen differently. Proponents of such valorization programs believed that governments could more effectively manage capitalism to prevent monopolistic impediments to the free market. Moreover, governments could help the free market to function more smoothly by reducing the naturally-occurring supply fluctuations resulting from weather conditions and other variables. Deeming it a success, Brazil expanded its valorization program. By the 1930s, the government oversaw the financing, sale, and transportation of Brazilian coffee.[59]

A decade before the Great Depression, John Maynard Keynes had laid the theoretical groundwork for such policies in a series of essays that rejected the idea of perfect competition based on unfettered supply and demand. Keynes believed competition led to the formation of cartels and oligopolies that manipulated the free market for their own benefit and prevented laissez-faire policies from effectively advancing the economy as a whole. To remedy such distortions, Keynes called for the state to intervene in markets, regulate competition, and direct the economy.[60] Such ideas resonated during the Great Depression. The economic crisis was especially intense in the United States, where real gross domestic product (GDP) fell by about 26 percent and unemployment reached as high as 25 percent. The government attempted to deal with these problems by adopting an unprecedented number of protectionist measures, including higher tariffs, import quotas, and foreign exchange controls.[61]

As the Great Depression hit Argentina, wheat and meat prices fell, foreign capital flows dried up, and revenues declined.[62] Between 1929 and 1932, the volume of world trade fell by around 30 percent, and between 1928 and 1932, the prices of Argentine exports declined by around 42 percent.[63] At first the Argentine government tried to double down on foreign trade, but after attempts to strengthen ties with Great Britain failed to reinvigorate the economy, the country increasingly turned inward. The move toward protectionism entailed a contested paradigm shift from laissez-faire ideology to a government-directed economic model. It also involved tradeoffs and compromises that benefited some domestic interests over others.

The Great Depression inevitably also had an impact on the yerba market in Argentina, particularly among the yerba growers who were already fighting Brazil's campaign to push them of out of business. In an effort to protect Argentina's yerba sector in the face of this competition from Brazil and the broader economic downturn, within two months after taking power President José Félix Uriburu (1930–1932) adopted radical steps in support of Argentina's yerba sector by following the growers association's recommendations from the previous year. Uriburu named three high-level government officials along with a representative of growers and another of processors to a new commission tasked with determining a ceiling for imports equivalent to the difference between domestic consumption and production, along with a price ceiling above the cost of production. While awaiting this information, Uriburu suspended yerba imports altogether. He justified these moves because "the government's first and foremost function is to defend and protect domestically-produced goods and the labor of its population," coupled with the argument that "almost all nations orient their political economy toward adopting means of defense and development of their respective products, impeding all competition by means of prohibitive tariffs or absolute prohibitions. . . ." Based on the commission's conclusions, the Argentine government limited yerba imports on March 14, 1931 to 60 million tons per year, divided between Brazil and Paraguay. A month later, the president issued a decree further limiting yerba imports based on its physio-chemical characteristics and composition.[64]

These moves to shore up the yerba sector demonstrate how far it had come since the first yerba plantations were established back at the turn of the century. With influence at the national level and a large constituency in Misiones, politicians clearly felt the yerba economy could not be ignored. Moreover, the nationalist rhetoric that politicians employed in defense of their opinions about the yerba sector can be traced back to some of the key debates and nationalist rhetoric of the nineteenth century surrounding mate's role in criollo identity and its status as an important working-class beverage. The protectionist measures of the 1930s, which many felt could lead to trade wars, showed how much yerba cultivation and its processing industries had become integrated into the Argentina economy over the prior three decades.

The higher import duties and hygiene standards that Uriburu instituted were a direct attack on Brazilian yerba. However, even as this policy helped Argentina's yerba producers, it led to controversy in other sectors. For example, later that year Brazil enacted a policy that prohibited flour imports for eighteen months beginning in August 1931, a move that Argentina's wheat interests argued was the result of the Argentine government's restrictions on yerba imports. These restrictions, they protested, had provoked a trade war.[65] Yerba was Brazil's most important export to Argentina, accounting for 30 percent of its total exports to Argentina in the 1930s, while wheat and flour were Argentina's most important export to Brazil, accounting for 77 percent of the country's total exports to Brazil over the same period. In 1931, Brazil was Argentina's second largest market (behind the United Kingdom) for its wheat exports, a fact that fueled the belief that Brazil had prohibited flour imports in retaliation for Argentina's restrictions on Brazilian yerba imports.[66] Such an assertion erroneously overlooked Brazil's underlying rationale for this action. In an effort to advance its coffee sales in the United States, the Brazilian government agreed in August 1931 to exchange over one million bags of coffee for twenty-five million bushels of American wheat. This action temporarily displaced Brazil's purchases of Argentine wheat.[67] As the Food Studies Institute at Stanford University assessed in 1932, "there is no prospect that the shift in trade will be permanent; American wheat shipped to Brazil ... cannot hope to compete in Brazil with Argentine wheat."[68]

Despite such predictions, Argentine congressmen completely ignored the significance of Brazil's coffee-wheat trade agreement when discussing whether or not to maintain the limits on yerba imports enacted the previous year. They blamed Brazil's temporary flour embargo entirely on their own country's yerba policy. According to Socialist party deputy Nicolás Repetto, who represented the city of Buenos Aires,

> The Brazilian government, painfully surprised by these decrees, reacted in a bit violent but justified form, or at least excusable, dictating in turn a decree that has all of the characteristics of retaliation. The government of Brazil prohibited all importation of wheat and Argentine flour into that country for a period of eighteen months.

This action had resulted in 800,000 tons of Argentina wheat not having a market, which was "a really significant loss for us."[69] In the same month that Repetto spoke before the chamber of deputies, the Argentine government revoked its quality standards and limits on yerba imports.[70] Such action did not resolve the impasse, but it did ensure the flow of cheap foreign yerba into Argentina.

The shifting positions by the Argentine government point to volatility in Argentina's economic policy, and also allude to broader economic debates about free trade and protectionism in Argentina at this time. These ideological debates were not, however, short-lived issues, and they grew in intensity over the next several years. Through it all, and for decades to come, the Argentine government overlooked and deprioritized the yerba sector in its national economic policies.

Some of the language from these debates in the early 1930s also emphasizes how class and Argentine identity continued to be an influencing factor in the discussions about yerba and yerba policy. For example, several weeks after the government rescinded its quality standards and limits on yerba imports, the Argentine Congress held lengthy and heated debates about the decision to revoke restrictions on yerba imports, and the rhetoric of elitism and classicism was notably present. Repetto, for example, promoted the dismantling of protectionist policies in order to keep yerba cheap and available for Argentine consumers, even though he personally disliked mate and associated it with backwardness. Despite presenting himself as a good Socialist, representing the working people of Buenos Aires, Repetto's opinions about yerba consumption reveal the underlying elitism and classism common among *porteños* (the people of Buenos Aires), then and now. Repetto asserted in congressional debates that yerba "is the very foodstuff of the poorly fed, of the chronically hungry," and thus, he predicted that "the consumption of yerba will diminish little by little in the South American continent as the living conditions of the population improves, as the people eat more meat, more bread, more legumes, more fruit." Moreover, Repetto believed mate to be a complete waste of time.

> Mate is a drink of people who have nothing to do and disdain the value of work. . . . This habit is only excusable in countries that, as I have said, disdain the value of work that does not compensate them. There, where people are well paid and men use their time well, there is no possibility of being distracted in this activity that simply implies a squandering or loss of time.[71]

Similarly, Federico Pinedo, Repetto's Socialist colleague from the city of Buenos Aires who became Minister of Finance a year later, discounted yerba's future in the country. "Yerba is a product whose consumption decreases. Every day we see people, who had long consumed mate in their homes, giving it up. People who abandon the use of this drink and replace it with another that they consider more convenient."[72] Even congressmen who advocated protectionist measures in support of Argentine yerba also looked down upon its consumption. Congressman Juan Simón Padrós of Tucumán from the conservative Partido Demócrata Nacional (the dominant party in the ruling Concordancia alliance) proposed some of the protectionist measures and acknowledged "for many, and for a large part of our population, it constitutes a genuine and traditional custom that we cannot ignore and that we are obligated to respect." But he also admitted that he did not drink mate and confirmed his agreement with Repetto that yerba mate was not "a good that we could consider a primary necessity."[73]

While the session drew out the congressmen's elitist ideas about yerba consumption, the main point of discussion was the impact of protectionism. Both Simón Padrós and another Partido Demócrata Nacional congressman (Herman Goméz of Corrientes) called for protecting Argentina's yerba sector, expressing concern for the thousands of Argentine yerba growers who had over 33 million plants and the twenty-five thousand laborers who subsisted exclusively from working in yerba.[74] In contrast, the Socialist Pinedo adamantly opposed protectionism, enthusiastically claiming, "the great Argentina, which has a special place in the world, is that of grains and meat" and eventually, manufactured and industrialized goods, all of which depended on an economic policy of "open doors, open for always, for all products, increasingly open doors." Pinedo abhorred any protectionist measures such as those being discussed for yerba growers. He acknowledged that "Argentina could be self-sufficient, enclosed with a Chinese wall" and "a miserly population, living a rudimentary existence," but "that would not be the great Argentina that we dream of!" Pinedo called for staying true to Argentina's longstanding policy of free trade, focusing on the noble products of cereals and livestock from the pampas and abstaining from protectionism to help other sectors such as yerba.[75] Like the earlier 1924 congressional debate, this contested debate also concluded after 11:00 p.m.

While opponents of yerba protection had the last word in this particular debate, Argentina's longstanding economic strategy based on free trade and exports was quickly losing its central place in Argentina's trade policies, as the ideologies of protectionism were becoming increasingly influential. In his testimony, congressman Simón Padós highlighted this shift. Arguing for Argentina to be more willing to use protectionist policies, he highlighted the worldwide spread of such policies: France had enacted import restrictions on wine, followed by a number of other products, and Brazil, Spain, Italy, and Germany had also taken steps to protect their domestic production.[76] It was time, he suggested, that Argentina recognize the value of these kinds of policies.

Despite the larger trend towards protectionism, congressional debates over economic policy in Argentina remained fierce. For example, yerba growers, and those advocating for their interests, lobbied ever more intensively for government assistance.[77] At the beginning of 1933, the government added yerba mate (both dried and processed) to an earlier list of goods being charged an additional 10 percent import tariff, which was intended to reduce budget shortfalls and the balance-of-payments deficit.[78] The higher tax on imported yerba provided some respite but did little to satisfy domestic growers.

The naming of Luis Duhau as Agriculture Minister and Federico Pinedo as Finance Minister in 1933 marked Argentina's definitive shift from an economic paradigm centered on exports and laissez faire policies to protectionism and government intervention. As Duhau explained, "The idea of economic self-sufficiency prevails everywhere . . . the country must seek relief from its present difficulties within itself and out of its own resources."[79] Pinedo even more clearly evidenced Argentina's sharp change in economic policy. As a Socialist deputy, Pinedo had enthusiastically asserted during 1932 congressional debates on yerba mate that Argentina must keep "open doors, open for always, for all products, increasingly open doors." But as Finance Minister, he instituted reforms that did the exact opposite. In consultation with Raul Prebisch who later became a foundational figure of dependency theory and protectionist economic policies, Pinedo took heterodox steps to increase state intervention and protectionism.

Recognizing the shift in their nation's economic paradigm, yerba growers—still heavily beleaguered by cheap imports from Brazil—sought to take advantage of the change. They lobbied intensely for government support by organizing, meeting with government officials, and staging protests to draw attention to their "disastrous" situation. They complained that the devaluation of Brazil's currency had led to extremely low yerba prices, leaving them unable to cover their production costs. In addition, the jobs of forty thousand laborers were in jeopardy.[80] On September 8, 1933, the PDN congressman from Corrientes emotionally appealed to his fellow legislators, "Misiones is dying! It is necessary to save her." He blamed competition from Brazilian yerba for endangering the standard of living of 143,000 inhabitants of Misiones who had invested 160 million pesos in growing yerba, and urging quick action by his fellow congressmen, he called for higher tariffs on imported yerba.[81]

Several days later, on September 12, 1933, Matías Sánchez Sorondo, a senator representing the province of Buenos Aires and member of the conservative PDN, introduced more comprehensive legislation to address the problem.[82] A decade earlier, Sánchez Sorondo had made various proposals for government intervention in support of Argentine cattle and then had served as Interior Minister under Uriburu (1930–1931).[83] Aiming to support domestic growers with higher prices, Sánchez Sorondo proposed that the Ministry of Agriculture head a regulatory board of twelve representatives composed primarily of Argentine growers, but also including processors, importers, and consumers. The commission's tasks would include the formation of a single national entity for buying dried yerba from Argentine growers and selling it to processors, establishing hygiene standards, regulating the harvesting season, and compiling statistics.

Corporatism, in the form of broad-based representative regulatory boards, arose in Argentina and elsewhere as a mechanism for responding to calls for greater government control over market forces. Such boards, organized under the state with both public and private representatives, aimed to promote national development by stabilizing particular sectors of the economy.[84] As such, regulatory boards were a middle ground between the extremes of late nineteenth century laissez-faire capitalism and complete state control over productive resources. In other words, it was a form of regulatory capitalism managed by the state. In the United States, the Agricultural Marketing Act of 1929 created the Federal Farm Board to promote American agricultural products, and a year later, the Cotton Stabilization Corporation, the Grain Stabilization Corporation, and the Wool Stabilization Corporation were formed to purchase surpluses and hold them until prices increased. With the New Deal, President Franklin D. Roosevelt took more aggressive corporatist steps.

In Argentina, rural growers experienced government intervention largely through such corporatist regulatory boards. The powerful Sociedad Rural lobbied for the creation of a national board to defend domestic livestock production, and President Justo and his Agriculture Minister sent such a proposal to Congress in 1932, along with another for the creation of a regulatory board for grains.[85] A month after Sánchez Sorondo proposed a regulatory board for yerba mate, Congress signed the first regulatory board (the Junta Nacional de Carnes) into law in October 1933. By the end of 1938, seventeen similar juntas existed for meat, grains, wine, yerba mate, milk, sugar, and cotton, among others. Just like the stabilization corporations in the United States and Brazil's coffee valorization program, proponents intended for the juntas to mitigate cyclical crises and promote price stability for domestic growers by financing production, purchasing surpluses, and coordinating marketing. The specific duties and powers of the juntas varied across sectors and over time.[86]

Although yerba mate would eventually have its own junta, the path towards this regulatory mechanism did not go smoothly, largely due to similar dilemmas as with past efforts to protect the industry—that is, international relations with Brazil. When Sánchez Sorondo initially made his proposition in 1932, enthusiasm for the bill seemed to imply it would be quickly approved. The senate president immediately forwarded it to the Commission on Agriculture, which ten days later recommended the passage of a slightly revised version.[87] Various parties from Misiones sent petitions asking the Senate to approve the bill,[88] and in an effort to address "the grave situation of Misiones," Sánchez Sorondo quickly brought the bill back to the Senate's attention. Suggesting that protectionism represented the wave of the future, the senator reiterated that the government needed to establish a remunerative price for yerba as "this is the ABC of modern political economy that all civilized nations of the world practice today." In response, fellow PDN senator Mariano Ceballos of Córdoba reassured Sánchez Sorondo, "today, governing boards for Argentine products are in fashion and one more junta protecting yerba would only be incorporated into the concert of all the juntas that already exist to regulate commerce and industries."[89] On the same day—September 29, 1933—the Senate approved the bill. However, it still needed to pass parliament, and a quick series of political events intervened in that easy passage.[90]

Less than two weeks after the Senate approved the bill, President Agustín P. Justo traveled to Brazil. During this trip, Argentine wheat and Brazilian yerba were key trade topics under discussion. Argentine newspapers extensively covered the trip, praising the two countries' friendship and the various treaties signed by Justo and Brazilian President Getúlio Vargas to promote mutual trade.[91] One noteworthy trade accord mandated that Brazil not institute any prohibitions or limits on wheat imports in return for the Argentine government agreeing to promote, in its first parliamentary sessions, the repeal of the 10 percent yerba mate tariff, and not to place any direct or indirect limitations on the import of Brazilian *Ilex paraguariensis*.[92] By prioritizing the removal of trade barriers on Brazilian yerba, the agreement doomed the passage of Sánchez Sorondo's legislation without serious revision.

A year after President Justo's trip to Brazil, reports about forthcoming yerba legislation emerged in Argentine newspapers.[93] About a week later, Justo and Agriculture Minister Duhau announced the proposal, which supplanted Sánchez Sorondo's yerba bill. It dismantled the 10 percent duty on imported yerba and created a yerba regulatory board. In a letter to Congress accompanying the proposal, the president and agriculture minister acknowledged the difficult problems facing this "noble and traditional product" and urged immediate action to help the yerba sector. While they recognized that the tariff "lessened these disastrous effects" on Argentine yerba, "the first project of law repeals [it]" because it was "essential [for Argentine wheat sales] that we can offer the great neighboring country a market for its yerba."[94] Clearly, their main goal was to advance Argentine wheat.

Instead of the tariff, the president and agriculture minister proposed a new tax assessed at the same rate on processed yerba, both domestic and imported, which they described as a positive policy tool, "similar to what the United Kingdom applies to millers, with the goal of helping domestic wheat producers without resorting to a customs tax."[95] Part of the proceeds from the new yerba tax would be channeled to domestic growers as a *sobreprecio* (premium) to make up the shortfall between the raw material sales price and the cost of production. The bill contained some other vague measures to help growers, such as encouraging the construction of processing facilities, greater access to credit, the establishment of hygiene standards, regulation of the harvesting season, and compilation of statistics. Unlike Sánchez Sorondo's proposal, the new bill also sought to curtail domestic production by taxing all new yerba plantings, which was a complete reversal of prior financial incentives for colonists to plant yerba trees.

The result of this legislation was something of a mixed bag. Although it was not the more robust support for yerba growers that Sánchez Sorondo's proposal would have provided, it did help the Argentine yerba processing industry by lowering the cost of importing raw material from Brazil, something that garnered little attention in public discussions. As of 1934, Argentine processed almost all of the yerba consumed domestically (approximately 99 million kilograms) and imported only a small amount of processed yerba from Brazil (a little more than 200,000 kilos). In contrast, Argentine processors still relied on large quantities of dried yerba from Brazil—more than 33 million kilos.[96]

After the proposed legislation was announced, Argentine newspapers shifted their attention to the domestic yerba sector and an intense period of lobbying ensued. Over the following months, growers organized and various groups sent petitions to Congress, requesting the passage of yerba legislation.[97] Most of the appeals came from groups directly related to the yerba sector or Misiones, but other groups connected to wheat, such as the Sociedad Rural and representatives of the province of Buenos Aires's agrobusiness federation, also petitioned Congress in support of the yerba legislation.[98]

Not everyone supported the bill. Editorials in *La Prensa* complained, "again the yerba mate problem is being raised, and the solution is looked for without taking into account the root of the problem, constituted by the disproportion between the prices that growers sell the product and those that prevail for consumers." The newspaper took the radical stance of blaming the yerba crisis on middlemen and processors who both underpaid small growers and overcharged consumers. As evidence, the editor explained that the previous year, dried yerba sold for between 12 and 20 cents per kilogram and that, according to information from the yerba mills, processing cost 5 to 6 cents per kilogram. Instead of charging consumers the fair rate of 18 to 26 cents per kilogram, consumers paid 80 cents, or even double that, for yerba. The editor predicted that based on this trend, the proposed legislation would be counterproductive. Consumers would pay higher prices for their yerba and growers would not benefit because middlemen and processors would pocket the money generated from the yerba tax.[99]

Concerns about consumers resonated with growing anxieties, especially during the Great Depression. According to some estimates, the unemployment rate had reached almost 30 percent, and in 1935, the National Labor Department estimated that the average salary covered only 77 percent of a family of five's minimum expenses.[100] Social scientists studying the standard of living and consumption patterns of working-class Argentines in the 1930s repeatedly concluded that workers did not earn enough to cover their basic needs, which included yerba mate. Argentine industrialists also supported raising the lower class's standard of living so that workers could consume more manufactured goods.[101] A yerba mate regulatory commission, combined with a new internal yerba tax to replace the yerba tariff, would likely lead to higher consumer prices for this important necessity and lower workers' standard of living. As a result, despite the precarity of the yerba growers and their need for relief, Congress did not act on President Justo's proposal to create this regulatory commission or yerba tax, leaving the sector marginalized and beleaguered within Argentina's economy.

DEBATE, COMPROMISE, AND THE CREATION OF THE COMISIÓN REGULADORA DE LA YERBA MATE

In 1935, a year after President Justo's had made his yerba proposal, Congress finally did act after large numbers of yerba growers, workers, and other interested parties in Misiones brought the matter to the nation's attention with a widely-publicized, forty-eight-hour general strike on August 11 and 12, 1935. The strikers insisted that Misiones was in crisis and that the government had to intervene on behalf of yerba growers.[102] An editorial in the pro-government newspaper *La Nación* the day before the strike described the yerba problem as "a serious question, almost the life or death for one of the wealthiest regions of the Republic" and one that "causes a drop in salaries and a reduction in the general living standards in all of the territory."[103] After the strike, the newspaper reported that more than twenty thousand people marched on the streets of Posadas, Misiones, and that various organizations reported about it in telegrams sent to the president, minister of agriculture, and other important government officials.[104] Another editorial in *La Nación* summarized that "it could be said, thus, that all of the population of Misiones shows solidarity with the yerba growers in this campaign" and concluded with the appeal that "those inhabitants should not be abandoned to the risks of such a precarious situation without the federal government doing what is in its power to remedy it."[105]

In the wake of the strike, the House of Deputies took up the proposed yerba legislation. A long, passionate debate ensued over three long days between a handful of deputies. The text of this debate totals 119 pages.[106] Socialist deputies representing the city of Buenos Aires dominated much of the debate, and from the outset, they announced their party's opposition to the yerba legislation, along with all other regulatory boards. They believed that these juntas served neither the interests of Argentines as a whole, nor small growers, but rather the country's well-connected landowning oligarchy.[107] As Manuel Palancín explained,

> We oppose the sanction of this law because it fits within the new modality of the old oligarchic political economy . . . a project that is nothing more than the repetition of past errors disguised with the snobbism of a new science. The directed political economy has now been discovered; it has been implanted in what is referred to as the viniculture sector; introduced with the milk sector; practiced in a precarious form with the new cotton sector; and we are preparing to sanction it for the yerba sector. But always at the service, not of the interest of the Argentine masses, but rather the dominating interests of small groups.[108]

Such rhetoric fit with the Socialists' active defense of urban industrialization and internationalism in opposition to nationalism and fascism.[109]

The Socialists not only opposed a yerba mate regulatory board, they disparaged Argentine yerba cultivation overall. As José Luis Peña explained on the second day of debate, "Argentina is the only country in the word that has embarked on planting trees that do not need to be planted, which he described as an absurd and anti-economic task that required enormous effort, investing considerable capital."[110] The Socialists even expressed doubts that a crisis in the yerba sector actually existed and that growers were in fact suffering. Instead, they claimed that oligarchic interests speculating in yerba were manipulating both the small growers and the Argentine public in their effort to realize immediate profits.

Given that the laissez-faire economic model had been discredited, the Socialists took a new approach in opposing the legislation. Now, the Socialists forcefully claimed they represented the interests of Argentine people, especially consumers. As voting rights expanded, consumers came to play an important role in political debates and the Socialists argued that tariffs made Argentine citizens suffer by having to pay higher prices at the point of sale.[111] As Nicolás Repetto explained, the proposed legislation aimed to advance yerba growers by "strangling the consumer."[112] Before voting on the bill, Manuel Palancín urged his fellow congressmen to consider "the interest of consumers, that is the interest of the Argentine nation." Palancín also voiced concern for yerba laborers, whose situation he believed was "truly lamentable," without suggesting any remedies.[113]

In contrast to the Socialists, members of the Partido Demócrata Nacional strongly believed that domestic yerba cultivation was in a state of crisis and that the government needed to intervene to save it. As Córdoba PDN deputy Miguel Ángel Cárcano explained, it was impossible "to negate reality of the yerba production problem." Cárcano had not intended to participate in the debate, but after hearing Socialist opposition to the legislation, he decided that he needed to voice his support for the government's nationalist agriculture policies. Cárcano believed that "the yerba problem has the same characteristics of all the problems that face the agrarian sector today. In reality, the root of the problem is this: it is that the sales price of the product does not stretch to cover the costs of its production." The solution, in his opinion, was direct government intervention in the economy, which all governments throughout the world were now practicing, including fascist dictatorships (Italy), socialists (Russia), labor governments (Great Britain), democratic governments (the United States), and conservative governments (Canada).

Specifically, Cárcano looked to Britain's situation with wheat and beef, concluding that

> this problem of yerba mate in Misiones seems very similar to me. . . . I think the presidency has chosen the less dangerous plan to address the actual yerba problem rather than the easier option of raising tariffs, an undoubtedly simple and effective method, but it is the less intelligent method.

Cárcano's preference for the president's plan to tax all yerba, not just imported yerba, reveals that that he too believed support for yerba should only be pursued after first defending Argentine wheat. As Cárcano clarified, the yerba problem "could not be resolved by thinking only about yerba mate growers without considering them in relation to . . . our business politics with Brazil, our main South American purchasers of wheat."[114]

Contention over the president's proposal to create a regulatory commission and yerba tax appeared not only in the congressional debates, but also in the extensive coverage by the Argentine press. The country's two most important newspapers assessed both the problem and the solution differently, and their biases showed in the amount of attention paid to those speaking in favor of or against the proposed legislation. The pro-government *La Nación* recounted more testimony in support of the bill, while *La Prensa,* which adhered more closely to liberal laissez-faire principles, did the opposite. Editorials published shortly after the debates even more clearly confirm these opposing stances.

La Nación's strong support of the proposed yerba legislation confirms Ricardo Sidicaro's finding that the newspaper shifted in the 1930s from promoting classical economic liberalism to advocating government intervention in the economy.[115] In the case of yerba, for example, none of *La Nación*'s three editorials published over two weeks in August 1935 included the typical warning that excessive state intervention distorted the economy.[116] The editorial on August 25 complained about the drawn-out congressional debate and emphasized the urgent need to pass the legislation "given that the life of the territory of Misiones depends on it." More importantly, the editorial claimed that the legislation would help Argentine wheat, asserting that the growth in domestic yerba production had offset Brazilian and Paraguayan yerba imports, and thus, created "a grave exchange problem" that led to "those countries los[ing] their economic capacity to acquire our wheat." As a result, "all that we win by not buying [their] yerba, we lose in duplicate by not selling cereals." The editor believed the most effective means for remedying the situation was for the government to intervene in the yerba sector, taxing both imported and domestic yerba and directing the proceeds to domestic growers so that they could cover their production costs, along with taxing new yerba plantings as a way to limit future supply.

La Prensa took a completely different stance toward the proposed yerba legislation. As Jorge Nállim argues, "*La Prensa* probably carried out the most consistent and articulated defense of classical economic liberalism and the traditional export economy, against the policies of state intervention implemented in the 1930s."[117] The newspaper's two editorials (September 1934 and July 1935) published prior to the congressional debates essentially blamed monopolistic exploitation (middlemen, processors, and latifundia) for the yerba problem and claimed that the interests of small growers and consumers had been heretofore ignored.[118] In a third editorial, published on August 27, 1935, *La Prensa's* editors took a strong stance against the legislation with a title that succinctly summarized the editor's concern: "A Legal Statute to Consolidate the Monopoly of Yerba Mate?" The editorial pointed out that the newspaper had consistently drawn attention over the past two years to the astounding disparity between the low price paid to growers in Misiones for the raw material and the high price that Argentine consumers paid for their yerba mate, but to no avail: middlemen and processors continued to take all of the profits. The editor believed that the legislation would only worsen the situation, creating a regulatory junta "where the principal interest, which is that of the consuming population, will be represented by an insignificant minority; one vote against twelve!" In sum, the junta would legally create a monopoly with "the same legislative abilities as a corporative or fascist regime."[119]

La Prensa's stance closely aligned with that of the Socialists, the main opponents of the legislation. Indeed, twice during the debates, deputies from the Socialist party specifically referred to articles published in *La Prensa* as evidence when they attacked the proposed legislation. On the first day of debate Palancín noted that *La Prensa* had for some years defended "liberal political institutions," paid "singular attention to economic problems," and collaborated "with public powers for the best solution." He then explicitly cited the aforementioned editorial as evidence that the main problem was profiteering by the protected yerba processors.[120] On the second day of debate, another Socialist deputy, José Luis Peña, referred to a November 1933 article in *La Prensa* as evidence that large-scale yerba growers had high production costs because they themselves did not work their plots and that they were now looking to the government for assistance in order to maintain high profit margins.[121]

The Socialists, however, were in the minority. The trend was toward greater government regulation and the massive protests in Misiones brought national attention to the yerba issue. About six weeks later, the Comisión Reguladora de la Yerba Mate (CRYM) was finally established by law. Like other regulatory boards instituted in Argentina and worldwide, the CRYM was founded on the belief that the unregulated agricultural sector experienced big price fluctuations and that the government could reduce such instability through intervening in the free market. For almost the next half century, it would fix yerba prices, adjust taxes to either restrict or encourage harvests and new plantings, oversee the sale of unprocessed yerba, and advance credit to growers. These decades had mixed results in meeting the intended goals of advancing Argentine yerba, helping small- and medium-sized growers, and maintaining price stability. From 1933 on, Argentine produced most of the yerba for its domestic market, and by the late 1940s, Argentina overtook Brazil as the world's largest yerba-producing country.[122] Unfortunately, global dominance did not translate into a vibrant yerba economy or resolve the sector's problems. Production increased slowly and cyclically over the next fifty years and the real price of yerba stagnated. But by intervening in yerba sales, facilitating credit, and targeting new plantings, the CRYM helped many small- and medium-sized yerba cultivators endure (one of the main publicized goals for creating the institution). As of 1988, most of Argentina's yerba growers (96 percent) continued to have small and medium-sized plots, although the sector was still dominated by a few very large players.[123]

The creation and implementation of the CRYM was symbolic of the great swerve that Argentine economic policy underwent in the 1930s, and it shows how the debates about yerba cultivation in the late nineteenth century, and the fever of investment that followed, set the stage for not only a new economic sector, but one that would become heavily entwined with the nationalist impulses of the government during the 1930s and the years that followed. It was a far cry from the kind of guaranteed success that Pablo Allain, the Swiss agricultural engineer who directed Argentina's first yerba plantation, had claimed would come to pass. Instead, it was what might be more accurately called a middling success, and one that relied on a broader turn towards protectionism and away from laissez-faire economics to survive. The next chapter explores how different political groups (including Socialists and later Peronists) used propaganda about yerba workers to advance their political ideas, illustrating how yerba mate and its role in Argentine culture would continue to be a key site for the negotiation of the country's political and social debates.

SEVEN

Yerba Workers as a Symbol of Capitalist Exploitation

LATE IN THE DAY on September 29, 1932, a heated debate erupted among elected officials in Argentina's Chamber of Deputies, the lower house of the National Congress. Juan A. Solari, the newly-elected Socialist deputy from Buenos Aires, hijacked the conversation and launched into a passionate monologue about the plight of the thousands of yerba workers in Misiones (see figure 12). Declaring that they "continue to be subjected to the arbitrary despotism and abuse from large companies," he argued that Argentina's national government must move forward on conducting a formal inquiry into yerba companies' noncompliance with the country's labor laws. These companies, Solari said, treat workers "with a heavy hand and keep them at the margin of human and civilized existence."[1]

Solari's speech that evening was a strong condemnation about the treatment of yerba workers, most of whom were Indigenous and mixed-race rural people from the surrounding region who lived in desperate circumstances as they labored in debt to the companies' owners. Just as sugar, cotton, rubber, and tea production relied on slavery and coerced labor, yerba workers also faced exploitation and abuse.[2] Despite his strong words, Solari also pointed out that everything he was saying about these working conditions was already well known, not an extraordinary revelation: "The long-suffering and hard-working 'mensú' (yerba harvester)," he said in his speech that night in Congress, "has been a theme, in this same venue, of exposés furnished with information by Socialist deputies who have preceded us in this work."[3]

Indeed, as Solari noted, for decades, journalists and politicians from the left and workers' rights advocates had been calling out the inhumane treatment of yerba workers in Misiones. *La Vanguardia,* the Socialist newspaper in Buenos Aires, for example, had published numerous articles denouncing labor abuses in the yerba harvest. These articles were part of early twentieth century muckraking journalism that connected yerba labor abuses in the tri-border region of Argentina, Paraguay, and Brazil to worldwide labor exploitation. By publicizing such abuses and portraying the yerba worker as a symbol of extreme capitalist exploitation, Socialists (and later Communists and Peronist populists) presented their party as the true defender of labor.

To draw attention to the plight of yerba workers and incite readers and politicians to action, investigative journalists wrote dozens of articles that were part of a broader wave of "muckraking journalism" around the globe at this time. As part of that project, the journalists often employed race, and specifically the idea of "white slavery," to inspire sympathy and a feeling of connection among readers in Buenos Aires to the exploited yerba workers. In the late nineteenth and early twentieth century, such terminology was widely used by journalists worldwide—to expose labor abuses, and most prominently, the prostitution of women of European descent. In contrast, yerba workers were instead generally Paraguayan, Brazilian, and mixed-race Argentine men. Calling yerba workers "white slaves" reveals an inclusive and broad understanding of whiteness, among certain intellectuals and left-wing journalists in Argentina, that encompassed mixed-race, Guaraní-speaking peoples. This racialization of the yerba worker was also part of a broader strategy for different political parties to drum up support for their labor cause—even as it reveals how whiteness as a measure of identity continued to determine class and culture in Argentina. It also points to the way arguments about identity remained important for the way urban readers viewed yerba workers and labor culture outside of Buenos Aires. Tracing how yerba workers came to represent these exploited rural laborers in Argentina, this chapter brings into view how issues of identity in the context of the exploitation of yerba workers would become part of a broader political and racial discourse in Argentina at this time.[4]

Some of the first major analyses of the exploitation of the yerba workers were by Rafael Barrett, a Spanish Anarchist writer living in Paraguay. First published in 1908, Barrett's descriptive essays on the subject earned him a place in studies of Latin American literature. However, while Barrett is recognized as the first to write about the plight of yerba workers, he was not, in fact, the first to do so. An earlier and now largely unknown author, Julian Bouvier, played an even more important role in exposing the labor exploitation of the yerba worker. Bouvier was a Socialist supporter and, like Barrett, based primarily in Paraguay. He published numerous articles during the first decades of the twentieth century about the exploitation of yerba workers in Argentine, Brazilian, and Paraguayan newspapers, many of which predate Barrett's work.

Together, both authors joined the worldwide muckraking movement in exposing extreme human rights abuses. In the decades ahead, as the yerba industry expanded, Bouvier's and Barrett's work would become part of a growing journalistic tradition in Argentina of writing about the exploitation of yerba workers. In 1941, for instance, almost as if nothing had changed, the Communist Argentine writer Alfredo Varela wrote similar articles. He also wrote a novel that covered this same theme of yerba worker exploitation, and Hugo del Carril, a Peronist, would adapt Varela's novel in 1952 into one of the top Argentine films of all time While Varela's novel promoted Communist insurrection as a solution to the exploitation, del Carril's film suggested that Peronism had solved such problems. However, as this chapter shows, Socialists, Communists, and Peronists alike mythologized the yerba worker to advance their own political agendas, even as they did little to actually help the blue-collar laborers who harvested yerba.

YERBALES AND MUCKRAKING JOURNALISM

In June 1908, Rafael Barrett, a Spanish journalist residing in Paraguay since 1904, published six essays in the Asunción newspaper *El Diario* about the extreme exploitation of yerba workers. The essays, titled "Lo que son los yerbales paraguayos" ("What the Paraguayan Yerbales Are"), exemplify early twentieth century muckraking journalism. In the United States, muckrakers brought to light corruption and human rights abuses during the Progressive Era (1890s-1920s). Their investigative journalism and realistic novels spurred public outrage, and in many cases, led to legal and policy reforms. Internationally, the most famous example of muckracking journalism was the exposure of the extreme exploitation of workers associated with rubber extraction in the Belgian Congo.[5] This effort to expose the labor abuses in the Belgian Congo was, like in Paraguay and Argentina, a journalistic one, and it was led by the British journalist E. D. Morel. But missionaries, politicians, and famous authors (including Joseph Conrad, Arthur Conan Doyle, and Mark Twain) also joined the effort.

In Paraguay, Barrett envisioned his writings about the yerbales as part of this broader movement. He began his essays with the claim, "It is necessary that the world knows once and for all what happens in the yerbales. It is imperative that when someone wants to cite a modern example of all that human greed can devise and execute, they don't only speak of the Congo, but also of Paraguay." Barrett built on international outrage over what was happening in the Belgian Congo, believing that his writings would impact the situation, as they were "destined to be reproduced in the civilized countries of America and Europe."[6] In 1910, the same year that he died from tuberculosis, Barrett's essays were re-published in Montevideo. In the following year, they were republished in Buenos Aires without the qualifier "*Paraguayos.*" This omission expanded the essays' relevance to include Argentina. Throughout the twentieth century, presses continued to republish Barrett's essays and they are known today as a classic of Latin American editorial journalism and an important work of Paraguayan history.

While Barrett is widely credited with being the first to publicize the exploitation of yerba workers, Julian Bouvier, a Frenchman who lived in Paraguay and the triple border region from 1891 until his death in 1916, predated Barrett in writing about the exploitation of yerba workers. Bouvier's more than twenty-five essays on the yerbales were both more numerous and more detailed than Barrett's six essays. Osvaldo Salinas Giménez, who had an excellent Facebook page dedicated to Bouvier, estimated that Paraguayan, Argentine, and Brazilian newspapers published some 1,500 pages of Bouvier's writing. And yet, scholars have overlooked Bouvier's work.[7] This is likely because Bouvier's writings remained confined to ephemeral publications and he himself stayed in Paraguay for twenty-five years as a journalist, teacher, and farmer. In contrast, Barrett's connections extended beyond the region. In 1908, the Paraguayan government deported Barrett for his political activities. While in exile in Montevideo, Barrett wrote articles for Uruguayan newspapers and met the literati who must have helped facilitate the publication of *Lo que son los yerbales paraguayos* in that city two years later. Bouvier, on the other hand, never saw his writings collected into a book, and his work would largely fall into obscurity after his death.

While Barrett's articles about the atrocities of the yerbales were originally published in a single Paraguayan newspaper, Bouvier published his writings in three newspapers in three different countries, reaching numerous publics: *A Noticia* published in Curitiba in Brazil, *Rojo y Azul* in Asunción, and *La Vanguardia* in Buenos Aires. From the onset, Bouvier was already known to readers of *A Noticia,* having sent numerous dispatches about various themes. Assuming that Brazilians could proficiently read Spanish, *A Noticia* published Bouvier's articles in Spanish, not Portuguese. The newspaper, which claimed to be independent and focused on business and news, began publishing Bouvier's dispatches about yerbales on January 31, 1908, with a series of eight articles that viciously attacked Domingo Barthe, an Argentine yerbatero and businessman with massive operations in the wild yerbales of the tri-border region. Bouvier informed readers that Barthe had brought death, destruction, and slavery to most of eastern Paraguay and was on the verge of doing so in the Brazilian state of Paraná. To make his *A Noticia* essays compelling to readers, Bouvier incited Brazilian nationalism and anti-Argentine sentiment. "It is a stain, and a great stain, to the dignity of the Brazilians that Barthe has been permitted, and is permitted, such abuses and such mockeries."[8] To spur further indignation, Bouvier presented Barthe as a racist who disrespected both Brazilians by calling them "baboons" (*macacos*) and a very derogatory term for Blacks (*macacos-cambás*), and Paraguayans, by calling them "thugs and savages."[9] To make clear that all of this abuse derived from a foreign source, Bouvier reminded readers, "do not forget that behind Barthe there is the Republic of Argentina."[10]

Three weeks later, *A Noticia* published another four articles by Bouvier. This time, Bouvier focused on conditions in the yerbales rather than on Barthe personally. In doing so, he described the work as "slavery" and highlighted race by emphasizing that abuses occurred against *blancos* (white people). "There is not a human word capable of describing without shocking the listeners about all the repugnant details of the treatment of whites that are carried out on a grand scale."[11] When referring to "slavery," Bouvier claimed that for the peon of Alto Paraná, "the forest is worse than a jail: it is a tomb."[12] He repeatedly added the descriptor "white" when using the word "slavery" even though most laborers in the yerbales were mixed-race Guaraní speakers. He did so in order to strike outrage into his Brazilian readership. Without such clarification, readers associated slavery with people of African descent, a less controversial practice that Brazil had only abolished twenty years earlier.

Almost five months after *A Noticia* first published Bouvier's essays about the yerbales, *La Vanguardia* also began publishing Bouvier's dispatches on the subject. As the official newspaper of Argentina's Socialist Party, *La Vanguardia* reached a large population with six printings per week and circulation throughout the country.[13] Bouvier's series began on May 10, 1908 with a splashy front-page article titled, "In Alto Paraná. Latifundio and Slavery. Horrors of Capitalism. What is the fate of the peon in the yerbales and logging enterprises. Assassinated workers. A call to civilization and justice. Will the government and the newspapers listen?" The article introduced Bouvier as a citizen vetted by a trusted Socialist colleague (Jacinto Coza), who would provide "tremendous revelations" that were "little or entirely unknown." Before transcribing Bouvier's long first letter, dated April 1908 from Encarnación, Paraguay, the newspaper committed itself to publicizing the conditions of "an enslaved proletariat, absolutely incapable of defending itself from its owners, the rich and greedy businessmen and all-powerful latifundia owners who rob them of liberty and life."[14] In taking up this charge, *La Vanguardia* published even more of Bouvier's essays on the subject than *La Noticia* (over twenty-five, most of which were published on a daily basis over a period of less than three months).

For his *La Vanguardia* essays, Bouvier built on what he had written for *A Noticia*. In some of his dispatches, Bouvier even explicitly quoted his articles published by *A Noticia* (but without mentioning that he had authored them). Just as he did for his Brazilian audience, Bouvier tailored his essays to the Argentine readers of *La Vanguardia*. Although he openly acknowledged that the atrocities occurred in Paraguay, Argentina, and Brazil alike, Bouvier focused his attention on Argentina. To attract readers, Bouvier began his first article by asserting that white slavery existed in Alto Paraná, where "slavers (*negreros*) convert the Argentine flag into a pirate flag." Then he appealed to both the pride and the ideals of his Buenos Aires readers in order to build further interest and concern. "Modern civilization will retreat horror-stricken knowing that such infamies are committed under the shadow of legality." To cultivate both compassion and outrage, Bouvier appealed to motherhood and charitable instincts, predicting that both Argentine mothers and immigrant mothers "will feel tears form in their eyes upon learning that there is an Argentine territory where children die of hunger . . . die without succor, without witnesses in the immense forests, in the forests that do not cry, in the forests where civilization enters in the form of a chain and leaves in the form of a cadaver." And more specifically, "the noble women of Buenos Aires who sustain the wherewithal or with the inexhaustible fountain of resources that flows without stopping from the great heart of public opinion or philanthropic institutions, will hear with stupor that in the Northwest . . . thousands of unhappy people yoked to the bondage of slavery groan." To drive home the idea of social activism, Bouvier referred specifically to the founding of social programs such as kindergartens and "Gota de Leche" before describing how men and children were "treated worse than the animals" in the yerbales.[15]

As with his articles in *A Noticia,* Bouvier repeatedly stated that abuses occurred in the Alto Paraná region of all three nations, but now he emphasized that Argentina was most under threat, claiming that in recent years, the center for the "recruiters of white slaves" or "slavers" had moved from Encarnación, Paraguay to Posadas, Argentina to better target Argentine youth. This occurred because "the south of Paraguay has been depopulated and its youth have been slowly assassinated. The territory of Misiones has been depopulated of youth, and now, the provinces of Corrientes and Entre Rios are going to be depopulated because the yerbateros do not tire and the slaves are dying slowly or they go to Brazil."[16] To make an even more compelling case, Bouvier appealed to national pride by pointing to Argentina's standing in the world. "What will they say in Europe when they know that slavery subsists, protected by the silence of the government? What will European nations say to know that there is an Argentine territory where, without any risk, the boss can assassinate or have assassinated the peon who owes him and tries to flee his obligation to pay with his body and his strength?"[17] Such a public portrayal of backwardness was humiliating and an affront to Argentines who strove to portray to the world that their country was civilized.

In his *La Vanguardia* articles, Bouvier repeatedly referred to slavery, and more specifically, *white* slavery, a characterization that he had proposed in his early articles for *A Noticia*. He summarized working conditions as "slavery" and used the term "slaves" to describe yerba workers. He also generalized the slaves or workers as *blancos:* "The slavery, the infamous treatment of whites, has been carried out for about thirty years without any moral repugnance against the slavers."[18] In calling yerba workers "white slaves," Bouvier connected his claims of abuse beyond northern Argentina to the international movement against "white slavery." In the 1830s and 1840s, labor activists in the United States used the term to condemn capitalist abuse of labor.[19] In 1870, Victor Hugo used the term to refer to the international traffic of women and children for sexual exploitation. Social reformers in Britain then used it to lobby against prostitution. In 1899, The International Association for the Suppression of the White Slave Trade formed and in 1904, twelve European states signed the International Treaty for the Suppression of the White Slave Trade.[20] European social reformers targeted Buenos Aires as a center of white slavery, especially because the city council had legalized prostitution within authorized bordellos as of 1875. In Argentina, the Socialist Party actively lobbied against forcing immigrant women into prostitution and introduced legislation in 1904 to punish anyone who forced a woman into prostitution.[21] The terminology for white slavery was different in Spanish than in English. Instead of the literal translation of "white slavery" into *"esclavitud blanca"* or *"esclavas blancas,"* the term "trade of white women" (*trata de blancas*), which referred more directly to the act of sale than to the condition of slavery, was used more frequently. When referencing yerba work, Bouvier sometimes used *"trata de los blancos,"* but mostly he used the more jarring terms "white slave" or "white slavery."

Calling exploited yerba workers "slaves" also linked Bouvier's message with the larger movement against abusive labor practices in Argentina. In 1888, when the Tucumán government debated the *ley de conchabo* (an anti-vagrancy labor law that forced anyone who did not earn rent or own property to carry papers proving employment or otherwise face imprisonment), senators called it slavery.[22] Within weeks of *La Vanguardia*'s inception in 1894, the Socialist newspaper had taken up the mantle of opposing slavery, which it continued to actively decry for decades. The newspaper first drew attention to modern slavery in Tucumán by focusing on the employment papers of workers who had to carry them based on the *ley de conchabo*.[23] Three months later, *La Vanguardia* expanded its discussion of slavery by publishing an article titled "The Slaves in the Yerbales of Misiones" that focused on the monetary advances that entrapped yerba workers to perpetually labor under abusive conditions because they could not repay their debts.[24] The newspaper continued to lobby against all forms of slavery, especially in northern Argentina, but it paid little attention to work in the yerbales until Bouvier's articles in 1908.

Bouvier meant for his rhetoric about white slavery to shock readers. Slavery was illegal and considered immoral and uncivilized. To claim that it existed in Argentina, one of the wealthiest countries in the world, where economic opportunities drew large numbers of immigrants, was scandalous. To the many readers of *La Vanguardia* in Buenos Aires who considered themselves white, and especially to those who were either European immigrants or their children, the idea of enslaving white people, people like themselves, was appalling. Bouvier cultivated a connection between *La Vanguardia* readers in urban Buenos Aires and yerba workers in distant Misiones by never clearly defining what he meant by "white." Most yerba workers were mixed-race people from Paraguay, the interior of Argentina, or Brazil. Many were Guaraní-speakers. Bouvier made a few references to contractors using the "subtleties of the Guaraní language" to attract laborers, implying that yerba workers had some non-white cultural traits, but he did not go into more detail.[25] At least once, Bouvier also clarified that the workers who he described as white were not Europeans because "not a single European would resist three days of that brutal labor."[26] Barrett also referred to yerba workers in the Paraguayan yerbales as "slaves." But unlike Bouvier, Barrett never described yerba workers as white, even though mixed-race Paraguayans had claimed white status since the mid-nineteenth century.[27]

The idea that mixed race Guaraní-speakers could be considered white complicates our understanding of race in Argentina. The myth of a white Argentina based on European immigration prevailed for much of the twentieth century, and is still widely believed today. Recent scholarship on the subject highlights Argentina's racial diversity and undermines the perception of Argentine exceptionalism as a largely white, European country in Latin America. For example, in the edited volume of essays *Rethinking Race in Modern Argentina,* published by Cambridge in 2016, several of the contributing scholars showed how people of Indigenous, African, and mixed-race ancestry did not disappear even as the country attracted large numbers of European immigrants. Furthermore, whiteness in Argentina included an array of racial origins, phenotypical variations, and shades of skin color.[28] For example, as Oscar Chamosa describes, sugar industrialists in Tucumán depicted their mixed-raced employees as white in the 1920s and the 1930s in order to receive tariff protection against cheap Cuban and Brazilian sugar produced by "inferior races."[29] Bouvier's reference to yerba workers as "white" while alluding to their mestizo backgrounds fit within such a framework. And yet, Bouvier went even further by excluding Europeans from his definition of white yerba workers. To rouse readers against capitalist exploitation, Bouvier used an ill-defined and expansive interpretation of whiteness, advancing an inclusive understanding that was distinct and separate from being European.

Like other muckrakers of the period, both Bouvier and Barrett used incendiary content and moralistic language to incite readers. For example, Bouvier described work in the yerbales as "killers of people and nothing more."[30] Throughout his dispatches, Bouvier repeatedly emphasized that youth were targeted for this work and quantified underage workers at 75 percent.[31] Elsewhere, he acknowledged that women, who he claimed were treated worse than a beast of burden, also worked in the yerbales.[32] Such exploitation of women and children clashed with Argentine family values that assigned men to work outside the home, women to be housewives, and children to go to school and play.

Bouvier further intensified his readers' emotional response by asserting that laboring in the yerbales not only physically destroyed workers, but also left them morally and emotionally ruined.

> The workers who don't die quickly are returned to society sickly, full of rheumatism, debilitated by malaria, with lungs eaten away, with the soul weakened, and with spirits deflated, dead in life, without even a single hope in the mind, and without a single beat of love in the heart.[33]

In describing the alcoholism, sexual promiscuity, incurable disease, and depression that resulted from yerba work, Bouvier extended his analysis to include the surrounding region where the worker is "completely sequestered from civilization."[34] The unhealthy natural environment of Misiones, with its extreme heat, cold, humidity, insects, and lush vegetation harbored sickness and diseases. Isolation made the wild yerbales inescapable, as did the system for contracting labor. Bouvier's claims of enslavement rested heavily on labor contracts that entailed a vicious cycle of indebtedness. Labor contractors in Posadas gave advances that encouraged profligate spending, drinking, and prostitution. Upon arrival in the distant yerbales, workers incurred more debt by having to purchase poor-quality goods from the company store at a markup of 300 percent. Then, in an attempt to pay off their debts, workers labored for months and months, earning grossly undervalued wages, and were shot dead with impunity if they attempted to flee. As Bouvier summarized, "the peon is always in debt."[35] Those who paid off their debts were immediately lured back into "slavery" by another advance. As Bouvier explained, "the entire system of slavery in Alto Paraná depends on alcohol and prostitution. The peon is advanced some money so that he can excessively enjoy himself"[36] for a few days.

> You will see him, drunk, staggering, fastened to the arm of a street prostitute enjoying a fictitious diversion, submerging himself in an erotic torpor, making up in a few days for the deprivations suffered during years in the forests where he has not had ... more joy than the brutal reminiscing of his past orgies.[37]

Debt peonage inextricably linked the yerbales with Posadas, the largest city of Misiones where peons signed their labor contracts. Bouvier portrayed the city as corrupt and full of vice and debauchery. In this veritable "Sodom and Gomorra,"[38] a "gang of loafers live off of the white slave."[39]

While Bouvier condemned prostitution and the role women played in the vice and debauchery that defrauded the yerba worker, he also implied that these women were themselves victims. Women had few options; they could support themselves by turning to prostitution or finding other ways to make money off of the spendthrift yerba workers. Those who tried to form a family had to find ways to support themselves for months on end while their man was working in the yerbales or join him in Alto Paraná, where

> these unhappy creatures never have a single diversion . . . not even the ability to raise chickens. Sequestered from civilization, reduced to the role of beasts of burden or a piece of furniture, they do not know what is joy, they cannot even make a home. They live, like all the rest, in tents worse than those of dogs. . . . Wretched, a thousand times more wretched if she has a child! She cannot raise [the child], and if she doesn't raise him, she will see [the child] die.

In such conditions, "the woman dragged to Alto Paraná by misfortune is sentenced to say good-bye to the world before reaching forty years of age . . . [and], at the age of twenty-five seem like they are fifty."[40]

By addressing women and the conditions in Posadas, Bouvier extended the yerbales' destruction to the Argentine nation and society. As Bouvier explained, workers became "lost always from progress because there they become befuddled and stupefied, limiting their aspirations to paying their debt to the slaver in order to return [to Posadas] and contract another one, and in this way, remain slaves their entire life." According to Bouvier, not only did workers suffer; the loss affected Argentine families, society, and even the nation. "The young peon is a man lost to civilization, to progress, to society, to his family, and to his own country."[41] From his perspective, Argentina not only lost any positive contribution to be made by yerba workers, the very integrity of society was undermined. "[The monetary advance] stupefies the individual; debases he who receives it; annihilates the family; destroys the home; and ruins the country."[42]

In part, Bouvier blamed yerba workers themselves. He belittled them for their profligate and wasteful spending on "shoddy, showy clothes, the clothes of a clown rather than the clothes of a working man."[43] Bouvier claimed that "ninety percent throw their money in a few days into rum, alcohol, cards, parties, dances, unusable clothing, baubles, foolishness."[44] While Bouvier derided the worker for selling his soul to have a good time, he also encouraged sympathy because the victims were almost always minors. Making matters worse, their ignorance was aggravated by a lack of education and good advice.[45] Elsewhere, Bouvier called the situation "the slavery of the ignorant who don't know their rights or the price of their work."[46]

Bouvier placed much of the blame on corrupt government officials who looked the other way.[47] Yerbateros bought off government officials to keep them from investigating abuses and enforcing laws. Such lack of oversight not only enabled "slavery," but also environmental loss. Overharvesting killed the trees, and as a result, Argentine yerba production had fallen precipitously from more than 400,000 arrobas (approximately 5,000 tons) to less than 30,000 arrobas (approximately 380 tons).[48]

To make readers take his articles seriously, Bouvier portrayed himself as an expert with firsthand experience in the yerbales, having worked for seven years as an assistant to a yerbatero.[49] He claimed that this experience allowed him to see things that others could not and that, based on these observations, he was the first to inform readers in Curitiba and Buenos Aires about the atrocities that had been happening for over thirty years. In contrast, the correspondents of the major newspapers, *La Prensa* and *La Nación,* "never worry themselves with these things and are dependent on their colleagues in Asunción." In sum, "All is ignored in Buenos Aires because the same thing is happening to the Republic of Argentina as cuckholded husbands in turning their heads: they are the last to know."[50] Bouvier believed that everyone who could speak out (government officials, journalists, judges, and tourists) was either bought off or too scared to do so. Some, like Socialist officials, who might want to shed light on the situation were not given access.[51]

Bouvier's exhaustive descriptions abound with details that lent credibility to his account. He described the yerba worker's daily schedule: waking every morning at 3:00 a.m. and working continuously for thirteen hours, from 4:00 a.m. until 5:00 p.m., without eating.[52] He provided detailed information about prices, profit margins, weights, and distances. He also copied a notebook that kept track of an individual worker's debt, and when he listed the content of a labor contract that a peon had to sign in order to receive a monetary advance, Bouvier asked, "And is this not slavery?" and then later answered, "This is not slavery: it is shameless robbery."[53]

Bouvier not only described the slavery and oppression that existed in Misiones, he also suggested a solution. Bouvier explained, biblically, that "your Mesopotamia has been sold to seven or eight traffickers . . . who bought it for a plate of lentils," and he went on to name some of those people "who have let those logging entrepreneurs and yerbateros exploit [the land] as they like."[54] As a result, Bouvier concluded, "seventy leagues bordering the river without even one farmer; seventy leagues bordering the river without a single free inhabitant."[55] Instead, "3,000 slaves to fill the pockets of twelve or thirteen individuals"[56] and "their capitalist tyranny has condemned the territory of Misiones to sterility."[57] All of this occurred in a place where Bouvier believed the climate, the quality of the land, the humidity, and other conditions would allow for several harvests each year and assure the well-being of a family on four or five hectares. He estimated that within the region there was at least eight hundred leagues of latifundia and if that land were distributed to families in ten-hectare plots, each league would have two hundred families generating at least 1,000 pesos per year, making for a total of 200,000 families producing 200 million pesos. More specifically, Bouvier called for government action.

> The Republic can return to expropriate those lands or part of them; establish populations in those places; establish centers of cultivated yerbales; open roads; name authorities. . . . In this way, yes, the Argentine republic could sing victory and intone hymns pondering its Mesopotamia, liberated of the plants of the pirates and the slavers because it will have recuperated an oasis where it could accommodate hundreds of thousands of families, and unite a humanitarian project with a work of progress, enhancement, and prosperity.[58]

In sum, Bouvier, like Barrett, believed the solution was to distribute land to small farmers who would cultivate yerba.[59]

While neither Bouvier nor Barrett convinced the Argentine government to expropriate land in Misiones, they did have an impact. Like muckraking journalism elsewhere, their writings brought attention to the problem and spurred outrage. Domingo Barthe, who Bouvier had described as a racist for the way he treated his workers in his massive yerba operations, felt compelled to visit *La Vanguardia* to defend himself while the mainstream press in Argentina published their own articles about abuse of peons working in yerbales.[60] Bouvier hoped his writings on the yerbales would have a global impact, something he believed the publication of his articles as a book would help achieve. In an article published in *La Vanguardia* on July 3, 1908, Bouvier announced, clearly excited, that the 8th Socialist Congress had ordered the publication of a booklet with all of his dispatches about Alto Paraná.[61] "By means of the book," he wrote earlier, "we will travel the world asking as an act of mercy from the civilized nations to raise their voice of protest."[62] Unfortunately, this book was never produced. Still, Bouvier's writings were not forgotten. Looking back in 1922, *La Vanguardia* claimed that Bouvier's dispatches "could form a thick volume," and although that had not been accomplished, the newspaper was certain that "among the erstwhile readers of our newspaper and longstanding affiliates of the Party, there certainly would not be anyone who has forgotten the tremendous revelations that the citizen Julian Bouvier published in these columns fourteen years ago, about the horrors and the crimes committed by the slavers who exploit the forests and yerbales of Misiones."[63]

THE GOVERNMENT, POLITICAL PARTIES AND YERBA WORKERS

Bouvier's plethora of articles also had a political impact. The Socialist Party rallied behind Bouvier, officially praising both him and *La Vanguardia* for publishing his accounts.[64] More importantly, Bouvier's articles pushed the Argentine government to investigate. In 1910, in one of his own writings on the subject, Rafael Barrett even acknowledged Bouvier's impact on the Argentine government.[65]

Less than two months after Bouvier published his first article in *La Vanguardia,* the Ministry of the Interior ordered a report from the governor of Misiones. Both the minister's request and the response by the interim governor José M. López (dated June 25, 1908) included a clipping of a *La Vanguardia* article by Bouvier. López framed his response around Bouvier's article, but he downplayed Bouvier's claims, pointing out that both the workers and the yerbateros complained about abuses by the other party. While López admitted that the monetary advance system was bad, he blamed ignorant and spendthrift workers. López concluded that a serious investigation of the matter was worthwhile, but claimed that his office did not have the ability to do so.[66] The Ministry of the Interior also asked López's successor, Justino Solari, to report on the accusations of abuse faced by peons in Misiones.[67] In a March 19, 1909 article for *La Vanguardia,* Bouvier discussed Solari's findings and concluded, "Governor Solari confirms all of what I said, with the difference that he does not call things by their true name." As an example, Bouvier explained, "the slavery, the kidnapping of the victims, Solari calls them: 'staying for more time.'"[68] Less than a week later, Bouvier concluded that his writings in *La Vanguardia* had had little impact: "it fell into the abyss." But he had still, he wrote, proved the government's corruption and complicity, and ultimately, he believed that Socialism would triumph.[69] Indeed, several days earlier, Bouvier predicted that a Socialist project to regulate work in Alto Paraná "is the only means to cut the slavery at its root."[70]

In 1914, the Department of Labor initiated an investigation into work in the yerbales, sending inspector José Elías Niklison to Alto Paraná for four months. Like Bouvier and Barrett, Niklison was highly critical of the working conditions in the yerbales and he employed shocking language in describing how the monetary advance resulted in "covert slavery, the deprivation of liberty." Despite such inflammatory language, Niklison also expressed the belief that some of the accusations about excessive violence had been exaggerated. Moreover, Niklison placed a significant portion of the blame on the workers, who he characterized as uneducated and lacking in moral values. In his conclusion, Niklison summarized the problems as resulting first from the worker who allowed himself to be a victim; second from the isolation of the yerbales, which hindered law enforcement; and third from the labor contractors who facilitated the monetary advances. In an attempt to address these complex problems, Niklison recommended special legislation adapted to regional conditions, along with government inspection.[71]

In response to Niklison's report, the Socialists again rallied against worker exploitation. In May 1914, *La Vanguardia* published a series of seven articles titled "Slavery in Alto Paraná." In one of the articles, the newspaper asserted that Niklison's report confirmed that "the denunciations made in *La Vanguardia* many years earlier have plainly been confirmed, and that the Socialist Party has been the first in protesting against the slavery prevailing in Argentine territory."[72] Less than a month later, Socialist Deputy Juan B. Justo took up the cause in the House. In a long address that continued for two days, Justo questioned Argentina's Ministry of the Interior and lectured about conditions in the yerbales. In doing so, Justo referenced the many articles in *La Vanguardia,* and especially those of Bouvier, and his address further perpetuated claims of "white slavery in Alto Paraná." Justo concluded by proposing legislation to address labor in the yerbales, which the House of Deputies sent to commissions for further study.[73] Three years later, in 1919, President Hipólito Yrigoyen again proposed legislation to regulate labor in yerbales, and in 1920, the Socialists did likewise.[74]

While the Argentine government failed to take concrete action, left-wing journalists, politicians, and writers continued to portray yerba workers as subjects of capitalist exploitation. The celebrated South American author Horacio Quiroga brought the subject to a broader audience in his popular short stories. Between 1903 and 1936, Quiroga spent extended periods of time living in the small town of San Ignacio, Misiones, where he engaged in various activities, including yerba cultivation. Writing during the final years of the wild yerbales and the onset of cultivated yerba, Quiroga portrayed the violence of both men and nature in this verdant environment.[75] While his writings were not overtly political, Quiroga was likely influenced by Markos Kanner, the main Communist activist in Misiones, with whom Quiroga had a friendly relationship and who he invited to spend summer vacation at his home.[76] Other authors also addressed labor in Argentina's yerbales and mentioned both Bouvier and Barrett in their writing.[77] At the same time, *La Vanguardia* continued to publish articles railing against "slavery" in the yerbales and praising its own efforts to draw attention to the matter for more than a decade.[78]

The repeated mention of slavery, and especially white slavery, fit with new ideas about cultural identity developing in Argentina in the late nineteenth and early twentieth century. While the gaucho continued to be an important cultural icon, the myth of Argentina as a nation of white European immigrants was also emerging. Yerba workers did not fit neatly fit with the concept of the gaucho. The gauchos' livelihood, and the very foundation of their way of life, centered around horses, cattle, and other livestock, and they were known to inhabit rural areas like the pampas, which were well-suited for ranching and cultivating grains. In contrast, livestock was not central to work in the yerbales and neither ranching nor grain farming flourished in the natural environment of Northeastern Argentina, a region that Argentines understood to be an exotic and foreign, and where the verdant jungle was a formidable enemy to their ideals of progress and civilization. The concept of white slavery in Misiones fit better with the developing narrative of a white Argentina, a nation of European immigrants. Between 1880 and 1930, Argentina received almost six million immigrants, many of whom came from Europe (and drank mate to show their assimilation). They came to Argentina because it was considered a country of opportunity with high wages and the promise of a better life. Because of the arduous labor, calling yerba workers in Misiones slaves fit with Argentina's emerging cultural identity as a civilized nation. And yet, calling them white slaves implied an impossible contradiction because whites should not be slaves; the terminology in itself was a call to action. Bouvier's writings about the yerba workers and the way Socialist politicians framed this debate show how the history of yerba mate and cultural identity would continue to intersect with broader political and social debates in Argentina

In the 1920s, as recounted in the previous chapter, yerba production in Argentina underwent fundamental changes. Wild yerbales disappeared due to overharvest and were replaced by cultivated yerba. After visiting Alto Paraná, Socialist politician Juan B. Justo described these changes in a 1922 interview with *La Vanguardia.* Justo acknowledged that "large capital" enterprises produced most of the yerba from wild yerbales, but German colonists were beginning to produce yerba on smaller plots of land. Reflecting these changes, Justo was much more sedate in describing the conditions facing yerba workers in 1922, as compared to his fiery testimony before the House in 1914. While he condemned the continued use of monetary advances, he no longer referred to yerba work as slavery. And he pointed out that cultivated yerba "permits workers to have a better quality of life" because it occurred in more accessible places.[79] Such thinking reflected the widespread belief that the conquering of nature resulted in progress and modernity.

Despite these changes, the cause of yerba workers continued to remain a core issue for others in the Socialist party. Throughout the 1930s, Juan A. Solari took up the cause, bringing bad living and working conditions in the yerbales to the attention of the House of Deputies. Solari also increasingly linked yerba labor problems to broader efforts to improve the conditions facing rural workers throughout northern Argentina, something that underlined how, after only two and a half decades of mass production, the yerba sector had become integrated into Argentina's evolving debates about class and labor. Solari subsequently compiled the debates and initiatives from 1932 to 1937 into a volume titled *Workers of the Argentine North,* which initially sold out and was republished in 1937 due to high demand. The volume began with Solari's monologue, discussed at the beginning of the chapter, about exploitation of yerba workers during 1932 congressional testimony about the nation's labor laws. Solari pointed out that the subject had been a "constant Socialist concern," referring to the complaints made by Barrett, *La Vanguardia,* Niklison, and Justo. Solari also acknowledged that yerba cultivation had created a better situation, some progress had been made, and that the conditions in the Argentine portion of Alto Paraná were now less tragic. Regardless, Solari claimed that slavery continued to exist as yerba workers still encountered monetary advances, unjust labor contracts, excessive working hours (twelve to thirteen a day), inadequate food, and unfair wages. To deal with the problems, the Socialists proposed labor legislation and more government spending on inspections to enforce labor laws. In 1934 and 1936, Solari proposed more legislation to complement his earlier proposal that had not been acted upon. Even though Solari began by framing his later proposal around the exploitation of workers in Misiones, he dedicated most of his attention to explaining how workers elsewhere in northern Argentina suffered similar conditions and deserved the same protections.[80] But again, the government did not act on Solari's proposals.

The fact that Socialist politicians did not focus specifically on improving the situation of yerba workers and instead used such discussions to draw attention to the overall exploitation of rural workers raises questions about their broader goals, and whether, like conservative politicians, they too drew on class or cultural prejudices in their political priorities. Indeed, each time Solari brought attention to the exploitation of yerba workers it was part of a broader discussion about rural workers. Furthermore, Socialists prioritized urban over rural workers. When the government created the Comisión Reguladora de la Yerba Mate in 1935 to oversee the yerba sector, Socialists paid scant attention to yerba workers. As described in the previous chapter, Socialists vehemently opposed the creation of the CRYM because Argentine consumers would suffer from higher-priced yerba. By focusing on the negative impact on consumers, instead of using this opportunity to lobby for better wages or working conditions for yerba workers or assistance for yerba growers, Socialists revealed their preference for urban workers over both rural workers and small farmers. Yerba workers were peon laborers in the country's distant hinterland, and not modern factory workers in the country's urban core. Prioritizing urban workers fit well with the country's elitist cultural history of focusing on its cities, and Buenos Aires with its Eurocentric aspirations in particular.

The prioritization of urban workers did not mean that Socialists ignored what was happening to yerba workers. They continued to sporadically draw attention to the sufferings of yerba workers, but without taking any strong action for real change. In 1941, Solari complained that conditions faced by yerba workers had actually worsened as a result of the CRYM. They were

> truly lamentable. While the industries and businesses have, by means of regulation, consolidated their gain, the workers receive insufficient salaries, diminished even more by the reduction in the amount [of yerba] harvested;

they must undertake workdays without moderation, subject as they are to piecework; they suffer exploitation in the canteens and company stores; they have a poor, precarious diet; they present a dismal sanitary situation, and without the possibility of permanent work or settlement, they mostly lead a nomadic and miserable existence.

In sum, Solari argued, "regulation, as can be seen, has brought enormous disadvantages to the workers" as a result of the more limited harvest season, the reduced harvests, and the lower prices. To improve the situation, Solari recommended labor laws and labor organizing, as he had done before.[81] But again, politicians failed to take concrete action to improve the plight of yerba workers.

1940S MUCKRAKING, COMMUNISM, AND PERONISM

Although Solari and the Socialist party continued to complain at various points about the plight of yerba workers, their hot and cold support high-lighted the lack of effective long-term commitment to improving working conditions. As a result, muckraking journalists continued to decry the conditions of the yerba workers. One important example is the work of Alfredo Varela. In the 1940s, Varela wrote a series of articles that vividly brought the plight of exploited yerba workers to a wider audience, as had Bouvier, Barrett and other muckraking journalists before him. Varela, a militant Communist Party member, had spent a couple months in Misiones at the invitation of Marcos Kanner, the Communist organizer in the region who was also friends with Horacio Quiroga. Kanner introduced Varela to the topic of yerba labor in Misiones, and the visit inspired Varela to write nine articles in 1941 for the magazine *Ahora*—a popular entertainment magazine with nationalist tendencies targeted to the working class—under the heading "Also in Argentina there are White Slaves!" These articles were followed by almost twenty more articles under the heading "Notes from Misiones" in the publication *La Hora,* the official newspaper of the Communist Party, whose audience was generally distinct from *Ahora's,* but that sometimes overlapped with it.

Varela's articles for these publications not only reflected what he had found during his visit to the region, they also extensively built on earlier works, especially those of Julian Bouvier from over three decades earlier. Like both Bouvier and Barrett, Varela used incendiary language to decry the living and working conditions of yerba workers in Misiones, and he proved himself knowledgeable on the subject by naming specific locations and the people who he accused of exploiting workers. Also like Bouvier, Varela described the yerba production process in detail, complete with Guaraní terminology, and he provided data, such as prices, weights, and hours, to back his claims of abuse. Similarly, Varela included examples of timesheets and account records as concrete evidence and made his stories come alive with references to the experiences of specific people. With the greater technical resources of the 1940s, Varela was also able to extend Bouvier's work, embellishing his articles with ample photographs depicting the people and environment of Misiones and different aspects of yerba production.

While Varela decried many of the same abuses as Bouvier and Barrett, he pointed out that the transition from distant wild yerbales to plots of cultivated yerba had led to some advances (see figure 13). In his first article for *Ahora,* Varela acknowledged, "the companies continued paying them the least amount possible, enough to not die of hunger," but he claimed that with permanent settlements, "the punishment of the laborers, the violent suppression of the peon, was not so easy as in the forest, where everything was hidden."[82] Reflecting a bias for modern landscapes and progress, Varela did not admit that workers could also more easily escape and hide in the forest, and that cultivated plantations facilitated greater oversight and restricted worker autonomy. In both series, Varela emphasized that the CRYM had made things worse for the workers. It raised the price of the raw material, but, he wrote, "the workers, in contrast, see their situation worsening without any palliative assistance."[83] Not only had their wages not increased, Varela complained that workers had fewer employment opportunities and faced extreme difficulty in finding ways to provide for their families due to the reduction in total yerba production and the more limited harvest season, both of which were intended to raise yerba prices. Still, Varela wanted readers to connect present-day yerba workers with the exploited yerba workers of the past. He did so, in part, by frequently using the term *mensú* (peon who worked in the *yerbales* or forests) that had been popularized by Quiroga.[84] In contrast, both Bouvier and Barrett used the more general terms "*obrero*" and "peon," likely because they did not want their readers to exoticize yerba workers.

In describing yerba workers, Varela took a noticeably different tone than earlier authors. While everyone portrayed them as victims, earlier authors had belittled them as ignorant, backward, and incapable. In contrast, Varela recognized workers' previous attempts to organize and protest against low

FIGURE 12. Yerba workers, 1910s. Carlos Girola, *Monografía sobre la yerba mate* (Buenos Aires, 1926).

FIGURE 13. Yerba workers standing in front of wild yerbales, 1910s. Carlos Girola, *Monografía sobre la yerba mate* (Buenos Aires, 1926).

FIGURE 14. Photograph of yerba plantation in Misiones, 1923. Source: AGN. AGAS01. Acervo Gráfico, Audiovisual y Sonoro. Departamento Documentos Fotográficos. No. 78912.

wages and poor working conditions, and he noted how such efforts had failed due to both repression and the workers' need to earn money to feed their families. Varela acknowledged that "the owners of the yerbales and educators and officials say, pointing to the depressing spectacle... There is nothing to do! All efforts are useless! They are lazy and left behind and all their life they will be the same.'" But Varela interpreted the problem differently. He claimed that workers' fatalism resulted from their belief that nothing could be done to change the situation. The mensú "knows his father and grandfather were exploited; the same is true for him. Whoever approaches him ... tends to take advantage of him in some form."[85] Although Varela blamed large capitalist enterprises and latifundia, he did not call for the government to redistribute the land to small farmers, like Bouvier and Barrett. Instead, Varela supported labor laws, and expressly called for the passage of Solari's proposed legislation to increase wages for yerba work.[86] Varela also emphasized the need for labor organizing. "The yerba workers are still not united in powerful labor entities that energetically voice their grievances," he wrote. "While this situation continues, they are condemned to be forgotten, to eternally be silent partners at the banquet of the large plantations and industrial companies."[87]

Highlighting how the politics of race and social identity remained key factors in the distribution of both public sympathy and financial resources in Argentina at this time, Varela, like Bouvier, employed racialized language to build sympathy for yerba workers and to cultivate outrage. By titling his articles for *Ahora* with the inflammatory claim "Also in Argentina There Are White Slaves!," Varela produced an emotional reaction in readers, connecting them with yerba workers while simultaneously emphasizing the workers' extreme exploitation. Just as Bouvier did decades earlier, Varela explicitly linked whiteness and slavery. The claim of white slavery was sure to rile readers in Buenos Aires who considered their country modern and European. But unlike Bouvier, Varela did not play up the yerba workers' whiteness. In at least two articles, Varela clarified that the mensús working in the yerbales were *"nativos, paraguayos, correntinos, misioneros,"* and he described how the overseers communicated with them in a mix of Guaraní and Spanish.[88] In the text of his *Ahora* articles, his preferred term was not "blanco" but "criollo," something that points to the ongoing use of racial and ethnic status in the Argentina's cultural and nationalist narratives.

Varela played up the Argentine identity of these "criollo" yerba workers by repeatedly describing them wearing the common attire of rural Argentine workers—*bombachas* (baggy trousers) and *alpargatas* (espadrilles). Varela also provided specific examples of yerba workers whom he described as criollo. Ramón Navarro, a "young Argentine," was a specimen of "that criollo people who know how to tame a foal and weed a yerbal, but are never able to earn enough pesos to buy some good bombachas or to replace their ragged alpargatas."[89] Elsewhere, Varela told the life story of Sinforiano Báez, who he described as an ideal yerba worker. "Someone said that around there that the criollo as a type of human is lazy, of little tolerance, but the case of Báez is evidence of the magnificent physical reserves of the race, despite suffering brutal treatment." Varela not only characterized Báez as a criollo, and not as white, he also noted that Báez was born in Paraguay.[90] In Argentina, the term "criollo" is widely understood to indirectly point to racial mixture and nonwhiteness or incomplete whiteness.[91] By acknowledging that a number of yerba workers like Báez had origins in Paraguay and Brazil, Varela described a more complex vision of Argentine identity than the typical Hispanic criollo and a more inclusive understanding of "white" that was not based primarily on European ancestry. By doing so, Varela nevertheless underscored how such designations played a role in the perceptions of the class of yerba workers at this time.

Despite highlighting how "mixed-race" yerba workers could and should be supported as quintessential Argentines, Varela's broad interpretation of "white" and his praise for criollos did not include people of African ancestry. Varela recounted his extensive interview with Vicente Matiaúda, "one of the darkest figures of Alto Paraná," who had worked as an overseer in Puerto

Paranambú. Before describing some of the extreme abuses Matiaúda had enacted upon the mensús, Varela graphically pointed out Matiaúda's African ancestry: "his thick lips stand out as occurs in descendants of negros and mulattos." In the same article, Varela again referred to African ancestry when describing another perpetrator of extreme abuse against yerba workers: "the overseer who they called '*el negro Cundí.*'"[92]

In addition to race, Varela employed ethnic stereotypes and xenophobia to denigrate those who exploited yerba workers, revealing the malleable and selective logic of his activism. In contrast to his positive descriptions of criollo yerba workers, Varela highlighted the foreignness of the exploiters. He identified the immoral labor contractors as "Syrians, Lebanese and Turks" and he explained that these "mostly Turkish" merchants establish friendly agreements with large yerba producers in order to swindle the mensús.[93] Varela thus played into derogatory stereotypes about merchants of Middle Eastern descent that had long circulated in Argentina. Elsewhere, Varela argued that foreign yerba companies and their foreign puppets not only abused yerba workers, they also corrupted the Argentine government. Varela called Martín y Cía., the first company to cultivate yerba on a large scale, "a foreign company" and an example of "how foreign consortiums act to defraud the State or municipalities," even though Julio Ulises Martín (the company's founder) was of Swiss origin, he had lived in Argentina from 1885 until his death in 1934, and the company marketed its yerba under the label "*Industria Argentina.*" In the same article, Varela described how the company bought accomplices, who were also often foreigners, to serve in local government, identifying a past mayor (also the administrator of Martín y Cía.) as "Decoppet, of French nationality" and the present mayor as "Dalmasso, Italian."[94]

Like a good Communist, Varela also blamed rich capitalists. He repeatedly referred to well-known members of the Argentine elite as part of the system that exploited yerba workers. Varela described abuses by Máximo Roca (relative of former president Julio Roca)[95] and the establishment owned by the Urquiza Anchorena family.[96] In one article Varela focused on the company Tierra y Yerbales S.A., owned by the Herrera Vegas family, which he described as a "characteristic type of the oligarchic fauna of Argentina." In addition to yerbales in Misiones, the family had wine operations in Mendoza, livestock operations in Buenos Aires, orange plantations in Paraguay, and land in all parts. In concluding his description of the family, Varela described them as part of the "*latifundista* and anti-national bourgeoisie."[97]

Varela purposefully mixed the present and the past when describing yerba labor in order to connect to the long history of yerba worker abuse. While the exploitation by Martín y Cía. and the yerba operation owned by the Herrera Vegas family occurred at the time of the articles, both Matiaúda and Báez, the two men who Varela featured as examples of the exploiter and exploited, belonged to the past, when the wild yerbales still existed. The same was true of the Moreyra brothers, who Varela briefly mentioned in one of his last articles for *Ahora*. After describing the labor abuse in Puerto Allica, Brazil, Varela recounted, "A few times the mensús resisted, thus producing truly pitched battles, like that which occurred with the Moreyra brothers who managed to escape with bullets. The laborers of Alto Paraná always remember with admiration the manly feat of those two men." Varela claimed that he had had the opportunity to talk with the brothers, who "provided a vivid picture of the prevailing conditions in the region back then," and he included in the article a photograph of one of the brothers, dressed in *bombachas*.[98]

Varela subsequently used the Moreyra brothers as the central characters in his 1943 novel *El río oscuro: La aventura de los yerbatales virgines*. Praised for its social realism and its structure based on three storylines, *El río oscuro* is an important work of literature about Misiones. In writing his only novel, Varela built on what he had learned during his time in Misiones and relied heavily on past writings about wild yerbales from decades earlier. Scholars have invariably recognized the influence of Barrett and Quiroga, but have failed to mention Bouvier.[99] Varela himself, however, was clearly aware of Bouvier's work and consulted it in his research. He even quoted Bouvier at the beginning of one of his chapters.[100]

Varela situated his novel in the past, in the early 1920s when yerba was still harvested from wild yerbales and yerba workers were most exploited. Doing so best allowed Varela to pursue his political agenda of highlighting both extreme capitalist exploitation and the potential for labor organizing to solve the problems. Varela based *El río oscuro* around the experiences of the Moreyra brothers, who he had met during his visit to Misiones. The story follows how the brothers encounter exploitation and abuse while working in the yerbales. Fed up, they lead a rebellion and then flee to the forest, where they get lost. One brother dies from illness while the other (Ramón) learns about unions, labor organizing and the Prestes Column of Brazilian rebels, who spent time in the tri-border region. Varela uses Ramón's experiences to address how the exploitation of yerba workers should be resolved: labor organizing, and if that does not work, armed revolt. Varela's emphasis is on labor organizing, which he makes clear in a section toward the end of the novel describing the history and realities of Misiones: "Over the ashes of the former mensú, of the muleteer, the conscious, organized peon begins to raise himself for the future. His thorny path has had a light for the future: the lantern of that humble shack of the Labor Union. . . ."[101] Varela further confirms this belief when Ramón leaves for "the cultivated yerbales and the Syndicate, to where men are still exploited but fight together in defense of their dignity."[102] The valorization of labor organizing, and armed if necessary, fit closely with Varela's Communist beliefs. Indeed, the novel resonated in Communist countries. It was translated into almost all of the languages of the Soviet bloc and tens of thousands of copies were printed. Domestically, sales were also strong. By 1960, 400,000 copies of *El río oscuro* had been printed.[103] The novel's success mythologized the yerba workers of the past who labored in wild yerbales but now no longer existed as a symbol of capitalist exploitation, much as gauchesque literature had mythologized the gauchos of the past as a symbol of Argentina's criollo identity.

Varela's focus on labor organizing not only fit with Communist priorities, but also with Peronism, which was gaining in strength in the 1940s. The success of Varela's novel and other writings on yerba workers shows how yerba mate and the economic and ideological issues surrounding it continued to intersect with Argentina's evolving political discourses. Juan Domingo Perón was a populist who served as president twice (1946–1955 and 1973–74) and rose to power with the support of workers and the lower class. As Secretary of Labor and as president, Perón worked through unions to improve the wages and standard of living of urban and industrial workers. Peronists also claimed that their reforms had uplifted, empowered, and improved living conditions for rural workers. In reality, the Argentine government had enacted some legislation on behalf of rural workers, starting before Perón took office, but the reforms had limited impact.

The 1942 "Statute for Seasonal Workers" addressed a variety of abuses faced by temporary workers in rural areas, but it did not tackle wages or benefits. In 1944, less than a year after being named Secretary of Labor and Social Security, Perón signed the "Statute for the Rural Worker," mandating a minimum wage, a six-day work week, paid vacation, and other benefits, but again, the law had limited impact as it only applied to rural workers in year-round employment. As of 1947, about a third of rural workers were employed temporarily, and thus, not covered under the legislation.[104] Perón further mitigated the law's impact by not requiring its strict enforcement "We have not wanted," he claimed, "with this *Estatuto del Peón,* to force anybody to do what they cannot do. We hope that slowly, everyone who has a peon in his service improves his living conditions."[105] Despite such limitations, Perón claimed, when looking back on his presidency, that the Estatuto del Peón had resulted in the salaries of rural workers increasing twice as much between 1945 and 1955 as compared to all workers.[106] Perón exaggerated. Rural workers' salaries grew only slightly more than workers' salaries overall during those years.[107] Beyond salaries, Perón pointed to sugar and yerba workers as examples of how rural workers were treated better, explaining that when he arrived in government "they were killed in cold blood in sugar mills and yerbales under a criminal labor regime."[108] Indeed, yerba workers had long symbolized extreme exploitation and abuse, and Perón used Varela's novel to showcase that the lives of rural workers had markedly improved under his tenure.

During this time, as mass media technologies began to expand, the politics surrounding yerba laborers and production in Argentina began to be exploited for profit and propaganda in new ways. For example, in 1952, Hugo del Carril, a prominent Peronist film director/actor and composer of the Peronist anthem, produced and acted in *Las aguas bajan turbias,* one of the top ten films of Argentine cinema.[109] The film was based on Varela's novel *El río oscuro,* and it underlined the way yerba production and yerba workers remained a central symbol for Argentines concerned about the wellbeing of workers and capitalist exploitation. Varela had concluded his novel on the hopeful note that Communist organizing would improve the plight of workers. However, the film implied that such transformation had already happened under Perón and that the exploitation of yerba workers was a thing of the past. At the film's premier people could be heard shouting, "Long Live Perón!"[110] While the Socialists had focused on the exploitation of the yerba workers in the 1930s to advance their broader political agenda, and Varela did so for his communist one, the Peronists were now eager to make their mark on the growing tradition of highlighting the yerba worker's struggles for political gain. But now, in contrast, Peronists wanted to use the exploited yerba worker as a political tool for trumpeting how they had ended the capitalist exploitation of rural labor.

In an interview decades after the film was produced, del Carril recounted how *El río oscuro* inspired the film.

> The book astonished me for the sincerity and boldness in its presentation of social phenomena that we, the Peronistas, were the first in combating. After reading it, I sent the book to general Perón at the house of government, along with a note that said that I considered the theme to be in accord with all of our doctrine. Days later, Perón sent me a telegram that only contained two words: *Déle marcha* (put it into action) and his signature.[111]

In making the film, del Carril had to reshape the conclusion to fit with Peronism and disassociate the film from Varela because of his Communist ties. Perón insisted that neither the author's name nor his novel be included in the list of credits. Still, del Carril consulted with Varela and received his approval for adapting the novel into a film.

Situating the events in the past, when yerba was harvested in wild yerbales, was critical for both Varela's Communist agenda and del Carril's promotion of Peronism. As Varela and others noted in writing about Misiones, yerba workers were most exploited when they worked in the distant and isolated forests of wild yerbales instead of cultivated yerbales. In order to emphasize that such abuse and exploitation predated Perón, del Carril juxtaposed the present with the past. The film begins with visuals and a brief voiceover about Misiones.

> The Alto Paraná, one of the richest Argentine territories. Fertile and boun-
> tiful soils. Yerba mate, green gold, has been and is a fountain of fabulous
> wealth. In this land, planted by his hand, a man is free and lives freely from
> the fruit of his harvest. The river is a path of civilization and progress, but it
> hasn't always been so. Some years ago, a few years ago, these were cursed and
> punishing lands.[112]

When the narrator calls yerba mate "green gold," the viewer sees rows and rows of neatly organized yerba mate trees extending into the distance (see figure 14). The brief scene stands in sharp contrast with the wilds of the forest where the rest of the film takes place (see figure 13). The cultivated yerbales appear modern, efficient, and prosperous, visually implying that working conditions have also improved. Later in the film, such a future is connected to labor organizing when the protagonist, Santos, reads from a letter written by a worker in the south about the formation of a labor union. "Here we are content. They treat us well and it is not like in Alto Paraná. . . . Neither the bosses nor the overseers dare to kill anyone, they don't even punish the peons because they know that the union will fight. Here we have stopped being slaves. We are men like the others."[113] The scene suggests that unionization had dramatically improved workers' lives.

While both *Las aguas bajan turbias* and *El río oscuro* call for labor organizing as a solution to the exploitation of yerba workers, the endings are different. In the film, the workers revolt, destroying the yerba operations, and Santos and his love interest Amelia escape. Instead of trying to reach the cultivated yerbales where a labor syndicate has formed like in the novel, the couple in the film flee to the south, where workers are already organized. Viewers leave the film not only hopeful that Santos and Amelia achieve a better life, but also believing that the situation had actually improved in Misiones because at the beginning of the film, the narrator had explained that the storyline occurred in the past and the cinematography proclaimed that civilization and progress had arrived in the region. Although the film did not explicitly explain how such changes occurred, its framing suggests that unions and Perón's reforms had solved the problems. By juxtaposing the mythologized yerba workers of the wild yerbales who suffered extreme exploitation with the modern cultivated yerbales, del Carril makes it seem like yerba workers' lives had improved as a result of Peronism while conveniently ignoring the persistence of poor working conditions and low wages.[114]

In subsequent years, authors and artists continued to depict the difficult lives of yerba workers, demonstrating that yerba workers remained a symbol for capitalist exploitation in Argentina's broader cultural imagination.[115] In 1955, Ramón Ayala wrote the song "El Mensú" describing the oppression faced by yerba workers and their desire for justice.

> River, old, river flowing downstream,
> I want to go with you in search of brotherhood,
> peace for my land,
> [that is] each day redder with the blood of the poor mensú.[116]

The song became an important part of the New Song Movement of political protest music. Ayala performed it in Cuba in the 1960s, where Che Guevara told the musician that Cuban revolutionaries sang the song when they were in the mountains trying to overthrow Fulgencio Bautista.[117]

In 1966, the Argentine journalist Rodolfo Walsh again brought yerba workers to the national stage as part of a series of articles about Misiones that he wrote for several Argentine magazines. Most of his essay focuses on the hardships endured by yerba workers. Like earlier muckraking journalists, Walsh used details to tug at readers' heartstrings. He identified specific workers: "There is María Antonia Torales, twelve years old, who should be in school but isn't and earns 125 pesos daily." Walsh also used workers' quotes to describe their poor living conditions.

—We have had it.
—We barely earn enough for bread.

—If one eats half a kilogram of meat per week, that is good.

—We are at the point of [only having] mate cocido.

—We do not have clothing.

Unlike both Varela and Bouvier, Walsh did not call yerba workers "white slaves." Instead, he explicitly identified them as mixed race. "There aren't any blond heads or exotic surnames among them. The yerba worker is always criollo, *misionero, paraguayao,* a migratory peon without land."[118] Despite efforts by Walsh and others to expose such suffering, yerba workers continued to face low wages, inconsistent work, and other hardships. To this day, they still symbolize the excesses of capitalist greed and exploitation, further demonstrating how the yerba sector, which remains the economic backbone of northeastern Argentina—exceeding perhaps even the dreams of Aimé Bonpland back in the 1800s—had, like the practice of yerba consumption itself, become profoundly interwoven into Argentina's political debates and cultural practices in the mid-twentieth century.

EIGHT

———

Modernity, Mass Politics, and Mate's Decline

IN THE 1940S, ARGENTINA ENTERED a new political and economic era, one whose effects on Argentine culture and national identity would reverberate for the next half-century. In 1946, Juan Domingo Perón was elected as president of Argentina. Born just outside of Buenos Aires, Perón joined the army after attending high school, making his way up the ranks before turning to politics, where he eventually served as Minister of Labor and Vice President in Argentina's military government in the 1930s and early 1940s. He ran for president in 1946 as part of the Partido Laborista, the Labor Party, on a platform aimed at supporting Argentina's working classes. His election, which would inaugurate the political movement known as Peronism, would redefine Argentina's economy and political culture, expand the nation's middle class, and instigate modern trends of consumerism across all social classes. It would also have a significant impact on the consumption and popularity of yerba mate in Argentina.

One of Perón's great political achievements was to inspire a growing sense of pride in proletarian identity. Perón's government instituted a number of policies that led to increased earnings and political power for Argentina's working class, and further fueled this pride. However, even as he promoted criollo nationalism, Perón also argued that the working classes should aspire to participate in modern consumer culture, a consumerism that, up until that point, had been reserved for the middle and upper classes. Peron's rhetoric fit with the cultural zeitgeist of midcentury Argentina, and as more people joined the consumer classes, they also aspired to a modern lifestyle. In doing so, they turned away from cultural practices long associated with traditions of rural living and poverty, including the consumption of yerba mate. Within less than five years after Peron's election, per capita consumption of yerba mate began a notable decline in Argentina, a decline that would last all the way until the late 1980s.

There were a number of factors that led to these events. Despite mate's historical importance in the lives of among many of his voters, Perón himself did not publicly promote the beverage, and there are no extant images of Perón drinking mate. Moreover, as this chapter shows, both Perón's ambivalence towards mate and the protracted decline in per capita mate consumption reflected a number of significant changes in Argentine identity, changes that can be directly understood by looking at mate's evolution as a cultural commodity during these years. One of the key goals of Peronism was to empower workers and turn them into middle-class consumers who would then become central actors in a new, modern Argentina. Mate's continued associations with poverty and an old-fashioned way of life put it into conflict with such a vision. Just as Europeans and Americans began to see tea as outdated and started turning to coffee and Coca-Cola instead, Argentines increasingly saw yerba mate as a relic of the past.[1] As the popular middle-class cartoon character Mafalda explained in a 1965 comic, ". . . these days mate doesn't give prestige. Could you imagine an executive in his office drinking mate? That's ridiculous!"[2]

As consumer culture spread in the 1940s and 1950s, yerba mate became increasingly seen as out of step with the evolving ethos of modernity to which a growing number of Argentines aspired. In the first half of the twentieth century, consumer culture was limited to the elite and a small emerging middle class who wanted prestige goods to mark their social advances and modernity. But under Perón, consumer culture expanded to include workers who wanted the modern comforts of a middle-class lifestyle. A belief in scientific and technological progress, industrialization, and urbanization, along with the state having a large role in directing the economy as it did with the Comisión Reguladora de la Yerba Mate, underlay this modernist zeitgeist.

As new modern lifestyle trends and consumer habits emerged in the 1930 and 1940s, advertising companies tried to reframe mate as a modern beverage. As this chapter discusses, in an effort to enhance mate's appeal among both middle- and upper-class consumers, as well as the emerging consumers from the working classes, mate companies printed hundreds of advertisements in major newspapers and magazines that presented modernized ways for consuming yerba mate. These efforts, however, did not catch on among any group, and Argentines who continued to drink mate did so in traditional ways. In the decades ahead, mate continued to be associated with poverty, rural living, and even backwardness, a reputation that drove down its popularity in the broader population.

One of the most notable efforts at rebranding mate as a modern drink at this time was by the yerba mate brand Salus. Salus, which was produced by Mackinnon y Coelho, one of the country's oldest and most important yerba processing companies, was one of the main Argentine brands of yerba mate. Between 1939 and 1958, Salus printed hundreds of advertisements in major newspapers and magazines. These advertisements reached a large portion of magazine readership by appearing in an assortment of publications including *Leoplán* (targeted to upwardly mobile sectors of Argentine society), *Para Ti* and *Chabela* (targeted to women), and *Gráfico* (targeted to men and sports fans). The advertisements also attracted attention because, starting in the mid-1930s, they were printed in color. Many filled an entire page, and they often appeared prominently on the back cover of the magazine. The approximately one hundred and fifty advertisements examined for this book over an extended period of twenty years provide a unique opportunity to study trends and changes in the representation and symbolism of yerba mate during these important decades in Argentine history. However, Salus's advertisements portrayed how the company *wanted* Argentines to consume yerba mate; actual consumption practices often differed. As such, the advertisements also reveal how marketing practices at a company like Mackinnon y Coelho tried to shape consumption practices in response to changing cultural and economic conditions.

MODERNITY AND CONSUMPTION PRIOR TO PERÓN

For people with money, Buenos Aires in the early 1940s was a dynamic, major urban center with every imaginable luxury. Foreign visitors would describe with awe the city and all of its offerings. During the first few decades of the twentieth century, the city had become a modern metropolis with tall buildings and wide boulevards filled with assorted stores, *confiterías,* and restaurants. Argentines with money, enthusiastically engaging in the growing consumer culture, went out and bought processed foods, clothing, furniture, and appliances; they ate out, watched films and theatre, read magazines, and engaged in other forms of entertainment. Although in the second half of the 1940s, advertisers would begin to target a growing worker population with disposable income, in the 1930s and early 1940s, only the Argentine elite and a small emerging middle sector of office workers, professionals, and business owners could afford such purchases. Consumption was a clear marker of social class.

During this period, Argentina's vibrant print media and advertisers began to shift their advertising practices, including those related to yerba mate, to include images that celebrated modernity in an effort to cultivate such consumerism among the elite and middle classes. By 1935, approximately two million copies of newspapers and magazines were printed daily in Buenos Aires, and they were filled with advertisements that catered to Argentine elite and the upwardly mobile.[3] These advertisements were part of a marketing strategy by companies to try to take advantage of burgeoning consumption in the city. Back in 1929, for example, sensing future opportunity, the American advertising firm J. Walter Thompson set up its first South American office in Buenos Aires. The company's marketing surveys found that the upper 25 percent of Argentine society were drawn to prestige goods associated with American-style modernity. Building on such information, advertisers marketed their products as a sign of good taste and respectability. Such advertisements inspired consumers' desire to purchase goods as a way to show social advancement.[4]

One of the best examples of this kind of marketing approach can be seen in almost fifty advertisements by the Salus brand of yerba mate between 1939 and 1944. In these advertisements, Salus emphasized Americanized consumption patterns, leisure and the good life, nationalism, and affordability. The company presented yerba mate consumption (in the form of tea, an iced beverage, and personal mates) as a beverage that fit with prevailing ideas about modernity and an upwardly mobile lifestyle. This representation of yerba mate as a "personal drink" rather than a shared one was a notable departure from the traditional method of drinking mate, which involved passing the beverage among a group. Although this modern way of drinking mate did not catch on among Salus's target audience (Salus subsequently returned to marketing the traditional manner of consuming mate), the effort underscores the broader trends influencing Argentina's commercial sector at this time, trends that were extremely popular and would remain so for decades to come.

In their initial efforts to push this modern style of drinking yerba mate in their advertisements to middle-class and elite consumers in the early 1940s, Salus most notably promoted American/European ways for consuming yerba mate. It was a far more sanitized style than in the past. The traditional *pava* (kitchen kettle), long associated with mate, did not appear in any of the images.[5] Instead, the more mobile and modern thermos took its place and was frequently shown prominently. Even more striking, whenever the advertisements showed people drinking mate, each person was almost always drinking from his or her own gourd. The individualized mate was the antithesis of the traditionally shared mate. But even though Salus portrayed the act of drinking as a personalized rather than a communal activity, the company continued to depict mate as a social activity that people did with others. Continuing health concerns, and especially those surrounding tuberculosis, likely inspired Salus to promote individualized mate consumption.[6]

Salus's advertisements also educated readers about other, different methods for consuming yerba mate. They promoted drinking yerba mate in the form of tea (*te-mate*) and iced tea (*refresco*), with or without milk or sugar. Argentines had long drunk yerba mate in the form of cocido, tea made by boiling approximately 50 grams of yerba in a liter of water that was then strained. But none of the advertisements used the term "cocido." Instead, they repeatedly used the term "te-mate" and showed pictures of teacups with saucers, and sometimes even teapots. The English term "tea," with all of its accoutrements, fit better with ideas of upward mobility, modernity, and the good life than the old-fashioned "cocido." In the early 1940s, Salus advertisements repeatedly showed happy, pretty people in well-appointed homes or other comfortable venues enjoying yerba mate as a tea or an iced beverage, in addition to, or even without mate. For example, "*Refresco Salus* to conserve the silhouette" shows three attractive young white women lounging comfortably in bathing suits and other informal clothing on patio furniture overlooking the beach while drinking big glasses of iced yerba mate through a straw (see figure 15).[7] Such representations fit with the international portrayal of the independent and fun-loving "modern girl" popularized during the interwar period.[8] In contrast, other advertisements from the period portrayed women as housewives and mothers. For example, "Te-mate Salus. Succulent breakfast for adults and children" shows a young mother and son conversing and drinking yerba mate tea from teacups and saucers while sitting at a table in front of a curtained window with a nice view (see figure 16).[9] A number of advertisements in the second half of 1941 promoted te-mate even more intensively by removing people from the images and showing a still-life setting with te-mate presented front and center, frequently with a thermos and a dessert, such as gâteau Salus, made with yerba mate. Salus was not the only company to market alternative ways of consuming yerba mate. In the early 1940s, for example, Martín y Cía. published a seventy-page color

FIGURE 15. Salus advertisement, *Leoplán,* February 14, 1940.

brochure to educate consumers about drinking yerba mate as tea, iced tea, and mate without the shared bombilla.[10] These marketing efforts had much in common with British and Dutch colonial tea growers' efforts to market tea in the United States in the 1930s. The International Tea Market Expansion Board promoted iced and hot tea as a modern and energizing beverage.[11]

FIGURE 16. Salus advertisement, *Leoplán,* June 5, 1940.

In educating readers about such new, modern ways of consuming yerba mate, a number of Salus advertisements in the early 1940s promoted yerba mate as a replacement for alcohol. Most notably, a 1942 advertisement titled, "Salus, the best aperitif," shows a small group of nicely dressed individuals sitting around drinking individual mates in a sitting room with a dining

FIGURE 17. Salus advertisement, *Chabela,* February 1942.

table in the background (see figure 17).[12] More frequently, the advertisements simply noted that drinking yerba mate reduced alcohol consumption (*aleja del alcohol*). Less overtly, Salus advertisements during the period frequently associated their yerba with a *sobrio* (sober) population.

Salus advertisements repeatedly highlighted affordability while still associating yerba mate with the upwardly mobile sector of society. Phrases like "only pure water is cheaper" and "Salus makes life cheaper" emphasized that Salus was inexpensive. The advertisements also frequently combined the ideas of quality and economy by highlighting that the flavor of yerba Salus lasted longer.[13] The idea of spending money wisely appealed to Argentina's emerging bourgeoisie, who saw the ostentatious spending of traditional elites as antimodern and decadent, especially in the context of the "Infamous Decade" (1930–1943) characterized by corrupt civilian rule.

Almost all of the Salus advertisements in the early 1940s showed images of an upper- or middle-class lifestyle. One notable example can be found in the magazine *Leoplán* on October 9, 1940 with the text: "Waking Up Happy." It centers on a young blonde woman in a nice bathrobe gazing out of a window while, in the background, a brunette servant with white skin brings her mate.[14] Throughout the advertisements, well-dressed people were placed in comfortable, modern settings. Several other advertisements from around this same period showed a man in a suit, along with a woman, drinking mate from a gourd while at work in an office. More frequently, Salus advertisements showed people engaging in leisure activities, playing sports or relaxing at the beach, on a picnic, or at home. When urban consumers drank yerba mate while relaxing in the countryside, a car was often in the background. At this time, only the wealthy could afford an automobile or live the lifestyle portrayed in these advertisements. In these images, the women were portrayed as confident, stylish, young, and attractive; this Argentine "modern girl" was part of global movement that began in the United States and Europe and was taken to its extreme with the flappers of the 1920s.[15] Salus advertising fit within the context of such universalizing trends based on the idea that Argentine consumers had the same preferences and wants as American consumers. They wanted prestige goods such as automobiles, radios and refrigerators along with personal hygiene and other consumer items that portrayed modern values and an up-to-date lifestyle.[16]

In addition to the "modern girl," Salus advertisements included an image of the Salus *Criollita* or *Paisanita*, who was the emblem of Salus yerba and the only image on Salus packaging. As a modestly dressed and sedate country woman who alluded to Argentina's rural past, she was the antithesis of the controversial "modern girl" portrayed in the representations of females described above. Instead, the Salus criollita was a *morocha argentina,* the unofficial national emblem and the quintessential Argentine woman. In Argentina, "*morocha*" means brunette or a person of dark complexion.[17] The Salus criollita was a light-skinned, long-haired brunette with blue eyes who was modestly dressed in a blue dress with a red scarf around her neck and a light-blue bow in her hair. In modern urban settings, the focus of most of Salus's early 1940s advertising efforts, the rural Salus criollita only appeared in the background as the brand's emblem. However, Salus also produced advertisements for its yerba products that sought to appeal to consumers' patriotic pride, and the rural Salus criollita was far more present in these designs. For example, one advertisement that appeared in *Leoplán* in 1939 with the text "200 million portraits of the criollita Salus!" had an image of the Salus criollita surrounded by various Yerba Salus items and the explanation,

> Salus is the most popular criollita in the world . . . All of the Country knows her and loves her . . . [she] is the emblem of the National Yerbatera Industry. The Salus criollita represents the Patria in yerba because it was the first that, proud of its lineage, proclaimed to the four winds its Argentine origins.[18]

By connecting the Salus criollita with the homeland and reminding readers that its brand was the first to market itself as using solely Argentine yerba, the advertisement turned the purchase and consumption of Salus yerba into a patriotic activity.

Emphasis on national pride was especially strong in advertisements published around the dates of the two independence holidays (May 25 and July 9). For example, "Toast to the homeland with Salus, which is ours!" had an image of the Salus criollita in the center. Holding an Argentine flag, she united for a toast a rural worker and a businessman in the countryside, on one side of her, and an urban worker and a businessman in the city, on the other.[19] While nationalism played a smaller role than depictions of a modern lifestyle in most of Salus's early 1940s advertisements, it was never entirely absent. The text in almost all of the Salus advertisements from the period concluded with either "build the homeland" (*haga la Patria!*) or "*viva la Patria!*" and almost every advertisement had "the flag covers the merchandise" (*el pabellon cubre la mercaderia*) at the bottom of the page. This patriotic undercurrent reveals the strength of Argentine nationalism among the country's population, and, additionally, the opportunity this nationalism offered as a sales tool for advertisers, which surprised researchers from J. Walter Thompson when they conducted their study of the Argentine market in 1930s.[20]

While Salus incorporated nationalism into its advertisements, references to criollo culture were almost entirely absent, with the exception of the Salus criollita. Of the almost fifty advertisements from the early 1940s, only one centered around a scene with a gaucho in a rural setting.[21] The general absence of the gaucho in Salus's advertising is especially striking given the longstanding importance of criollo nationalism and mate's historic ties to the gaucho. Tango, for example, had long used the connection between mate and the gaucho to culturally bridge rural and urban Argentina. From their inception, tango songs incorporated criollo nationalism and alluded to mate's close association with Argentine identity and its central role in daily life. A precursor to the tango, a *habenera* from the late 1850s, was titled "Drink mate" with the lyrics, "drink mate, friend, drink mate, because in the land of the pampas, chocolate is not in fashion."[22] The tango legend Carlos Gardel, who was considered the epitome of a criollo *porteño* (inhabitant of Buenos Aires), sang about mate and was widely seen drinking mate in photographs. In his first tango recording ("My Sad Night" in 1917), Gardel sang about drinking mate with the woman who spurned him. In the 1930s, the yerba mate company SAFAC capitalized on Gardel's popularity by advertising cans of Yerba Mate Gardel with a photo of the singer in gaucho attire.[23] Similarly, one of the most famous folklore musicians of the twentieth century and a pioneer for the militant song movement, Atahualpa Yupanqui, made his first recording in 1936 for a company marketing yerba mate, and he dressed like a gaucho for public performances.[24]

If mate's connection to criollo nationalism was so strong, why didn't Salus incorporate the gaucho into its early 1940s advertisements? The basic reason is that Salus was interested in developing its consumer base among the country's urban and middle-class populations, populations who did not historically consume mate near the rate of the rural populations, but who had more money to spend on it. Particularly during the 1930s and early 1940s, as consumerism was expanding among the professional and elite classes, Salus, eager to profit from this audience, sought to promote yerba mate as a product suitable for a modern, urban lifestyle. By focusing on images of upper-class individuals consuming yerba mate in new ways, Salus tried to appeal to these consumers and show that its product had relevance beyond rural settings and was more than a nostalgic criollo activity. At the time, advertising companies in general focused on selling prestige goods to the country's upper and aspiring middle classes, especially in Buenos Aires, and they largely ignored lower class consumers due to their extremely limited buying power.[25] Even though Argentina had experienced some industrialization and became more urban between 1935 and 1946, the majority of Argentines still did not earn enough to participate in this consumer culture portrayed in the Salus advertisements.[26] A standard of living study published by the National Department of Labor in 1937 reported that the monthly expenses of a typical working-class family in Buenos Aires surpassed a wage laborer's salary by 30 percent. The study underscored,

> The Statistics Division takes great efforts to make it comprehensible that this situation *is the real situation of the families that do not count on more than 120 pesos monthly, and that [the Statistics Division] in no way affirms that it is a sufficient standard of living needed by the working family.*[27]

An even larger study of 10,000 working class families in 1943 suggested a slight improvement (the gap between the average working-class family's expenses and income had fallen to nineteen percent), but the improvement was overstated. The typical working-class family in the 1943 survey was smaller (with two instead of three children) and high inflation also meant that wages had less buying power.[28] Yerba mate played an important role in the daily life for many of these working-class families struggling to make ends meet. Salus's advertising, however, which drew on other modernizing cultural trends of that period, sought to present the culture of yerba mate as a luxury activity, beyond this kind of struggle.

This depiction of mate was an attempt to shift the history of yerba mate in Argentina, as it had long been integrated into rural, working culture as a necessity, not a luxury. Indeed, all of the standard-of-living surveys demonstrate the importance of yerba mate for Argentine workers. Yerba mate always appeared in the "food" (*alimentación*) category. Early 1930s surveys also included coffee and tea, likely because the surveys were based on European consumption models, but later Argentine surveys stopped including tea. This never happened for yerba mate. In fact, when summarizing changes in living standards between 1914 and 1945, the government's social statistics office included yerba mate as one of the ten indispensable consumer articles.[29] The Department of Labor estimated that in 1935 the hypothetical monthly budget for a working-class family with three children under fourteen and earnings of 120 pesos purchased 2.5 kilos of yerba mate estimated at 1.73 pesos. According to the budget, working class families consumed less and spent less on other beverages with the exception of wine: coffee (.6 kilos costing .87 pesos), wine (12 liters costing 5.16 pesos), and soda (5 bottles costing .25 pesos).[30] In the same year, working class families reported that yerba mate was their eleventh largest food expenditure.[31] By 1943, the government's next hypothetical monthly budget for a working class family (this time with two juvenile children and higher earnings of 149.20 pesos) included less yerba mate (2.03 kilos as compared to 2.5 kilos) and more coffee (.8 kilos as compared to .6 kilos) plus 0.1 kilo of tea, reflecting the growing importance of these other caffeinated drinks. The Argentine government continued to use these quantities for measuring standard of living until 1960.[32]

Worldwide interest in calculating workers' standard of living intensified concern about the living conditions of Argentine workers. People on both ends of the political spectrum worried that the earnings of urban workers barely covered their family's subsistence, but until the 1940s, government officials focused their efforts on trying to grow the economy through efforts like the CRYM, which was meant to advance the entire yerba sector, rather than directly addressing the situation of workers. Until the mid-1940s, Argentina's labor movement was fragmented and only a small proportion of workers formally belonged to a union. The political establishment further weakened the labor movement by keeping it marginalized.[33] But change was on the horizon. Argentine newspapers and politicians increasingly discussed topics related to workers' living standards in the 1940s.[34] Social agitation increased as workers communicated their dismay over low wages with strikes, which were increasingly resolved through collective negotiation.[35] These movements, which emerged at the same time as industrialization and modernization trends swept the country, would ultimately transform yerba mate's situation in Argentina's culture, and, despite Salus advertising efforts to the elite and urban middle class, lead to a long period of decline in the coming years.

PERÓN, WORKERS, AND YERBA MATE

Urban labor's living standards and political power markedly improved with Juan Domingo Perón's ascent to power, first as Secretary of Labor and Social Security in 1943 and then as president in 1946. These changes should have meant greater yerba mate consumption given that drinking mate had long been an important part of workers' daily life. Furthermore, one would think that Perón's embrace of workers and the lower class, along with criollo nationalism, should have made him a public proponent of mate. But as this section shows, mate's continued associations with poverty and rural Argentina did not fit with the zeitgeist of modernity and a middle-class lifestyle.

After participating in the military coup in 1943 that ended the so-called "Infamous Decade," Perón appealed to Argentine workers who felt left out and disenfranchised from their share of Argentine wealth, and he parlayed their support into political power.[36] To do so, Perón utilized his position as head of the National Department of Labor, a heretofore minor government body that had primarily been occupied with producing statistical reports. Under Perón, it grew to become the Secretariat of Labor and Welfare, which was equivalent in the cabinet hierarchy to the Secretariat of Industry and Commerce. In this role, Perón advocated on behalf of unions and instituted a number of measures benefiting Argentine workers, such as increasing salaries by decree, establishing minimum wages for certain industries and granting a number of other benefits such as severance, retirement, and paid vacation.[37] Perón also cultivated followers in hundreds of speeches that called for improving the living standards of Argentine workers as a way of uniting and advancing the nation. He claimed that higher domestic demand for goods would spur economic growth and counter the threat of communism.[38]

Perón's actions had a material impact on workers. His Secretariat of Labor assisted in the signing of about a thousand collective labor agreements in 1944, contributing to a 12 percent average rise in the real wages of unskilled workers between 1943 and 1945. Not only did workers' wages increase, the number of Argentines eligible for state welfare and protection quintupled from approximately 400,000 to 2 million.[39] Many workers credited Perón for making these changes possible. Looking back at the period, Doña María Roldán, a worker in the Swift meatpacking plant and a union delegate, remembered how by 1944 the company had conceded to a number of her union's demands, including measures to improve working conditions such as giving workers a break for cocido every afternoon. Roldán credited Perón with facilitating these advances and inspiring a newfound sense of self-respect among workers.[40]

After winning the presidential elections in 1946 with 53 percent of the vote as head of the newly formed Labor Party, Perón implemented a corporatist economic model that was neither communist nor free-market capitalist.[41] Rather, the state intervened throughout the economy to stimulate growth and more equitably distribute the nation's wealth among its population. Industrial expansion played a key role in such a vision. For Perónist policymakers, industrialization and improving workers' standard of living went hand-in-hand in a "cycle of prosperity:" raising workers' wages increased their capacity to consume, which meant they bought more goods, thereby leading to more production and higher income for all. Such thinking focused on the domestic economy, blending fascist corporatism with the Keynesian economic theory that the government should increase workers' purchasing power during periods of underemployment in order to stimulate demand and return the economy to full employment. In sum, Perón promoted higher wages, mediated through the government, not only as a way to improve workers' standard of living, but also as a mechanism to further industrialize and grow the Argentine economy as a whole.[42] Such a model implied that purchases of yerba mate would grow along with the rest of the economy.

In its first years, Perón's administration used abundant foreign exchange, accumulated during the war years as a result of falling imports, to support this model of industrialization, consumption, and full employment. Such spending spurred industrial expansion and economic growth for the first years of Perón's presidency. Between 1946 and 1954, the number of manufacturing enterprises grew from 85,000 to 148,000. For the three years between 1946 and 1948, Argentine production increased an average of 8.4 percent per year, which as of that date was the second highest rate over a three-year period. Workers benefited as real wages grew by 72 percent between 1945 and 1950, an increase unparalleled in the world in both scale and pace. While the economy expanded, such growth was unsustainable through 1950. And then, as foreign exchange surpluses dried up, inflation became problematic, and the economy fell into recession. Perón's administration responded with belt-tightening measures. In an effort to tackle inflation, the government restricted wage growth and encouraged Argentines to limit their spending. As a result of such efforts, the economy improved, but at the cost of workers' income. Real salaries fell dramatically in 1951 and 1952, and then increased and stabilized in 1954 and 1955, but without returning to the high of 1950.[43]

Many of these wage increases and social provisions were channeled through union contracts, which spurred the development of working-class identity. By the early 1950s, Perón had centralized Argentine unions into a single Confederación General de Trabajo under state oversight. Support of unions grew and membership increased from just over 500,000 in 1946 to over 2.3 million in 1951. Workers embraced their class identity. In remembering the period, workers described their consumption not as an attempt to raise their social class, but rather as personal gratification and a sign of social achievement that reinforced class belonging. Workers took pride in being workers as they assumed a more important role in Argentine society. As Daniel James wrote, "the people, the nation and the workers became interchangeable."[44]

Not all of Argentine society embraced the emphasis on workers and the lower class. The Argentine elite mocked Perón's supporters, calling them *descamisados* (shirtless ones) and *cabecitas negras* (little blackheads). The slurs backfired; Peronist identity was so strong that workers turned these derogatory insults into positive political terms.[45] Recognizing that Peron's supporters identified as "descamisados," Santa Teresita brand yerba targeted this population by giving purchasers a free medallion with the image of Perón along with the saint, and by explicitly marketing itself as "the yerba of the descamisados."[46]

Perón's efforts to uplift Argentine workers extended beyond wages and basic necessities to the democratization of well-being across Argentine society. His paradigm of dignified life (*vida digna*) extended the standard idea of welfare to include the right to material comforts.[47] Perón enshrined such values in his 1949 constitutional reform. Workers had "the right to well-being" that guaranteed access to "housing, adequate clothing and nutrition, to satisfy without worry, their needs and those of their family in a manner that [would] allow them to work with satisfaction, rest free of preoccupations and enjoy in a measured fashion spiritual and material gains."[48] Perón pushed for legislation to turn such a goal into reality. Minimum wage regulation and year-end bonuses (*aguinaldos*) provided workers with more spending money; subsidies and price ceilings made purchases more accessible; the eight-hour workday, half-day on Saturday, and paid vacations gave workers more time to enjoy their purchases; and public housing and tourism infrastructure provided workers with modern accommodations.

The improved standard of living promoted middle-class consumption patterns among workers.[49] The homes, appliances, clothing, and leisure activities of blue-collar workers were often indistinguishable from those of white-collar workers. As Juan Carlos Torre and Elisa Pastoriza point out, images of working-class families from the period showed a "worker, sitting in a comfortable armchair in the living room of his home, with a jacket and a tie, reading the newspaper or listening to the radio in the presence of his family, which corresponded to the idealized representation of the middle classes."[50] Torre and Pastoriza include a picture of a man drinking mate that mostly fit with idealized representation of middle-class life. The image, by the popular artist Luis J. Medrano, who was known for depicting prototypes of Argentine culture, matches Torre and Pastoriza's description of a working-class family under Peronism, except that this man is wearing a smoking jacket without a tie; he is reading a book instead of a newspaper; but most notably, he is drinking

FIGURE 18. Luis J. Medrano, "El hombre que no va al fútbol," *Argentina,* October 1, 1949.

mate and his family is not present (see figure 18). These differences add irony to the image. In Medrano's rendering, the sociability of the family is absent. In its place is the private consumption of mate. Both family and shared mate had long been cornerstones of Argentine identity. In contrast, Medrano's image emphasized individuality. Indeed, Medrano did not intend for the image to represent a typical Argentine setting. Instead, he included the image with a 1949 essay about an atypical male resident of Buenos Aires, "the man who does not go to see football" but rather seeks refuge at home.[51] Medrano's image hints at the difficulty of integrating mate into the middle-class lifestyle promoted under Perón. Salus's early 1940s advertisements depicting leisure and modern ways of consuming yerba mate implied that the yerba sector had already started reshaping yerba mate consumption to better fit with a middle-class lifestyle, but in fact the company failed to change Argentine consumption patterns. In the Peronist era of modernity, yerba mate became an antiquated symbol of Argentine identity despite such marketing efforts.

Starting in the mid-1940s, after years of directly targeting Argentina's elite and professional classes with a modernized vision of yerba mate, advertising companies took note of workers' increased buying power under Perón. With this new and growing consumer population in mind, companies began to expand their marketing strategies to appeal to lower-class Argentine consumers, incorporating images of workers, humor, and idealized women into their advertisements.[52] As with the advertisements that predominated prior to the mid-1940s and were aimed at upper and middle class consumers, advertisements during this time continued to highlight modernity, but now, as Salus shifted to target working class consumers, they no longer focused on an upper-class lifestyle. Realistic representations of people in luxurious and well-appointed settings were gone. Instead, almost all of the people were cartoon images with plain or non-existent backgrounds. The emphasis on promoting an urban middle-class lifestyle did not only occur in Argentina; in Mexico, advertisers took the same approach in order to sidestep radical nationalism and sell American goods.[53]

One of the main shifts that Salus made in its marketing strategies during this time was to return to exclusively promoting mate, the quintessential workers' drink, instead of other yerba mate products. Clearly, the company had concluded that its efforts to show modern ways of consuming yerba mate had failed to resonate with consumers. Gone was the intensive marketing of other forms of consuming yerba mate. With very few exceptions, te-mate and refrescos no longer appeared in either images or text after 1944.[54] Salus also abandoned its efforts to promote innovations in mate consumption, and instead, portrayed mate in its traditional form. Rather than highlighting people drinking from their own mates, the advertisements showed people sharing mate. Even the thermos, a sign of modernity and innovation, disappeared after 1945. Instead, the more traditional kettle increasingly appeared in Salus advertisements.[55] Salus's return to portraying longstanding ways of consuming mate was an acknowledgement that Argentine consumers had rejected new ways of consuming yerba mate, continuing instead to share their mate.

While Salus abandoned its efforts to educate consumers about modern ways for consuming yerba mate, it continued to promote the brand's modernity by highlighting the company's use of technology. Such an approach fit with Perón's industrial strategy and portrayed Salus as a high-quality brand with a superior product. For example, between 1949 and 1951, Salus emphasized that it was the only brand to use pressurized packaging, and in 1953–1954, the company launched a campaign titled "Reasons that Justify the People's Preference for Salus" with eight points about how Salus used advanced approaches in producing its yerba. Four of the reasons described industrial processing; two focused on cultivation; one centered on nationalism; and the last reason summarized all seven.[56] The nationalist claim that focused on Salus being superior because it was Argentine stood out from Salus's overall advertising efforts during this period.

Although nationalism was widely viewed by Argentine companies as an important marketing tool during Perón's time in office, in fact, Salus's advertisements for yerba mate during that time tended to avoid using nationalism to help sell its product, a departure from its own past practices. From 1944 until Perón's fall from power in 1955, Salus's advertising efforts generally focused on conveying the idea that mate was part of a middle-class lifestyle, and it paid less attention to nationalism than in the earlier period. Such an approach differed from overall marketing trends. Natalia Milanesio has described how nationalist themes, along with economy and durability, monopolized Argentine advertising in the 1950s.[57] Yet Salus bucked this trend. Likely, the company avoided emphasizing Argentine nationalism and criollo culture in order to avoid the divisiveness of Peronist nationalism and not alienate middle-class consumers who abhorred Peronism. Gone were the phrases "*viva/haga la Patria!*" and "the flag covers the merchandise" that appeared in almost all of Salus's advertising in the early 1940s, and the company published very few explicitly patriotic advertisements around the dates of Argentine independence. Salus's advertisements between 1944 and 1955 also generally overlooked prime opportunities for highlighting Argentine identity. For example, one advertisement with the words "Salus was elected" described how Salus was chosen by all types of people (*campesinos,* small townspeople, mate-drinking city dwellers, rich and poor, and mothers and children), but without ever using the term "Argentina" or "Argentines." Furthermore, the image portrayed a very idealized version of these people: they were all white men and women wearing suits and nice clothing. None were dark-skinned or wore the work attire of blue-collar laborers or rural folk.[58] Likewise, only a few of the advertisements from the period explicitly mentioned criollo culture and only two showed images of a gaucho.[59] After Perón lost power, however, the company did wade more explicitly into national politics in its advertisements, and, in 1956, in striking contrast to its 1944 to 1955 advertisements, Salus published a series of three advertisements that emphasized Argentine nationalism and criollo identity, likely in an effort to unite Argentines in the wake of Perón's fall from power.

While many yerba mate advertisements, such as those of Salus, tried to connect the beverage with an urban, middle-class lifestyle, a few reinforced the association of mate with gauchos and rural life. For example, the brand Nobleza Gaucha not only made this connection explicit in its name, it

FIGURE 19. Nobleza Gaucha advertisement, *Chabela,* September 1955.

visually represented humble, rural folk enjoying mate in three 1955 advertisements (see figure 19). All show smiling dark-skinned men dressed in unassuming attire like gauchos.[60] These advertisements took a strikingly different approach compared to Salus's, which included very few gauchos before 1956, and only rarely did they look like common folk.[61] The three Nobleza Gaucha advertisements show how some images from the period did not fit with the prevailing myth of Argentina as a white-European nation.[62] Still, such images were the exception; other Nobleza Gaucha advertisements from the 1950s show white people engaging in a modern middle-class lifestyle like those portrayed in Salus advertisements.

After 1945, when the company began to cultivate an empowered working class, one of the main ways that Salus's advertising had distanced the brand from Argentina's rural past was by modernizing the Salus emblem—the Salus criollita. The text in Salus advertisements no longer referred to her as "criollita," and even the term *paisanita* (fellow countrywoman) disappeared. These shifting depictions of this figure in the advertisements highlight evolving ideas about women and modern society, and how these images might be used to sell yerba mate to consumers aspiring to a middle-class lifestyle. In the post-1945 period, in the few advertisements where the criollita appeared in the countryside or with a rural man, she generally seemed more like a girl from the city than a gaucho's companion. The updated version of the Salus criollita was ubiquitous in the company's advertisements between 1945 and 1955, even though her image remained the same as the pre-1945 depiction on Salus packaging. The new sanitized version was white, willowy, youthful, and attractive, a cartoonish version of the pretty woman described by Milanesio.[63] She had a new hairstyle (two long braids), manicured nails, red lipstick, and a gold bracelet. She wore an apron and looked like the modern girl-next-door. This modern criollita was the centerpiece of Salus's advertisements between 1946 and 1954. Unlike in the earlier period, where the Salus criollita mostly appeared as an emblem of the Salus brand, the modern criollita was an active participant in the advertisements. Moreover, she was smiling and having fun, in contrast to the older sedate image. The modern criollita took on the role of educator, actively teaching about Salus yerba. For example, the criollita points to the advertisement's title, "To deeper enjoy the pleasure of having mate . . . fill your mate with Salus, the only yerba packaged by pressure" (see figure 20).[64] When she offered mate, the criollita appeared as an equal to the consumers, not as a servant. In "Yerba Salus: Traveling Companion," from 1948, the modern criollita sits on a train with a couple

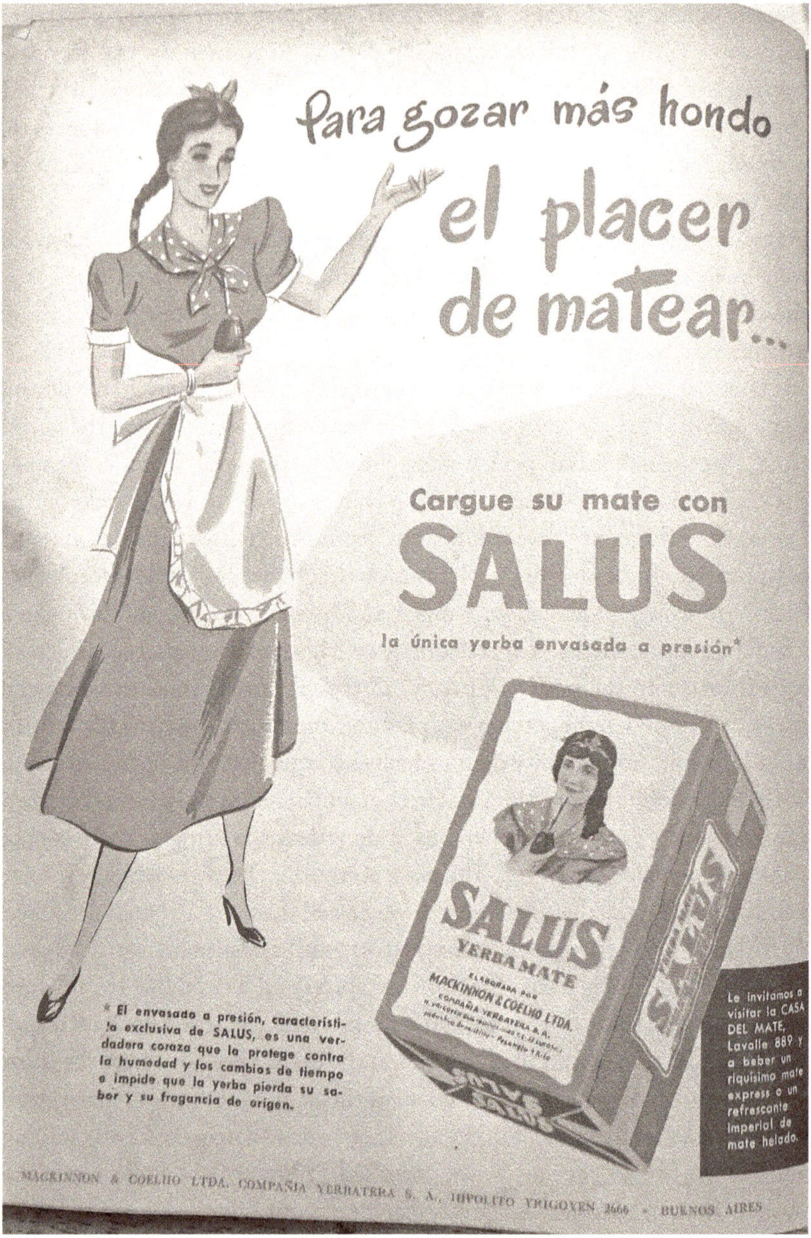

FIGURE 20. Salus advertisement, *El Gráfico,* February 15, 1952.

going on vacation while serving them mate; the text provides readers with information about how mate made vacations more enjoyable.[65]

Depictions of the criollita in Salus advertisements for yerba mate, however, continued to evolve as the decades passed and social ideologies continued to change. Indicating the importance of trends of paternalism among its audiences in the mid-1950s, the Salus paisanita disappeared entirely after 1955, with the exception of the old-style criollita on the packaging. Advertisements now showed the bodiless face of a modern woman with big eyes (most often blue or green), big jewelry, and a short hairstyle accompanied by manicured hands either offering mate holding a box of Salus. Often, the text explicitly mentioned housewives choosing mate for their families. Such advertisements clearly delineated gender roles—women as housewives serving mate and men working outside of the home. "With Salus: the dense and white froth" (1958) shows the arm of a woman extending a mate to her husband returning from work.[66] Such advertisements fit with the paternalistic ideas about family life propagated during the Perón era. Even though women gained the right to vote and more women entered both higher education and the job market in the 1940s, Argentines still thought of men as breadwinners and women as homemakers. Higher wages made it possible for married women to stay home and dedicate themselves to being wives, mothers, and homemakers. Such gendered expectations meant that Argentine women continued to engage in paid labor, but the percentage of women who identified as unpaid housewives remained constant (around 75 percent) between 1947 and 1960. In contrast, the percentage of married women who worked outside of the home in the United States doubled between 1940 and 1960.[67]

Salus's numerous full-page color advertisements in various popular magazines worked to sell the company's yerba by associating it with changes occurring in Argentine society. In doing so, the company tried to insert mate into a modern, urban, middle-class lifestyle and downplay its connection to Argentina's rural past. While Salus's expensive marketing efforts (almost one hundred different advertisements between 1944 and 1958) reached a wide audience, they had limited success. Per capita yerba mate consumption in Argentina peaked in 1948 and began a precipitous drop after 1952. This trend is especially surprising because criollo nationalism, which was closely associated with mate, experienced an upsurge under Perón.

As head of state, Perón expanded government support for criollo nationalism by funding folklore research projects, radio broadcasts, educational programs in schools, and festivals throughout the country. His first five-year plan, issued in 1947, included the assertion, "only with the cultivation of traditions will the nation be preserved," and a section of it was dedicated to culture. As a result of such measures, criollo folklore reached broad audiences.[68] Mate stood to benefit given its Indigenous origins and rural connections. Yerba mate's origin story connecting it with Ca'a Yari (the goddess of yerba) resonated with the folklore movement's interest in Indigenous myths and stories.[69] The practice of drinking mate and all of its associations also appealed to folklorists. The writer and journalist Amaro Villanueva published his first book about the popular culture surrounding mate in 1938 and his complete findings in the 1960s, and it was republished various times.[70] Between 1942 and 1950 over 50,000 copies of Luzán del Campo's *Cancionero del mate* taught readers about mate folklore.[71] Attempting to cultivate local pride and attract tourism, the Nacional Territory of Misiones officially hosted the Fiesta of Yerba Mate in 1944, one of the many national festivals begun in the 1940s, but the effort failed to take off until years later. The next festival did not occur until 1967 and it did not become a yearly event until 1972.[72] As Oscar Chamosa has shown, folklorists focused most of their efforts on northwest Argentina rather than the yerba-producing northeast.[73] Even so, criollo folklore continued to emphasize the gaucho, a figure who had long been associated with mate.

With respect to food, Perón promoted criollo cuisine such as *locro* (stew), *mazamorra* (sweet corn pudding), *humita* (savory corn pudding served like a tamale), grilled *anchuras* (offal or organ meat), and *puchero* (stew), after an initial emphasis on beef consumption.[74] In a 1949 speech inaugurating a conference on Argentine food politics organized by the Public Health Ministry, Perón explained that his administration had already solved the problem of access to food, "but the problem is still not resolved. It is not all about [getting enough to] eat; [a person] must eat well."[75] Such thinking not only fit with the Peronist emphasis on providing workers with a dignified life, it was also in line with growing international interest in vitamins, nutrition, and proper diet.[76] In his speech, Perón promoted the consumption of "protective foods" (*alimentos protectors)* with vitamins and minerals, and praised criollo cuisine. Strikingly, even though yerba mate had long been thought to provide critical vitamins and minerals as part of the traditional criollo diet of beef, hardtack, mate, and no vegetables, Perón did not mention the substance, nor did most of the presenters at the conference.[77] Such an omission points to Perón's ambivalence towards mate, and in particular, its problematic associations with a substandard diet and poverty.

Perón paid slightly more attention to yerba mate when the country experienced an economic downturn. In 1952, Perón released a second five-year plan that emphasized developing agriculture, but it only briefly mentioned assistance to small- and medium-sized yerba producers and an expansion of the nation's yerba production.[78] Elsewhere, Perón referenced cocido, but not mate, as a cost-cutting measure during hard times. He stopped entertaining visitors to the presidential office with imported coffee or whisky and instead offered them cocido.[79] In radio transmissions, Perón frequently used the analogy of offering cocido to ambassadors instead of imported coffee as a simple way to explain to the general public how to stabilize the economy.[80] Perón admitted to regularly drinking coffee and cocido depending on the circumstances.[81] In contrast, he did not mention mate. Neither Perón nor Evita can be seen in photographs with mate, even though it was the beverage of the workers and common people who they claimed to represent.[82] Despite the noticeable lack of imagery showing Perón with mate, one member of a meat-packer's union remembered that when Perón met with the delegates informally, he shared mate and talked with them in their language. As she recounted, this interaction made her feel that "[Perón] was very criollo."[83] And yet, again, even though many photographs show Perón and Evita in informal settings, none depict them drinking mate.

Perón was not the only major Argentine figure who drew heavily on criollo culture, but did not drink mate (at least where he could be photographed). Jorge Luis Borges, Argentina's most famous author, recognized yerba mate as one of the three things that defined Argentine identity (the others were a guitar and metaphysics), and yet he also admitted that he himself was not a big fan of mate.[84] In a 1968 interview, Borges acknowledged, "I've not tasted mate for forty years. At one time I used to drink it and was proud of my addiction. . . . After the death of my grandfather, who was a mate drinker, we gave it up."[85] Like Borges, many Argentines reduced their yerba mate consumption or gave up the practice altogether during the mid-twentieth century.

DECLINING CONSUMPTION

On average, Argentines consumed less and less yerba mate after mid-century. Consumption peaked in 1948 at over 8 kilos per person per year, and most definitively declined after 1952, a trend that continued until the late 1980s when consumption fluctuated at around 5 kilos per person per year. In sum, between 1948 and 1984, per capita yerba mate consumption declined an average of 40 percent.[86] Similarly, tea consumption declined in Britain beginning in the late 1950s. British consumers saw tea as dull and outdated and were attracted instead to coffee and soft drinks, which they thought of exciting and modern.[87] A similar dynamic seems to have been at work in Argentina. The decline in yerba mate consumption is especially striking when compared to that of wine, which grew during the 1940s and 50s and boomed in the following two decades. Argentines consumed an average of 55 liters of wine per capita in the mid-1940s, and when consumption peaked in 1977, the people of Buenos Aires drank an average of 99 liters, making it one of the world's biggest wine-drinking cities.[88] Why did per capita wine consumption almost double in Argentina while yerba mate consumption declined by about 40 percent? As a criollo custom and the drink of the people who Perón had empowered, mate consumption should have increased. The answers can be found in the other associations Argentines made with mate.

Despite Salus's efforts to portray mate as a modern beverage suited to an urban middle-class lifestyle, mate continued to be associated with poverty and the countryside, and the social markers associated with yerba mate failed to bridge the urban and the rural, the traditional and the modern. Mate had long been culturally connected to poverty, and this association did not go away. In his 1933 book *X-Ray of the Pampa,* which won Argentina's National Prize for Literature, Ezequiel Martínez Estrada wrote, "Those poor of the countryside, that live on mate and biscuits, procreate poverty." As for the yerba-producing region of Misiones, Martínez Estrada wrote, "entire populations never taste meat; the children are raised on manioc, oranges and mate; three quarters of the population is illiterate; the percentage of men exempted from military service for thoracic deficiencies or endemic diseases . . . is frightful."[89] This association between mate and poverty was described in mainstream films. For example, the 1938 film *La Rubia del Camino* highlighted mate as a custom of the working class and not the elite. The film shows the rich as being out of touch with popular culture; the working-class male protagonist has to teach the wealthy, spoiled female protagonist how to drink mate.[90] Tango songs also associated mate with poverty. "Yira . . . yira," a popular song recorded by Carlos Gardel in 1930, proclaimed,

> when you have nothing, not even faith
> nor yesterday's yerba mate drying in the sun;

when you wear out your shoes searching for those few coins
so that you can get a little to eat.[91]

A little over a decade later, the lyrics of another popular tango song, "Three corners," remembered a humble neighborhood as a place "where we drink mate beneath the shade of the vines."[92] In an interview years later, that song's composer described it as a postcard depicting a neighborhood of a bygone era.[93]

Unlike mate, the tango moved beyond its urban lower-class roots to become part of broader Argentine culture. Upper- and middle-class Argentines initially disdained the tango because of its origins among the lower class and prostitutes, but after it became popular among Europeans and North Americans, tango promoters made it more palatable to upper- and middle-class Argentines by sanitizing the lyrics and moving the tango out of the bordellos. By the 1930s, lyricists wrote more universal tangos that were less rooted in the world of the poor, and in 1944, the government passed legislation to censor lyrics in an effort to avoid corrupting public morals. Such changes intensified under Perón, who believed that themes of hunger, poverty, and prostitution were no longer relevant to the new Argentina.[94] By distancing itself from such negative associations, tango took on a larger role in Argentine culture, not only bridging the countryside and the city, but also connecting the traditional and the modern.

In contrast, Peronists continued to associate mate with poverty. In highlighting how the Perón administration helped people in the countryside, a pre-1952 poster showed a humble old man of the countryside drinking mate with a nice country home in the distant background and the text, "You deserve a tranquil old age. Become [the] owner of the countryside that you work. The government will give you what you need."[95] The image associated mate with an old-fashioned, impoverished way of life that contrasted with the modern, prosperous future shown in the distance. The marketing of yerba mate as an inexpensive product further reinforced such ideas. An article about yerba mate published by the *Journal of the Economic Science* in 1951 emphasized the product's affordability by concluding with the claim, "the consumer will always have within his reach the pseudo nutritious, healthy, agreeable, and economic product."[96] Such perceptions conflicted with the Peronist vision of modern Argentina.

While Perón celebrated the poor as the true Argentines, he emphasized upward mobility.[97] Mate was caught in between. By remaining associated with poverty, mate did not fit with the goal of upward mobility. It also conflicted with modernity, hygiene, and efficiency. Mate had long been considered a way to pass the time and was often associated with laziness. For example, Pedro Aulino's short story "Slacker" (*Haragán*), published in *Caras y Caretas* in 1930, provided the following introduction to the protagonist: "Ciriaco was a great slacker. His principal pleasure was drinking mate and sleeping on a cot." Lying on his cot, "Ciriaco would call one of the children and have him serve him mate until he fell asleep."[98] Years later, in his 1968 interview, Borges also associated mate with laziness. "I think they see it as a way of passing time, like cards. It's a form of idleness, not of nourishment."[99]

While Argentina's blue-collar workers found that mate did not fit with the idealized middle-class life to which they aspired, the country's white-collar workers also abandoned mate in their desperate attempts to differentiate themselves from blue-collar workers. Along with the elite, Argentine professionals, office workers, and business owners were affronted that blue-collar workers had entered, as citizens and consumers, public spaces that had heretofore been limited to the upper and middle sector of the population. The workers went shopping, saw the movies, frequented restaurants, and took vacations in greater numbers. For example, the average number of monthly ticket sales for Buenos Aires movie theatres more than tripled between January 1940 and 1952, from approximately 1.6 million to almost 4.9 million, spurring high-class ladies to complain about working-class viewers patronizing downtown theatres.[100] Likewise, Argentine elites saw their seaside resort of Mar de Plata flooded with working-class vacationers as the number of tourists jumped from 380,000 to 1.4 million between 1940 and 1955.[101] Blue-collar workers not only entered spaces that Argentina's elite and white-collar populations had previously monopolized, but the greater buying power of blue-collar workers enabled them to dress, consume, and look like their social superiors.

The blurring of social difference disturbed the upper and middle sectors of Argentine society who wanted to distinguish themselves from workers and immigrants from the country's interior.[102] The middle class felt especially threatened because of its own short history. Until the 1930s, the term "middle class" was not commonly used in Argentina, and a shared common identity distinct from upper class aspirations only developed in the 1940s as a response to Peronism.[103] In response to their anxiety about social leveling, members of the middle class tried hard to find ways to distinguish themselves from the common people. They looked for markers of quality and paid attention to detail.[104] In doing so, they spurned mate due to its association with poverty, laziness, and the common people.

Mate's negative associations mounted and per capita consumption further declined over the following decades. A 1977 study commissioned by the province of Misiones described yerba mate an "inferior good." Based on economic data from the previous thirty years, the authors found that Argentines purchased less yerba mate when incomes rose, and that consumption only increased when coffee or tea prices increased relative to the price of yerba mate. In other words, Argentines preferred both coffee and tea to yerba mate, but they turned to it during times of financial hardship.[105] Two cartoons from the 1960s and 1970s shed light on public opinion about mate. Tellingly, *Mafalda,* a very popular comic strip from the 1960s and 1970s that portrayed urban middle-class life, never showed mate consumption. But in the 1965 comic mentioned at the beginning of the chapter, Mafalda asked her friend Felipe if his family drank mate. It was not an innocuous question. Felipe was insulted and he beat up Mafalda. When Felipe angrily told her that the president drank mate, Mafalda was not impressed.[106] In his cartoons, Quino portrayed president Arturo Umberto Illia in a negative light and as inefficient.[107] This particular episode reinforced this idea, and confirms that mate did not have a positive image among Argentina's urban middle class.

In the 1970s, Roberto Fontonarrosa's satirical comic strip *Inodoro Pereyra,* about a gaucho in the pampas, reinforced similar ideas in its references to mate. One cartoon from 1978 makes fun of modern, urban Argentines for disdaining mate consumed in the interior of the country. When Superman (a man who says he's from Metropolis, but who Inodoro's dog calls a *porteño* from Buenos Aires) finds himself not feeling well after visiting Córdoba, Inodoro offers him some mate. Superman is convinced that the mate contains the debilitating substance kryptonite. "That! That must have been it! I had that in Córdoba, and now I see what it has inside: KRYPTONITE!"[108] Ironically, Superman believes mate causes a loss of energy even though mate's caffeine content makes it a stimulant. For Superman, thought to be a *porteño* by Pereyra's dog, mate is like poison and something to be avoided at all costs. These and other depictions reveal that even though mate continued to be part of criollo culture, and was drunk by many Argentines, especially blue-collar workers and people in the countryside, it was increasingly marginalized among urbanites between the 1950s and 1980s.

This decline was a sad fate for yerba mate in Argentina. Despite having been a central custom in Argentina and the region for hundreds of years, modern trends of speed, efficiency, and individualism pushed the beverage out of fashion, largely due to its historical associations with rural and impoverished populations. The higher wages and more social provisions that arrived under Perón had improved workers' standard of living and promoted working-class identity, and this empowerment pushed them to abandon cultural practices not associated with the vision of Argentina as a modern nation of middle-class consumers. The persisting association of mate with poverty and backwardness put it in conflict with such a vision. Although mate had long been associated with workers and was widely considered a basic foodstuff, mate consumption fell during the 1950s, and continued to decline all the way to the 1980s. Yerba companies and others tried unsuccessfully to modernize yerba mate, reshaping perceptions of mate to fit with ideas about a middle-class lifestyle. But those who did drink yerba mate continued to do so in the traditional way, as a shared beverage, and mate retained its longstanding associations with penury, poor hygiene, and laziness. The failure of yerba mate to evolve suggests that the country's ethos of modernity turned Argentines off yerba mate. It also illustrates how Argentina's criollo culture was sanitized during the shift to that ethos of modernity. But this decline of yerba was not a permanent one, and, as the next chapter discusses, Argentina's recurring economic problems and the loss of the middle class would eventually lead to mate's remarkable resurgence.

NINE

The Rebirth of Mate with Democracy, Economic Crisis, and Globalization

IN ITS NOVEMBER/DECEMBER 1989 ISSUE, *NACLA Report on the Americas,* a quarterly magazine with articles providing information and analysis from activists, journalists, and scholars, published an article about Argentina's new president, Carlos Menem, that included a photo of Menem drinking mate and the remarkable caption: "Menem drinks *mate:* A regular guy." The article described Menem's efforts to be seen as a "people's candidate." As one voter quoted in the article explained, people saw him as "The person in the street, who understands his fellows, who drinks mate."[1]

This depiction was remarkable because Menem was hardly a "regular guy." Born in La Rioja province to a Muslim family from Syria, Menem became active in Peronist politics and converted to Catholicism in his youth. In 1973, he was elected governor of La Rioja, but was deposed during the 1976 coup that brought the military to power. He was then imprisoned for two years for corruption and links with guerrilla movements. With the return to democracy Menem was again elected governor of La Rioja. Tanned and frequently sporting bushy sideburns, Menem was a bon vivant who, as president, regularly appeared in gossip columns with models, Formula One drivers, and other celebrities, and with his flashy, red Ferrari.

But in 1989 Menem was running for president on an anti-elitist, populist platform, and he carefully crafted an image as someone who understood ordinary people—a regular guy, albeit much wealthier. By this time, drinking mate, with its rural and working-class roots, was once again becoming a symbol of patriotic pride in Argentina, and Menem sought to exploit this symbolism to gain votes. His carefully crafted image was successful: Carlos Menem won the election by a wide margin (47 percent of the popular vote in a nine-way race).

Menem's effort to use mate as a marketing tool to win a presidential election highlighted a notable comeback for mate in Argentina in the final decades of the twentieth century. As the prior chapter discussed, mate began a long decline as a cultural practice in Argentina back in the 1950s, a decline that continued well into the 1980s. This chapter looks in more detail at how this decline unfolded, explaining how drinking mate continued to be largely seen as old-fashioned and taboo in the 1950s, 1960s, and 1970s, before finally making a resurgence in the 1980s and 90s, right at the time when Carlos Menem was running for office in the 1989 presidential election. In the end, the story of mate's resurgence at this time is one that, like so often before with yerba mate in Argentina, is closely intertwined with Argentina's ongoing and often dramatic political and economic changes.

From the 1950s until the 1980s, Argentina went through several decades of rapid cultural, economic, and political change. These changes crossed over all economic sectors and social classes, and they altered daily life and culture in Argentina in profound ways. Major cultural changes during the 1960s and 1970s were driven by the arrival of American music and new media, leading to new forms of youth culture and countercultural movements. At the same time, major political changes were about to occur. In the 1970s, a repressive military dictatorship took over the country, leading to a chaotic and violent period that eventually gave way to a democratic transition in the 1980s. But during the economic turmoil that accompanied this transition back to democratic rule, hyperinflation devastated the country's economy, driving more than 50 percent of the country into poverty. As this poverty spread, the country's elected leaders instituted vast free market reforms during the 1990s in an effort to stabilize and reinvigorate the economy.

During these tumultuous and dramatic decades in Argentina, the consumption and production of yerba mate also went through major changes. Increasingly marginalized culturally during the years of Peron's rule, yerba mate was further ignored by most of the youth culture movements in the 1960s, and its reputation as an old-fashioned beverage endured. The resulting decline in yerba mate consumption continued all the way through the military dictatorship in the 1970s and into the 1980s. But mate's popularity would start to make a comeback in the years ahead. As hyperinflation drove down incomes, people stopped buying coffee and tea, and instead bought more yerba mate. Similar to the way that, during the economic depression in Japan after World War II, people turned to inexpensive foodstuffs like ramen, mate consumption grew in Argentina during these years because it was an inexpensive staple at a time when the population was suffering serious economic hardship.[2] Furthermore, as poverty spread, mate regained a cultural importance beyond simply being a necessary foodstuff in people's diets. The social aspect of mate consumption contributed to its resurging popularity. Both mate's rising popularity and its persistence over the years was also due to the fact that common, ordinary people embraced it and integrated it into their lives. This association with the "common people" and "regular guy," as Carlos Menem tried to present himself to voters, played an important role in mate's newest wave of popularity, and during the bourgeoning economic crises in the 1980s, mate become a symbol of the Argentine people's resilience and suffering during a period of national crisis, gaining new political and cultural cache.

Yerba's dramatic return to popularity during this period of economic hardship would ultimately set the stage for its newest transformation in the 1990s during the free market economic era, as an authentic beverage of choice. It was a remarkable comeback for mate. After several decades of being denigrated as an out-of-date, antiquated symbol of Argentine identity, mate would become an idealized and performative marker of Argentine cultural identity as the country entered an era of globalization at the turn of the twenty-first century.

ROCK N' ROLL, YOUTH CULTURE, AND MATE ON THE DECLINE: 1950–1970S

Beginning in the late 1950s, after Perón's overthrow, young people in Argentina increasingly identified with the modern, international youth scene. Rock music from the United States initially drove the movement, but Argentine musicians soon made their own songs in Spanish. Rock music was a cultural and social practice; Argentine youth gathered to listen and dance together as part of a broader generational shift. In contrast to tango, now considered outdated and associated with the urban working class, rock music epitomized Argentine youth, cutting across social classes and gender lines.[3] Similarly, blue jeans also became a marker of Argentine youth culture, even though class distinctions remained. Both rock and blue jeans united Argentine youth by setting them apart from older generations and cultivating a sense of belonging and participation in international youth culture.[4]

Within this flourishing youth culture, drinking mate was largely seen as boring and outdated. Although there were a few left-wing subcultures that maintained interest in mate at this time, the growing youth culture did not generally embrace yerba mate. There were some notable efforts to try to reinvigorate mate consumption, although they generally failed. During the 1960s and early 1970s, for example, the yerba sector and its government allies initiated a marketing campaign to target younger customers. In 1970, a large-scale marketing project called the "National Mate Campaign" released a forty-second television commercial that featured happy and energetic urban youth. The video begins with the pouring of mate and a young blonde man dressed in a suit energetically breaking into song: "What swing mate gives me!" (*Ah . . . Qué swing que me da el mate!*) As the catchy lyrics play in the background, an assortment of young couples joyfully share mate in different middle-class settings. The commercial ends with "Where there is mate, there is love!"[5]

Soon thereafter, the Ad Council for Yerba Mate Consumption, a branch of the Agriculture Ministry joined with the Ministry of Education to host a national student essay competition focused on yerba mate. The campaign culminated in celebrations attended by the student writers and their families, government officials, and representatives of the media in both Iguazú, Misiones, and Buenos Aires. A full-page *La Nación* article titled "Mate Conquers the Youth" described the campaign and published the winning essay. Despite the ad council's goal of increasing interest in mate among Argentine youth, the winning essay nevertheless revealed that the yerba sector still had a long way to go toward modernizing and popularizing yerba mate among this population. Written by a fifth-year student at a Catholic high school in the posh Buenos Aires neighborhood of Belgrano, the essay, titled "I am yerba mate," focused on the past, both history and tradition. Even though the essay praised mate, it concluded on a far less optimistic note by acknowledging that mate did not fit well with a modern lifestyle: "the hectic existence of today, the crazy rhythm of modern life that unfortunately does not leave much time for the warmhearted leisure of hospitality." And the narrator, playing the role of mate, implored the reader, "do not leave me, youth."[6]

As this essay reveals, at this time, mate was still heavily mired in associations with tradition that did not fit well with the mid-century youth culture that was exploding in Argentina—rock music, blue jeans, international social movements. Back in the 1950s, the American musician Bill Haley had traveled to Argentina and posed with a poncho while drinking mate. This photo marked Haley as a foreigner and an outsider trying to fit into local culture.[7] In contrast, the Argentine rockers of the 1960s looked like Western

European or American rock stars. Their fans met in bars or cafes and drank alcohol or coffee, not mate. Similarly, Argentine hippies—also part of the broader youth and countercultural movements emerging at this time—tried to be more like hippies in the United States than to be uniquely Argentine. In 1967, the popular Argentine journalist José de Zer spent forty-eight hours with hippies in Buenos Aires and wrote about how their appearances, actions, and attitudes broke Argentine societal norms. The journalist described how the hippies hung out for hours on end, sharing cigarettes and food while chatting and singing. This social environment was the perfect setting for sharing mate, so its absence is striking.[8] The drink was old-fashioned and not part of the modern international youth scene. Indeed, a number of left-wing activists and intellectuals complained that clothing firms and imperialist propaganda had hijacked the hippie movement in Argentina so that it was more about ambiance than anti-consumerism and political activism.[9]

Although the major youth movements in the 1960s did not embrace mate, yerba mate did continue to appeal to a subset of social reformers and leftist activists. Concerns about persistent poverty and inequality spurred people throughout Latin America to get involved with on-the-ground efforts to affect change in the late 1960s. Especially influenced by Catholic liberation theology, they worked in solidarity with the poor. In line with the research technique of participant observation employed by anthropologists, getting to know their target population often entailed spending time sharing mate with inhabitants of urban slums and impoverished rural areas. Jose Míguez Bonino, a Methodist theologian and a major contributor to liberation theology, learned about poverty by spending time drinking mate with dock workers in their tenement houses.[10] The bishop of La Rioja, Enrique Angelelli, who was assassinated in the late 1970s because of his involvement in social issues, was remembered as having a close relationship with the poor that was epitomized by sharing mate: "He went to drink mate in the houses of the people, above all those of the poorest."[11]

Mate also played a role in the New Song Movement of protest music that developed in the 1960s. Mercedes Sosa led the New Song Movement in Argentina, and she had a large following outside of the country. In Chile, where the New Song Movement was more popular, Victor Jara became one of the most famous victims of Pinochet's brutal regime after singing protest music in the soccer stadium where he was interrogated, tortured, and executed with thousands of others. Both Jara and fellow Chilean Violeta Parra sang about drinking mate as part of daily life. For example, in the song "La

Cocinerita" ("The Little Cook") Jara answers his own question "where is my little cook? Ah, [she] is drinking mate." Likewise, in the song *"El Ají Ma'uro"* ("The Ripe Chili"), Parra compares life to the spicy chili pepper and asks her listeners to bring yerba: "I'm going to make mate for my grandmother."

Many of the Argentine leftists who drank mate in their cultural circles were part of the groups who were later persecuted during military rule (1976–1983) and killed or driven underground or into exile. The Argentine-Mexican guitarist Alejandro Marcovich remembered that he and other leftist youth "obviously" packed yerba mate for a camping excursion in 1975. They drank mate cocido while singing protest songs around the fire. Marcovich was fifteen and on the verge of entering the youth section of the Communist Party. Less than a year later, just days after the military coup, Marcovich and his family fled Argentina for exile in Mexico.[12] Under the guise of the Cold War, the military dictatorship tortured and disappeared tens of thousands of social reformers, leftist activists, and others. In Misiones and Corrientes, a number of yerba growers and workers were imprisoned, tortured, and disappeared for their efforts at organizing and demanding higher prices and better pay.[13] In response to such flagrant human rights abuses, many leftist yerba drinkers fled the country and those who remained lived in fear.

Mate's decline continued into the 1980s under military rule, and perceptions of mate as an out-of-fashion cultural practice did not change. When *La Nación* investigated what seven well-known Argentine authors thought about yerba mate in 1981, it found that all were familiar with mate, but only one of the seven (Gregorio Weinberg) drank it regularly. Three (Jorge Luis Borges, Silvina Bullrich, and Ernesto Sabato) had drunk a lot of it when they were younger, but were no longer in the habit. Most of the authors described specific times or settings when they drank mate, further confirming that it was not a part of their regular daily routine. Several associated mate with the countryside and nostalgia. As the writer Bernardo Kordon said, "The truth is that mate is the national drink that the Argentine cultivates outside of the country, like tango."[14]

Two years earlier, in 1979, a correspondent for the same newspaper had written a two-part article about the future of yerba mate, which was apparently bleak. An avid mate drinker himself, Santiago Ferrari expressed serious concern about its future. "I am a drinker of unsweetened yerba mate with a bombilla and I never will see mate cocido as true mate. Still, I think that the economic future of yerba is in mate cocido." To further investigate the matter, Ferrari interviewed Adolfo Navajas Artaza, the head of one of the country's largest yerba operations (Las Marías). Navajas Artaza admitted that "mate with the bombilla loses ground in the country as it did some time ago in parts of Brazil and Chile. There are those that say, with pessimism, that within a generation, mate won't be drunk in Argentina." As the article pointed out, "even the mate-drinker in the countryside, accustomed to drinking mate in all of the huts (*ranchos*), can feel a little resistance to sharing the bombilla with a stranger." Navajas Artaza was also pessimistic about mate's future; he predicted that it would only continue as an individual practice, or perhaps be shared among married couples.[15]

During these years, official governmental reports repeatedly concluded that Argentine consumers preferred coffee and tea to yerba mate. A 1976 report by the government of Misiones predicted a long-term decline in per capita consumption because when "the population earns higher incomes, people replace yerba with other products (coffee, tea, etc.)" and "when the price of coffee and tea falls, less yerba is consumed."[16] A year later, the government published a more extensive report. This time the report clarified that yerba mate exhibited the characteristics of an inferior good: the economic term for a product whose sales increase, in contrast to normal goods, when people's incomes fall. The report attributed such atypical behavior to Argentines' preference for both coffee and tea over yerba mate, all of which were substitutes for each other. It concluded that "the tendency of per capita consumption of yerba mate is declining, and it only increased when the prices of coffee and tea rose."[17]

Yerba companies responded to such preferences by marketing yerba mate products like coffee. In 1977, Navajas Artaza's company launched a number of television commercials that showed how Taragüi brand yerba mate could be brewed in a filter and drunk like a cup of coffee. In the same year, the Salus brand launched instant yerba mate that would also be drunk like Nescafe, backed by a strong publicity campaign in radio, television, and print media. Just like in the 1930s-40s, such marketing efforts had limited results as consumers continued to consume yerba mate primarily from a bombilla and gourd. Although yerba mate's decline was sustained across many decades, among the rural communities outside of the urban centers and far from the youth cultural movements, mate continued to maintain an important place within many people's lives. Moreover, mate remained fixed in the broader population's imagination across social classes as a historical Argentine cultural practice rooted in the country's national myths. Although this did not necessarily help its popularity during the mid-century era, the economic turmoil in the years ahead spread poverty around the country and the association with the country's heritage would eventually help set the stage for mate's resurgence.

Lasting from 1976 until 1983 when Raúl Alfonsín was elected president, the military dictatorships in Argentina oversaw a period of repression and violence that left enduring trauma throughout the country. The return to democracy was a major moment in Argentina's history, and it quickly shifted every political calculation across the country. It was also a period in Argentina when new economic ideas were coming to the fore, and debates about future liberalization of the economy intensified. Although neoliberal economic ideas would eventually become national policy, in the early 1980s, as Argentines moved to embrace democracy, there was still a strong belief in an interventionist state that could direct the economy and mediate the free market.[18] One of the best illustrations of this was in the yerba mate sector where, since the 1930s, the Comisión Reguladora de la Yerba Mate had set prices, planting strategies, and harvest protocols, all in an effort to mediate cyclical extremes of oversupply and shortages. The CRYM also advanced credit to help small and medium sized growers, and for decades was considered a crucial aspect of the yerba economy. After the transition back to democracy in 1983, when Argentina's economy was in tatters, yerba growers turned to the CRYM to help them stabilize financially. This effort, however, failed miserably, and the failure would turn out to be an important reason why many former beneficiaries of government regulation generally accepted, and even embraced, the neoliberal reforms of the 1990s.

In the months following the end of military dictatorship and Raúl Alfonsín's election, economic duress continued to spread throughout Argentina. Over the previous three years, GDP per capita had fallen by almost 10 percent.[19] Like most sectors, yerba mate was struggling. Yerba growers complained about low prices and yerba processors worried about a raw material shortage. People felt that the CRYM should do something to secure the yerba market. But at the same time, almost everyone agreed that the agency also needed significant reform. Many of the debates surrounding how best to do this, coming on the heels of the brutal dictatorship, centered on ideas about equality and inclusion, and regularly employed rhetoric about democracy and representation. It was a collision between older ideas about the importance of government intervention to protect less powerful market actors, and increasingly popular ideas that suggested things would be best if the market was left to fend for itself.

Small- and medium-sized growers, urging intervention, believed that a few big industrial companies dominated the sector. They pointed out that only four companies processed, marketed, and sold over half of all yerba consumed in Argentina. Moreover, all four were based in Buenos Aires or Rosario rather than in the yerba-producing region of Misiones and Corrientes.[20] As part of their argument for reform and intervention, small- and medium-sized growers argued that even though they had an equal number of representatives on the CRYM's governing board as the large industrial processing companies, those large industrial companies had formed a bloc to effectively promote their shared interests, while smaller growers remained disorganized. As one informant described,

> A grower told me that he went to the CRYM meeting from his farm, all sweaty and driving an old cart (*catafalco*), and he ran into four men from Buenos Aires, who had arrived the night before and slept in hotels. They ate dinner together, conversed, established strategies, and when they arrived refreshed in the morning (because they had gotten up at eight, while he had [woken up] at five to come from where he came), they gave him shit. He didn't have any opportunity, furthermore, five minutes before, to meet with the others to know what to do. The other guys came as a body, they also conversed with the official that came from Buenos Aires. That was the reality of the CRYM. They were growers without any preparation, without strategies, against professionals with great economic and political power who already had everything negotiated.[21]

The disgruntled growers who felt left out made up a sizeable portion of Misiones' voting population. In proposing legislation to reform the CRYM, Peronist politicians highlighted that there were 13,000 yerba growers and that over half of them had small plots with ten or fewer hectares.[22] Both the ruling Radical Party and the opposition Justicialista Party (the Peronist Party) called for reforming the CRYM, but they disagreed about how to do so. The large processors, however, were strongly against any of these groups' suggested reforms, as they believed doing so would reduce their profits and regulatory influence.

At this time, however, the government of Misiones was dominated by the ruling Radical Party, and, as a result, it was the reforms proposed by that party that carried the day. The government went ahead and asked president Alfonsín to order a government takeover of the CRYM and to name a controller (*interventor*) to replace the governing board and oversee the entity until formal legislation reformed the CRYM. Such action entailed a deepening of the interventionist state. By taking over the CRYM, the government assumed direct oversight of the yerba sector. Radical deputies justified this plan based on democratic principles. As one explained, the CRYM's governing board "does not defend the interests that the citizens of Misiones voted for on October 30," the date of the elections that marked Argentina's return to democracy, "for a democracy in defense of public interest over sectorial interests."[23] The Radical Party used the rhetoric of democracy and representation to call for government intervention in the CRYM because doing so would ostensibly benefit small- and medium-sized growers.[24]

Opponents of government intervention claimed the opposite. For them, a government takeover was inherently undemocratic. In congressional proceedings, a Justicialista deputy argued, "The intervention of the CRYM would be the return of procedures that we thought eradicated with the disappearance of the military dictatorship." A government takeover was undemocratic because it sidestepped "established constitutional procedures, through the modification of law."[25] Ironically, calls for government intervention in the CRYM came just months after the Alfonsín administration ended prolonged government intervention in the wine regulatory board as a result of pressure to normalize the institution after the return to democracy.[26]

Despite opposition from the Peronist Party and large yerba companies, Alfonsín and Economic Minister Bernardo Grinspun ordered a government takeover of the CRYM and named Misiones's Minister of Agricultural Affairs (José Oswald) as controller on August 29, 1984. Intended as a short-term measure to give greater representation to small- and medium-sized growers and processors in Misiones and Corrientes, the government takeover made the CRYM less democratic in practice by removing all representatives from the governing board. Instead, all decision-making power resided in the hands of a single government official for almost four years.

A little under two years into the intervention, the government of Misiones announced a highly controversial plan to give itself an even bigger role in managing the yerba economy. The CRYM already regulated new plantings, decided on harvest dates, and set the price for dried yerba. In the past, through its subsidiary, the Mercado Consignatario (MC), the agency had also acted as an intermediary for yerba growers by acquiring and paying an advance for their dried yerba and then selling it to processing companies when the price was good. Under the new plan, however, the government of Misiones decided to take things further. If it had been successful, this move would have had a radical impact on the yerba sector, expanding government intervention into the processing, marketing, and selling of yerba mate through the creation of its own brand, Ñande Yerba. No longer would government involvement in the yerba economy be limited to establishing regulations and acting as an intermediary between growers and processers. Now, government intervention would extend vertically, from buying the raw material to selling the finished product. The Misiones government promoted the plan as benefiting consumers, growers, and small processers by disrupting the unequal oligopolistic yerba market. Governor Barrios Arrechea asserted that insufficient financial, marketing, and management capabilities prevented small brands from entering the market. He claimed that by processing and selling yerba on their behalf, the government would help growers and small processers create a brand that could compete in the national market, leading to higher profits for small producers and better quality for consumers.[27] In doing so, the government would initially compete directly with private yerba companies, but once well established, the government planned to cede operations to an organization of small processers.

The yerba industry quickly and vehemently spoke out against the plan. The Federation of Yerba Processors got the national press to write about its opposition to Ñande Yerba well before covering the government's side of the story. In contrast to earlier debates about government intervention in the CRYM, opposition to Ñande Yerba did not focus on democracy. Rather, the Federation of Yerba Processors emphasized that Ñande Yerba contradicted the country's recent push for a neoliberal economic strategy, asserting that the initiative "clearly is in contrast to the thinking of the President of the Nation" regarding the reduction of state intervention in activities better done by the private sector.[28] The federation claimed that the plan was a "statist adventure" that ran counter to the national politics of privatizing the economy.[29] A plethora of newspaper articles ensued over the following months, with the country's main newspapers providing mostly negative coverage. As an editorial in *La Nación* concluded, "The new project for state-run business is the reiteration of a vision for the State that has long proven its inefficiency and its contradiction with the spirit of the Magna Carta, in addition to being in conflict with the privatizing intentions outlined on more than one occasion by the presidency."[30]

Ñande Yerba was doomed from the start. The government of Misiones did not have the money, and the national government would not provide the necessary financing. In sum, the economic model of an interventionist state did not fit with the changing times. The country had immense financial problems at that time and was struggling with high levels of foreign debt. These problems were systemic and vast; Argentina's economy contracted for five of the ten years of the 1980s.[31] In addition to revenue problems, Argentina had limited access to credit. Ever since Mexico had declared a moratorium on its debt in 1982, the International Monetary Fund (IMF) and commercial banks had made new loans to developing countries contingent on austerity measures that cut government spending. While Alfonsín and his economic team resisted such neoliberal reforms as long as they could, his government tepidly applied austerity measures in the second half of the 1980s. Hence, they could not provide enough funding for the MC to acquire dried yerba from small- and medium-sized producers.

Without this funding, the Misiones government's broader reform efforts for the yerba sector fell apart. By 1986, the MC not only had very little money for purchasing dried yerba, it had also accumulated significant debt from previous yerba purchases. In August 1986, newspaper articles estimated the debt at 5 to 6 million *australes* (5.8 to 7 million dollars).[32] Several months later, Governor Barrios Arrechea asked the president of the Central Bank to give the MC 8 million dollars. In doing so, Barrios Arrechea acknowledged, "it is shameful what happened in 1986. It is the first time that [the MC] almost did not acquire the product."[33] In that year, the MC acquired only 8.1 million kilos of dried yerba (6 percent of the total amount produced in 1986), and as a result, Ñande Yerba lacked the necessary raw material. By the end of that year, the government of Misiones gave up on Ñande Yerba and transferred it to the Federation of Agricultural Cooperatives of Misiones. But the situation just continued to worsen. In 1987, the MC purchased only .3 million kilos (less than 1 percent of all production) and estimates of its debt skyrocketed to 15 to 17 million *australes* and beyond.[34] At this point, the CRYM—the regulatory mechanism that had been in place for more than half a century—ceased to be meaningful, and the entire yerba sector was about to move into unknown territory, with many consequences for the future of yerba consumption in Argentina.

The election of the opposition Justicialista Party candidate as governor of Misiones in 1987 paved the way for the end of provincial oversight. After the elections, yerba processors stepped up their calls for the end of Misiones's intervention in the CRYM, and in May 1988, President Alfonsín signed legislation that ended the takeover, returning control to a governing board led by representatives of various government entities and delegates from entities representing yerba growers and industry.[35] The CRYM continued to exist for another couple years, but it was barely operational.[36]

Despite having pushed hard for more state intervention to protect their interests during the time that the CRYM was falling apart, growers did relatively well by selling their unprocessed yerba in the private market. There had been a decline in the supply of the raw material, and this led to higher prices for dried yerba. In early 1988, a representative of yerba processors described a spectacular price increase of 500 percent over three months.[37] Growers prospered from the higher prices. As the ex-controller of the CRYM explained, in 1983 a yerba grower could purchase a F-100 pickup truck with 55,000 kilos of dried yerba, a tractor with 31,000, and a liter of gas with 420 grams, but in December 1987, a grower could make the same purchases with only 12,800 kilos, 10,800, and 170 grams, respectively.[38] Several months later, a journalist reported, using racially insensitive language, that after four years the yerba economy of Misiones was doing well. "The gypsies, the traditional vehicle salesmen, have invaded Misiones. Car dealerships and stores that sell tractors and equipment for yerba work have become active again after having been forgotten."[39]

While the yerba sector benefited from higher yerba prices, consumers suffered by having to pay more for their yerba. An influential journalist of Argentine agribusiness reported that the price of yerba mate had jumped from 3.5 *australes* per kilo in October 1987 to over 20 *australes* in April 1988.[40] This equated to a monthly growth rate of over 34 percent, significantly higher than the monthly inflation rate of between 3 and 20 percent.[41] Soon, though, the country exploded into hyperinflation. The Austral Plan, instituted in 1985, had brought inflation under control for a couple of years, but it did not last. Between March 1989 and March 1990, prices increased by an unfathomable 20,000 percent. Inflation accelerated even more over the next year, reaching record levels.[42]

Inflation had a devasting impact on the country's already teetering economy, helping drive more than 50 percent of the country's population into poverty. In an effort to mediate the impact of inflation on the poor, the government instituted price controls on the various basic necessities that formed the official market basket of goods necessary for a family (known as the *"canasta familiar"*). Within this *canasta familiar,* government officials included yerba mate as a basic need for a family, a decision that hearkened back to prior arguments in the nineteenth and early twentieth centuries that had framed yerba mate as a core part of Argentine diet and culture. Although these fixed prices helped more people buy yerba mate, they also hurt yerba growers' profits. Newspapers articles described how the price set by the government did not cover production costs and the yerba sector repeatedly requested that yerba mate be removed from the *canasta familiar* so that they could receive a higher price for their yerba.[43] But the government maintained its perspective that yerba mate was a fundamental part of the Argentine family's diet, and did not remove the yerba from the list.

Despite their complaints, the situation was not so bad for the yerba sector. According to Juan Szychowski (owner of the yerba company *La Cachuera* and director of the body that represented the yerba-processing companies of the region), dried yerba sold for $.75 US as of December 1990, which was significantly lower than the peak of $1.30 US six months earlier, but also significantly above the historic price of $.35 US.[44] Given that the CRYM was largely ineffective and free market prices were still relatively good, growers lost confidence in the regulatory board and government oversight, and, in the years ahead, they began to produce more yerba, hoping to generate even greater profits. But in free markets, more production does not always lead to more profits, and overproduction can drive lower prices, which is what happened next. Indeed, as discussed in the rest of this chapter, the arrival of remarkably low consumer prices for yerba mate intersected with growing national unrest over surging poverty, creating an opportunity for yerba mate to suddenly re-emerge in political and popular discourse as a symbol of national unity and Argentine resilience.

IMPOVERISHMENT AND RISING YERBA CONSUMPTION IN THE 1980S

With the return to democracy in 1983, Argentines were hopeful, but suffering economically. As of 1982, over half of the population lived below the poverty line, and during one month alone (February 1983), the cost of living increased by 13 percent.[45] To win the presidential elections, Alfonsín channeled both democratic and economic concerns. He especially emphasized the goal of ending hunger in Argentina, as his popular campaign slogan made clear: "With democracy, one eats, one is educated, one is cured." While hunger was not new to rural and impoverished areas, in the early 1980s Argentines were shocked by reports that urban working-class people were going hungry. They had long thought that their country, with its industrial sector and rich agricultural and livestock production, had moved beyond such problems.[46]

Despite some periods of improvement, Alfonsín's government failed to solve hunger or resolve the country's economic problems. Between 1980 and 1990 GDP decreased by about 10 percent. Millions of people lost their jobs and could not find enough work.[47] At the same time, a growing proportion of the population worked in the informal economy, getting paid under the table.[48] Even those lucky enough to be employed in the formal sector experienced lower real wages due to inflation.[49] In greater Buenos Aires, average household income declined by 22 percent over the decade.[50] Prices were almost always increasing, and by the end of the decade, hyperinflation made life especially difficult. While sitting in front of his typewriter writing an article about hyperinflation, a journalist noted that, during the time it took him to write the article, the price of cigarettes increased from eleven to fourteen *australes*.[51] Inflation generally hurt the poor the most since they relied heavily on cash and had few assets.

When complaining about the economy, public figures highlighted the connection between yerba and poverty. To emphasize the general desperation throughout Argentina in 1980, a leader of the Peronist party asserted, "the only thing that is doing well is yerba mate, because mate cocido has become, in this stage that the country lives, the main dish in humble homes."[52] A year later, during a sermon about the problem of hunger in Argentina, the bishop of Quilmes (an industrial city close to Buenos Aires) complained that extreme poverty had turned yerba mate into a mainstay for many Argentines. "Brothers and sisters, there is hunger. Today many families get by on yerba mate and a bit of bread and crackers."[53] When describing the prevalence of malnutrition, newspaper articles explained that marginalized sectors of society only ate one meal a day (often at a soup kitchen) and for the rest of the day drank mate or mate cocido, sometimes with some bread.[54]

To address the problem of hunger head on, Alfonsín created a temporary emergency food program, the Programa Alimentario Nacional (PAN). Between 1984 and 1990, the Argentine government distributed monthly food boxes containing approximately thirty pounds of nonperishable foodstuffs such as powdered milk, cooking oil, noodles, polenta, flour, corned beef, lard, and sugar, with the goal of providing 30 percent of the monthly calorie requirement for a family of four. At its height in 1986, the PAN produced 1.3 million food boxes per month for about 5.6 million Argentines (up to 17 percent of the population).[55] Notably, PAN boxes did not include yerba mate. PAN recipients complained about its absence, and when they were surveyed, yerba mate was their most requested item.[56]

The combination of higher prices and reduced incomes in the 1980s meant that Argentines had less purchasing power. People adjusted their spending accordingly, and those living far below the poverty line found they had to reduce the money that they spent on food. An article in *Clarín* from October 1988 referred to yerba mate when describing some of these tradeoffs.

> Mate is a foodstuff that provokes habit. Thus, addiction constitutes the principal reason that assures its elimination from the daily diet will never be absolute. However, the limits on the population's purchasing power exert pressure on what is not considered essential. . . . The failure of salaries to rebound and the continued high prices at the consumer level have made it so that the population has adopted a selective criterion for purchasing foodstuffs. In this selection, yerba has passed to second place in the face of the priority that flour, milk, beef, and other basic products for survival have.[57]

The article was correct that impoverished Argentines made tough choices about their food purchases, but it overstated their de-prioritization of yerba mate. As another article in *Clarín* reported, "many inhabitants of Buenos Aires sharpen their resourcefulness in order to not abandon the tradition of mate," and as a result, numerous shops offered consumers smaller quantities of unpackaged yerba.[58] For the most desperate, PAN boxes provided some basic foodstuffs, soup kitchens served meals, and mate numbed hunger. Almost everyone went to various stores, strategically searching for deals. Recognizing this practice, major supermarkets regularly placed newspaper advertisements about special temporary price breaks on popular consumer items such as yerba mate. Unscrupulous businesses also took advantage of the situation, selling cheap yerba mate diluted with leaves from other plants.[59] Small producers felt so threatened by adulterated yerba that the Federation of Agricultural Cooperatives of Misiones officially complained to government authorities about the problem.[60]

Argentines, and especially those with less resources, prioritized yerba mate purchases because mate was a mainstay of their diet. A study of food consumption patterns in Argentina from 1974 to 1984 acknowledged the importance of yerba for the poor and coffee for the middle classes and above. In doing so, the authors took a condescending tone toward both mate and the poor, describing it as the foodstuff of the unemployed and families with very low incomes who do not have enough to eat. These people, they claimed, "'relax' in large part over mate, which has no nutritional value but is gratifying."[61] In contrast, an anthropologist who extensively studied Argentine food consumption patterns included yerba mate as one of the twenty-two food items (and the only caffeinated beverage) that made up a shared common diet for Argentines of all social classes.[62] Similarly, a nutritionist who compiled a basic diet for a family of four during hyperinflation for the newspaper *Clarín* included yerba mate as the only beverage and described it as a fundamental item for nutrition.[63] During hyperinflation, newspapers regularly reported on the cost of living by highlighting the prices of yerba mate and other basic necessities. For example, a July 1989 article titled, "How much does it cost to survive in Argentina?" included a table that identified the emergency necessities for a family of four. The table listed seventeen items under foodstuffs, including 2 kilos of yerba mate, but no meat or fruit.[64] In an effort to make emergency foodstuffs more accessible, the government instituted price ceilings. In doing so, it selected ten items "of massive consumption that make up the family basket [of basic necessities]." And again, the list included yerba mate.[65]

Concern about the accessibility of basic foodstuffs made sense given the situation of the 1980s. In Buenos Aires and its suburbs, impoverished households (defined as households with incomes below the poverty line and/or one or more unmet basic need) grew over the decade from 19.8 percent to 34.6 percent of the population. Notably, the percentage of structurally or chronically poor remained a fairly constant, even as their living standards deteriorated. In contrast, the percentage of households with incomes below the poverty line increased significantly.[66] Almost everyone saw their incomes decline, except for the wealthiest Argentines. As a result, inequality grew. Between 1974 and 1988, the top 20 percent of the population saw their share of the national income expand while everyone else's share fell.[67]

Concurrent with growing poverty and inequality, the shrinking of the middle class was especially disconcerting to Argentines. The country had long been proud of its large middle class, especially as compared to other Latin American countries. As of 1980, the urban middle class made up almost half (47 percent) of the country's population, but by 1991 the percentage had fallen to 38 percent.[68] Growing numbers of people who had been part of the middle class found themselves earning incomes below the poverty line.[69] To distinguish the poor who were formerly middle class from those who were structurally poor, researchers began writing about the "new poor."[70]

Even though their socio-economic circumstances meant that they were no longer officially part of the middle class, many of the "new poor" continued to associate themselves with the middle class. They made great efforts to maintain their social standing and to hide their financial hardships.[71] To reduce spending, the "new poor" ate at home more frequently and went out less. They also drank mate. Celso, a formerly middle-class industrial worker who lost his job and saw hyperinflation eat up his money in the late 1980s, explained:

> We turned to polenta without meat, to noodles without meat. Sometimes I bought half a kilo of meat and made a pasta sauce to pour a shabby bit of it on the food for several days: on rice, peas, polenta, noodles. The kids were already big and didn't ask me for milk. We only ate at mid-day and at night we only made mate cocido.[72]

During hyperinflation, even the middle class resorted to drinking yerba mate, although they preferred coffee or tea. Such a preference is clear in a July 1989 *Clarín* article about how the middle class was dealing with the economic crisis. The subtitle of the article explained that the middle class employed such strategies as switching from using cars to buses and from using taxis to bicycles. When detailing various expenses, the journalist first highlighted how the middle class was substituting tea for coffee (due to its lower price), while still drinking coffee "with a vengeance" in restaurants by having it as the dessert. Later, the journalist pointed out, "And reappearing under the desks, the kettles and heaters for bags of mate cocido and tea, or if money allows, instant coffee." A table summarizing spending changes elucidated the middle-class hierarchy of caffeinated beverages: "Before: Coffee; Now: Tea," and separately, "Before: Brand-name yerba in 1-kilo package; Now: Loose yerba or cheap yerba in half-kilo package."[73]

As discussed earlier, during the second half of the 1980s, before the neoliberal reforms were enacted with a vengeance, consumer prices for mate grew significantly. Although yerba growers had earlier sought intervention from the CRYM to protect their interests, and despite the failure of that intervention, the yerba sector was booming, with prices rising faster than inflation. This boom in yerba prices in the midst of a broader economic depression represents an important moment in the larger evolution of the consumption of yerba mate in Argentina, as it was around this time that mate began to be regularly spotlighted in the press and in popular culture as an important cultural symbol for more than just rural poor people, but also for the urban and middle-classes. This was a status that mate had not had for decades.

FIGURES 21 AND 22. Dobal, "Precios," *De la crónica diaria, Clarín*, March 12, 1988 (top), and Dobal, "Tiempos," *De la crónica diaria, Clarín*, March 28, 1988 (bottom).

In the late 1980s, as the CRYM was falling apart and the yerba industry was about to move towards a free market model, yerba mate became a touchstone for high prices and financial difficulties. Newspapers repeatedly referred to yerba mate when describing cost-saving measures and calculating the cost of living. *Clarín* also published a large number of cartoons about yerba mate, particularly in 1988, when yerba mate prices were rising faster than inflation. The cartoons not only revealed widespread awareness and concern about the high price of yerba mate, they also showed how yerba mate was used in the media as a humorous way to complain about the overall hardships of the period.

The cartoons included both men and women, focusing primarily on people who looked middle class and who complained about how expensive yerba mate was. For example, in a vignette called "Prices," published in March of 1988, the cartoonist Dobal shows two downcast women leaving a corner store while one says, "I never imagined that it would cost me so much to drink mate *amargo* (without sugar)!" while the other responds, "... Think about me, I drink it *dulce* (with sugar)!" (see figure 21).[74] Just over two weeks later in another Dobal vignette called "Times," two men excitedly converse on the phone after not having been in communication for a long because one of

SE ENRIQUECIÓ CON LA YERBA...

¿COCAÍNA? ¿MARIHUANA?

...MATE

RECURSOS

...NO SÉ QUÉ VA A SER DE NOSOTROS, LOS DE LA CLASE MEDIA!

SITUACION

FIGURES 23 AND 24. Dobal, "Recursos," *De la crónica diaria, Clarín*, March 29, 1988 (top), and Dobal, "Situación," *De la crónica diaria, Clarín*, July 19, 1989 (bottom).

them had been months without a telephone. The other asks him for his address so they could talk and share mate like old times. The man who recently got phone service back happily responds, "I'm delighted. [You] bring the yerba!" (see figure 22).[75] Both vignettes point to the high price of yerba mate and the overall economic hardships facing both the middle class and the poor. But they also point to mate's position at this time as a cultural symbol that could be used in stories in a way that would appeal to Argentina's middle class. This is reflective of an important, broader evolution in the perception of mate in Argentina's cultural imagination at this time.

Although most of Dobal's cartoons centered on the middle class, he also addressed other sectors of society. In several cartoons he included shabbily dressed men who looked like vagabonds to emphasize extreme destitution. He also depicted the rich and implied that people in the yerba sector had dishonorably gotten wealthy off of yerba mate. In a vignette titled "Resources," two men in suits talk as a big, fancy car passes with a man smoking a cigar. One of the men whispers, "He got rich with yerba...." The other asks, "Cocaine? Marijuana?" and the first responds "... Mate" (see figure 23).[76] During the same month, a cartoonist named Crist also ran two cartoons about yerba mate in *Clarín*. One showed a gaucho drinking mate and saying

"this is the famous mate-less. Mate almost without yerba." The second cartoon implied that the yerba sector was exploiting the economic situation.
One man with a tie who seems to be reading the newspaper asks another man
who is also wearing a tie, "Is it possible that they have discovered that yerba
has new properties and that's why it costs so much?" The other man, who is
drinking mate, responds, "Precisely so. And all are private properties."[77]

A little over a year later, in June and July of 1989 during hyperinflation,
Clarín again printed cartoons by both Dobal and Crist with similar themes.
A vignette by Dobal titled "Situation" points to the disappearance of the middle class. It shows two ragged vagabonds sitting at a campsite and sharing
mate while one says, ". . . I don't know what is going to happen to us, those of
the middle class!" (see figure 24).[78] This and other cartoons of the time used
yerba mate as a vehicle for discussing economic hardships. If yerba mate,
which should be affordable, was not, this was evidence that middle class people were really struggling to make ends meet. For consumers who had to pay
super high prices for yerba (and almost everything else), it was natural to
assume that producers were benefiting. Although this was partly true, the full
story was more complex. The yerba sector was undergoing significant changes,
moving rapidly towards a period of vast deregulation and neoliberal reforms
that would soon help send yerba mate back into the cultural mainstream.

DEREGULATION AND NEOLIBERAL
REFORMS IN THE 1990S

The hyperinflation that arrived at the end of the 1980s transformed Argentina.
It caused people to once again recalculate longstanding prevailing political
and economic ideas, and to reimagine how they viewed the history and future
of the country. In 1989, Argentines went to the polls to elect a new president,
and, many hoped, to reinstate some degree of economy stability after so much
recent uncertainty and hardship. Argentines elected Carlos Menem as president. As a candidate, Menem had promised a mix of reforms and a return to
basics. His platform adhered to the standard Peronist strategy of promising
salary increases to cultivate working class support, while at the same time he
promised to modernize and reform the economy. Even though the economy
was a wreck, with 70 percent of Argentines believing that their country was
in a bad or very bad state, the population did not elect Menem primarily
because they thought he would solve the country's problems. Argentines were

disillusioned and had little faith in any politician. A poll of two thousand potential voters in large urban centers one month before the elections revealed that only 34 percent thought Menem had done a good job as governor of La Rioja and only 37 percent believed that he could be the leader that the country needed. Instead, Menem appealed to voters primarily because they viewed him as a "regular guy," although in fact he was more of a faux populist. Still, 71 percent of those polled praised Menem for being close to the people and 65 percent characterized him as unpretentious (*es una persona simple*).[79]

Drinking mate epitomized Menem's ability to connect with common people. As the voter quoted at the beginning of the chapter explained, "Radicals were all from the better-off class, people who intellectualized politics, and who spoke about workers but never understood them. Peronism was the normal thing, of ordinary people. . . . Peronism is what is normal. The person in the street, who understands his fellows, who drinks mate."[80] And yet, as a lawyer and politician, Menem was not a member of the working class. He was flamboyant—as president, he drove fast cars, flew planes, and partied with glamorous women. By drinking mate, Menem showed that he was of the people even though his income and standard of living made him elite. Menem won the election with a 12 percent margin over the Radical Party candidate.

The crisis of hyperinflation gave Menem an opening to take drastic action. During the elections, Menem indicated that he would reform the economy, and he followed through. Almost immediately after taking office, Menem laid the groundwork for radically altering the Argentine economy. Within one month, his administration passed emergency legislation that gave the president the power to privatize almost all public companies, and the following month, another bill allowed the presidency to enact additional economic reforms by decree.[81] These laws set the stage for drastic reforms to open the Argentine economy and austerity measures that weakened the benefactor state. To sidestep complaints about the hardships caused by these reforms, Menem repeatedly reminded Argentines about hyperinflation and emphasized that these measures would stabilize prices.[82] One of the most radical reforms was the April 1991 Convertibility Plan that tied the Argentine peso to the US dollar so that 1 peso AR equaled $1 US.

At 8:30 p.m. on October 31, 1991, Menem announced a massive deregulation package. Accompanied by his cabinet, Menem gave an eighteen-minute speech that was broadcast live throughout the country on national television and radio stations. Menem began by describing the reforms as "a series of historic decisions. Very concrete. Truly revolutionary." He declared that the reforms would transform the country's economic and social system. "As of today, we break the spider's web of a perk-giving (*prebendario*), asphyxiating and arbitrary State that obstructed the national productive life with an assortment of unnecessary regulations." Menem claimed that the changes would lead to stability, growth, investment, employment, and production within a framework of justice and liberty. The principal beneficiaries would be the most dispossessed.[83]

With 122 articles and two annexes, the presidential decree reached almost all sectors of the economy. It deregulated trade and capital markets, reduced and eliminated a number of taxes, and reformed collective negotiations and the social security system. In addition, the decree eliminated regulatory entities, including those that oversaw the production and sale of agricultural products such as yerba mate, grains, beef, wine, and sugar. Its text succinctly stated that all regulation of yerba mate cultivation, harvest, industrialization, and marketing ended, and within ninety days, the Comisión Reguladora de la Yerba Mate had to be liquidated. The decree included similar instructions for the other regulatory boards. The government predicted that deregulation would drastically improve the economy. According to official estimates, industry, agriculture, and exports would benefit by $120 million, $200 million, and $120 million, respectively.[84]

The following day, reactions to Menem's announcement saturated the newspapers. *La Nación* not only published Menem's speech, it also published the entire decree. Editorials and news articles described overwhelming support for the decree. Socialist and Communist politicians and a few regional politicians who wanted protection for their local products complained about deregulation, but they were in the minority.[85] Almost everyone else seemed to agree that deregulation needed to occur. The only disagreement was about how the decision was made. Instead of having Congress democratically create legislation, the Executive had issued a decree. Moreover, instead of proposing to Congress a series of laws addressing the separate aspects of deregulation, Menem had wrapped everything into a single deregulation decree. Economic Minister Domingo Cavallo believed that to do otherwise would lead to the neutralization of the reforms "by the lobbies of the sectors that would see their privileges disappear."[86] Menem concluded that "there is no other solution than to send a decree."[87]

The day after the announcement, Cavallo shared news of the reform package with world financial leaders, having taken an overnight flight to New York City. There, he presented the decree to the Group of Thirty, an influential body of financial leaders headed by the former chairman of the US Federal Reserve, Paul Volcker. The deregulation package closely aligned with the goals of Wall Street bankers and the International Monetary Fund. Less than two weeks later, Menem traveled to the United States to lobby the IMF for a $3 billion loan and request debt forgiveness.[88] The *New York Times* described Argentina's stabilization program as "little more than orthodox economics," while acknowledging that it was "fast becoming the envy of other Latin American governments."[89]

To many in Argentina, the deregulation decree seemed sudden. But in fact, functionaries had been working in secret on the project for at least five months.[90] And for over a year, people involved in the yerba sector had been discussing whether or not the CRYM should be disbanded. Large growers and processors generally called for deregulation, while cooperatives and small growers and processors argued that the CRYM should continue. Even those who called for deregulation wanted it to happen gradually and thoughtfully so that growers would avoid bankruptcy.[91] The response in Misiones to Menem's decree dismantling the CRYM was muted, however. No major protests occurred. In the days that followed, some government officials expressed concern that the suddenness of the measure would create problems for small and inefficient yerba growers, but others claimed it would not hurt small growers because they were well organized and would adapt.[92]

With deregulation, the yerba sector was now subject to the laws of supply and demand. As a result, yerba production jumped significantly: from less than 175,000 tons prior to 1992 to well over 250,000 tons by the mid-1990s. The big increase in supply made prices fall.[93] Small- and medium-sized yerba growers felt especially squeezed as the price for the raw material plummeted, and by the mid-1990s, they were staging protests in Misiones.[94] At the same time, big yerba companies spent money to modernize and advertise their product in order to keep up in the marketplace. Some of the largest yerba mate brands lost market share, while a few smaller brands seized the opportunity to become major players.[95] Large supermarkets opened, offering consumers more choices, while new marketing techniques educated consumers and promoted products. Overall, neoliberal reforms and globalization invigorated consumer culture, leading to nothing less than a renaissance for yerba mate in the coming years.

By many measures, the Argentine economy improved in the 1990s. The Convertibility Plan stopped hyperinflation, and between 1991 and 1998, Argentina experienced its highest growth rates since World War I. Cheap money (*plata dulce*) benefited wealthy and middle-class Argentines who took out loans and bought consumer goods on payment plans. Drinking champagne with pizza symbolized the period. But not all Argentines prospered. Poverty decreased in Greater Buenos Aires between 1991 and 1994, but inequality remained high, and by the mid-1990s, the divide between winners and losers became increasingly apparent. Most Argentines felt insecure about their standing. By 2000, many middle-class Argentines added qualifiers such as "impoverished middle class" or "lower middle class" that alluded to their tenuous circumstances, and a majority of Argentines believed that their parents' generation had had a better standard of living.[96]

Indeed, despite the economic growth, Argentina experienced high unemployment in the 1990s. Tens of thousands of Argentines lost their jobs due to privatization and deregulation, and high growth rates failed to create enough employment opportunities to compensate for such losses. In 1993, the unemployment rate reached a record high of 9.5 percent. It then jumped to 19 percent in 1995 and remained high for the rest of the decade. Significantly greater numbers of people worked in the informal economy, increasing from 27 percent in 1989 to 37 percent in 1998. Even those employed were not satisfied. In 1997, some 23 percent of people in Buenos Aires with jobs were also looking for employment. After 1994, earnings declined. Salaries in 1999 equated to 83 percent of 1986 salaries after accounting for inflation. Many people struggled to make ends meet. In 1997, over 600,000 people in the city of Buenos Aires earned between 126 and 407 pesos, far less than the projected family budget of 1,018 pesos and insufficient to cover basic food and drinks (459 pesos) for a family.[97]

Making matters worse, food was no longer as cheap in the 1990s. Food prices had risen to levels similar to Europe and the United States. Poorer Argentines once again had to change their diets in response to financial difficulties and the high cost of food. A divide appeared between the food of the rich and the food of the poor, which the national statistics office recognized for the first time in its 1996 survey of household spending. Households with lower incomes concentrated their spending on foodstuffs rich in energy, consuming more carbohydrates and sugars. They ate more low-income foods ("*alimentos de carestía*") such as bread, potatoes, dried pasta, cheap cuts of meat, and pasta and less fruits, vegetables, and dairy. They also consumed more yerba mate and tea, and less coffee. In contrast, coffee consumption remained dominant in high-income households.[98]

Families with stretched finances might have turned to mate at this time initially because it was cheaper than coffee, but they also found other aspects of it appealing. As a drink, mate is typically shared, and sharing mate created conditions for sociability. People built social connections as they drank mate together. Family time in Argentina had long centered around meals, but financial difficulties challenged such practices. With stretched budgets, Argentines ate more outside of the home (at schools and soup kitchens) and limited their large family meals. To safeguard family time, Argentines turned to yerba mate, which allowed sociability without a formal meal. At the time of dinner or the afternoon snack, families had mate or mate cocido. According to a scholar of nutrition in Argentina, when poor families could no longer afford to buy enough food for a meal, "those that still had some income concentrated their purchases on a few products (yerba mate, sugar, milk, bread, and crackers) that permitted them to maintain commensality in the home around the table at key moments in the day. . . . To have a home is to have food to share, even if it is only mate."[99] The practice of sharing mate and drinking it at home further connected the beverage to the family and built intimacy as compared to coffee and tea, which were also drunk in cafés or restaurants.

In her late 1980s study of a rural community in Entre Rios, Kristin Ruggiero described the way mate served this important social function. "Wherever maté is made and drunk, it creates an automatic center of community feeling. Of all the activities that take place in the home and community, drinking maté occupies the most time and is the most communal. It is more than a drink; it is a ritual of sociability."[100] Mate is a communal drink. People not only consume it together, they share the mate, drinking from the same bombilla and gourd. Through close contact and sharing, participants create intimacy. They need to remain present, aware of who is the server and whose turn it is in order to keep the mate round going. As a result, participants tend to be actively engaged in the moment. Mate lends itself to bringing people together at a deeper level than other food or beverages.

At the same time that Argentines were increasingly drawn to mate because of its low price and sociability, the Misiones government embarked on a major marketing campaign to promote yerba mate. In December 1991, Ramón Puerta, a close political ally of Carlos Menem, became the governor of Misiones.

As a major player in the yerba sector, Puerta had a vested interest in yerba mate. *Clarín* reported that Puerta had 800 hectares planted in yerba mate and the fourth largest processing plant in the country, which produced 20 million kilos per year in the late 1980s.[101] Furthermore, promoting yerba helped Puerta politically because a significant portion of Misiones' voting population was involved in yerba production. A different *Clarín* article estimated that, in addition to yerba farmers, the 55,000 laborers who harvested yerba, along with their families, accounted for almost a third of the province's population.[102]

Within a year of Puerta taking office, the Misiones government initiated a two-year marketing campaign funded primarily by $5 million from the national government.[103] The project smacked of cronyism. Menem's government gave generous funds to Misiones to support its efforts to promote the yerba sector during the height of spending cuts and deregulation. In contrast, only several years earlier, Alfonsín's government had refused to financially support the Misiones government in its interventionist efforts on behalf of the yerba sector. The Programa de Promoción del Consumo de Yerba Mate sought to increase domestic consumption of yerba mate by 24 percent over four years, so that per capita consumption in Argentina would reach 6 kilos per capita (211 million kilos) in 1995. The campaign focused on television (80 percent), but it also used radio, newspapers, posters, and signs. It aimed to re-shape the image of mate by addressing a wide array of themes: sports, friendship, family, modern life, social hierarchy, solidarity, national identity, regional identity, health, environment, history, culture, youth, and globalization. Even so, the campaign targeted its marketing efforts primarily to youth (45 percent), uplifting mate's social status (35 percent), and associating it with traditional values (20 percent). The campaign thus had two objectives: to introduce mate consumption to the sectors of society most distant from mate consumption (youth and people with high incomes) and to consolidate consumption among the sectors of society where the custom of mate had solid roots.

The publicity campaign based its goals on a survey of 1,400 people in Greater Buenos Aires. Of those surveyed, 27 percent did not consume yerba mate. Men (59 percent) were more likely than women not to drink yerba mate, which the report attributed to the "association of mate consumption with 'domesticity'" and time spent at home. The report also found that younger Argentines (fifteen to thirty years old) consumed less yerba mate than Argentines over thirty, and consumption quantities declined with higher levels of income. It rationalized lower mate consumption by the youth, in part, because a good part of their activities occur outside of the home (studies, sports, and gatherings) and they are more exposed to substitutes, such as sodas or beer, that have a much more aggressive advertising presence. Furthermore, it is the age when the individual tries to extend emotional ties and 'break from the protective shell of the family,' and that includes the domestic habit of having mate.

Regarding higher income levels, the report attributed declining consumption to two fundamental factors: first, the perception of mate as an item of low social standing its association with the popular class and second, the conflict between "the 'lack of time' and the hustle and bustle that modern life imposes on the ruling classes." Hence, for the youth, the marketing campaign focused on "associating mate consumption with activities pertaining to this stage of life: studies, recreation, dance, music." To reach the upper classes, the marketing campaign tried to "identify yerba consumption with values associated with success in modern life: youthful dynamism, beauty, business, vacations, travel, sports, health, self-assurance, happiness, etc."[104]

Soon thereafter, the Secretary of Trade and Integration sent a fax that praised yerba mate. It described the recent launch of the publicity campaign, during which President Menem had "referred to [mate] as the principal reason for his vitality, along with the practice of numerous sports. 'Companion during times of isolation and loneliness. . . . Also it was with me during the times that I had to make transcendental decisions for the future of the Nation.'" Ironically, rather than openly acknowledge that the publicity campaign targeted youth and people of upper income levels, the fax claimed that both groups were already fervent mate consumers. "[The youth] have defined, with their preference, a strong increase in yerba mate consumption in the country by incorporating it as a companion to all types of activities. From studies, to sport or work, mate has been transformed into a principal protagonist." Regarding upper income levels, the fax reported, "Businessmen and executives have resumed the traditional custom of the infusion of yerba mate, rediscovering it as energizing and an ideal combination to resist the pressures of daily life."[105] The fax concluded with eight pages of propaganda material titled "Yerba Mate of Misiones: The Drink that Gives Life," in the format of a magazine insert.[106]

By 1994, Governor Puerta reported that the marketing campaign had early success. Consumption had increased about 5 percent in 1992 and more than 8 percent in 1993.[107] A reporter for *La Prensa* attributed the increase not only to the government's promotional campaign, but also to major efforts by yerba mate companies to modernize their packaging and have "a presence in social, economic, and cultural events, and also in festivals, exhibitions, and commercial missions abroad."[108] The available data indicates that per capita consumption markedly increased in the mid-1990s. In 1989, Argentines consumed 4.1 kilos per capita. Consumption then jumped from 4.7 kilos in 1992 to 5.9 kilos in 1993 and 6.4 kilos in 1994.[109] Statistics about yerba consumption in the 1980s and 1990s are not very reliable due to the dismantling of the CRYM. While we cannot be certain exactly when per capita consumption increased, however, we know it happened in the late 1980s and/or 1990s.

As yerba mate consumption grew once more, perceptions also changed. Many Argentines who faced financial difficulties initially substituted cheaper yerba mate for more expensive coffee and tea as a cost-saving measure. Even though they found themselves in reduced circumstances, many did not see themselves as "poor people" or identify with the structurally poor.[110] And thus, as more urban middle-class (and formerly middle class) Argentines drank mate, its associations with poverty diminished and it became more socially acceptable. Demonstrating this shift, a 1987 article in *La Nación* refuted the ideas spread by "gossiping tongues" that "mate is a privilege of ancient early morning risers, an advantage of retired folk who have extra time, or 'the drink of the poor.'" Instead, the article claimed, "a walk around the neighborhoods of Villa Luro, San Telmo, Barracas, Liniers, Belgrano, and Recoleta showed that demand and consumption of yerba is equivalent among diverse ages and different socioeconomic sectors." This emphasis on age and socioeconomic status mirrored the marketing campaign that stressed the need to increase mate consumption among Argentine youth and the upper class. To show that mate appealed across socioeconomic groups in 1987, the article quoted the manager of a corner store who admitted that tea and coffee did well in his upper-class neighborhood of Barrio Norte, but also "yerba sells very well. . . . Equally, the doormen as well as home owners partake in the cult of this beverage."[111]

Likewise, the article set out to measure mate's appeal among the youth by focusing on three famous Argentine "rockers" as their "representative voices." All three of these rockers had learned the custom of mate from their families while growing up, but as adults, they drank it with varying degrees of regularity. One of the musicians, Charlie García, drank mate only once in a while: "I don't share it with my friends because they don't drink it." Marcelo Cantero of Los Enanitos Verdes drank mate during tours; "I consider mate as an ever-present (*infaltable*) companion on the roads of Argentina." The third musician interviewed for the article, Raul Porcheto, described himself as a fervent mate drinker. "I drink mate every day and with a bombilla. . . . I love having the ritual of mate among friends, whether it be in my home, in their home or while on tour." The article drew the conclusion that "everything indicates that [mate] has the youth as enthusiastic followers of its core values: drinking it in a relaxed environment and using it as a motive for gathering together."[112]

Less than a year later, *Clarín* published a review of a Punta del Este beach that associated nonconformist youth with mate consumption. As the subtitle of the article described, "At La Mansa some people 'tan' the 'my way' (*'curte' el 'my way' (hace la suya))* without tying themselves to fashion." The photograph accompanying the article focused on a shirtless young man drinking mate with a thermos nearby and a t-shirt on his head. The caption described, "mate, radio and whatever thing that serves for protection from the terrible sun with little ozone. T-shirts on the head or creams on the face. The most important is to have a good time and relax. Living attentively to fashion can provoke 'stress.'"[113] By the end of the 1990s, mate had once again moved out of the home and was regularly consumed in public parks and outdoor spaces. By sharing mate in green spaces, youth and people of all ages built social connections while getting fresh air and escaping the hustle and bustle of daily life.[114] Such activity directly addressed common anxieties. A small survey in 1997 of middle-class Argentines between the ages of seven and fifty-five found that they felt burnout and exclusion and "exhibited a passive longing for tranquility, of the ideals of solidarity and engagement, of security and social protection."[115] Sharing mate built solidarity and engagement, while drinking it in green spaces offered relaxation and tranquility. Mate not only lessened stress and created a sense of connectedness at the level of the individual, it also reduced societal tensions. As a common practice that cut across socioeconomic levels, mate consumption united Argentines and was an important part of Argentine identity. Sharing mate had become a performance of Argentinidad.

By 1999, mate consumption was so widely accepted that *La Nación* felt it newsworthy to educate readers about past efforts to suppress the drink. As the byline to the article explained, "With its unique flavor, [mate] captures a large part of the Argentine and Uruguayan population, but even so, there were many attempts to clamp down on its consumption for various reasons. . . ."[116] Mate had become so common that many had forgotten about the degree to which it had been denigrated in the not-so-distant past.

Afterword

ON THE RAINY AUTUMN DAY of June 6, 2001, a parade of tractors, trucks, and farm machinery from all over Misiones entered the provincial capital of Posadas. After driving through the city, and snarling traffic along the way, the vehicles stopped at the central plaza in front of the *casa del gobierno* and cathedral. The numerous tractors, many of which showed the wear and tear of decades worth of hard work, made for a strange sight. Accompanying the vehicles were hundreds of rural folks wearing mended and wet clothing. They came from all over the province and many had caravanned together for several days to get to the capital. The event had some precedent: a week earlier, around one thousand rural folk had gathered in a similar protest in Oberá (Misiones's second largest city), and several days earlier they had closed off a major highway. Once in Posadas, an estimated five hundred protesters stayed on, refusing to leave until the government listened to their grievances. Some slept in an old room at the cathedral and received handouts of food from charity groups. A week later, more than two hundred additional tractors and trucks arrived as reinforcements, again parking in front of the casa de gobierno. The police estimated that the caravan extended more than four kilometers. To promote public safety, and maybe to limit the number of protesters, the police prohibited people from riding in the back of trucks on provincial highways. Organizers responded by getting a dozen buses to transport supporters. A protest of this scale had not been seen in Misiones for years. Known as the Tractor Protest (*Tractorazo*), the demonstrations disrupted life in the province and gained national attention.[1]

Who were the protesters and what did they want? Called "colonos," they were small- and medium-sized yerba growers who wanted a higher price for their yerba and a return to government regulation of the yerba sector. In

Misiones, some 20,000 yerba growers produced around 90 percent of the yerba consumed domestically. Due to a supply glut, the price of the raw material had dropped dramatically since the mid-1990s, and growers felt squeezed.[2] As of June 2001, unprocessed dried yerba sold at around 20 cents per kilo, while packaged yerba cost between 1.6 and 2 pesos per kilo in the supermarket. To help the growers, the government agreed to a price floor for unprocessed yerba, followed by the creation of a new regulatory agency, the Instituto Nacional de la Yerba Mate (INYM), to oversee the yerba sector.[3] After ten years of deregulation, the Argentine government's approach to the yerba sector had come full circle. Days later, however, the Argentine economy collapsed. Concerned that the Central Bank might not have enough dollars in reserve to support dollar-peso parity, the government instituted a *corralito* on December 2 that froze most bank account withdrawals, and protests erupted throughout the country. On December 21, president Fernando de la Rúa (Carlos Menem's successor) fled office after less than two weeks on the job. Four presidents succeeded him over the next ten days. In the years ahead, during the presidencies of Néstor and Cristina Kirchner (2003–2015)—part of the "Pink Tide" in Latin America—government intervention and social welfare returned to the center of Argentina's economic policy. This shift was the newest result of the persistent dialectical tension between regulation and free market economic policies in Argentina. Despite having been one of the initial success stories of neoliberal economic reform in the 1990s, Argentina's shift in the early 2000s (along with most of Latin America) back to state intervention bucked the broader trend of neoliberal economic policies elsewhere in the world during an age of globalization. Although shifts in Argentine economic policy often correlated with shifts in the consumption and population of yerba mate, this time, mate's popularity did not waver, and its popularity continues to grow.

. . .

By the 2000s, Argentina wholeheartedly embraced mate as an emblem of Argentinidad, much like how foie gras became a symbol of French identity.[4] In 2013, the Argentine government designated mate as the official national infusion (wine is the national drink), and in 2016, it formalized "Yerba Mate Argentina" as an official geographic indication, like French champagne and Mexican tequila. With these measures, the Argentine government formally recognized yerba mate as a symbol of national identity while consumers use mate's unique accoutrements to perform an Argentinidad full of contradictions. Argentines embrace mate for its authenticity, and yet yerba mate's Indigenous roots, discussed in the early chapters of this book, are sidelined as consumers are more likely to associate mate's origins with the gauchos and the pampas rather than the Kaingang or Guaraní of the triple frontier region. Furthermore, yerba mate, despite its remarkable and expansive history in Argentina, is inherently transnational. It is deeply meaningful to people in Paraguay, southern Brazil, and Uruguay—places where, like Argentina, it is consumed widely. Paraguay and Brazil, moreover, are also major producers of yerba mate.

Ironically, while mate has grown in popularity and notoriety in Argentina over the past two decades, the amount of yerba mate that Argentines consume has actually decreased. According to Argentina's national statistics office, Argentines purchased 10 percent less yerba mate in 2012–13 as compared to the peak in 1996–1997.[5] Indeed, INYM concluded that consumption per capita fell by 6 percent between 2005 and 2020, from 6.3 kilos to 5.9 kilos.[6] Furthermore, as described in the introduction, the snob of Nordelta's 2017 WhatsApp message and the congressman's 2020 tweet demeaning mate consumption expose persisting social and class divisions within the country. As this book shows, despite being idealized by politicians and marketers, mate's power to unite Argentines is frequently exaggerated, and its appeal across social classes has risen and fallen according to broader cultural and political trends. The importance of mate to Argentine culture has always been controversial, and based on contested understandings of Argentine identity.

During the last two decades, the influence of globalization has led Argentines to embrace yerba mate as autochthonous, while foreign consumers in international markets "glocalize" the beverage, adapting it to local tastes. Yerba mate is sold and marketed globally as a South American drink, but in a form that rarely corresponds to the traditional method of drinking it from a shared bombilla and gourd. The most popular brand of yerba mate in the United States, for example, is Guayakí Yerba Mate, which embraces yerba mate's South American origins and promotes itself as a lifestyle beverage for "personal, social, ecological and cultural regeneration."[7] The name alludes to yerba mate's Indigenous roots, albeit invoking an Indigenous group distinct from the Guaraní and Kaingang who discovered it.[8] In promoting yerba mate as an energy drink, US and European companies exoticize the drink as a mystical premodern relic from South America—which is totally distinct from how it's currently thought of in Argentina. Instead of the shared mate with all of its specialized paraphernalia, people consume their own iced tea or carbonated beverage from disposable, single-use bottles and cans. Carbonated yerba mate drinks have been around in Germany and Cuba since the early twentieth century and they have been growing in popularity. Club-Mate is a favorite of techies and partiers in Europe because of its high caffeine content, and among Cuban expatriates, the pre-revolutionary drink Materva remains popular.[9] But even as yerba mate consumption evolves and changes based on consumer preferences, shared mate with its Indigenous technologies persists in Argentina and much of South America, even as continually evolving cultural and social conditions lead it to take on new meanings.

· · ·

The history of yerba mate is the history of Argentina. Yerba mate originated among the Guaraní or Kaingang people of Paraguay, and under Spanish rule, it evolved into a colonial staple whose trade incorporated a peripheral frontier and its people into the Spanish Empire. After independence, Brazil surpassed Paraguay as the major producer, while Argentina's struggle to define the nation-state and its frontiers impeded the country's ability to develop yerba production. Over the course of the nineteenth century, mate became the drink of the gaucho and a clandestine practice among the urban elite of Buenos Aires. In the early years of the twentieth century, the promise of large profits and nationalist rhetoric drew European colonists and capitalist investors to Misiones to cultivate yerba.

These investments and the expansion of the yerba industry, along with the political debates surrounding them, played a central role in the broader evolution of the country and its debates about cultural identity and national goals. It was an influence that continued in the decades ahead. In the 1930s, nations worldwide implemented protectionist measures. Following suit, Argentina created a regulatory agency for managing the yerba sector as a compromise measure that placated yerba growers and processors while prioritizing Argentine wheat. No matter whether yerba was harvested from wild yerbales (from the colonial era through the nineteenth century) or from cultivated trees (in the twentieth century), yerba workers labored in poor conditions for low wages and they came to symbolize capitalist exploitation and greed for Anarchists, Socialists, Communists, and Peronists alike. In the middle of the twentieth century, Juan Perón sought to empower these very workers and his policies helped turn them into modern, middle-class consumers.

Although yerba mate would be seen as antiquated and associated with poverty in the coming years, and per capita mate consumption declined for decades, the importance of mate to Argentina's cultural myths and national heritage remained strong. As the country experienced economic crises in the 1980s, Argentines turned to yerba mate because it was cheaper than coffee and tea, and because sharing it facilitated sociability. As middle class (and former middle class) consumers increasingly drank mate, its reputation improved. A mate renaissance ensued and Argentines publicly embraced it as a marker of national identity. Yerba mate's history is a centuries-long story that bridges empires, evolving political debates, and dramatically different economic and social eras—it is, in short, the story of Argentina itself.

Yerba mate is a caffeinated beverage that, unlike coffee, tea, and chocolate, largely resisted globalization until the twenty-first century. As such, it is also a story of persistence, resistance, acculturation, and amalgamation. This book is a commodity history that studies consumption and the evolving meanings of yerba mate for both consumers and detractors. In doing so, it brings everyday common people into the history of Argentina. The book also investigates the production of yerba mate and the insights it provides about the nation-state, international relations, and economic policies. Books about Argentina often focus on Buenos Aires. However, the story of yerba mate in Argentina is a national story, including the often overlooked northeastern borderlands in the tri-border frontier region that connects Argentina, Paraguay, and Brazil. To understand the history of yerba mate in Argentina, it is important to look at its consumption and production through numerous scholarly lenses, particularly those of cultural studies and political economy: two different approaches that are rarely used together. My goal has been to shine a light on mate's extraordinary history of continuity and change—from pre-Columbian times to the turn of the twenty-first century. It's a story that, as this book shows, not only reveals the way yerba mate production and consumption has evolved, but also the complicated and contested nature of national identity in Argentina. The history of yerba mate exposes the deep and enduring tensions—and the political consequences of such tensions—between the desire to be modern and "civilized," and the desire for authenticity.

NOTES

INTRODUCTION

1. "Audio oficial cheta de Nordelta," https://www.youtube.com/watch?v= XJGs21mzxsI.

2. "Fernando Iglesias, diputado de Cambiemos salió a pedir disculpas . . .," *Misiones Online,* March 12, 2020.

3. Nouzeilles and Montaldo, *The Argentina Reader,* provides an overview of Argentina's history, culture and society and yet yerba mate is not included in its index.

4. Rappaport, *A Thirst for Empire*; Clarence-Smith and Topik, *The Global Coffee Economy*; Beckert, *Empire of Cotton*; Mintz, *Sweetness and Power*; Elmore, *Citizen Coke.*

5. Pilcher, "Eating á la Criolla."

6. Norton, *Sacred Gifts, Profane Pleasures.*

7. "Medicines in my Home: Caffeine and Your Body," https://www.fda.gov /downloads/ucm200805.pdf, accessed April 20, 2017.

8. Heck and Mejia, "Yerba Mate," 140.

9. Heck and Mejia, "Yerba Mate," 138.

10. Markowicz Bastos et al., "Yerba Maté," 38.

11. Diccionario de la Real Academia Española, http://dle.rae.es/?id = KMZGtT3.

12. Letter by Martín González, July 1, 1556, as quoted in Candela, *Entre la pluma y la cruz,* 116–17; "Relación de Juan Bautista Corona," February 12, 1603, AGI, Charcas 48. Leasing of the "coca" or yerba of Maracayú, Sección Copias, ANA, 1603, Vol. 14, f. 63–64.

13. Ruiz de Montoya also made the other connection: "its odor and taste (that of sumac), in which it closely resembles the Peruvian herb called *coca*" (*The Spiritual Conquest,* 43).

14. León Pinelo, *Question moral,* 34; Gemelli Careri, "A Voyage," 4:28; Cobo, *Historia del nuevo mundo,* 2:97; du Biscay, *An Account,* 10.

15. *Daily Post,* January 19, 21, and 22, 1741.

16. Joyce, "Yerba mate," 326–27.

17. Pedro de Montenegro, "Libro primero de la propiedad y virtudes de los árboles y plantas de las Misiones y Provincia del Tucumán," 1711, BNE, MSS/10314, 37.

18. Ruiz de Montoya, *Tesoro*, 165.

19. Vega, *Primera parte*, Libro 8, 208–9.

20. According to Javier Ricca, Spaniards found it difficult to pronounce the Guaraní term for the vessel for drinking yerba, and thus adopted a variation of the Nahatl term "matl" that was used in Perú. See Ricca, "En el origen fue el mate, part 1," *El Federal*, February 10, 2011, 42–44; "En el origen fue el mate, part 2," *El Federal*, February 17, 2011, 44–46.

21. Clavigero, *The History*, 438. A 1685 book published in London reported that Mexicans used *tecomate* to describe the cup or goblet for drinking chocolate (Dufour, *The Manner*, 106).

22. Frézier, *A Voyage to the South-Sea*, 252.

23. Ulloa, *A Voyage to South-America*, 1:284; Betagh, *A Voyage Round the World*, 290–91; Byron, *The Narrative*, 227.

24. J. Aguirre, "Diario del capitán," 19:245.

25. Saint-Hilaire, "Aperçu d'un voyage," 350–51.

26. Saint-Hilaire, *Histoire des plantes*, xlj; Saint-Hilaire, "Note sur l'herbe," 30.

27. Saint-Hilaire, "Aperçu d'un voyage," 44–45 ; Saint-Hilaire, "Note sur l'herbe," 32.

28. Miers, "On the History." Bell, *A Life in Shadow*, 171–72.

29. A strange exception is the appearance of "yerba mate" between 1637–1643. See the distribution at https://books.google.com/ngrams/graph?content=yerba+mate&year_start=1600&year_end=2008&corpus=10&smoothing=3&share=&direct_url=t1%3B%2Cyerba%20mate%3B%2Cco#t1%3B%2Cyerba%20mate%3B%2Cco and https://books.google.com/ngrams/graph?content=yerba+del+Paraguay&year_start=1600&year_end=2008&corpus=10&smoothing=3&share=&direct_url=t1%3B%2Cyerba%20del%20Paraguay%3B%2Cco#t1%3B%2Cyerba%20del%20Paraguay%3B%2Cco.

30. Giberti, "Maté." Worldwide there are about four hundred species of *Ilex* with six species in Paraguay; see Giberti, *Flora del Paraguay*, 8.

31. Sánchez Labrador, *El Paraguay Católico*, 245–51; Aguirre, "Diario del capitán," 19:254–57.

32. "Las yerbas importadas," *La Prensa*, December 20, 1911.

33. "La yerba-mate," *La Vanguardia*, December 21, 1911.

34. "La industria yerbatera," *La Prensa*, December 23, 1911.

35. A number of yerba species in Brazil had popular names that referenced congonha. Linhares, *História econômica*, 86–87.

36. Saint-Hilaire, "Aperçu d'un voyage," 351.

37. Saint-Hilaire, "Note sur l'herbe," 31.

38. Spelled as *paraguayensis* (Segovia, "Cultivo," 67–69).

39. Scala, "Contribución," 101.

40. "Decreto del poder ejecutivo nacional."

41. Law 4,084, August 21, 1930, in Cámara de Comercio Argentino-Brasileña, *La yerba mate,* 79. According to the Codigo Alimentaria Argentino, *Ilex para-guariensis* is the only species authorized for use in yerba mate products (Argentina law, Act 18.284, articles 1192–1193).

42. "Misiones: La difícil situación . . .," *La Prensa,* April 7, 1930.

43. "Protesta de la embajada . . .," *La Prensa,* August 23, 1935.

44. Kongóin—herva matte. See Val Floriana, "Dicionário Kaingang-Portuguez," 58; Linhares, *História económica,* 69–70. Some sources assert that *congonha* is a Tupi term, but that is doubtful. Eduardo de Almeida Navarro's dictionary of old Tupi does not include anything similar to *congonha* or *côgôî* (*Tupi antigo,* 207). Antônio Geraldo da Cunha's historical dictionary of Portuguese with Tupi origins includes *congonha* as the "common name of diverse plants of the genus *Ilex,* similar to mate" but the earliest reference dates to the late colonial period (1783) (*Dicionário histórico,* 112).

45. Amaral, "Conhecimento e uso de plantas," 29; Tempski, "Caingângues," 167 and 367–68.

46. Segovia, "Cultivo de la yerba mate," 67.

47. Shua and Prada, *La leyenda*; Córdova, *Leyendas,* 51–53; Galeano, "Maté."

48. Ambrosetti, "Segundo viaje," 73–74; Cambas, *Leyendas,* 40–53; Morales, *Leyendas,* 12–16.

49. Hill and Hurtado, *Ache Life History,* 41.

50. According to its label, "Yachack is the name the Indigenous Kichwa people of the Sarayaku in the Ecuadorian Amazon give to their shamans."

CHAPTER 1

1. *Tratado del recto uso de la yerba del Paraguay,* 1667, Lima. Although extensively quoted, Zevallos's book has not been located by modern scholars. Lozano, *Historia de la conquista,* 1:203, 1:210–12.

2. Lozano, *Historia de la conquista,* 1:213.

3. Norton, *Sacred Gifts.*

4. Galeano, "Mate," 1:29–30.

5. Joyce, "Yerba Mate," 326–27.

6. By the late nineteenth century, the name "Kaingang" signified all non-Guaraní Indigenous peoples living in southern Brazil (Marrero et al., "Demographic and Evolutionary," 301–2). Colonial era sources call them Gualacho or Guayaná/Guaianá. I use Kaingang for consistency.

7. Ruíz de Montoya also believed yerba deserved condemnation due to "the hardship involved in its cultivation, the high esteem it enjoys, its sustaining and stimulating effect on workers, the high price it commands . . . and even for its odor and taste (that of sumac), in which it closely resembles the Peruvian herb called *coca*" (*The Spiritual Conquest,* 43).

8. Ruíz de Montoya, *Arte, y bocabulario,* part 2, p. 54; Ruíz de Montoya, *Tesoro,* 83, 98.

9. Email correspondence from Guaraní linguist Leonardo Cerno, June 25, 2018.

10. Kongóin—herva matte. De Val Floriana, "Diccionario Kaingang-Portuguez," 58; Linhares, *História econômica,* 69–70; Becker, "O índio Kaingáng," 96.

11. Segovia, "Cultivo," 67.

12. "Sí, este autor es al parecer muy reacio a incluir palabras no tupí-guaraníes en sus diccionarios" (email correspondence from Guaraní linguist Leonardo Cerno, June 25, 2018).

13. "Relação," 1630, in Cortesão, *Jesuítas e bandeirantes no Guairá,* 350. "Hechicero" is also spelled "hechizero" and "hichizero" by various colonial authors.

14. "Carta anua de Antonio Ruíz," 1628, in Cortesão, *Jesuítas e bandeirantes no Guairá,* 298.

15. Lozano, *Historia de la conquista,* 1:427.

16. Serrano, *Etnografía de la antigua provincia,* 45.

17. Ruíz de Montoya, *The Spiritual Conquest,* 42–43.

18. Austin, *Colonial Kinship,* 136–37.

19. Austin, *Colonial Kinship,* 147.

20. "Relação," 1630, in Cortesão, *Jesuítas e bandeirantes no Guairá,* 350.

21. Pedro de Montenegro, "Libro primero de la propiedad y virtudes de los árboles y plantas de las Misiones y Provincia del Tucumán," 1711, BNE, MSS/10314, 37–38.

22. Lozano, *Historia de la conquista,* 1:203.

23. Ruíz de Montoya, *The Spiritual Conquest,* 43.

24. "Carta anua de Antonio Ruíz," 1628, and "Carta de Padre Simão Masseta," January 25, 1629, in Cortesão, *Jesuítas e bandeirantes no Guairá,* 279, 282, 288–90, and 301–2.

25. "Carta Anua de Pedro de Oñate," April 22, 1618, DHA 20:142.

26. "Carta Anua de Diego Ferrer," August 21, 1633, in Cortesão, *Jesuítas e bandeirantes o Itatim,* 30.

27. Navajas, *Caá porã,* 36.

28. "Relação de Justo Mancilla y Simão Masseta," November 10, 1629, in Cortesão, *Jesuítas e bandeirantes no Guairá,* 312.

29. Ruíz de Montoya, *Tesoro,* 13, 266, 312, 351, 84, and 196.

30. Ruíz de Montoya, *Tesoro,* 84, 49, 356, and 257. Elsewhere, Ruíz de Montoya claimed, "the native Indians take it with moderation once a day" (*The Spiritual Conquest,* 43). In 1637, the Augustinian priest Gonzalo del Valle wrote, "the Indians ordinarily consume it almost all day, and they have it for sustenance" (quoted in Bouza, "El arbitrio," 80).

31. Ruíz de Montoya, *Tesoro,* 84.

32. De Souza Pereira et al., "Ecologia histórica."

33. Ruíz de Montoya, *Tesoro,* 157 and 209.

34. Ruíz de Montoya, *Tesoro,* 49, 84, 141, 196, and 252; Ruíz de Montoya, *Arte,* 54 and 266.

35. Da Luz, "Caruhis e barbaquás."

36. Prous, "Arqueologia tupiguarani"; Milheira and Alves, "O sítio guarani."

37. Da Silva Mayer, "Bomba de chimarrão"; Villanueva, "El arte de cebar," in *Obras Completas,* 143–74; Oberti, *Historia y folklore,* 207–42; Barbosa Lessa, *História do chimarrão,* 12.

38. Nordland, *Brewing,* 78–117; Griffith, "A Drinking Siphon"; Lindblom, "Drinking-Tubes"; Birket-Smith, "Drinking Tube."

39. Frézier, *A Voyage to the South-Sea,* 252.

40. Vidal, *Picturesque Illustrations,* 108. Juan Bautista Ambrosetti noted that the Kaingang used the straw without the filter ("Los indios cainguá," 725).

41. Norton, "Subaltern Technologies"; Nimmo and Miró Medeiros Nogueira, "Creating Hybrid Scientific Knowledge and Practice."

42. The first shipment of goods from Paraguay to the king of Spain around 1556 did not include yerba mate (J. Aguirre, *Discurso histórico,* 143).

43. Earle, *The Body of the Conquistador.* Other early modern Europeans prized the exotic and foreign, including foodstuffs. See W. Smith, *Consumption and the Making of Respectability,* 75; Cowan, *The Social Life of Coffee.*

44. Schmidt, "Voyage of Ulrich Schmidt."

45. The first printed reference to coffee in a European text was 1575 (Cowan, *The Social Life of Coffee,* 16). The first known reference to tea in a European text appeared in the 1550s (Rappaport, *A Thirst for Empire,* 31).

46. Cowan, *The Social Life of Coffee;* Schivelbusch, *Tastes of Paradise,* 15–84; W. Smith, *Consumption and the Making of Respectability,* 121–29.

47. " . . . [C]oca que es hierba para beber los indios con agua y también los cristianos" ("Carta de Martín González," July 1, 1556, quoted in Candela, *Entre la pluma y la cruz,* 116–17). A gourd for yerba was listed in the estate inventory of a deceased Spaniard in Paraguay. See estate records of Pedro Montañez, August 13, 1541 and December 4, 1550, *El Archivo Nacional de la Asunción,* 8:278 and 17:648.

48. "Carta de Juan Romero," September 1594, BRAM, Jesuitas, Tomo 81, 51, folios 57–58.

49. Alonso de la Madrid, February 10, 1596, quoted in J. Aguirre, *Discurso histórico,* 325.

50. De la Madrid made a sixth objection about yerba production and how it caused great suffering for Paraguay's Indian population (quoted in J. Aguirre, *Discurso histórico,* 324–26).

51. Quoted in J. Aguirre, *Discurso histórico,* 326.

52. Ricca, *El mate,* 29.

53. "Carta anua de Diego de Torres," June 6, 1610; "Carta anua de Diego de Torres," April 5, 1611; and "Carta anua de Diego de Torres," February 15 to May 10, 1612, DHA 19:42–43, 85, 87–88 and 494.

54. "Carta anua de Diego de Torres," June 6, 1610, DHA 19:42.

55. Norton, *Sacred Gifts, Profane Pleasures,* 131 and 232.

56. Copy of Diego de Torres to the Inquisition of Peru, September 24, 1610, AHNM, Inquisición, Libro 1037, p. 193; "Carta anua de Diego de Torres," June 6, 1610, DHA 19:42.

57. Appeal by the cabildo of Asunción, November 7, 1602, AGI, Charcas 48.

58. Austin, *Colonial Kinship*; Roulet, *La resistenci,* 175–93; Potthast-Jutkeit, "The Creation."

59. Potthast-Jutkeit, "The Creation," 128–129.

60. De Gandía, *Indios y conquistadores,* 91.

61. Reginaldo de Lizárraga, April 28, 1608, quoted in Austin, "Beyond the Missions," 66n157.

62. De Saavedra, "Carta al rey."

63. "Decisión real," Madrid, October 10, 1618, in P. Hernández, *Misiones del Paraguay,* 2:679.

64. "Informe," December 1, 1620, in Cortesão, *Jesuítas e bandeirantes no Guairá,* 174.

65. "Carta anua de Nicolas Mastrillo Duran," November 12, 1628, DHA 20:306–7.

66. "Carta de Francisco Retz," December 13, 1732, BNM, Mss. 6976, p. 268–269.

67. "Ordenes del P. Provincial Jaime de Aguilar," July 3, 1735, BNM, Mss. 6976, p. 275.

68. "Carta de Antonio Machoni," June 28, 1740, BNM, Mss. 6976, p. 292–293.

69. Bouza, "El arbitrio," 79. Gaspar de Escalona attributed yerba to Saint Bartholomew rather than Saint Thomas (*Gazofilacio,* 267).

70. Ruíz de Montoya, *The Spiritual Conquest,* 43.

71. As quoted in Lozano, *Historia de la conquista,* 1:203, 1:210–12.

72. Cowan, *The Social Life of Coffee,* 20–29; Schivelbusch, *Tastes of Paradise,* 15–84; W. Smith, *Consumption and the Making of Respectability,* 121–29.

73. Stillé, *Therapeutics,* 2:433.

74. Dobrizhoffer, *An Account of the Abipones,* 1:103–4.

75. Arzáns de Orsúa y Vela, *Historia de la villa imperial de Potosí,* 1:7.

76. J. Aguirre, "Diario del capitán," 18:370.

77. Each arroba passing through Santa Fe was to be taxed half a peso and one peso for Peru and Tucumán, with the revenue funding the defense of Buenos Aires's port ("Cedula real," February 26, 1680, AGI, Charcas 282).

78. Testimony in the petition by Pedro del Casal, procurador general of Santa Fe, May and June 1681, AGI, Charcas 282.

79. Petition by Alonso de Herrera y Velasco, teniente de gobernador y capitan de guerra of Santa Fe, 1681, AGI, Charcas 282.

80. Response by Fiscal Bernal, Lima, February 7, 1683, AGI, Charcas 282.

81. "Carta de Francisco de Monforte," November 1, 1689, AGI, Charcas 131.

82. Bando del Virrey Cevallos, November 17, 1777, DHA 1:223.

83. J. Aguirre, "Diario del capitán," 18:370; Johnson, *Workshop of Revolution,* 333n27.

84. Saguier, "El mercado del cuero," 121.

85. "Cabildo de Buenos Aires," January 14, 1732 and February 26, 1732," in Biedma, *Acuerdos,* 6:2, 6:431–32, and 6:444–46.

86. Petition by Alonso de Herrera y Velasco, teniente de gobernador y capitan de guerra of Santa Fe, 1681, AGI, Charcas 282. Over one hundred years later, a traveler came to the same conclusion (*Notes on the Viceroyalty of la Plata,* 35).

87. Pernety, *The History of a Voyage to the Malouine (or Falkland) Islands,* 135–36.

88. "Carta anua de Nicolas Mastrillo Duran," November 12, 1628, DHA 20:306.

89. Gonzalo del Valle quoted in Bouza, "El arbitrio," 81.

90. Lozano, *Historia de la conquista,* 1:208; Dobrizhoffer, *An Account of the Abipones,* 1:102.

91. Wilde, *Buenos Aires,* 4.

92. R. Palma, "Un zapato acusador," 841.

93. Gay, *Atlas de la historia,* vol. 1, image 30.

94. Dobrizhoffer, *An Account of the Abipones,* 1:102.

95. Cardiel, *Las misiones del Paraguay,* 89; Dobrizhoffer, *An Account of the Abipones,* 1:103.

96. Phipps, Hecht, and Esteras Martín, *The Colonial Andes,* 345–51.

97. De Lafuente Machain, *Buenos Aires,* 148.

98. *Notes on the Viceroyalty of la Plata,* 38.

99. Garavaglia, *Mercado,* 40–41.

100. "Carta anua de Nicolas Mastrillo Duran," November 12, 1628, DHA 20:307.

101. Escalona Agüero, *Gazofilacio real,* 267.

102. Du Biscay, "An Account," 10–11 and 51.

103. Du Biscay, "An Account," 50–51.

104. "Informe del arzobispo de la Plata," July 27, 1690, AGI, Charcas 282; Arzáns de Orsúa y Vela, *Historia de la villa,* 1:7. Frézier, *A Voyage,* 253. Betagh, *A Voyage,* 290–291.

105. Byron, *The Narrative,* 227.

106. Garavaglia, *Mercado,* 90–91.

107. De Ulloa, *A Voyage to South-America,* 1:285.

108. Rätsch, "Ilex Paraguariensis," 290–93; Giberti, "Maté," 245–52.

109. "Ordenes de Francisco de Alfaro," October 12, 1611, AGI, Charcas 33.

110. "Decisión real," October 10, 1618, in P. Hernández, *Misiones del Paraguay,* 2:679.

111. Lozano, *Historia de la compañía,* 2:301.

112. Copy of Diego de Torres to the Inquisition of Peru, September 24, 1610, AHNM, Inquisición, Libro 1037, p. 194; "Carta Anua de Diego de Torres," June 6, 1610, and "Carta Anua de Diego de Torres," April 5, 1611, DHA 19:43 and 19:87.

113. "Carta de Ignacio Defrias," November 30, 1699, BNM, Mss. 6976, 196–197.

114. Lenguas generales de América del Sur, "Respuesta que dieron los yndios . . .," http://www.langas.cnrs.fr/#/consulter_document/extraits/109.

115. Garavaglia, *Mercado,* 308–17.

116. The viceroy of Peru, Francisco de Toledo, instituted the mita in the 1570s in response to a shortage of Indigenous laborers and declining output in the Potosí

silver mines. See "Carta anua de Antonio Ruíz," 1628, in Cortesão, *Jesuítas e bandeirantes no Guairá,* 290–91. In defending the beneficio, the governor of Paraguay highlighted in 1655 that it complied with Toledo's rules regarding mita labor, and furthermore, he claimed that the beneficio was less onerous because it was restricted to only part of the year and the work was incomparably easier. See "Carta de Juan Diez de Andino," October 10, 1665, AGI, Escribania 899C, fjs. 571–573.

117. "Carta de Antonio de Vera Moxija," November 11, 1684, AGI, Escribania 899C.

118. Bouza, "El arbitrio," 84.

119. De Azara, *Geografía, física,* 408.

120. "Carta de Juan Rodriguez Cota," April 13, 1698, AGI, Charcas, 216. See also "Carta de Juan Diez de Andino," April 30, 1682, AGI, Charcas 279.

121. Garavaglia, *Mercado,* 371.

CHAPTER 2

1. *A Proposal for Humbling Spain,* 8 and 19–20.

2. "Carta de Andres de Rada," December 19, 1667, BNM, Mss. 6976, p. 51; "Relación de la misiones guaraníes," in Hernández, *Misiones del Paraguay,* 1:264.

3. Cardiel, *Declaración de la verdad,* 271–72.

4. "Carta de Andres de Rada," December 19, 1667, BNM, Mss. 6976, p. 51.

5. "Carta de Thomas Bonavidas," December 10, 1685, BNM, Mss. 6976, p. 127–130.

6. Sarreal, *The Guaraní and Their Missions,* 171–84.

7. Paucke, *Hacia allá,* 2:93–97 and 2:103–6.

8. Paucke, *Hacia allá,* 3:322.

9. "Memorial de José Arce," 1701, AGN, as quoted in Furlong, *Misiones,* 415–16.

10. "Carta anua de Nicolas Mastrillo Duran," November 12, 1628, DHA, 20:306–307.

11. "Recurso de los Jesuítas de Paraguay," in Muriel, *Historia del Paraguay,* 369.

12. Rodero, *Hechos,* 1743, BNM, R/38794, p. 4.

13. Sarreal, "Jesuit Missions," 6.

14. "Carta de Andres de Rada," December 19, 1667, p. 51, BNM, Ms. 6976.

15. "Memorial de José Arce," 1701, AGN, as quoted in Furlong, *Misiones,* 415–16.

16. Sarreal, *The Guaraní and Their Missions,* 83–84 and 226.

17. The missions accounted for 15–25 percent of all yerba mate sales (Garavaglia, *Mercado,* 68–72).

18. Dobrizhoffer, *An Account,* 1:100–1.

19. Sarreal, *The Guaraní and Their Missions,* 82–84, 87–89.

20. "Carta anua de Pedgro Ignacio Frías," 1689–1700, as quoted in Page, *El colegio,* 256.

21. "Carta de Francisco Garcia," in Jarque, *Insignes,* 375.

22. Dobrizhoffer, *An Account,* 3:160.

23. Paucke, *Hacia allá,* 2:93–97.

24. Paucke, *Hacia allá,* 2:103–6.

25. "Acto del cabildo," Santa Fe, February 18, 1654, Tomo III B, *I-1–1/III-F.352-I-1–1/III-F.354, https://www.santafe.gov.ar/actascabildo/default/buscar/2/01_01_1573–31_12_1810/yerba; "Acto del cabildo," Santa Fe, March 30, 1656, Tomo III B, *I-1–1/III-F.484-I-1–1/III-F.485, https://www.santafe.gov.ar/actascabildo/default/buscar/3/01_01_1573–31_12_1810/yerba.

26. "Copia de memorial de José García Inclán," November 8, 1720, AGI, Charcas 237.

27. "Tratado de Paz," 1732, in Biedma, *Acuerdos* 6:2, 6:468.

28. Campo de Bloqueo, 1757–08–06 and 1757–08–06, AGN Sala IX, 4–3-1.

29. "Testimonio de Baltasar de Pucheta," May 29, 1636, AGI, Escribania 892A.

30. "Razon de lo que dice el Yndio," Montevideo, November 13, 1751, f. 794, AGN, IX. 2–1-4.

31. "Diario de la expedición a Salinas," 1808, as quoted in Nacuzzi, *Diarios,* vol. 3, no. 2, p. 14.

32. Aguirre, "Diario del capitán," 19:357.

33. Biedma, *Acuerdos,* 2:144; "Acto del cabildo," Santa Fe, August 12, 1658, tomo III B, *I-1–1/III-F559v-I-1–1/III-F560v, https://www.santafe.gov.ar/actascabildo/default/buscar/3/01_01_1573–31_12_1810/yerba.

34. Furlong, *José Cardiel,* 149.

35. Lozano, *Historia de la conquista,* 1:410.

36. Haenke, *Viaje,* 63.

37. Rengger, *Viaje,* 127–28.

38. Garavaglia, *Mercado.*

39. "Carta del cabildo," Asunción, December 22, 1620, AGI, Charcas 33.

40. "Informe del arzobispo de la Plata," July 27, 1690, AGI, Charcas 282.

41. Aguirre, "Diario del capitán," 18:368–69.

42. Garavaglia, *Mercado,* 68–69.

43. De Massiac, *Plan francés,* 74.

44. Garavaglia, *Mercado,* 70 and 75.

45. Biscay, *An Account,* 10.

46. Testimonies in the petition by Pedro del Casal, procurador general of Santa Fe, May 24, 1681, AGI, Charcas 282.

47. "Informe del Real Audiencia de la Plata," June 5, 1696, AGI, Charcas 282.

48. "Carta de la real audiencia de Charcas," August 3, 1706, AGI, Charcas 282. A similar statement is in "Dictamen del Fiscal," Madrid, September 1, 1701, AGI, Charcas 282.

49. Richard and Giráldez, "An Appetite for Small Change"; Shell, *Wampum.*

50. Valenze, *Social Life,* 44–50; Avery, *The Tea Road,* 33–34; Einzig, *Primitive Money,* 107–9 and 300–3.

51. Richard and Giráldez, "An Appetite"; Ennis, "Shortages," 3–5.

52. Carrió de la Vandera, *El lazarillo,* 178.

53. Zavala, "Apuntes históricos"; Pusineri Scala, *Historia de la moneda.*

54. Gonzalo del Valle and Juan Bautista de Elorriaga as quoted in Bouza, "El arbitrio," 83 and 87.

55. "Cédula real," February 26, 1680, ANA, Sección de Historia, vol. 8, no. 2; "Testimonio de Francisco Resguin," May 24, 1681, AGI, Charcas 282; Dobrizhoffer, *An Account,* 1:108–9.

56. "Carta de los pobladores de Curuguaty," August 21, 1717, AGI, Charcas 216; "Carta de los pobladores de Curuguaty," June 12, 1719, AGI, Charcas 216.

57. "Visita de Manuel Antonio de la Torre," 1761, AGI, Buenos Aires, 166 ; "Carta de Andres Cornejo," 1662, AGI, Charcas 1622, vol. 148B.

58. Report about Francisco Obet's estate, November 22, 1729, AGI Charcas 117; various documents discussing Francisco Obet's estate, Madrid, 1731, AGI Charcas 217.

59. Telesca, "La colonia," 95.

60. Aguirre, "Diario del capitán," 18:294.

61. Griego, *The Politics of Giving,* 110.

62. "Todo hombre es yerba; con esta yerba, dejan los Paraguayos de ser hombres; cuando con ella se hacen hombres otros; y porque este punto es el enigma de Paraguay." For this and the following description see "Informe de Manuel Antonio de la Torre," September 31, 1761, AGI, Buenos Aires 166.

63. "Informe de Raphael de la Moneda,"April 18, 1744, AGI, Charcas 217; Sánchez Labrador, *El Paraguay Católico,* 2:212; de Pinedo, "Informe del Goberrnador del Paraguay," 3–10.

64. "Respuesta del fiscal and Consejo de Indias," December 23, 1763 and March 17, 1764, AGI, Buenos Aires 166.

65. Herzog, *Frontiers;* Cardim et al., *Polycentric Monarchies*; Grafe and Irigoin, "A Stakeholder Empire."

66. Irigoin and Grafe, "Bargaining for Absolutism."

67. Flynn and Giráldez, "Born with a 'Silver Spoon,'" 202.

68. Grafe and Irigoin, "A Stakeholder Empire."

69. "Testimonio de Antonio Canañas Ampuero," October 2, 1697, AGI, Escribania 899C.

70. "Carta de Diego de los Reyes E. Almaseda," August 28, 1717, AGI, Charcas, 216.

71. "Carta de los poblanos de Curuguaty," June 12, 1719, AGI, Charcas 216; "Informe de Raphael de la Moneda," April 18, 1744, AGI Charcas 217; "Carta de Jaime Just," Asunción, February 20, 1752, AGI, Charcas 217.

72. Aguirre, "Diario del capitán," 18:372 and 19:254.

73. Bigelow, *Mining Language,* 33, 264–65.

74. Whigham, *The Politics of River Trade,* 110.

75. "Bando de Vera Muxica," 1684, mentioned in Garavaglia, *Mercado,* 246.

76. Pinedo, "Informe del goberrnador del Paraguay," 11–12.

77. "Informe del cabildo," Santa Fe, March 6, 1745, Tomo XI, https://www.santafe .gov.ar/actascabildo/default/manuscrito/6675-6_de_Marzo_de_1745; various documents about the proposal of an estanco of yerba, 1764 AGI, Buenos Aires 166.

78. "Carta de Juan de Porral de la Amarilla," November 7, 1602, AGI, Charcas 48.

79. Leasing of the "coca" or yerba of Maracayú, Sección Copias, ANA, 1603, Vol. 14, f. 63–64.

80. Garavaglia, *Mercado,* 69; López, "The Economics," 504.

81. Bouza, "El arbitrio.'"

82. A *beneficio general* permitted yerba production for ten months of the year, while a *beneficio simple* allowed it year-round. "Carta de Juan Diez de Andino," April 30, 1682, AGI, Charcas 279; Governor Juan Rodriguez Cota, October 22, 1697 and December 23, 1697, AGI, Escribania 899C; Garavaglia, *Mercado,* 229–380.

83. "Testimonio de Juan Mendez de Carvajal," 1686 AGI, Escribania 899C; "Carta del cabildo," Asunción, October 2, 1697, AGI, Escribania 899C.

84. "Cedula real," September 15, 1679, AGI, Charcas 33. See also Garavaglia, *Mercado,* 68–69.

85. "Carta de Joseph Martínez de Salazar," June 16, 1664 and Real Cedula, February 26, 1680, AGI, Charcas 278; Charcas 279; and Charcas 282.

86. Melchor de Navarro, October 24, 1683, AGI, Charcas 282 ; Rivarola Paoli, *La economía colonial,* 1:363.

87. Royal Cedula, December 31, 1701, AGI, Buenos Aires, 4, L. 12; Royal Cedula, January 17, 1717, as described in Contreras and Cortés, eds. *Catalogo,* 2:191; Real Cedula issued in Madrid, October 27, 1728; "Acta del cabildo," Santa Fe, May 11, 1729, Carpeta 14 B 74, Carpeta 14B, https://www.santafe.gov.ar/actascabildo /default/buscar/4/01_01_1573–31_12_1867/sisa%20de%20yerba; Simon Tagle Bracho, Procurador General of Buenos Aires, April 25, 1733, AGI, Charcas 33.

88. Royal Cedula, August 18, 1726, as quoted in Cervera, *Historia de la ciudad,* vol. 1 appendix 26, 100–101; "Actas del cabildo," Santa Fe, March 6, 1745, Tomo XI, https://www.santafe.gov.ar/actascabildo/default/manuscrito/6675–6_de_Marzo_ de_1745; Rivarola Paoli, *La economía colonial,* 1:373 ; Contreras and Cortés, *Catalogo,* 3:311; request by the governor, Madrid, October 11, 1775, AGI 122–3-13, as described in *Catálogo de documentos del Archivo de Indias,* 2:239.

89. Dobrizhoffer, *An Account,* 3:100 and 3:103.

90. Mathias Flores Bohórquez and others to the king, Potosí, February 4, 1762, AGI, Charcas 59.

91. "Carta de Ambrosio O'Higgins," November 5, 1788, AGI, Chile 210.

92. "Carta de Ambrosio O'Higgins," November 5, 1788, AGI, Chile 210.

93. "Informe de Manuel Peres Cotapos," September 18, 1788, AGI, Chile 211.

94. "Informe de Manuel Peres Cotapos," September 18, 1788, AGI, Chile 211.

95. Barros Arana, *Historia general,* 7:17 and 7:48.

96. Born in Tucumán and raised in South America, de León Pinelo likely came into contact with yerba mate in South America. See de León Pinelo, *Question moral,* 64–65.

97. Cobo, *Historia del nuevo mundo,* 2:97.

98. Gemelli Careri, "A Voyage," 4:503.

99. Sorsby, "British Trade," 285.

100. *Daily Post,* January 19, 21, and 22, 1741.

101. De Jaucourt, "Herbe du Paraguay."

102. Southey, *History of Brazil,* 2:356–59.

103. Massiac, *Plan francés,* 74.

104. The author wrote his proposal in 1711, but the document was published in 1739. See *A Proposal for Humbling Spain,* 14–15, 19–20, and 42.

105. William Temple, "Letter to the Editor," Trowbridge, July 19, 1762, *Lloyd's Evening Post,* July 21, 1762.

106. *A Summary Account,* 22–23.

107. Pernetty, *The History,* 135; Malisset, *La Parfait Intelligence,* 277.

108. de Ulloa, *A Voyage to South-America,* 178.

109. "Carta de D. Jorge Escobedo," *Lima,* November 5, 1787, AMCN, Microfilm, roll 6: "Flora Peruana y Chilense," Ref. 126–151.

110. "Prosigue la materia de Buenos-Ayres," *Diario Noticioso, Curioso, Erudito y Comercial Público y Económico* 93 (April 25, 1760): 185–86.

111. "Explicación de la yerba del Paraguay," *Diario Noticioso, Curioso, Erudito y Comercial Público y Económico* 108 (May 13, 1760): 215–16.

112. "Prosigue la materia," *Diario Noticioso, Curioso, Erudito y Comercial Público y Económico* 125 (June 4, 1760): 249–50.

113. Dobrizhoffer, *An Account,* 1:107

114. De Azara, *Geografía, física,* 332.

115. Southey, *History of Brazil,* 3:297.

116. Rappaport, *A Thirst for Empire,* 48–50; Lawson, *A Taste for Empire,* 1–21; S. Smith, "Accounting for Taste," 196; Burnett, *Liquid Pleasure,* 53.

117. Aguirre, "Diario del capitán," 18:370. Jesuit authors also wrote that the English purposefully tried to stop the spread of yerba mate in Europe (Lozano, *Historia de la conquista,* 202).

118. This quote was not included in the English translation. See Dobrizhoffer, *Historia de los Abipones,* 1:203–4.

119. Kowaleski-Wallace, "Tea, Gender."

120. Gillespie, *Gleanings and Remarks,* 157–58.

CHAPTER 3

1. Bonpland, "Nota sobre la utilidad," 270.

2. For simplicity, I will use the term "Argentina" even though it was not a single, united country until 1880. Between 1810 and 1831, a union of provinces was called the United Provinces of the Río de la Plata. From 1831 to 1852, the provinces organized into the Argentine Confederation, but did not include the province of Buenos Aires between 1853 and 1861. In 1860, a presidential decree gave the country the name that continues to be used today, "Argentine Republic."

3. Robertson and Robertson, *Letters on Paraguay,* 1:182, 343, and 359.

4. Robertson and Robertson, *Francia's Reign of Terror,* 21.

5. Whigham, *The Politics of River Trade.*

6. Pastore, "Trade Contraction."

7. Whigham, *The Politics of River Trade.*

8. Whigam, *The Politics of River Trade,* 120 and 127.

9. Rengger, *Viaje,* esp. 159, 342 and 348.

10. One year the quantity exported exceed the 1816 peak. See Whigham, *The Politics of River Trade,* 127; Reber, "Commerce," 47.

11. Parish, *Buenos Ayres,* 234–35.

12. Whigham, *The Politics of River Trade,* 71, 127, and 148.

13. Miers, *Travels in Chile and La Plata,* 1:70; Caldcleugh, *Travels in South America,* 1:255, 1:261, 1:283, 2:121, 2:124, 2:146, 2:172; Schmidtmeyer, *Travels into Chile,* 197 and 249.

14. Parish, *Buenos Ayres,* 349.

15. Pickett, "Mate," 31; Brackenridge, *Voyage to Buenos Aires,* 56.

16. Caldcleugh, *Travels in South America,* 1:133. Schmidtmeyer, *Travels into Chile,* 38–39.

17. Parish, *Buenos Ayres,* xi-xiii. In 1825, Woodbine Parish got permission from Francia for various British subjects (who took large quantities of yerba mate) to leave the country. See Robertson and Robertson, *Francia's Reign,* 2:63–64.

18. Rengger, *Viaje,* 343.

19. Caldcleugh, *Travels in South America,* 1:132.

20. Linhares, *Historia económica,* 76, 91, 105.

21. Bolsi, "El primer siglo," 128.

22. Galarza, "La yerba-mate," 79.

23. Bolsi, "El primer siglo," 134.

24. Departamento de Hacienda, *Memoria presentada,* viii and xii.

25. Misiones was part of the province of Corrientes until 1881 when it became a National Territory. In 1953, Misiones became a province.

26. Bell, *A Life in Shadow,* esp. 39.

27. "Carta de Aimé Bonpland," November 6, 1854, in Pujol, *Corrientes,* 4:254–255; Bell, *A Life in Shadow,* 40.

28. Bonpland, "Nota sobre la utilidad," 270.

29. See for example, Aimé Bonpland, "Letter to Fr. Delessert, Montevideo, Dec. 26, 1853," in Hemy, *Aimé Bonpland,* 179; "Notas de Bompland," Sept. 30, 1854," in Pujol, *Corrientes,* 4:199–210.

30. De la Fuente, *Children of Facundo*; Halperín Donghi, *Historias de caudillos argentinos.*

31. Whigham, "Cattle Raising."

32. Bell, *A Life in Shadow,* 51. On November 9, 1832, Corrientes issued a decree attempting to establish an official yerba mate industry in Misiones by inviting all Argentines, after obtaining a government-issued license, to exploit yerba mate in the forests of the former Jesuit missions (Eidt, *Pioneer Settlement,* 60).

33. Bell, *A Life in Shadow,* 42–64.

34. Robertson and Robertson, *Letters,* 2:132–134.

35. "Carta de Francisco Ramírez," September 4, 1820, as quoted in Machón, *Misiones,* 166–67.

36. León Esquivel, Commander of Caá-Catí, November 13, 1820, as quoted in Gómez, *Corrientes,* 71.

37. "Carta de Francisco Javier Sití," November 17, 1820, as quoted in Machón, *Misiones,* 183–84.

38. Poenitz and Poenitz, *Misiones,* 205–9.

39. Lynch, "From Independence," 9–10.

40. "Ley de Aduana," December 18, 1835, in *Registro Oficial de la República Argentina,* 2:359–61.

41. "Carta de Juan Manuel de Rosas," July 20, 1836, as quoted in Levene, ed., *Historia de la nación,* 7:182–83.

42. *El Comercio,* May 3, 1850, as quoted in Hemy, *Aimé Bonpland,* 194; Parish, *Buenos Ayres,* 226 and 347.

43. "Carta de Justo J. de Urquiza," November 15, 1854, in Pujol, *Corrientes,* 4:268.

44. Bonpland proposed his plan for yerba to Pujol in writing. See "Carta de Aimé Bonpland," September 30, 1854, and "Carta de Aimé Bonpland," October 27, 1854, in Pujol, *Corrientes,* 4:197–210 and 243–45; Bell, *A Life in Shadow,* 182–207.

45. Whigham, "Cattle Raising," 332.

46. "Carta de Guillermo Rawson," June 13, 1863, as quoted in F. Palma, "Un momento," 208.

47. Whigham, *The Road to Armageddon.*

48. Burmeister, *Memoria sobre el territorio,* 44.

49. República de Argentina, *Primer censo,* 608; Eidt, *Pioneer Settlement,* 79.

50. De Basaldúa, *Pasado, presente,* 182–83; Cambas, "Historia de la Provincia," 292–93; Provincia de Misiones, *Planeamiento de la Provincia* 2:25 ; Peyret, *Cartas,* 100–2.

51. Ambrosetti, "Los indios cainguá," 713–14, 724–25, and 727.

52. Julio A. Roca, "Discurso ante el congreso al asumir la presidencia," October 12, 1880, in Halperín Donghi, *Proyecto y construcción,* 437.

53. The census report blamed the population loss on the wars of 1817 and 1820 (República de Argentina, *Primer censo,* 608).

54. "Carta de Julio A. Roca," July 5, 1881, in Sanches Negrete, *Cuestión-Misiones,* 1.

55. "Carta de Julio A. Roca," July 5, 1881, in Sanches Negrete, *Cuestión-Misiones*, 4 and 5.

56. Eidt, *Pioneer Settlement,* 66–68 ; Bartolomé, *Los colonos,* 93–94.

57. Rock, *Argentina, 1516–1987,* 137; Gori, *Inmigración.*

58. "Carta de Julio A. Roca," July 5, 1881, in Sanches Negrete, *Cuestión-Misiones,* 4.

59. Law 1149—Federalización del Territorio de Misiones.

60. "Carta de Antonio Gallino," January 16, 1882; "Severo Fernandez to Julio Roca," January 14, 1882, AGN, Sala 8, Fondo General Julio A. Roca, Legajo 21; "Ley

sobre venta de tierras públicas," June 22, 1881, in Provincia de Corrientes, *Recopilación completa,* 2:39; Ministerio de Agricultura de la Nación, *Memoria de la Dirección General,* 16.

61. "Carta de Rudecindo Roca," January 14, 1882, AGN, Sala 8, Fondo General Julio A. Roca, Legajo 21.

62. Ministerio de Agricultura de la Nación, *Memoria de la Dirección General de Tierras,* 16; Eidt, *Pioneer Settlement,* 74–77 and 84.

63. Juan Balestra, "Informe elevado al Ministerio del Interior," January 1894, in Gobernación de Misiones, *La tierra pública y su colonización,* 18; "Colonización y fomento de la yerba mate, proyecto de ley," in DSCD, *1919* 5 (1919): 495.

64. Article 14 of Law 817 *Ley de Inmigración y Colonización* passed on October 6, 1876.

65 Law 1,265. "Ley de venta de tierras y división de los territorios nacionales," November 3, 1882, in Gobernación de Misiones, *La tierra pública,* 53–61.

66. Title 3, article 13 of the law; see Gobernación de Misiones, *La tierra pública,* 58.

67. Eidt, *Pioneer Settlement,* 60, 64, and 80. Corrientes passed legislation in 1880 that allowed in specific cases for the sale of land with yerbales, but no sales were ever made. See "Ley sobre venta de terrenos con yerbales, Corrientes, January 3, 1880," in Provincia de Corrientes, *Recopilación completa de códigos, leyes y decretos reglamentarios,* 30–34; Balestra, "Informe elevado," in Gobernación de Misiones, *La tierra pública,* 14.

68. Balestra, "Informe elevado," in Gobernación de Misiones, *La tierra pública,* 13 and 17. Miner (*minero*) was a common term for yerba workers (Ambrosetti, "Segundo viaje," 73–78).

69. Eidt, *Pioneer Settlement,* 84; Germani, "Mass Immigration," 166.

70. Ministerio de Agricultura, *Memoria de la Dirección General de Tierras,* 188.

71. "Informe del Gobernador Lanusse," October 1, 1898, 1898, AGN, Archivo Intermedio, MI, 1898, L. 10, Expediente 4438.

72. Balestra, "Informe elevado al Ministerio del Interior," in Gobernación de Misiones, *La tierra pública,* 3–23.

73. Gobernación de Misiones, *Memorias correspondientes,* 11 and 37.

74. Bartolomé, *Los colonos,* 99–110; Abínzano, "Procesos de integración."

75. Yssouribehere, "Investigación agrícola," 192.

76. Niederlein, *Mis exploraciones,* 4 and 7.

77. República de Argentina, *Segundo censo,* 2:643, 2:657, 2:660, and 2:662; Balestra, "Informe elevado al Ministerio del Interior," in Gobernación de Misiones, *La tierra pública,* 4; Bolsi, "El proceso," 29–33; "Informe del Gobernador Lanusse," October 1, 1898, AGN, Archivo Intermedio, MI, 1898, L. 10, Expediente 4438.

78. Yssouribehere, "Investigación agrícola," 50.

79. Bolsi, "El proceso," 33.

80. Rau, *Cosechando,* 40.

81. Bolsi, "El primer siglo," 142; República de Argentina, *Segundo censo,* 2:648 and 2:651; Eidt, *Pioneer Settlement,* 82.

82. Bolsi, "Misiones," 29.

83. Mulhall, *Handbook,* 1:4.

84. Antonini, "La yerba mate," 115; Girola, "Cultivo de la yerba mate. . .Comercio," 491; Billard, *Economía,* 8, 68, and 73.

85. Alcaráz, *Una etnografía,* 127.

86. Magalhães, *Retratos;* Alcaráz, *Una etnografía,* 121–50.

87. Alcaráz, *Una etnografía,* 93–120; Reber, "Commerce," 48–53; "Actualidad paraguaya,'" *Caras y Caretas* 7 (1904).

88. Alcaráz, *Una etnografía,* 65–92.

89. Julian Bouvier, "El oeste paranense," *A Noticia,* April 10, 1908.

90. Hernández, *Cartas,* 115.

91. "Appendix B: Report on Yerba Mate or Paraguay Tea," in Bureau of the American Republics, *Handbook of Paraguay,* 99.

92. Ministerio de Agricultura, *Ley de bosques,* 19.

93. Bolsi, "Misiones," 50–51; Gobernación de Misiones, *La tierra pública.*

94. Queirel, *Misiones,* 302–3; Bolsi, "El primer siglo," 146–49; Gobernación de Misiones, *La tierra pública.*

95. Explotación de Yerbales, January 3, 1896, 10th sesión de prórroga, DSCD, *1895,* vol. 2 (1896): 978.

96. Sarreal, "Disorder."

97. Dirección General de Agricultura y Defensa Agrícola, *Debates de la conferencia,* 13.

98. Gobernación de Misiones, *La tierra pública.*

99. Balestra, "Informe elevado al Ministerio del Interior," in Gobernación de Misiones, *La tierra pública,* 17 and 21; Queirel, *Misiones,* 306–7; Dirección General de Agricultura y Defensa Agrícola, *Debates de la conferencia,* 8, 2–6, and 30.

100. Barreyro, *Ideas de gobierno,* 21

101. Bernárdez, *De Buenos Aires,* 84–85.

102. Dirección General de Agricultura y Defensa Agrícola, *Debates de la conferencia,* 4.

103. Barreyro, *Ideas de gobierno,* 12 and 24.

104. "Informe del Gobernador Lanusse," October 1, 1898, AGN, Archivo Intermedio, MI, 1898, L. 10, Expediente 4438.

105. Leguizamón, *Yerba-mate,* 12–13.

106. Luis N. Barbagelata, "La Yerba," *La Prensa,* August 27, 1894.

107. Bermúdez, *Informe del gobernador,* 55.

108. Queirel, *Misiones,* 306.

109. Queirel, *Misiones,* 308; "Informe del Gobernador Lanusse," October 1, 1898, AGN, Archivo Intermedio, MI, 1898, L. 10, Expediente 4438; Burmeister, *Memoria.*

110. As quoted in Queirel, *Misiones,* 308.

111. *Decreto sobre explotación de yerbales, Dec. 18, 1903* and *Reglamento of 1907.*

112. Yssouribehere, "Investigación agrícola," 95–96.

113. "Por el Alto Paraná," *La Prensa,* December 18, 1911.

114. Ministerio de Agricultura, *Ley de bosques,* 36.

115. Carlos D. Girola, "Cultivo de la yerba mate... Comercio," 494.

116. Rau, *Cosechando,* 40.

CHAPTER 4

1. Brant, *Viaje,* 83–84.

2. Pilcher, *¡Que Vivan los Tamales!,* 45–98.

3. Carretero, *Vida cotidiana,* 1:65.

4. Love, *A Five Years' Residence,* 59.

5. Isabelle, *Viaje,* 200; Beaumont, *Travels in Buenos Ayres,* 62; Brackenridge, *Voyage to Buenos Aires,* 56.

6. Bacle y Cía lithograph, "No.1. Trajes y costumbres de Buenos-Aires. Señora porteña por la mañana," 1833, in González Garaño, *Trages y costumbres.*

7. Carlos Enrique Pellegrini, *Minué en los Altos de Escalada,* 1834; Carlos Enrique Pellegrini, *Minué en casa de Villarino,* approximately 1831; Carlos Enrique Pellegrini, *Tertulia porteña,* approximately 1831, colección Minetti de Rosario.

8. Love, *A Five Years' Residence,* 59.

9. "Parada para hacer noche" and "El asado," in Palliere, *Albúm Palliere;* "El rancho," in Pellegrini, *Recuerdos.*

10. "El gato, baile campestre," in Palliere, *Albúm Palliere;* "Media caña" and "Cielito," in Pellegrini, *Recuerdos.*

11. Pueyrredón, "Un alto en el campo," 1861, and "Un domingo en los suburbios de San Isidro," 1864, at Museo Bellas Artes, Buenos Aires, Argentina.

12. For example, Caldcleugh, *Travels in South America,* 1:255, 1:261, 1:283, 2:121, 2:124, 2:146, 2:172; Schmidtmeyer, *Travels into Chile,* 197 and 249; Miller, *Memoirs,* 1:151–52; Armaignac, *Viajes,* 42; Vidal, *Picturesque Illustrations,* 75 and 77; Beaumont, *Travels in Buenos Ayres,* 64 and 66.

13. Prieto, *Los viajeros ingleses;* Cicerchia, *Journey.*

14. Lehman, "The Gaucho"; Hobsbawm, "The American Cowboy"; Slatta, *Gauchos,* 20–29; Buss, *Winning,* 43–47.

15. Sarmiento did not even have any firsthand knowledge of the gauchos and had not crossed the pampas by the time he wrote *Facundo* (Slatta, *Gauchos,* 182).

16. Adamovsky, *El gaucho indómito.*

17. Gutiérrez, *The Gaucho Juan Moreira,* xii.

18. Bartolome Hidalgo, "Un gaucho de la guardia del monte contesta al manifiesto de Fernando VII," 1820, in Ludmer, *The Gaucho Genre,* 62–63.

19. Until recently, most scholars attributed the idea of a divide between civilization and barbarism to Sarmiento, while in fact such descriptions circulated in the 1820s and 1830s. See de la Fuente, "'Civilización y barbarie.'" The underlying belief that the Buenos Aires elite were superior to the rest of the population had even older roots (N. Shumway, *The Invention*).

20. As quoted in Slatta, *Gauchosa,* 180–81. See N. Shumway, *The Invention,* 265.

21. Sarmiento, *Facundo,* esp. 16–17; Lehman, "The Gaucho," 154–59; Slatta, *Gauchos,* 180–83; Delaney, "Making Sense of Modernity," 443–45.

22. MacCann, *Two Thousand Miles,* 1:24 and 1:156–58.

23. Gutiérrez, *Historia de Juan Manuel de Rosas,* 85.

24. Cayetano Descalzi, *Boudoir Federal,* circa 1845, https://commons.wikimedia .org/wiki/File:Boudoir_federal_de_Cayetano_Descalzi.jpg.

25. Raymond Monvoisin, *Soldado de la guardia de Rosas,* 1842, https://es .wikipedia.org/wiki/Archivo:Monvoisin,_Raymond_-_Soldado_de_la_guardia_ de_Rosas_-1842.jpg.

26. Barbará, *Diabluras,* 38.

27. Sarmiento, *Facundo,* 157.

28. "Carta de Juan Manuel de Rosas," August 7, 1864 as quoted in Raed, Rosas: *Cartas confidenciales,* 52.

29. "Escenas de los tiempos pasados," 1882, in Quesada, *Memorias,* 1:207.

30. "La juventud en la época de Rosas," 1883, in Quesada, *Memorias,* 1:319–22.

31. "Mi tío Blas: recuerdos del tiempos pasados," January 1883, in Quesada, *Memorias,* 1:293 and 309.

32. Wilde, *Buenos Aires,* 244 and 234.

33. Beck-Bernard, *El Río Paraná,* 88.

34. Gay, *Atlas de la historia física,* vol. 1, No. 30 and 31.

35. Couyoumdjian, "El mate."

36. "Notas de mi viaje," *La Prensa,* February 20, 1911. Similar descriptions are in Clemenceau, *South America To-Day,* 44–45, and Georges Clemenceau, "'The Oriental Band,'" *New York Times,* February 12, 1911.

37. Obligado, *Tradiciones argentinas,* 65–69. There is no indication of any working-class cafés in Buenos Aires before the second half of the nineteenth century (González Bernaldo de Quirós, *Civility and Politics,* 61).

38. Article dated November 29 (year unknown), as quoted in United States Consul Baker, "Appendix B: Report on Yerba Mate or Paraguay Tea," in Bureau of the American Republics, *Handbook of Paraguay,* 103.

39. Elliott, *The Argentina of To-Day,* 162. An 1899 law prohibited policemen from using mate while on duty. Twenty-seven years later, policemen were again allowed to drink mate, but without sharing and only outside of public view (Pau Navajas, *Caá porá,* 253).

40. Pellegrini, "Mate," 55.

41. *Cultivo de la yerba mate (Ilex Paraguariensis St. Hil.): Consumo,* 2.

42. Mariquita Sánchez to Enrique Lezica, December 6, 1854, as quoted in Shumway, *A Woman,* 237.

43. In a letter to *La Prensa,* a doctor promoted mate because it was a cheap and indirect means for getting people to drink sterilized (boiled) water ("La guardia nacional en campaña," *La Prensa,* April 16, 1896).

44. "La matenia," *La Prensa,* December 31, 1919. For more about tuberculosis see Armus, *The Ailing City.*

45. Uzal, "La yerba mate como bebida higiénica," 65.

46. Granada, *Reseña,* 233–34.

47. Ebelot, *La Pampa,* 224–25.

48. William Acree generously shared various primary sources that are only accessible in Argentine archives.

49. Torrejón, *Lectura de economía doméstica.*

50. A. Palma, *El hogar modelo,* 17, 147–49.

51. Elsewhere in the book when topics related to mate were discussed, yerba mate was not mentioned (*Economía doméstica al alcance de las niñas,* 46 and 41, and 22).

52. Fragueiro, "Lectura XXX," 97–100.

53. Pulido, *Urbanidad y cortesía,* 23.

54. Corrado, *Contribución,* 12. The Mate Museum in Tigre, Argentina showcases an example of a hygienic bombilla, called "mate higiénico alemán."

55. "El mate," *Caras y Caretas,* December 23, 1916, 91.

56. "Nuestras costumbres viejas," *El Soldado Argentino,* April 15, 1923.

57. Villanueva, *Obras completas,* 135.

58. "El mate," *Caras y Caretas,* December 23, 1916, 90.

59. Daireaux, *La cría,* 72.

60. Slatta, *Gauchos,* 49.

61. Ebelot, *La Pampa,* 205–6 and 226–27.

62. Delaney, "Making Sense of Modernity."

63. Hora, *The Landowners,* 45–67.

64. Slatta, *Gauchos.*

65. Germani, "Mass Immigration," 166.

66. Adamovsky, *El gaucho indómito*; Delaney, "Making Sense of Modernity"; Slatta, *Gauchos,* 191; Chamosa, *The Argentine Folklore Movement,* 22–26.

67. Adamovsky, *El gaucho indómito,* 26–31.

68. Hernández, *The Gaucho Martín Fierro,* 15–16.

69. Hernández, *El gaucho Martín Fierro; La vuelta,* 29, 140, and 146.

70. Hernández, *El gaucho Martín Fierro; La vuelta,* 149, 157, 164, 178, and 206.

71. Gutiérrez, *The Gaucho Juan Moreira,* 7, 8, 11, 17, 21, 57–59, 63, 67, 68, and 76.

72. Gutiérrez, *The Gaucho Juan Moreira,* 20.

73. Acree, *Staging Frontiers,* 27. *El mate y los gauchos* shown at the Teatro Argentino in 1857 was a precursor of gauchesque themes in the Argentine circus (Seibel, *Historia del circo,* 28).

74. Acree, *Staging Frontiers.*

75. Acree, *Staging Frontiers,* 129–58.

76. Prieto identified the first three functions (*El discurso criollista*); Adamovsky identified the fourth function ("La cuarta función").

77. Cunninghame Graham and Cunninghame Graham, "A Vanishing Race," in *Father Archangel of Scotland,* 180.

78. Armaignac, *Viajes,* 42.

79. MacCann, *Two Thousand Miles,* 1:156.

80. Hammerton, *The Real Argentina,* 319.

81. Ebelot, *La pampa,* 217–18.

82. Silva, *Costumbres campestres,* esp. 102–3 and 121–27.

83. Pite, "The Rural Woman."

84. Humberto Cairo, Ernesto Gunche, and Eduardo Martínez de la Pera, dirs., *Nobleza gaucha,* 1915.

85. Carmen Gazcon de Vela, "El mate," in Gorriti, ed., *Cocina ecléctica,* 390–92.

86. Emilio (surname illegible), "Letter to the Editor, Berlin Aug. 1905," *La Nación,* September 23, 1905.

87. Pellegrini, "Mate," 55.

88. Larson, *Our Indigenous Ancestors.*

89. Vidal, *Picturesque Illustrations*; Beaumont, *Travels in Buenos Ayres,* 54; Mac-Cann, *Two Thousand Miles,* 41, 112, and 135.

90. "Nuestras costumbres viejas: El mate," *El Soldado Argentino,* April 15, 1923.

91. Daumas, "El problema," 49–50; Antonini, "La yerba mate," 115.

92. Gupta, "The History of the International Tea Market."

93. G. Clemenceau, "Notas de mi viaje," *La Prensa,* February 20, 1911; Clemenceau, *South America To-Day,* 45.

94. "La yerba mate," *La Nación,* March 27, 1912; "Informe del Gobernador Lanusse," October 1, 1898, AGN, Archivo Intermedio, MI, 1898, L. 10, Expediente 4438; "Impuestos de Aduana, July 22, 1891," DSCD, *1891* 1 (1891): 351–66.

95. Departamento Nacional del Trabajo, *Boletín del Departamento Nacional,* 241–44. Subsequent publications by the Department of Labor that discussed cost of living almost always included yerba mate as one of the basic necessities.

96. "Carta del Presidente Roca," in Martín & Compañía, *Julio U. Martín,* 48.

97. Granada, *Reseña,* 233.

98. Gallardo, *La industria,* 227.

99. Arata, *El mate,* 15.

100. Various editions of Sastre's book were published and it was adopted as an acclaimed book for public schools. See Sastre, *El tempe arjentino,* 13.

101. Arata, *El mate,* 5, 10, and 15.

102. Ambrosetti, *Tercer viaje,* 99–100.

103. Arata, *El mate,* 14 and 23; Gallardo, *La industria,* 227.

104. Carmen Gazcon de Vela, Contributor, "El mate," in Gorriti, *Cocina ecléctica,* 157.

105. Queirel, *Misiones,* 301; Corrado, *Contribución,* 10–11.

106. Hicken, "La yerba-mate," 56 and 66.

107. Brant, *Viaje,* 83–84.

108. Hale, "Yerba Mate," 469; Elliott, *The Argentina of To-Day,* 197–98.

109. Chamosa, *The Argentine Folklore Movement,* 39–46.

110. Alvarez also claimed that mate was not truly Argentine because he attributed its discovery to the Jesuits and not the Guaraní ("La nacionalidad y el mate," *La Prensa,* May 10, 1925).

111. Julio Díaz Usandivaras, "La nacionalidad y el mate," *Nativa,* May 31, 1925.

112. "Hermanos en la gloria!," *La Nación,* June 14, 1928.

113. "Nuestras costumbres viejas," *El soldado Argentina,* año II, no. 43, April 15, 1923.

114. Arata, *El mate,* 14.

115. Juan Alvarez, "La nacionalidad y el mate," *La Prensa,* May 10, 1925.

116. Similarly, immigrants and their children were the main producers and viewers of criollo theatre (Acree, *Staging Frontiers*).

117. Julio Díaz Usandivaras, "La nacionalidad y el mate," *Nativa,* May 31, 1925.

118. Alberto Gerchunoff, "Tomemos mate," *Caras y Caretas,* March 1930.

119. Karush, *Workers or Citizens,* 62–89.

120. Quoted in Hale, "Yerba Mate," 471.

121. "Carta de Verónica Capurro," June 12, 1912, quoted in Cortese, "Inmigrantes italianos," 15.

122. In writing "camp," the author probably means *campo* (or countryside) (Koebel, *Argentina,* 104).

123. Alberto Gerchunoff, "Tomemos mate," *Caras y Caretas,* March 1930.

124. "Impuestos de aduana, July 22, 1891," DSCD, *1891* 1 (1891), 356; Hernández, *Cartas,* 114.

125. J. Puga, *Así fue nuestro destino* (Buenos Aires: s. ed., s. l., 1988), 171, quoted in Núñez Seixas and Farías, "Las autobiografías," 69. Gerchunoff, "Tomemos mate," *Caras y Caretas,* March 1930.

126. Seoane, *Rumbo Argentino,* 40.

127. Lynch, *Massacre.*

128. Mintz, "Eating Communities."

129. Hinchliff, *South American Sketches,* 49.

130. As quoted in Wilde, *Buenos Aires,* 107–8.

131. Quoted in Moya, *Cousins and Strangers,* 54.

132. Nouwen, *Oy, My Buenos Aires,* 3–4, 55–56, and 60.

133. Zago, *Pioneros,* 126 and 167.

134. Glusberg, "Mate amargo," 70 and 74; Nouwen, *Oy, My Buenos Aires,* 34–36.

135. Civantos, *Between Argentines and Arabs*, esp. 1–2.

136. Folch, "Stimulating Consumption," 26.

137. Zago, *Pioneros,* 126.

138. Ignacio Excurra, "Tradición gaucha en Medio Oriente," *La Nación,* January 23, 1966; Folch, "Stimulating Consumption," 29.

139. García Mata and Silva Carneiro, "Consideraciones sobre la exportación," 191; "List of importing countries for the selected product: 0903 Mate," International Trade Statistics, https://www.trademap.org/Country_SelProduct_Map.aspx?nvpm = 1%7c%7c%7c%7c%7c0903%7c%7c%7c4%7c1%7c1%7c1%7c1%7c2%7c1%7c1%7c3, consulted December 21, 2021.

CHAPTER 5

1. Allain, *Proyecto,* 10–11.

2. Larguia, *Misiones—Itapúa,* 125.

3. Allain, *Proyecto,* 4.

4. Della Paolera and Taylor, *A New Economic History,* 3.

5. Stein, *Vassouras*; Sedgewick, *Coffeeland.*

6. Asociación Argentina de Plantadores de Yerba Mate, "El establecimiento 'San Juan' del Señor Otto Bemberg," *Revista Yerbatera* 1, no. 8 (July 1929): 15.

7. Germani, "Mass immigration"; Ministerio del Interior, *Censo general,* 1:135.

8. Abínzano, "Procesos"; Bartolomé, *Los colonos.*

9. Adelman, *Frontier Development*; Taylor, "Latifundia."

10. Scobie, *Revolution,* 51. *Colono* has varied meanings in Latin America. In some places, it has been synonymous with sharecropper, and in others, it means a small-scale landowner. See Schulman, "The Colono System."

11. Navajas, *Caá porã,* 94.

12. Beltrame, "Industria," 163.

13. Pedro Yssouribehere, "Notas," *La Nación,* July 22, 1908.

14. Luis N. Barbagelata, "La yerba," *La Prensa,* August 27, 1894. Other individuals were also credited with the discovery: Juan Bautista Ambrosetti, "La yerba mate," *La Prensa,* August 29, 1894; Huergo, "La yerba mate," 637; letter by Benito Zamboni to *L'Italia del popolo* of Buenos Aires, October 14, 1944, in Zamboni, *Escenas familiares,* 269–70.

15. Burmeister, *Memoria,* 34.

16. Eidt, *Pioneer Settlement,* 103.

17. "Instrucciones para la siembra de la yerba mate," *Boletín de Agricultura y Ganadería* 1, no. 13 (1901): 15; "Aclimatación de la yerba mate," *La Prensa,* July 2, 1901; "Cultivo de la yerba mate," *La Prensa,* July 29, 1901.

18. Queirel, *Misiones,* 299.

19. Bernárdez, *De Buenos Aires,* 84.

20. Burmeister, *Memoria,* 33–34.

21. "Carta de Julio Roca," Martín & Compañía, *Julio U. Martín,* 48.

22. Larguia, *Misiones,* 125–126.

23. Beltrame, "Industria," 163.

24. Allain, "Memorándum," 23. According to a 1904 report, Martín y Cía spent 250,000 pesos to start the enterprise (Yssouribehere, "Investigación," 82–83).

25. Yssouribehere, "Investigación," 82–83.

26. Pedro Yssouribehere, "Notas misioneras," *La Nación,* July 22, 1908.

27. Roger, "Cultivo," 63.

28. Burmeister, *Memoria,* 34; Bernárdez, *De Buenos Aires,* 85–86.

29. Roger, "Cultivo," 47 and 63–64.

30. Uzal, "La yerba mate," 64.

31. "La industria yerbatera," *La Prensa,* January 7, 1907.

32. "La yerba-mate,'" *La Prensa,* January 30, 1909.

33. "Las importaciones de yerba-mate," *La Prensa,* April 28, 1910.

34. "La yerba mate," *La Prensa,* December18, 1911; "Por el Alto Paraná," *La Prensa,* November 2, 1911; "La yerba mate," *La Nación,* March 27, 1912; "Cultivo de la yerba mate," *La Prensa,* March 2, 1914.

35. Cohen, *Pure Adulteration.*

36. Rappaport, *A Thirst,* 120–82.

37. "La industria yerbatera," *La Prensa,* December 23, 1911.

38. Bell, *A Life,* 171–72.

39. Segovia, "Cultivo," 67–69.

40. Scala, "Contribución," 101.

41. Lesage, "Efectos," 98 and 101.

42. Leguizamón, "La yerba-mate," 330.

43. Such descriptions extended Taylorist scientific management ideas about machine-like rationalization beyond labor productivity to the human body (Maier, "Between Taylorism and Technocracy"). Colombian intellectual elite also conceptualized the body as a machine and discussed the what diet would optimize worker efficiency and productivity (Pohl-Valero, "'La raza'").

44. "Yerba Mate Rigoletto (Mackinnon y Coelho)," *La Nación,* December 18, 1915.

45. "La yerba mate," *La Nación,* June 3, 1915.

46. Gallardo, *La industria,* 227–234; Lenoble, "La yerba mate"; Hicken, "La yerba-mate," 65–66; Antonini, "La yerba mate," 112.

47. "A los obreros," *La Vanguardia,* August 31, 1907.

48. "Letter to the Editor," *La Vanguardia,* July 6, 1895.

49. Leguizamón, "La yerba-mate," 335.

50. Galarza, "La yerba-mate," 88.

51. "La Guardia Nacional en campaña," *La Prensa,* April 16, 1896.

52. "Colonización y fomento de la yerba mate. Proyecto de ley," September 24, 1919, DSCD, 5:499.

53. Oestreich-Janzen, "Caffeine," 556; Gootenberg, *Andean Cocaine,* 15–54.

54. Sprecher von Bernegg, *Tropische,* 3:414–17.

55. Gallardo, *La industria,* 227–234; Corrado, *Contribución,* 9–18; Galarza, "La yerba-mate," 88–94.

56. R. Hernández, *Cartas misioneras,* 114.

57. Queirel, *Misiones,* 301; Antonini, "La yerba mate," 112.

58. "An Apparently Harmless Stimulant," 1081.

59. "Yerba Mate," 303; "A Seemingly Harmless Stimulant," 660; Walker, "Yerba Mate."

60. Estlin Grundy, "Carta de Londres," *La Nación,* August 17, 1914.

61. "Yerba-mate para Europa," *La Nación,* February 15, 1918.

62. Baker, "Yerba-Maté"; "Appendix B: Report on Yerba Mate or Paraguay Tea," in Bureau of the American Republics, *Handbook of Paraguay,* 96–104.

63. "'Yerba-Mate' as a Drink," *The News and Herald,* Winnsboro, SC, June 30, 1883; "Yerba-Mate. A South American Beverage That May Supplant Tea and Coffee," *New York Journal,* republished in the *Wichita Daily Eagle,* December 12, 1893 and in the *Griggs Courier,* Griggs, CO, December 15, 1893.

64. Seeger, "Agricultural and Industrial"; Ruffin, "Yerba-Mate Cultivation."

65. Carlos R. Santos, "The Commercial Conditions of Paraguay," and J. Cordeiro da Graça, "Brazil and its Resources," in Butler, *Official Proceedings,* 249–250 and 272–275.

66. "Drinkers of Yerba," *New York Tribune,* republished in *The Yakima Herald,* October 26, 1899; "A Chance for Investors," *The Evening Times,* November 5, 1899; "Of Interest to Americans," *Northern Wisconsin Advertiser,* December 7, 1899; Untitled article published in *The Red Cloud Chief,* February 16, 1900; *Kansas Agitator,* February 16, 1900; *Meade County News,* February 22, 1900; *Rocky Ford Enterprise,* February 22, 1900; and others.

67. Butler, *Paraguay,* 60.

68. Butler, *Yerba Maté,* 31–34.

69. "Yerba Maté."

70. Hale, "Yerba Mate," 1911; Albes, "Yerba Mate," 1916; Cameron, "Maté," 1929.

71. Albes, "Yerba Mate," 643.

72. "Mate May Soon Become Popular Beverage," *The American Bottler*, December 1920, 67.

73. "Latin-American Drink," *Waterbury Evening Democrat,* May 5, 1905; "A New Kind of Tea," *The San Francisco Call,* May 23, 1905; "A Wonderful Herb," *The St. Mary Banner,* September 30, 1905; "Yerba-Mate," *The Columbian,* October 5, 1905; "A Meritorious Latin-American Drink," *Vermont Phoenix,* December 29, 1905; "Yerba Mate Popular as Drink in Argentina," *Evening Star,* October 21, 1916; Victor Elliott, "May Introduce New Drink Here," *South Bend News-Times,* November 24, 1916; "Here's a New Morning Drink," *The Washington Post,* December 25, 1916.

74. Uzal, "La yerba mate," 65; Uzal, "La yerba-mate," 792.

75. Hale, "Yerba Mate," 487.

76. "La yerba mate su producción y consumo," *La Nación,* January 8, 1915; "La yerba mate," *La Nación,* June 3, 1915.

77. "La yerba mate en el ejército Británico," *La Nación,* November 7, 1915.

78. Girola, *Cultivo de la yerba mate. . . Consumo,* 5.

79. Carpenter, "Dependence of Life," 258; Clemenceau, *South America,* 46.

80. Seeger, "Agricultural and Industrial Conditions," 43–44.

81. Zahm, *Through South America's Southland,* 115; reprinted in "Here's a New Morning Drink," *The Washington Post,* December 25, 1916.

82. Albes, "Yerba Mate," 628 and 643.

83. Seeger, "Agricultural and Industrial Conditions," 44.

84. Zahm, *Through South America's Southland,* 115.

85. "Yerba Maté," 259.

86. "Yerba Maté Tea," *The Saturday Evening Post*, May 12, 1900, 1058.

87. "El alcohol y la yerba-mate," *La Nación,* January 31, 1919.

88. Graciela Mandujano, "Mate Tea Popular in Latin Americas," *The Sun,* April 28, 1919; William R. Sanborn, "Will Mate Be Popular Drink after July 1?," *The Richmond Palladium and Sun Telegram,* June 20, 1919.

89. Frederic R. Tibbitts, "So. America Offers Drink for Wets," *The Sun,* June 23, 1919.

90. "A New Temperance Drink," *The American Review of Reviews,* April 1921, 441.

91. "Preparations: New and Old. A New Non-Alcoholic Beverage," *The British Journal of Inebriety* 12, no. 2 (Oct. 1914): 92.

92. "Not Beer or Near Beer But TAY. The New Beverage," *Great Falls Daily Tribune,* July 12, 1919.

93. Advertisements in *The Bemidji Daily Pioneer,* July 27, 1920 and *Grand Folks Herald,* July 26, 1920.

94. Materva advertisement, Villapol and Martínez, *Cocina.*

95. Wong, "Materva."

96. Heimat-und Ortsverein Bad Köstritz e.V., https://www.heimatverein-bad-köstritz.de/ar-bronte.htm.

97. "La yerba mate en Argentina," *La Nación,* February 7, 1910.

98. Girola, *Cultivo de la yerba mate. . .Consumo,* 2.

99. Corrado, *Contribución,* 11.

100. Kaerger, "La introducción," 839–41.

101. "El tabaco, el arroz y la yerba mate," *La Prensa,* October 9, 1911; Fernández Ramos, *Misiones,* 110; Allain, "Proyecto," 6.

102. Baldassarre, "Informe," 171.

103. "Misiones: Enviado del Ministerio de Agricultura," *La Prensa,* July 20, 1908; "La yerba mate en Misiones," *Anales de la Sociedad Rural Argentina* 43 (1908), 193.

104. Yssouribehere, "Investigación," 82–85; Baldassarre, "Informe," 171; Antonini, "La yerba mate," 118 and 120.

105. "Instrucciones para la siembra," 15; Huergo, "La yerba mate"; Galarza, "La yerba-mate"; Oliveira, "Métodos."

106. Molfino, "Carlos D. Girola."

107. Museo Agricola de la Sociedad Rural Argentina, "Publicaciones efectuadas por el Director Honorario Ing. Agr. Carlos D. Girola."

108. "Museo Agrícola: Concurso de yerba mate," *La Prensa,* December 8, 1918; "Sociedad Rural Argentina: plantación de yerba mate," *La Nación,* January 4, 1920.

109. Barreyro, *Ideas de gobierno,* 25–26 and 38–39.

110. "Colonización y fomento de la yerba mate. Proyecto de ley," September 24, 1919, DSCD, 5: 494–501; "Colonización y fomento de la yerba mate," *La Prensa,* September 25, 1919.

111. In contrast to most colonization projects, this legislation did not favor European immigrants. Preference was given to native Argentines, then to naturalized Argentines, then to married foreigners living in Argentina and with children born in Argentina, and then to hard-working immigrants who showed good behavior. See

"Colonización y fomento de la yerba mate. Proyecto de Ley," September 24, 1919, DSCD, 5: 494–501.

112. Ministerio de Agricultura, *Memoria de la Dirección General,* 188.

113. Eidt, *Pioneer,* 143–44; L. Rodríguez, "Estado," 47–48.

114. Gallero, *Con la patria,* 84–89.

115. Gallero, *Piporé,* 16–17.

116. Allain, *Proyecto,* 4.

117. Daumas, "El problema," 21, 49–50.

118. Dirección de Estadístisa Social, *Nivel de vida,* 7; Daumas, "El problema," 54.

119. Allain, *Proyecto,* 3 and 11. Allain, "Memorandum," in Pastoriza, *Conferencia,* 26.

120. Roger, "Cultivo," 63–64.

121. Allain, *Proyecto,* 10–11 and 20; Allain, "Memorándum," 26; Antonini, "La yerba mate," 119–120; Girola, "Cultivo de la yerba mate... Costo de la yerba mate, 19–21, 27–28, and 29; Cámara Argentina de Cultura, Comercio, Industria y Producción, "Una fuente," 22.

122. "El cultivo de la yerba mate y su rendimiento," *La Prensa,* November 18, 1912.

123. Antonini, "La yerba mate," 117.

124. "La industria yerbatera," 220.

125. Bolsi, "Misiones," 91; Bartolomé, *Los colonos,* 150–51.

126. Ministerio del Interior, *Censo general,* 1:207; Girola, *Yerba mate,* 16 and 41.

127. Bolsi, "Misiones," 117.

128. Girola, *Cultivo de la yerba mate... 2nda encuesta,* 19; Barreyro, "Censo," 1625, and Girola, *Cultivo de la yerba mate... quinta encuesta,* 8 and 23–36; Duhau, *Censo.*

129. Barreyro, "Censo," 1626.

130. Fernández Ramos, *Misiones,* 150–63; Eidt, *Pioneer,* 143.

131. Germani, "Mass Immigration," 166; Devoto, *Historia de la inmigración,* 248.

132. República de Argentina, *Segundo censo,* 2:643 and 660; Ministerio del Interior, *Censo general,* 1:135; Presidencia de la Nación, *IV Censo general,* 1:538–39.

133. Meding, "Procesos," 66; Gallero, *Con la patria.*

134. Ministerio de Agricultura, *Censo nacional agropecuario,* 1937, 2:86 and 108.

135. Such ethnic categories are situational, overlapping, and contradictory; see Bryce, *To Belong.*

136. "Orden del día número 135," August 14, 1935, DSCD, 2:644.

137. Abínzano, "Procesos," chapter 1, page 3.

138. Bartolomé, *Los colonos,* 17.

139. Puerto Rico and Liebig (Corrientes) are known as German colonies, Santo Pipó is known as a Swiss colony, and Apóstoles is known as a Polish-Ukranian colony.

140. Girola, *Cultivo de la yerba mate...Porvenir,* 4; Benito Zamboni, "Escenas...del Alto Paraná," September 27, 1926 in Zamboni, *Escenas,* 127.

141. "La industria yerbatera," 222.

142. "Las actividades de la Casa Tornquist desde su iniciación," Biblioteca Tornquist, Bancos 831-18040. The Compañía Eldorado Colonización y Explotación de

Bosques Ltda. produced a number of informational booklets, in a variety of languages, with descriptive information and photos about the colonies.

143. T.B., "In Eldorado, a Modern Colony, Profit and the Picturesque," *Buenos Aires Herald,* June 17, 1931.

144. Ziman and Scherer, *La selva vencida,* 167–68; Gallero, *El llamado,* 15; Johann Christian Theler, "Pionero en la selva virgen," in Gallero, *El llamado,* 27; Gallero, *Piporé,* 22; Sprecher von Bernegg, *Tropische,* vol. 3.

145. Gallero, *Piporé,* 24–25.

146. Gallero, *El llamado,* 14.

147. National Mortgage Bank, *National Territory*; Banco Ipotecario Nazionale, *Territorio nazionale.*

148. Advertisement in *The American Weekly of Buenos Aires* 13 (September 25, 1926), 7.

149. *Argentinisches Tageblatt,* 1924 in Gallero, *Querida misiones,* 85; Compañia Eldorado, *Dieentwicklung*; Compañia Eldorado, *Eldorado: 15 Aniversario.*

150. "La colonización en Misiones," December 1, 1925 and "La vida en Misiones," October 10, 1923, in Zamboni, *Escenas,* 119 and 93.

151. Antonini, "La yerba mate," 119–120.

152. Roger, "Cultivo," 63–64; Oliveira, "Métodos," 10; Antonini, "La yerba mate," 119–120.

153. Bolsi, "Misiones," 96.

154. As quoted in *La industria yerbatera,* 36. See Beltrame, "Industria," 162–65.

155. Gallero, *El llamado,* 15; Gallero, *Piporé,* 33.

156. Ziman and Scherer, *La selva,* 235.

157. "La vida en Misiones," Santa Ana, October 10, 1923 in Zamboni, *Escenas,* 94 and 120.

158. Cámara Argentina de Cultura, Comercio, Industria y Producción, "Una fuente," 23; Daumas, "El problema," 20.

159. "La yerba mate en Argentina," *La Nación,* February 7, 1910.

160. Figures for 1920 from Girola, *Cultivo de la yerba mate. . .2nda encuesta*, and Ministerio del Interior, *Censo general,* 1:207. Figures for 1933 from Duhau, *Censo.*

161. Instituto Nacional de la Yerba Mate, *Plan estratégico para el sector yerbatero Argentino, 2013–2028,* 2013.

162. Lindsay, *Eldorado,* 17.

163. Bartolomé, *Los colonos,* 190.

CHAPTER 6

1. "Yerbateros de Misiones reclaman medidas para defender la industria," *La Prensa,* September 1, 1933.

2. Guy, *When Champagne became French,* 6.

3. This was an early example of cascading tariffs, which the Argentine government used to promote the industrialization of certain sectors.

4. González, *Recopilación,* 2:857 and 3:1023.

5. "Impuestos de aduana," July 22, 1891, DSCD, *1891,* 1:354–57.

6. "Yerba mate: Impuesto de inspección," December 6, 1907, DSCD, *1907,* 2:28.

7. "Explotación de yerbales en Misiones," *La Prensa,* August 17, 1897; Dirección General de Agricultura y Defensa Agrícola, *Debates,* 13.

8. Imported dried yerba incurred higher taxes relative to that produced domestically from wild yerbales for several months in 1923/1924 (Billard, *Economía,* 91–93).

9. "No Hay Otro!," *Caras y Caretas,* January 24, 1931, p. 95.

10. *Molino de yerba mate "La Yerbatera Paraguaya," Estevez & Cia. Rosario y Buenos Aires,* undated, https://www.youtube.com/watch?v = yS_VfyIhzFA.

11. Cimó Queiroz, "A Companhia Mate Laranjeira," 207–9 and 217.

12. Daumas, "El problema," 49; Billard, *Economía,* 8, 68, and 72.

13. "Industria de la yerba mate," *La Prensa,* January 15, 1917.

14. Daumas, "El problema," 59.

15. "Panamericanismo y guerra de tarifas," *La Prensa,* April 5, 1916.

16. "La yerba mate," *La Vanguardia,* March 9, 1916; "Industria de la yerba mate," *La Prensa,* January 15, 1917.

17. *La industria yerbatera,* 10–11.

18. Daumas, "El problema," 33.

19. Billard, *Economía,* 74, 76, 84, and 86, and tables 7 and 8.

20. Gerchunoff and Llach, *El ciclo,* 92–93; Billard, *Economía,* 91–92.

21. "Decreto del Poder Ejecutivo Nacional disminuyendo los derechos de importación a la yerba mate brasileña," *Boletin Oficial,* March 27, 1924.

22. Dirección de Estadística Social, *Nivel de vida,* 7.

23. Alberdi, *El crimen,* 121. "Proyecto de ley," July 4, 1924," DSCD, *1924,* 2:372.

24. "Peticiones particulares," August 13, 1924," DSCD, *1924,* 3:189–90.

25. "Decreto del Poder Ejecutivo Nacional prohibiendo la importación de palo de yerba y de congonilla sueltos," *Ministerio de Relaciones Exteriores y Culto— Circular Informativo Mensual* 80 (September 10, 1924): 555–56.

26. "Importación de yerba mate," December 17, 1924, DSCD, *1924,* 7:184–246, esp. 200.

27. "Decreto del Poder Ejecutivo Nacional referente a la importación de yerba mate," *Ministerio de Relaciones Exteriores y Culto—Circular Informativo Mensual* 92 (January 22, 1925): 805.

28. Daumas, "El problema," 33–34.

29. Daumas, "El problema," 25; Billard, *Economía,* 72 and 87; Barreyro, "Censo," 1627–28.

30. "A reunião de hontem, na Associação Comercial do Paraná," *O Dia,* July 26, 1927.

31. Daumas, "El problema," 34.

32. Cameron, "Maté," 988.

33. Daumas, "El problema," 21 and 43.

34. "En Bonpland se constituyó la 'Sociedad Argentina de Plantadores de Yerba Mate,'" *El Territorio,* February 3, 1927, p. 1.

35. "Primera Asamblea General de delegados de todas las zonas yerbateras . . .," *Revista Yerbatera,* May 1929, 3.

36. "Yerba mate brasileña adulterada," *Revista Yerbatera* 1, no. 4 (March 1929): 1; "Peticiones particulares," September 17, 1928, DSCD, *1928,* 4:322.

37. "En Bonpland se constituyó la 'Sociedad Argentina de Plantadores de Yerba Mate,'" *El Territorio,* February 3, 1927; Girola, *Cultivo de la yerba mate . . . estadística,* 24.

38. Barreyro, "Censo," 1627–28.

39. "Defensa de las industrias," *Revista Yerbatera,* December 1928, 1–2.

40. "Asociación Argentina de Plantadores de Yerba Mate," *Revista Yerbatera,* June 1929, 2.

41. In 1929, Argentina imported from Brazil just over 13 thousand kilograms of processed yerb as compared to over 53 kilos of dried yerba (Billard, *Economía,* 72–74).

42. Articles in *Revista Yerbatera* between December 1928 and December 1929.

43. "Nuestro régimen arancelario," *Revista Yerbatera,* June 1929, 1.

44. "La producción de yerba mate argentina," *Revista Yerbatera,* July 1929, 1.

45. "La critica situación yerbatera," *Revista Yerbatera,* September 1929, 1.

46. "Se gestiona la defensa de la industria yerbatera," *Revista Yerbatera,* December 1929, 1–6.

47. Billard, *Economía,* 86.

48. "Se gestiona la defensa de la industria yerbatera," *Revista Yerbatera,* December 1929, 1–3.

49. Muello, *Yerba mate,* 165–71.

50. "Misiones: La difícil situación de los productores de yerba mate del territorio," *La Prensa,* April 7, 1930, p 20.

51. Billard, *Economía,* 91–92.

52. "Comentario: Indiferencia o desprecio al pueblo consumidor," *La Prensa,* April 12, 1930.

53. "Comentario: La solución racional del problema yerbatero," *La Prensa,* April 18, 1930.

54. Cámara de Comercio Argentino-Brasileña, *La yerba mate,* 79–80.

55. Dirección de Estadística Social, *Nivel de vida,* 7–8.

56. Gerchunoff and Llach, *El ciclo,* 117.

57. United States Patent Office, Trade-Mark 251,758, registered January 15, 1929, http://tsdr.uspto.gov/documentviewer?caseId=sn71266255&docId=ORC20051027235423#docIndex=0&page=1.

58. "Salus: la primer yerba que proclamó su origen nacional," 1930. See http://www.magicasruinas.com.ar/publicidad/piepubli350.htm.

59. Holloway, *The Brazilian Coffee.*

60. Crotty, "Was Keynes."

61. Irwin, *Trade Policy,* viii and 2.

62. Romero, *A History of Argentina,* 65–69.

63. Gerchunoff and Llach, *El ciclo,* 112–13.

64. Cámara de Comercio Argentino-Brasileña, *La yerba mate,* 81–93; Billard, *Economía,* 100–2.

65. Billard, *Economía,* 102.

66. Madrid, "Argentina y Brasil," 137–39.

67. *Financial Chronicle,* August 29, 1931, 1329.

68. "Survey of the Wheat Situation," *Wheat Studies of the Food Research Institute* 8, no. 3 (January 1932): 225.

69. "Proyecto de Resolución," May 16, 1932, DSCD, *1932,* 2:357.

70. Cámara de Comercio Argentino-Brasileña, *La yerba mate,* 95–96; Billard, *Economía,* 104–5.

71. "Vigencia de decretos sobre la yerba," May 30, 1932, DSCD, *1932,* 2:595–96.

72. "Vigencia de decretos sobre la yerba," May 30, 1932, DSCD, 2:637.

73. "Vigencia de decretos sobre la yerba," May 30, 1932, DSCD, 2:630–31.

74. "Vigencia de decretos sobre la yerba," May 30, 1932, DSCD, 2:617, 620, and 632–33.

75. "Vigencia de decretos sobre la yerba," May 30, 1932, DSCD, 2:637 and 641.

76. "Vigencia de decretos sobre la yerba," May 30, 1932, DSCD, 2:626–27.

77. "Asamblea de plantadores de yerba mate en Apóstoles," *La Prensa,* July 13, 1932; various petitions between July and November 1932, DSCD, 1932.

78. Billard, *Economía,* 94–95.

79. As quoted in Hora, *The Landowners,* 195–96.

80. "Yerbateros de Misiones reclaman medidas para defender la industria," *La Prensa,* September 1, 1933; "En favor de los yerbateros se piden medidas," *La Nación,* September 7, 1933; "Misiones pidió el apoyo oficial para la yerba del país," *La Nación,* September 9, 1933; "Los productores de Misiones piden la ayuda del P.E.," *La Nación,* September 10, 1933.

81. "Ante el senado el P.E. opinó sobre el momento económico," *La Nación,* Sept. 13, 1933.

82. "Inserción solicitada por el Señor Diputado Gomez," September 8, 1933, DSCD, *1933,* 4: 123–4.

83. Smith, *Politics,* 88–94.

84. Williamson, *Varieties.*

85. Smith, *Politics and Beef,* 150–53; Persello, "Partidos políticos," 92–93.

86. Persello, "Partidos políticos."

87. "Comisión Reguladora de la Producción y Comercio de la Yerba Mate," September 22, 1933, DSCS, *1933,* 2:386–90.

88. DSCS, *1933,* 2:160, 248, and 464.

89. "Mociones," September 29, 1933, DSCS, *1933,* 2:742 and 743.

90. "Proyecto de ley," September 29, 1933, DSCS, *1933,* 2:756–58.

91. Numerous articles, October 11 to 13, 1933, in *La Nación* and *La Prensa.*

92. Articles 2 and 4, "El protocolo adicional al Tratado de Comercio y Navegación . . .," October 10, 1933; "Firmose el modus vivendi que completa el Tratado de Comercio y de Navegación," *La Nación,* October 12, 1933.

93. "Se publicó en Río el acuerdo acerca de la yerba mate," *La Nación,* September 14, 1934; "El P. Ejecutivo propicia la derogación del impuesto de 10% a la yerba brasileña," *La Prensa,* September 16, 1934; "Editorial: El convenio sobre la yerba mate," *La Nación,* September 18, 1934.

94. "Asuntos entrados," September 20, 1934, DSCD, *1934* 7:757.

95. "Asuntos entrados," September 20, 1934, DSCD, *1934* 7:758.

96. Billard, *Economía,* 68, 74, and 76.

97. "En Posadas, Misiones, se efectuó una importante reunión de yerbateros," *La Nación,* July 8, 1935; "Territorios: Hubo una asamblea de yerbateros en la zona de Apóstoles, Misiones," *La Nación,* July 13, 1935; "Misiones: La Comisión pro Defensa Económica," *La Prensa,* July 21, 1935.

98. Various petitions between January 31 and September 26, 1935, DSCD, *1935.*

99. "Actualidad: El problema de la yerba mate," *La Prensa,* September 22, 1934.

100. Gerchunoff and Llach, *El ciclo,* 120.

101. Elena, *Dignifying Argentina,* 34–42.

102. Various articles in *La Nación* and *La Prensa* between August 10 and 14, 1935.

103. "Editorial: Misiones y la yerba mate," *La Nación,* August 10, 1935.

104. "Toda la población de Misiones hizo ayer causa común . . .," *La Nación,* August 13, 1935; "Misiones: Continuó ayer el paro general," *La Prensa,* August 15, 1935.

105. "Editorial: La situación de Misiones . . .," *La Nación,* August 13, 1935.

106. "Comisión Reguladora de la Yerba Mate," August 14, 21, and 22, 1935, DSCD, *1935,* 2:601–49; 781–812; and 840–76.

107. A. Mateu, "El modelo," 31–32.

108. "Comisión Reguladora de la Yerba Mate," August 14, 1935, DSCD, *1935,* 2:621.

109. Nállim, *Transformations,* 54–59.

110. "Comisión Reguladora de la Yerba Mate," August 21, 1935, DSCD, *1935,* 2:793.

111. Alonso, *Between Revolution and the Ballot Box.*

112. "Comisión Reguladora de la Yerba Mate," August 22, 1935, DSCD, *1935,* 2:865.

113. "Comisión Reguladora de la Yerba Mate," August 14, 1935, DSCD, *1935,* 2:628–29 and 634.

114. "Comisión Reguladora de la Yerba Mate," August 21, 1935, DSCD, *1935,* 2:781–88.

115. Sidicaro, *La política, 123–49.*

116. "Editorial: Misiones y la yerba mate," *La Nación,* August 10, 1935; "Editorial: La situación de Misiones," *La Nación,* August 13, 1935; "Editorial: La yerba mate," *La Nación,* August 25, 1935.

117. Nállim, "An Unbroken Loyalty," 44–46.

118. "Comentario: El problema de la yerba mate," *La Prensa,* September 22, 1934; "Editorial: El problema de la yerba mate," *La Prensa,* July 28, 1935.

119. "Editorial: Un estatuto legal para consolidar el monopolio de la yerba mate?" *La Prensa,* August 27, 1935.

120. "Comisión Reguladora de la Yerba Mate," August 14, 1935, DSCD, *1935,* 2:630–31.

121. "Comisión Reguladora de la Yerba Mate," August 21, 1935, DSCD, *1935*, 2:803–4.

122. Billard, *Economía,* tables 1 and 6.

123. Instituto Nacional de Estadistica y Censos, *Censo Nacional Agropecuario, 1988*, table 27.

CHAPTER 7

1. Solari, *Trabajadores,* 8–9.

2. Mintz, *Sweetness and Power*; Beckert, *Empire of Cotton*; Stanfield, *Red Rubber*; Hochschild, *King Leopold's Ghost*; Besky, *The Darjeeling Distinction.*

3. Solari, *Trabajadores,* 9.

4. Even today, as the yerba sector is transitioning to mechanized harvesting, outcries about the mistreatment of yerba workers continue to appear in the news.

5. Schiffrin, ed., *Global Muckraking.*

6. Barrett, *Lo que son los yerbales,* in *Obras completes,* 2:7.

7. I have found only a brief reference to Bouvier in a book about one hundred people who contributed to the history of Misiones: Salinas Giménez, "18—Julián S. Bouvier, Santiago Misiones."

8. Julian Bouvier, "La ola que avanza. El incorregible avariente. ¡Sentinela alerta!," *A Noticia,* February 3, 1908.

9. Julian Bouvier, "La ola que avanza. El incorregible avariente. ¡Sentinela alerta!," *A Noticia,* February 6, 1908.

10. Julian Bouvier, "Carta. Villa Encarnación del Alto Paraná, January 9, 1908," *A Noticia,* February 26, 1908.

11. Julian Bouvier, "El oeste paranense," *A Noticia,* March 19, 1908.

12. Julian Bouvier, "El oeste paranense," *A Noticia,* March 27, 1908.

13. Walter, "The Socialist Press," 12; Buonuome, "Los socialistas," 147–79.

14. Julian Bouvier, "En el Alto Paraná. El latifundio y la esclavitud," *La Vanguardia,* May 10, 1908.

15. Julian Bouvier, "En el Alto Paraná. El latifundio y la esclavitud," *La Vanguardia,* May 10, 1908.

16. Julian Bouvier, "Los misterios del Alto Paraná," *La Vanguardia,* June 14, 1908.

17. Julian Bouvier, "Los misterios del Alto Paraná," *La Vanguardia,* June 22–23, 1908.

18. Julian Bouvier, "Los misterios del Alto Paraná," *La Vanguardia,* June 22–23, 1908.

19. Roediger, *The Wages,* 65–92.

20. Gorman, "Empire," 197.

21. Guy, "White Slavery," esp. 60 and 66.

22. Campi and Vignoli, "La emergencia."

23. "La esclavitud en el norte de la república," *La Vanguardia,* July 28, 1894.

24. "Los esclavos de los yerbales en Misiones," *La Vanguardia,* October 27, 1894.

25. Julian Bouvier, "Los misterios del Alto Paraná," *La Vanguardia,* May 15 and June 6, 1908.

26. Julian Bouvier, "Los misterioso del Alto Paraná," *La Vanguardia,* June 14, 1908.

27. Huner, "How Pedro Quiñonez."

28. Alberto and Elena, *Rethinking Race,* esp. 11.

29. Chamosa, "Indigenous or Criollo," 100–1.

30. Julian Bouvier, "Los misterios del Alto Paraná," *La Vanguardia,* June 22–23, 1908.

31. Julian Bouvier, "En el Alto Paraná," *La Vanguardia,* May 10, 1908.

32. Julian Bouvier, "Los misterios del Alto Paraná," *La Vanguardia,* June 15–16, 1908.

33. Julian Bouvier, "Los misterios del Alto Paraná," *La Vanguardia,* June 22–23, 1908.

34. Julian Bouvier, "Los misterios del Alto Paraná," *La Vanguardia,* June 8–9, 1908.

35. Julian Bouvier, "Los misterios del Alto Paraná," *La Vanguardia,* June 14, 1908.

36. Julian Bouvier, "Los misterios del Alto Paraná," *La Vanguardia,* May 29, 1908.

37. Julian Bouvier, "Los misterios del Alto Paraná," *La Vanguardia,* May 15, 1908.

38. Julian Bouvier, "Los misterios del Alto Paraná," *La Vanguardia,* May 15, 1908.

39. Julian Bouvier, "Los misterios del Alto Paraná," *La Vanguardia,* June 6, 1908.

40. Julian Bouvier, "Los misterios del Alto Paraná," *La Vanguardia,* June 15–16, 1908.

41. Julian Bouvier, "Los misterios del Alto Paraná," *La Vanguardia,* May 15, 1908.

42. Julian Bouvier, "Los misterios del Alto Paraná," *La Vanguardia,* June 24, 1908.

43. Julian Bouvier, "Los misterios del Alto Paraná," *La Vanguardia,* May 15, 1908.

44. Julian Bouvier, "Los misterios del Alto Paraná," *La Vanguardia,* June 24, 1908.

45. Julian Bouvier, "Los misterios del Alto Paraná," *La Vanguardia,* June 6, 1908.

46. Julian Bouvier, "Los misterios del Alto Paraná," *La Vanguardia,* May 29, 1908.

47. Julian Bouvier, "Los misterios del Alto Paraná," *La Vanguardia,* June 28, 1908.

48. Julian Bouvier, "Los misterios del Alto Paraná," *La Vanguardia,* May 30 and June 12, 1908.

49. Julian Bouvier, "En el Alto Paraná," *La Vanguardia,* May 10, 1908.

50. Julian Bouvier, "Los misterios del Alto Paraná," *La Vanguardia,* May 30, 1908.

51. Julian Bouvier, "Los misterios del Alto Paraná," *La Vanguardia,* May 16, 1908.

52. Julian Bouvier, "Los misterios del Alto Paraná," *La Vanguardia,* June 12, 1908.

53. Julian Bouvier, "Los misterios del Alto Paraná," *La Vanguardia,* June 24, 1908.

54. Julian Bouvier, "Los misterios del Alto Paraná," *La Vanguardia,* June 13, 1908.

55. Julian Bouvier, "Los misterios del Alto Paraná," *La Vanguardia,* June 25, 1908.

56. Julian Bouvier, "Los misterios del Alto Paraná," *La Vanguardia,* June 14, 1908.

57. Julian Bouvier, "Los misterios del Alto Paraná," *La Vanguardia,* June 13, 1908.

58. Julian Bouvier, "Los misterios del Alto Paraná," *La Vanguardia,* June 22–23, 1908.

59. Rafael Barrett, "La tierra," in *Obras completas,* 2:298–99.

60. Barthe visited *La Vanguardia* on June 5, 1908. Julian Bouvier, "Los misterios del Alto Paraná," *La Vanguardia,* June 24, 1908; "Misiones. Los peones del Alto Uruguay," *La Prensa,* June 14, 1908; "Los peones en el Alto Paraná," *La Prensa,* August 30, 1908; "Misiones," *La Vanguardia,* June 17, 1908.

61. Julian Bouvier, "Los misterios del Alto Paraná," *La Vanguardia,* July 3, 1908.

62. Julian Bouvier, "Los misterios del Alto Paraná," *La Vanguardia,* June 25, 1908.

63. "Humanitarismo en retardo," *La Vanguardia,* April 15, 1922.

64. "Por los peones del Alto Paraná," *La Vanguardia,* June 19, 1908; "Movimiento social. Partido Socialista," *La Vanguardia,* July 12, 1908.

65. Barrett, "La cuestión social en el Paraguauy," in *Obras completas,* 2:254.

66. "Los horrores del Alto Paraná," *La Vanguardia,* August 16, 1908; "La esclavitud en el Alto Paraná," *La Vanguardia,* August 18, 1908.

67. "La esclavitud en Misiones," *La Vanguardia,* December 9, 1908.

68. Julian S. Bouvier, "Los misterios del Alto Paraná," *La Vanguardia,* March 19, 1909.

69. Julian S. Bouvier, "Los misterios del Alto Paraná," *La Vanguardia,* March 24, 1909.

70. Julian S. Bouvier, "El trabajo en el Alto Paraná," *La Vanguardia,* March 20, 1909.

71. Niklison, "Alto Paraná," esp. 26 and 231–33.

72. "La esclavitud en el Alto Paraná," *La Vanguardia,* May 20, 1914.

73. "Congreso diputados," *La Vanguardia,* June 13 and 16, 1914; "El 'contrato' de Trabajo," *La Vanguardia,* July 1, 1914.

74. "Trabajos en obrajes y yerbatales," June 25, 1919, DSCD, *1919,* 3: 196–98; Enrique Dickmann, "Contra el 'truck system,'" *La Vanguardia,* June 20, 1920.

75. Stephanis, "From Resurrection," 66–107.

76. Martínez Chas, *Marcos Kanner,* 132.

77. Naboulet, *La justicia*; Cavazzutti, *Misiones.*

78. "La esclavitud de hecho," *La Vanguardia,* February 21, 1920; "Humanitarismo en retardo," *La Vanguardia,* April 15, 1922.

79. "Conversando con el Doctor Justo," *La Vanguardia,* May 7, 1922.

80. Solari, *Trabajadores.*

81. Solari, "Trágicas," 11–12.

82. Alfredo Varela, "También en la Argentina hay esclavos blancos," *Ahora,* February 14, 1941.

83. Alfredo Varela, "Notas misioneras," *La Hora,* March 22, 1941.

84. The term was an abbreviation of *mensual* that was phonetically adapted based on Guaraní language practices. It also applied to peons working in logging in the jungles of the region. See Vidal de Battini, "El léxico," 1:484.

85. Alfredo Varela, "También en la Argentina hay esclavos blancos," *Ahora,* February 28, 1941.

86. Alfredo Varela, "También en la Argentina hay esclavos blancos," *Ahora,* February 25 and 28, 1941.

87. Alfredo Varela, "Notas misioneras," *La Hora,* March 22, 1941.

88. Alfredo Varela, "También en la Argentina tenemos esclavos blancos," *Ahora,* February 14 and March 14, 1941.

89. Alfredo Varela, "Notas misioneras," *La Hora,* April 4, 1941.

90. Alfredo Varela, "Notas misioneras," *La Hora,* April 8, 1941.

91. Chamosa, "People as Landscape," 54.

92. Alfredo Varela, "También en la Argentina tenemos esclavos blancos," *Ahora,* March 14, 1941.

93. Alfredo Varela, "También en la Argentina hay esclavos blancos," February 14, 1941. Alfredo Varela, "Notas misioneras," *La Hora,* March 25, 1941.

94. Alfredo Varela, "Notas misioneras," *La Hora,* March 27, 1941.

95. Alfredo Varela, "Notas Misioneras," *La Hora,* April 5 and 6, 1941.

96. Alfredo Varela, "También en la Argentina tenemos esclavos blancos," *Ahora,* March 19, 1941; Alfredo Varela, "Notas Misioneras," *La Hora,* April 4, 1941.

97. Alfredo Varela, "Notas Misioneras," *La Hora,* March 30, 1941.

98. Alfredo Varela, "También en la Argentina tenemos esclavos blancos," *Ahora,* March 14, 1941.

99. Korn and Trímboli, *Los ríos profundos*; C. Mateu, "Encuentros."

100. Varela, *El río oscuro,* 53.

101. Varela, *El río oscuro,* 254–55.

102. Varela, *El río oscuro,* 259.

103. Korn and Trímboli, *Los ríos profundos,* 188–89.

104. Lattuada, *La política,* 1:65–66, footnotes 30 and 34.

105. Juan Domingo Perón, November 30, 1944 as quoted in Lattuada, *La política,* 1:49–50.

106. Perón, *La fuerza,* 23.

107. Newland and Cuesta, "Peronismo," 93.

108. Perón, *La fuerza,* 15.

109. The film remained on top of the box office for nine weeks and earned 1.3 million pesos. It received numerous awards in Argentina and abroad, including an Academy Award nomination for best foreign film. See Kriger, *Cine,* 187.

110. España, "*Las Aguas,*" 9.

111. "Los artistas prohibidos cuando Perón gobernaba," *Cambio,* approximately 1982, Caja 2.1, carpeta #3, BNA, Archive Alfredo Varela.

112. Borrás, *Las aguas bajan,* 33.

113. Borrás, *Las aguas bajan,* 145.

114. Mario Scoffici's film, *Prisioneros de la tierra,* also dealt with the exploitation of yerba workers in Misiones, but did not end on a positive note. The protagonist's love interest is shot dead by her father, who has been driven crazy by the natural environment of Misiones. Then the protagonist is shot dead after a workers' revolt. In contrast to *Las aguas bajan turbias,* viewers of *Prisioneros de la tierra* are left hopeless about any chance of overcoming nature and human exploitation in the yerbales.

115. Laferrére, *Aguas turbias*; Magrassi, *La caá yarí*; Alterach Peralta, *Mensú*; Barrios, *El "mensú."* The important Paraguayan author Augusto Roa Bastos wrote various short stories and novels that discussed the exploitation of the yerba mate worker.

116. As transcribed in Orquera, "Paisaje social," 20.

117. Orquera, "Paisaje social," 13 and 29.

118. Walsh, "La Argentina," 157.

CHAPTER 8

1. Rappaport, *A Thirst for Empire,* 376–409.

2. Quino, Mafalda cartoon, March 2, 1965, in *Todo Mafalda,* 550.

3. Sarlo, *Una modernidad,* 21.

4. Salvatore, "Yankee Advertising," 221 and 232; Elena, *Dignifying Argentina,* 18–34; Adamovsky, *Historia de la clase media,* 66–77; Milanesio, *Workers Go,* 54–58; Karush, *Culture of Class,* esp. 19–42; Rocchi, "La americanización."

5. Only two advertisements referred to the kettle in text: "Salus es sabrosa, fragante y aguantadora," *Leoplán,* January 17, 1940; "Salus. Silueta, aguantadora, económica, limpia y pura," *Leoplán,* January 3, 1940.

6. Instructions for the first year of domestic science at the Liceo Nacional de Señoritas listed "the bombilla for mate, above all when used by several people at the same time" as an activity that spread tuberculosis. See Arcelli, *Ciencias domésticas,* 46; Armus, *The Ailing City,* esp. 148–49 and 155.

7. "Refresco Salus para conservar la silueta," *Leoplán,* February 14, 1940.

8. Tossounian, *La Joven Moderna.*

9. "Te-mate Salus suculento desayuno para grandes y chicos," *Leoplán,* June 5, 1940.

10. Martín y Cía., *¿Qué es la yerba mate?*

11. Rappaport, *A Thirst for Empire,* 284–88.

12. "Salus el mejor copetín," *Chabela,* February, 1942 and *Leoplán,* February 11, 1942.

13. This approach challenges Natalia Milanesio's findings that advertising prior to the 1950s emphasized exclusivity and prestige goods that conveyed social class rather than an emphasis on affordability (*Workers Go,* 89–95).

14. "Alegre despertar. Salus," *Leoplán,* October 9, 1940.

15. Tossounian, *La Joven Moderna.*

16. Salvatore, "Yankee Advertising"; Rocchi, "La americanización."

17. Adamovsky, "A Strange Emblem."

18. "200 millones de retratos de la criollita Salus!," *Leoplán*, August 2, 1939.

19. "Brinde a la patria con Salus, que es nuestra," *Leoplán*, July 3, 1940.

20. Salvatore, "Yankee Advertising," 229.

21. "Salus en el mate del estribo," *Leoplán*, February 15, 1939.

22. Drago, *Dos en uno*, 58; Goldman, *Lucamba*, 129.

23. "Toda una evocación en un mate," Yerba Mate Gardel advertisement, 1936, *Caras y Caretas*, December 5, 1936. Museo del Mate in Tigre, Argentina has items related to Carlos Gardel and mate. The Museo Casa Carlos Gardel had an exposition about mate, tango, and Carlos Gardel; see http://noticiasdelaruta.blogspot.com/2014/05/comenzo-en-ba-la-exposicion-con-el-mate.html.

24. Molinero and Vila, "Atahualpa Yupanqui," 168.

25. Milanesio, *Workers Go*, 54–62.

26. Comisión Económica para América Latina, "El desarrollo económico de la Argentina. Anexo: Algunos estudios especiales y estadísticas macroeconómicas preparados para el informe," June 30, 1958, Table 2, p. 4 and Table 3, p. 5 ; García, *Peronismo*, 62; James, *Resistance*, 8; Ranis, *Argentine Workers*, 18; Gerchunoff and Llach, *El ciclo*, 145.

27. Departamento Nacional de Trabajo, *Condiciones de vida*, 14 and 27–28 ; Departamento Nacional de Trabajo, "Costo de la vida."

28. Dirección de Estadística Social, *Condiciones de vida*, esp. 37; Ranis, *Argentine Workers*, 18.

29. Dirección de Estadística Social, *Nivel de vida*.

30. Departamento Nacional de Trabajo, "Costo de la Vida," 22.

31. Departamento Nacional de Trabajo, *Condiciones de vida*, 32 and 37.

32. Dirección de Estadística Social, *Condiciones de vida*, 37.

33. James, *Resistance*, 8–9; Adelman, "Reflections."

34. Elena, *Dignifying Argentina*, 34–41 and 54–60.

35. Gaudio and Pilone, "El desarrollo"; Adelman, "Reflections," 247.

36. "Introduction," in Karush and Chamosa, *The New Cultural History of Peronism*.

37. García, *Peronismo*, 76.

38. Elena, *Dignifying Argentina*, 67–74.

39. Elena, *Dignifying Argentina*, 64; Tamarin, *The Argentine Labor Movement*, 191–92; Gaudio and Pilone, "El desarrollo," 44.

40. James, *Doña María's Story*, 47–48, 50 and 54.

41. Nohlen, *Elections*, 85–86; Romero, *A History of Argentina*, 98–99.

42. Belini, *La industria*; Gerchunoff and Llach, *El ciclo*, 182; Elena, *Dignifying Argentina*, 75–81.

43. Gerchunoff, "Peronist Economic Policies," 62–79; Gerchunoff and Llach, *El ciclo*, 183; Elena, *Dignifying Argentina*, 76, 166–75, and 221–50; Milanesio, "'The Guardian Angels.'"

44. James, *Resistance*, 9–10 and 22; Milanesio, *Workers Go*, 193.

45. Milanesio, "Peronists," 53–84.

46. Gambini, *Historia del peronismo,* 90–91.

47. Torre and Pastoriza, "La democratización." For more on *vida digna* see Elena, *Dignifying Argentina.*

48. *Constitutición de la nación Argentina* (Buenos Aires, 1949), p. 28–29.

49. Torre and Pastoriza, "La democratización," 307–8; Elena, *Dignifying Argentina,* 119–20.

50. Torre and Pastoriza, "La democratización," 307; Gené, *Un mundo feliz,* 119–29.

51. Luis J. Medrano, "El hombre que no va al fútbol," *Argentina,* October 1, 1949.

52. Milanesio, *Workers Go,* 54–63 and 83–122.

53. Moreno, "Marketing."

54. Salus published two advertisements with instructions for preparing te-mate in 1950 and four advertisements in 1952 that invited consumers to try mate express or an imperial de mate helado at the company's Casa de Mate. None of the advertisements mentioned cocido.

55. "Salus. Usted ceba . . . ceba . . . ceba . . .," *Chabela,* March 1951.

56. "Razones que justifican la preferencia del pueblo por Salus. 80 Razón," *Para Ti,* April 20, 1954 and *El Gráfico,* August 20, 1954. The second reason focused on the colonies that cultivated yerba mate and did not mention either Argentina or Misiones, instead referring to the location as "a zone where Nature seems to help a man produce more and better." See "Razones que justifican la preferencia del pueblo por Salus. 20 Razón,'" *El Gráfico,* August 21, 1953, and *Para Ti,* September 1, 1953.

57. Milanesio, *Workers Go,* 89–95.

58. "Salus fué la elegida," *Leoplán,* April 17, 1946.

59. "Cada mate Salus: Es un pedazo de sol," *El Gráfico,* October 15, 1948 ; "Mate cebado con Salus," *El Gráfico,* October 9 and October 26, 1951.

60. "!Diez años sin cambiar la yerba!" *Chabela,* no. 237, September 1955; "Mis primeros 500.000 mates," *Para Ti,* June 7, 1955; "!En mi boca se hace canto!," 1955.

61. "Salus tiene y da energía," *Leoplán,* November 7, 1945; "El mate 'Salus.' Santo y seña de criollismo," *El Gráfico,* June 8, 1951; "Mate cebado con Salus," *El Gráfico,* October 9 and 26, 1951.

62. Adamovsky, "Race."

63. Milanesio, *Workers Go,* 104–5.

64. "Para gozar más hondo el placer de matear . . .," *El Gráfico,* February 15, 1952.

65. "Yerba Salus: Compañera de viaje," *El Gráfico,* March 12, 1948

66. "En Salus la espuma apretada y blanca," 1958.

67. Pite, *Creating,* 108–9; Milanesio, "'The Guardian Angels'"; Gené, *Un mundo,* 130–40; Harrison, *On Account of Sex,* xi.

68. Chamosa, "Criollo and Peronist," 113–14.

69. For references to Ca'a Yari, see Ambrosetti, "Segundo viaje," 73–74; Cambas, *Leyendas,* 47–50; Morales, *Leyendas,* 12–15.

70. Villanueva, *Obras completas.*

71. Del Campo, *Cancionero del mate.*

72. *Antecedentes: Fiesta Nacional Yerba Mate,* n.d., Archivo de la Provincia de Misiones. The Perón administration absorbed and co-opted many of these festivals. See Chamosa, "Criollo and Peronist," 127–34.

73. Chamosa, *The Argentine Folklore Movement,* 26.

74. Milanesio, "Food Politics"; Gerchunoff and Llach, *El ciclo,* 203–9.

75. Ministerio de Salud Pública de la Nación, *Política alimentaria,* 12.

76. In 1941, the United States released its first Recommended Dietary Allowances to educate consumers about proper nutrition (Biltekoff, *Eating Right,* 45–79).

77. Perón considered eggs, dairy, fish, vegetables, and fruits protective foods. Ministerio de Salud Pública de la Nación, *Política alimentaria,* 14–15, 24–25.

78. Presidencia de la Nación, *20 plan,* 181.

79. Elena, *Dignifying Argentina,* 229.

80. Gerchunoff and Antúnez, "De la bonanza," 175.

81. While in exile in Spain, Perón was known to drink decaffeinated coffee when with Spaniards and cocido when with Argentines (Pavón Pereyra, *Los últimos días,* 67).

82. The archivist at the Biblioteca Museo Evita knew of only one image showing a young Eva Duarte drinking mate. He did not know of any images of Juan Perón drinking mate. Photograph in Fundación Tiempo Social, *17 de Octubre,* 78.

83. James, *Doña María's Story,* 65–66.

84. Wilson, *Jorge Luis Borges,* 62.

85. Guibert, "Jorge Luis Borges, 1968," 95.

86. Baracat, *Yerba mate,* Table A-2.

87. Rappaport, *A Thirst,* 375–410.

88. Stein, "Essence," 216.

89. Martínez Estrada, *Radiografía,* 84 and 127.

90. Karush, *Culture of Class,* 169–72.

91. Carlos Gardel, "Yira . . . Yira," in Misemer, *Secular Saints,* 56.

92. "Tres esquinas," 1941 with lyrics by Enrique Cadícamo, https://poesiadegotan.com/2012/05/24/tres-esquinas-1941.

93. Zlotchew, "Tango," 137.

94. Guy, *Sex and Danger,* 145–60; Karush, *Culture,* 136–50; Bockelman, "Between the Gaucho," 578–79.

95. Poster by Aristo Téllez, no date; Téllez died in 1951. See Quintana and Manrupe, *Afiches del peronismo,* 32.

96. Repetto et. al, "La yerba mate," 1462.

97. Karush, "Populism," 28 and 45.

98. Pedro Aulino, "El Haragán," *Caras y Caretas,* March 22, 1930.

99. Guibert, "Jorge Luis Borges, 1968," 95.

100. The January 1940 number included both movie and theatre tickets (Milanesio, *Workers Go,* 127–28 and 136).

101. Torre and Pastoriza, "La democratización," 301.

102. Elena, *Dignifying Argentina,* 156–66; Milanesio, "Peronists and Cabecitas"; Milanesio, *Workers Go,* 123–47.

103. Adamovsky, *Historia de la clase,* 26 and 121–35; Garguin, "'Los Argentinos.'"

104. Milanesio, *Workers Go,* 147–56.

105. Provincia de Misiones, *Evolución de la yerba mate,* 47–75. An earlier report had similar findings (Galharretborde, *Análisis*). A later study had less conclusive findings (Bolsi, "Misiones," 157–61).

106. Quino, Mafalda cartoon, March 2, 1965, in *Toda Mafalda,* 550.

107. Cosse, *Mafalda,* 31–32.

108. "Tu nombre me sabe a yerba," [1978] Fontanarrosa, *20 años,* 257. The title of the cartoon, "Tu nombre me sabe a yerba," was an ironic riff on the popular 1960s love song "Tu nombre me sabe a hierba" by the Spanish musician Joan Manuel Serrat.

CHAPTER 9

1. Fox, "Argentina," 6.

2. Solt, *The Untold History of Ramen.*

3. Cambra and Raffo, "A Newer Tango."

4. Manzano, *The Age of Youth*; Manzano, "The Blue Jean Generation."

5. Juan José Jusid, *Donde hay mate hay amor (Ah . . . Qué swing que me da el mate!),* 1970, Campaña Nacional de Mate, https://twitter.com/MuseoDelCineBA/status/1042823570752266242.

6. "El mate conquista a la juventud," *La Nación,* July 2, 1972.

7. Manzano, *The Age of Youth,* 74.

8. José de Zer, "48 Horas Con Los Hippies," *Atlántida,* December 1967, 42–46.

9. Manzano, *The Age of Youth,* 150.

10. Ferm, *Profiles,* 130.

11. "Interview with Fray Antonio Puigjané," in Madres de la Plaza de Mayo, *Memoria,* 230.

12. Marcovich, *Vida,* 79–80.

13. Copani, "Terrorismo"; Rodríguez, "Los radicalizados."

14. M.E.V., "El mate," *La Nación,* August 9, 1981.

15. Santiago Ferrari, "Crónicas Argentinas. La aventura del mate (I y II)," *La Nación,* March 13 and 16, 1979.

16. Gobierno de la Provincia de Misiones, *Posibilidades,* 7.

17. Gobierno de la Provincia de Misiones, *Evolución,* 74–75.

18. Veigel, *Dictatorship,* 130–31.

19. Veigel, *Dictatorship,* 131.

20. Bolsi, "Misiones," 202–3.

21. As quoted in Schamber, "Barajar," 133.

22. "Proyecto de Ley: Sobre CRYM, April 21, 1987," DSCD, 1986, 11:8747.

23. "Fundamentos y reacciones," *El Territorio,* August 12, 1984.

24. "Justicialistas propongan reformas para las leyes de la yerba mate," *El Territorio,* September 1, 1984.

25. "Luego de un prolongado debate . . .," *El Territorio,* August 12, 1984.

26. Juan Jesús Hernández, "El Instituto Nacional."

27. "Misiones: Un proyecto conflictivo para la producción de yerba mate," *La Nación,* May 27, 1986; "Declaraciones del gobernador Barrios Arrechea," *La Nación,* May 31, 1986; "Declararon de interés provincial el proyecto denominado Ñande Yerba," *La Nación,* July 8, 1986; "Ñande Yerba," *La Razón,* July 13, 1986.

28. "Participa Misiones en la comercialización de yerba," *La Prensa,* May 24, 1986.

29. "Misiones," *La Nación,* May 27, 1986; "Declaraciones del gobernador Barrios Arrechea," *La Nación,* May 31, 1986.

30. "Editorial. El estado, nuevamente empresario," *La Nación,* June 4, 1986.

31. Powers, "The Politics of Poverty," 91; Maute, *Hyperinflation,* 28.

32. "Yerba mate," *Clarín,* August 6, 1986; "Yerba mate y té en Misiones," *Clarín,* August 30, 1986.

33. "Reclaman apoyo para el sector yerbatero," *Clarín,* October 24, 1986.

34. By comparison, the MC had acquired 75 percent of dried yerba in 1975; see Liliana Pagliettini, "Principales limitantes en los canales de comercialización de algunos productos regionales," Préstamo Banco Mundial 2712 -AR, 1988, page 92 and 107. "Yerba mate," *Clarín,* May 7, 1988; "Proyecto de Ley: Sobre CRYM," March 19, 1987, DSCD, *1986,* 11:8506; Alberto Mónaca, "Grave crisis inquita al sector yerbatero misionero," *Ámbito Financiero,* May 6, 1987.

35. "Cesan intervenciones en organismos yerbateros," *La Nación,* June 2, 1988.

36. "Mercado Consignatario debe 700 millones de australes," *El Territorio,* April 5, 1989.

37. "Preocupa la caída de la producción de la yerba mate," *La Nación,* January 3, 1988.

38. "Refutan acusaciones por la crisis yerbatera," *La Nación,* March 6, 1988.

39. Domingo di Nucci, "Desfasaje entre la oferta y la demanda," *Clarín,* May 7, 1988.

40. Domingo di Nucci, "Problema antinguo agravado," *Clarín,* April 18, 1988; "Complejo panorama de la yerba mate," *La Nación,* August 20, 1988.

41. Kiguel, "Inflation," 972–973.

42. Powers, "The Politics of Poverty," 91; Maute, *Hyperinflation,* 28.

43. "Pedirán liberación del precio de la yerba," *El Territorio,* May 11, 1989; "Precios máximos,'" *El Territorio,* May 12, 1989; "Piden que se libere el precio de la yerba mate," *La Nación,* May 13, 1989; Domingo di Nucci, "Distorsiones y problemas de abastecimiento," *Clarín,* Sept. 11, 1989.

44. "'La CRYM no debe existir más,'" *El Territorio,* December. 11, 1990.

45. Veigel, *Dictatorship,* 131. Adair, *In Search,* 36.

46. Adair, *In Search,* 23 and 36–37.

47. Beccaria and Carciofi, "Argentina," 187 and 192.

48. López and Romeo, *La declinación,* 23–24.

49. Beccaria and Carciofi, "Argentina," 193–94.

50. Lvovich, "Colgados," 77.

51. Osvaldo Soriano, "Living with Inflation," in Nouzeilles and Montaldo, *The Argentine Reader,* 485.

52. First vice president of the Partido Justicialista as quoted in Troncoso, *El proceso,* 5:65.

53. As quoted in Adair, *In Search,* 23.

54. Ostiguy and Armstrong, *La evolución,* 50.

55. Adair, *In Search,* esp. 46–49.

56. P. Aguirre, "El P.A.N.," 48–49.

57. "La yerba mate paga los platos rotos," *Clarín,* Oct. 23, 1988.

58. Jumbo advertisment, *Clarín,* June 14, 1989, sec. Política; "Los altos precios y la escasez . . .," *Clarín,* March 2, 1988.

59. "Dos detenidos en GLEW," *Clarín,* June 4, 1988.

60. "Protesta en Misiones por la adulteración de yerba mate," *La Nación,* November 4, 1988.

61. Ostiguy and Armstrong, *La evolución,* 50.

62. P. Aguirre, "How the Very Poor Survive," 301–2.

63. Omar Báez, "La supervivencia," *Clarín,* June 22, 1989.

64. "¿Cuánto cuesta sobrevivir en la Argentina?," *Clarín,* July 23, 1989.

65. "Precios máximos para 10 productos," *Clarín,* July 16, 1989.

66. Beccaria and Carciofi, "Argentina," 196; Powers, "The Politics of Poverty," 92–93.

67. Beccaria, "Cambios," 95.

68. Torrado, "Estrategias," 1:41; López and Romeo, *La declinación,* 12.

69. Beccaria and Carciofi, "Argentina," 197 ; Beccaria, "Cambios," 106.

70. Minujin and Kessler, *La nueva pobreza,* 41.

71. Minujin and Kessler, *La nueva pobreza,* 217–30.

72. As quoted in Halperín, "¿Hay una cultura," 216.

73. "Al mal tiempo buena cara," *Clarín,* July 16, 1989.

74. Dobal, "De la crónica diaria: Precios," *Clarín,* March 12, 1988.

75. Dobal, "De la crónica diaria: Tiempos," *Clarín,* March 28, 1988.

76. Dobal, "De la crónica diaria: Recursos," *Clarín,* March 29, 1988.

77. Crist, comics, *Clarín,* March 9 and 30, 1988.

78. Dobal, "De la crónica diaria: Situación," *Clarín,* July 19, 1989.

79. Catterberg and Braun, "Las elecciones," 364–65 and 369.

80. Alberto Delgado as quoted in Fox, "Argentina," 6.

81. Viegel, *Dictatorship,* 173–74.

82. Powers, "The Politics of Poverty," 118.

83. "Menem dijo que se acabó el estado prebendario," *La Nación,* November 1, 1991.

84. "El texto del decreto de desregulación," *La Nación,* November 1, 1991; Eduardo de Simone, "Un decreto que abre puertas a nuevas medidas," *La Nación,* November 1, 1991.

85. "Repercusiones entre los políticos," *La Nación,* November 1, 1991.

86. Eduardo de Simone, "La decisión maduró en secreto," *La Nación,* November 1, 1991.

87. "Crónica de un día agitado en gobierno," *Clarín,* November 1, 1991.

88. Eduardo de Simone, "La decisión maduró en secreto," *La Nación,* November 1, 1991. Gary Marx, "Argentine Leader Takes Economy by the Horns," *Chicago Tribune,* November 10, 1991.

89. Nathaniel C. Nash, "Making a Difference; Argentina's Mr. Fix-It," *The New York Times,* November 17, 1991.

90. Eduardo de Simone, "La decisión maduró en secreto," *La Nación,* November 1, 1991.

91. "'La CRYM no debe existir más', afirmó Szychowski," *El Territorio,* December 11, 1990; "La CRYM debe continuar, afirmó cooperativista," *El Territorio,* December 14, 1990; "Los molineros apoyan continuidad de la CRYM," *El Territorio,* January 19, 1991; Abel R. Rodríguez, "Preocupa a la industria que se abandonen los yerbatales," *El Cronista Comercial,* January 22, 1991; "Yerba mate: 'Hay que desregular, pero de a poco,'" *El Territorio,* January 27, 1991.

92. "Sostienen que la desregulación creará problemas sociales," *El Territorio,* November 1, 1991; "La desregulación desde la óptica misionera," *El Territorio,* November 3, 1991; "Desregulación 'no afectará' a los pequeños productores," *El Territorio,* November 3, 1991.

93. Rau, *Cosechando,* 104; unpubished report by Asociación Argentina de Consorcios Regionales de Experimentación Agrícola, *Agroalimentos Argentinos,* 2003, 143 and 146.

94. "Resistencia por el cambio en la yerba," *Ámbito Financiero,* April 15, 1994; César L. Sánchez Bonifato, "Continúan los reclamos de los yerbateros misioneros," *La Nación,* April 27, 1994; "Depreciación de la cosecha yerbatera," *Clarín,* May 2, 1994.

95. Vicente Martínez, "Creciente competencia en el mercado de la yerba mate," *La Nación,* April 29, 1994.

96. Veigel, *Dictatorship,* 184–85, 193; López and Romeo, *La declinación,* esp. 19; Svampa, *Desde abajo.*

97. Powers, "The Politics of Poverty," 99–101; Veigel, *Dictatorship,* 192; López and Romeo, *La declinación,* 23–25; Torrado, "Estrategias," 1:60; Lvovich, "Colgados," 64–65."

98. P. Aguirre, *Estrategias,* 46–47, 102, 155 and 186.

99. P. Aguirre, *Estrategias,* 124 and 137.

100. Ruggiero, *And Here,* 151.

101. M. P. Krasnob, "El diputado que donó el sueldo a su pueblo," *Clarín,* June 25, 1989.

102. Armando E. Domínguez, "Brusca caída de la producción," *Clarín,* March 2, 1988.

103. Gobernación Provincia de Misiones, "Programa de promoción del consumo de yerba mate," undated (viewed at the Archivo de Redacción, *Clarín*).

104. Gobernación Provincia de Misiones, "Programa de promoción del consumo de yerba mate," undated (viewed at the Archivo de Redacción, *Clarín*).

105. "Fax from Secret. de Com. e Integración. Una costumbre siempre actualizada. El mate. Siempre actualizado. Ahora en la onda de la juventud," 1990s (viewed at Archivo de Redacción, *Clarín).*

106. Gobierno de la Provincia de Misiones and Secretaría de Comercio e Integración, "Yerba mate de Misiones. La bebida que da vida," 1990s, advertisement included in a document at the Archivo de Redacción, *Clarín*.

107. "El Gobernador, Federico Puerta, sostuvo que no será importada," *Ambito Financiero,* April 25, 1994.

108. Liliana Fariña, "Situación actual," *La Prensa,* March 26, 1995.

109. Gobierno de la Provincia de Misiones, *Misiones: Relevamiento yerbatero,* 2002, page 31.

110. Powers, "The Politics of Poverty," 118.

111. "Temas cotidianos. El mate," *La Nación,* June 13, 1987.

112. "Temas cotidianos. El mate," *La Nación,* June 13, 1987.

113. Mario Rodríguez Muñoz, "En La Mansa, alguna gente 'curte' el 'my way' (hace la suya) sin atarse a la moda," *Clarín,* January 9, 1988.

114. Arizaga, "Ciudad," 151–54.

115. "Una radiografía de los consumidores," *Clarín,* May 5, 1997.

116. "Los detractores del mate," *La Nación,* October 2, 1999.

AFTERWORD

1. "'Tractorazo' en Posadas," *El Territorio,* June 4, 2001; "Los yerbateros cortan rutas en Misiones," *La Nación,* June 5, 2001; "Sigue trabado el conflicto yerbatero," *La Nación,* June 8, 2001; "Piden una suba del valor de la yerba," *La Nación,* June 13, 2001; Alejandro Ramírez, "Gobierno apura medidas por la crisis yerbatera," *Ámbito Nacional,* June 13, 2001; "La crisis de las economías regionales," *Ámbito Financiero,* June 21, 2001.

2. De Bernardi, Kricun, and Secretaría de Agricultura, Ganadería, Pesca, y Alimentación, *Cadena alimentaria* esp. 14–16.

3. "Los productores reclamaban un aumento," *La Nación,* June 23, 2001; Alejandro Ramírez, "Crisis del sector yerbatero en Misiones," *Ámbito Financiero,* July 17, 2001; "Una ley a contramano," *Clarín,* December 1, 2001.

4. DeSoucey, *Contested Tastes.*

5. Argentines purchased an average of 455 ml of yerba mate per year in 1996–1997, 376 ml in 2004–2005, and 406 ml in 2012–2013. In all periods, they consumed significantly more yerba mate as compared to both coffee and tea (Zapata, Rovirosa, and Carmuega, *La mesa,* 155).

6. "Al caer el consumo de yerba mate per cápita, el INYM planea campañas orientadas a los jóvenes," *AgroLink,* November 17, 2021.

7. https://guayaki.com/our-vision, accessed August 20, 2021.

8. As mentioned in the introduction, Guayaki is actually a derogatory Guaraní term for the Ache Indians (Hill and Hurtado, *Ache Life History,* 41).

9. Luke Lewis, "Club Mate Is the Hipster Energy Drink You Need to Try," *BuzzFeed,* January 28, 2016; Rábade Roque, *The Cuban Kitchen,* 6.

BIBLIOGRAPHY

ARCHIVAL SOURCES

Archivo del Museo Nacional de Ciencias Naturales, Spain	AMCN
Archivo General de Indias, Spain	AGI
Archivo General de la Nación, Argentina	AGN
Archivo Histórico Nacional, Spain	AHNM
Archivo Nacional de Asunción, Paraguay	ANA
Biblioteca Nacional, Argentina	BNA
Biblioteca Nacional de España, Spain	BNE
Biblioteca de la Real Academia de Historia, Spain	BRAM
Diario de Sesiones de la Cámara de Diputados	DSCD
Diario de Sesiones de la Cámara de Senados	DSCS
Documentos para la historia Argentina. Vols. 1–20. Buenos Aires: Talleres s.a. Casa Jacobo Peuser ltda, 1912–1927.	DHA
El Archivo Nacional de La Asunción. 17 vols. Talleres Nacionales de H. Kraus, 1901–1902.	

PRINTED SOURCES

"A Seemingly Harmless Stimulant." *Public Opinion* 35, no. 21 (November 19, 1903).

Abínzano, Roberto. "Procesos de integración en una sociedad multiétnica. La Provincia Argentina de Misiones." PhD diss., Universidad de Sevilla, 1985.

Acree, William Garrett. *Staging Frontiers: The Making of Modern Popular Culture in Argentina and Uruguay*. Albuquerque: University of New Mexico Press, 2019.

Adair, Jennifer. *In Search of the Lost Decade: Everyday Rights*. Berkeley: University of California Press, 2020.

Adamovsky, Ezequiel. *El gaucho indómito: De Martín Fierro a Perón, el emblema imposible de una nación desgarrada*. Buenos Aires: Siglo Veintiuno Editores, 2019.

———. "A Strange Emblem for a (Not So) White Nation: 'La Morocha Argentina' in the Latin American Racial Context c. 1900–2015." *Journal of Social History* 50, no. 2 (2016): 386–410.

———. "Race and Class through the Visual Culture of Peronism." In *Rethinking Race in Modern Argentina*, edited by Paulina Alberto and Eduardo Elena, 155–83. Cambridge: Cambridge University Press, 2016.

———. "La cuarta función del criollismo y las luchas por la definición del origen y el color del ethos argentino." *Boletín del Instituto de Historia Argentina y Americana "Doctor Emilio Ravignani"* 41 (2014): 50–92.

———. *Historia de la clase media argentina: Apogeo y decadencia de una ilusión, 1919–2003*. Buenos Aires: Planeta, 2009.

Adelman, Jeremy. *Frontier Development: Land, Labour and Capital on the Wheatlands of Argentina and Canada, 1890–1914*. Oxford: Oxford University Press, 1994.

———. "Reflections on Argentine Labour and the Rise of Perón." *Bulletin of Latin American Research* 11, no. 3 (1992): 243–59.

Aguirre, Juan Francisco. *Discurso histórico sobre el Paraguay*. Edited by Ernesto J. A. Maeder. Buenos Aires: Academia Nacional de la Historia, 2003.

———. "Diario del capitán de fragata d. Juan Francisco Aguirre." In *Revista de la Biblioteca Nacional*, Vol. 17–19. Buenos Aires: Ministerio de Educación, 1948–1950.

Aguirre, Patricia. *Estrategias de consumo: Qué comen los argentinos que comen*. Buenos Aires: Miño y Dávila srl, 2005.

———. "El P.A.N.—Programa Alimentario Nacional—Informe sobre su implementación entre los años 1984 y 1989." Buenos Aires, May 1990.

———. "How the Very Poor Survive—The Impact of Hyper-Inflationary Crisis on Low-Income: Urban Households in Buenos Aires/Argentina." *GeoJournal* 34, no. 3 (1994): 295–304.

Alberdi, Juan Bautista. *El crimen de la guerra [1870–1895]*. Buenos Aires: n.p., 1934.

Alberto, Paulina, and Eduardo Elena, eds. *Rethinking Race in Modern Argentina*. Cambridge: Cambridge University Press, 2016.

Albes, Edward. "Yerba Mate—The Tea of South America." *Bulletin of the Pan American Union (Washington)* 42, no. 5 (1916): 625–43.

Alcaráz, Alberto Daniel. *Una etnografía de las élites del Alto Paraná durante la explotación yerbatera-madera (1870-1930)*. Buenos Aires: Prometeo Libros, 2019.

Allain, Pablo. "Memorándum sobre la yerba mate." In *Conferencia sobre explotación de yerbales*, edited by Luis Pastoriza, 19–26. Montevideo: Universidad de Montevideo, 1921.

Allain, Pablo. *Proyecto de una plantación de yerba-mate en Misiones*. Buenos Aires: Imprenta Kidd, 1910.

Alonso, Paula. *Between Revolution and the Ballot Box: The Origins of the Argentine Radical Party in the 1890s*. Cambridge: Cambridge University Press, 2000.

Alterach Peralta, Miguel Angel. *Mensú: Vida y costumbres en el legendario Alto Paraná*. Buenos Aires, 1948.

Amaral, Argeu Mĭg. "Conhecimento e uso de plantas pelos Kaingang na terra indígena guarita RS." Licenciatura en historia, Universidade Federal de Santa Catarina, 2015.

Ambrosetti, Juan Bautista. *Tercer viaje a Misiones*. Buenos Aires: Editorial Albatros Saci, 2008.

———. "Los indios cainguá del Alto Paraná (Misiones)." *Boletín del Instituto Geográfico Argentino* 15 (1894): 661–744.

———. "Segundo viage a Misiones por el Alto Paraná é Iguazú." *Boletín del Instituto Geográfico Argentino* 15 (1894).

"An Apparently Harmless Stimulant." *The British Medical Journal* 2, no. 2234 (October 24, 1903): 1081–82.

Antonini, H. J. "La yerba mate." *Boletín del Ministerio de Agricultura* 18, no. 2 (1914): 105–21.

Arata, Pedro. *El mate en nuestras costumbres*. Buenos Aires: Imprenta el Diario, 1881.

Arcelli, María. *Ciencias domésticas: Apuntes de higiene de la habitación*. Buenos Aires: Moly, 1936.

Arizaga, Cecilia. "Ciudad y usos del espacio en los jóvenes: El consumo juvenil desde dos escenarios urbanos." In *Pensar las clases medias: Consumos culturales y estilos de vida urbanos en la Argentina de los noventa,* edited by Ana Wortman, 141–56. Buenos Aires: La Crujía Ediciones, 2003.

Armaignac, Henry. *Viajes por las Pampas Argentinas, 1869–74*. Translated by Isabel Molina Pico. Buenos Aires: EUDEBA, 1974.

Armus, Diego. *The Ailing City: Health, Tuberculosis, and Culture in Buenos Aires, 1870–1950*. Durham, NC: Duke University Press, 2011.

Arzáns de Orsúa y Vela, Bartolomé. *Historia de la villa imperial de Potosí, [1705]*. Edited by Lewis Hanke and Gunnar Mendoza. 3 vols. Providence, RI: Brown University, 1965.

Austin, Shawn Michael. *Colonial Kinship: Guaraní, Spaniards, and Africans in Paraguay*. Albuquerque: University of New Mexico Press, 2020.

———. "Beyond the Missions: Ethnogenesis in Colonial Paraguay, 1556–1700." PhD diss., University of New Mexico, 2014.

Avery, Martha. *The Tea Road: China and Russia Meet Across the Steppe*. Beijing: China Intercontinental Press, 2003.

de Azara, Félix. *Geografía, física y esférica de las provincias del Paraguay y misiones guaraníes*. Edited by Rodolfo R. Schuller. Montevideo, 1904.

Baker, E. L. "Yerba-Maté or Paraguay Tea." In *Reports from the Consuls of the United States on the Commerce, Manufactures, Etc.,* 27:245–52. Washington, DC: US Department of State, Government Printing Office, 1883.

Baldassarre, Juan F. "Informe sobre la importancia de los cultivos de yerba mate y tártago en el Territorio de Misiones." *Boletín del Ministerio de Agricultura* 10 (1908): 169–77.

Banco Ipotecario Nazionale. *Territorio Nazionale di Misiones; Coltivazione della "Yerba-Mate."* Buenos Aires: Compañía Impresora Argentina, 1927.

Baracat, Elías. *Yerba mate: Cincuenta años de ciclos alternativos de promoción y prohibición.* Buenos Aires: Fundación Mediterránea, 1986.

Barbará, Federico. *Diabluras, diversiones, y anécdotas de Juan Manuel de Rosas.* Buenos Aires: Imprenta la Reforma, 1859.

Barbosa Lessa, Luíz Carlos. *História do chimarrão.* Porto Alegre: Livraria Sulina, 1953.

Barrett, Rafael. *Obras Completas.* Edited by Francisco Corral. 3 vols. Asunción: RP Ediciones, 1988.

Barreyro, Héctor. "Censo de las plantaciones de yerba mate en el Territorio de la Gobernación de Misiones." *Revista de Ciencias Económicas* 16 (1928): 1624–29.

———. *Ideas de gobierno: Memorial presentado al Ministerio del Interior por el Gobernador de Misiones.* Talleros Gráficos Argentinos de L.J. Rosso y Cía, 1919.

Barrios, Valentín José. *El "mensú" que triunfó en la selva.* Buenos Aires: Librería Perlado, 1951.

Barros Arana, Diego. *Historia general de Chile.* Vol. 7. Santiago: Editorial Universitaria, 2000.

Bartolomé, Leopoldo J. *Los colonos de Apóstoles: Estrategias adaptivas y etnicidad en una colonia eslava en Misiones.* Posadas, Argentina: Editorial Universitaria, 2007.

de Basaldúa, Florencio. *Pasado, presente, porvenir del Territorio Nacional de Misiones.* La Plata, 1901.

Beaumont, J. A. B. *Travels in Buenos Ayres, and the Adjacent Provinces of the Río de La Plata.* London: James Ridgeway, 1828.

Beccaria, Luis A. "Cambios en la estructura distributiva 1975–1990." In *Cuesta abajo. Los nuevos pobres: Efectos de la crisis en la sociedad Argentina,* edited by Alberto Minujin, 93–118. Buenos Aires: Editorial Losada, 1992.

Beccaria, Luis A., and Ricardo Carciofi. "Argentina: Social Policy and Adjustment during the 1980s." In *Coping with Austerity: Poverty and Inequality in Latin America,* edited by Nora Claudia Lustig, 187–236. Washington, DC: Brookings Institution, 1995.

Beck-Bernard, Lina. *El Río Paraná: Cinco años en la Confederación Argentina, 1857–1862.* Buenos Aires: Emecé Editores, 2001.

Becker, Ítala Irene Basile. "O índio kaingáng no Rio Grande do Sul." *Pesquisas: Antropologia* 29 (1976): 1–331.

Beckert, Sven. *Empire of Cotton: A Global History.* New York: Vintage Books, 2014.

Belini, Claudio. *La industria peronista, 1946–1955: Políticas públicas y cambio estructural.* Buenos Aires: Edhasa, 2009.

Bell, Stephen. *A Life in Shadow: Aimé Bonpland in Southern South America, 1817–1858.* Stanford, CA: Stanford University Press, 2010.

Beltrame, Alfredo. "Industria y cultivo de la yerba mate en la Argentina." *Revista de Eonomía Argentina* 10 (1923): 162–66.

Bermúdez, Manuel A. *Informe del Gobernador del Territorio, Señor Manuel A. Bermúdez.* Corrientes: Imprenta y Encuadernación de Teodoro Heinecke, 1907.

Bernárdez, Manuel. *De Buenos Aires a Iguazú.* Buenos Aires: Imprenta de "La Nación," 1901.

de Bernardi, Luis Alberto, and Sergio Dante Prat Kricun. *Cadena alimentaria de "yerba mate," "ilex Paraguariensis."* Secretaría de Agricultura, Pesca y Alimentación, 2001.

Besky, Sarah. *The Darjeeling Distinction: Labor and Justice on Fair-Trade Tea Plantations in India.* Berkeley: University of California Press, 2014.

Betagh, William. *A Voyage Round the World.* London: Bible and Dove, 1728.

Biedma, José Juan, ed. *Acuerdos del extinguido cabildo de Buenos Aires.* Buenos Aires: Talleres Gráficos de la Penitenciaría Nacional, 1907.

Bigelow, Allison Margaret. *Mining Language: Racial Thinking, Indigenous Knowledge, and Colonial Metallurgy in the Early Modern Iberian World.* Chapel Hill: University of North Carolina Press, 2020.

Billard, Juan J. *Economía de la industria yerbatera argentina.* Buenos Aires: Imprenta de la Universidad, 1944.

Biltekoff, Charlotte. *Eating Right in America: The Cultural Politics of Food and Health.* Durham, NC: Duke University Press, 2013.

Birket-Smith, Kaj. "Drinking Tube and Tobacco Pipe in North America." *Ethnologische Studien* 1 (1929): 29–30.

du Biscay, Acarate. *An Account of a Voyage up the River de la Plata and Thence over Land to Peru (1658).* London: S. Buckley, 1698.

Bockelman, Brian. "Between the Gaucho and the Tango: Popular Songs and the Shifting Landscape of Modern Argentine Identity, 1895–1915." *American Historical Review* 116, no. 3 (2011): 576–601.

Bolsi, Alfredo. "Misiones (una aproximación geográfica al problema de la yerba mate y sus efectos en la ocupación del espacio y el poblamiento)." *Folia Histórica del Nordeste* 7 (1986–1987): 9-253.

———. "El primer siglo de economía yerbatera en Argentina." *Folia Histórica del Nordeste* 4 (1980): 119–82.

———. "El proceso de poblamiento pionero en Misiones (1830–1920)." *Folia Histórica del Nordeste* 2 (1976): 9–70.

Bonpland, Amado. "Nota sobre la utilidad de trabajar los." November 3, 1854. *Revista Farmacéutica* 5 (1867): 270–76.

Borrás, Eduardo, ed. *Las aguas bajan turbias.* Buenos Aires: Editorial Biblos, 2006.

Bouza, Fernando. "El arbitrio de la hierba 'provechosa' del Paraguay de 1637. Experiencia y práctica en la construcción de saberes locales de Indias a través del Atlántico." *Anos 90: Revista do Programa de Pós-Graduação em História da Universidade Federal do Rio Grande do Sul* 24, no. 45 (2017): 73–100.

Brackenridge, H. M. *Voyage to Buenos Aires in the Years 1817 and 1818.* London: Sir Richard Phillips and Co., 1820.

Brant, Mario. *Viaje a Buenos Aires [1916].* Translated by Roberto Romero Escalada. Buenos Aires: Botella al Mar, 1980.

Bryce, Benjamin. *To Belong in Buenos Aires: Germans, Argentines, and the Rise of a Pluralist Society.* Stanford, CA: Stanford University Press, 2018.

Buonuome, Juan. "Los socialistas argentinas ante la 'prensa burguesa.' El semanario *La Vanguardia* y la modernización periodística en la Buenos Aires de entresiglos." *Boletín del Instituto de Historia Argentina y Americana "Doctor Emilio Ravignani"* 3, no. 46 (2017): 147–79.

Bureau of the American Republics. *Handbook of Paraguay.* Washington, DC: US Government Printing Office, 1892.

Burmeister, Carlos. *Memoria sobre el Territorio de Misiones.* Buenos Aires: J. Peuser, 1899.

Burnett, John. *Liquid Pleasure: A Social History of Drinks in Modern Britain.* New York: Routledge, 1999.

Buss, James J. *Winning the West with Words: Language and Conquest in the Lower Great Lakes.* Norman: University of Oklahoma Press, 2011.

Butler, William Mill. *Paraguay: A Country of Vast Natural Resources, Delightful Climate, Law-Abiding People, and Stable Government, Rightly Called the Paradise of South America.* Philadelphia: Paraguay Development Company, 1901.

———. *Yerba Maté Tea.* Philadelphia: The Yerba Maté Tea Co., 1900.

———, ed. *Official Proceedings of the International Commercial Congress.* Philadelphia: Philadelphia Commercial Museum, 1899.

Byron, John. *The Narrative of the Honourable John Byron.* London: S. Baker and G. Leigh, 1768.

Caldcleugh, Alexander. *Travels in South America During the Years 1819–20–21.* 2 vols. London: John Murray, 1825.

Cámara Argentina de Cultura, Comercio, Industria y Producción. "Una fuente de riqueza nacional: La yerba mate." *Boletín de la Cámara Argentina* 1, no. 5 (1926): 18–23.

Cámara de Comercio Argentino-Brasileña. *La yerba mate, el problema económico y fiscal.* Argentina: Futura, 1933.

Cambas, Aníbal. "Historia de la Provincia de Misiones y sus pueblos (1862–1930)." In *Historia argentina contemporánea, 1862–1930,* vol. 4, 2nd section: 283–324. Buenos Aires: Libreria "El Ateneo" Editorial, 1967.

———. *Leyendas misioneras.* Posadas, Argentina: Eco de Misiones, 1938.

Cambra, Laura, and Juan Raffo. "A Newer Tango Coming from the Past." In *Music and Youth Culture in Latin America: Identity Construction Processes from New York to Buenos Aires,* edited by Pablo Vila, 243–60. Oxford: Oxford University Press, 2014.

Cameron, C. R. "Maté: Important Brazilian Product." *Bulletin of the Pan American Union (Washington)* 63, no. 2 (1929): 988–1005.

Campi, Daniel, and Marcela Vignoli. "La emergencia de la cuestión social en Tucumán. Un concurso de la Sociedad Sarmiento de 1892." *Nuevo Mundo Mundos Nuevos,* July 7, 2016. https://doi.org/10.4000/nuevomundo.69361.

del Campo, Luzán. *Cancionero del mate.* Rev. edition. Buenos Aires: Editorial Tupã, 1950.

Candela, Guillaume. *Entre la pluma y la cruz: El clérigo Martín González y la desconocida historia de su defensa de los indios del Paraguay.* Asunción: Editorial Tiempo de Historia, 2018.

Cardiel, José. *Las misiones del Paraguay [1771].* Madrid: Dastin, 2002.

———. *Declaración de la verdad [1758].* Buenos Aires: Imprenta de Juan Alsina, 1900.

Cardim, Pedro, et al., eds. *Polycentric Monarchies: How Did Early Modern Spain and Portugal Achieve and Maintain a Global Hegemony.* Portland: Sussex Academic Press, 2012.

Carpenter, William M. "Dependence of Life upon Water." *The Scottish Temperance Review,* June 1849, 256–64.

Carretero, Andrés M. *Vida cotidiana en Buenos Aires.* 3 vols. Buenos Aires: Editorial Paidós SAICF, 2013.

Carrió de la Vandera, Alonso. *El lazarillo de ciegos caminantes: Desde Buenos Aires hasta Lima [1773].* Buenos Aires: Ediciones Argentinas Solar, 1942.

Catálogo de documentos del Archivo de Indias en Sevilla referentes a la historia de la República Argentina, 1514–1810. Vol. 2. Buenos Aires: Taller Tipográfico de la Penitenciaría Nacional, 1903.

Catterberg, Edgardo, and María Braun. "Las elecciones presidenciales argentinas del 14 de Mayo de 1989: La ruta a la normalidad." *Desarrollo Económico* 29, no. 115 (1989): 361–74.

Cavazzutti, Esteban. *Misiones. Naturaleza, labor humana, crimenes.* La Plata: Talleres Gráficos Olivieri y Domínguez, 1923.

Cervera, Manuel M. *Historia de la ciudad y provincia de Santa Fe, 1573–1853.* Vol. 1. Santa Fe: La Unión, 1908.

Chamosa, Oscar. "People as Landscape: The Representation of the Criollo Interior in Early Tourist Literature in Argentina, 1920–30." In *Rethinking Race in Modern Argentina,* edited by Paulina Alberto and Eduardo Elena, 53–72. Cambridge: Cambridge University Press, 2016.

———. *The Argentine Folklore Movement: Sugar Elites, Criollo Workers, and the Politics of Cultural Nationalism, 1900–1955.* Tucson: University of Arizona Press, 2010.

———. "Criollo and Peronist: The Argentine Folklore Movement during the First Peronism, 1943–1955." In *The New Cultural History of Peronism: Power and Identity in Mid-Twentieth-Century Argentina,* edited by Matthew B. Karush and Oscar Chamosa, 113–42. Durham, NC: Duke University Press, 2010.

———. "Indigenous or Criollo: The Myth of White Argentina in Tucumán's Calchaquí Valley." *Hispanic American Historical Review* 88, no. 1 (2008): 71–106.

Cicerchia, Ricardo. *Journey, Rediscovery and Narrative: British Travel Accounts of Argentina.* London: Institute of Latin American Studies, 1998.

Cimó Queiroz, Paulo Roberto. "A companhia Mate Laranjeira, 1891–1902: Contribução á história da empresa concessionária dos ervais do antigo sul de Mato Gross." *Revista Territórios & Fronteiras* 8, no. 1 (2015): 204–28.

Civantos, Christina. *Between Argentines and Arabs: Argentine Orientalism, Arab Immigrants, and the Writing of Identity*. Albany: State University of New York Press, 2006.

Clarence-Smith, William Gervase, and Steven Topik, eds. *The Global Coffee Economy in Africa, Asia and Latin America, 1500–1989*. New York: Cambridge University Press, 2003.

Clavigero, Francesco Saverio. *The History of Mexico*. Translated by Charles Cullen. Vol. 1, book 7. London: G. G. and J. Robinson, 1787.

Clemenceau, Georges. *South America To-Day*. London: T. Fisher Unwin, 1911.

Cobo, Bernabé. *Historia del nuevo mundo, 1653*. Vol. 2. Seville: E. Rasco, 1891.

Cohen, Benjamin R. *Pure Adulteration: Cheating on Nature in the Age of Manufactured Food*. Chicago: University of Chicago Press, 2019.

Compañia Eldorado. *Eldorado: 15 aniversario de la fundación de la colonia, 1919–1934*. Buenos Aires, 1934.

———. *Dieentwicklung der Eldorado-Kolonien, 1919–1929*. Buenos Aires, 1929.

Contreras, Remedios, and Carmen Cortés, eds. *Catalogo de la colección Mata Linares*. Vol. 2. Madrid: Real Academia de la Historia, 1970.

Copani, Andrea. "Terrorismo de estado y trabajadores: La potencialidad del testimonio para pensar la represión a la clase obrera durante la última dictadura argentina." *Historia, Voces y Memoria* 10 (2016): 81–94.

Córdova, Fernando. *Leyendas, mitos, cuentos y otros relatos guaranies*. Buenos Aires: Longseller S.A., 2005.

Corrado, Alberto J. *Contribución al estudio de la yerba mate*. Buenos Aires: La Semana Médica, 1908.

Cortesão, Jaime, ed. *Jesuítas e bandeirantes no Guairá (1549–1640)*. *Manuscritos da Coleção de Angelis*, vol. 1. Rio de Janeiro: Biblioteca Nacional, 1951.

———. *Jesuítas e bandeirantes o Itatim (1596–1760)*. *Manuscritos da Coleção de Angelis*, vol. 2. Rio de Janeiro: Biblioteca Nacional, 1952.

Cortese, Luis O. "Inmigrantes Italianos en Buenos Aires a través de documentos privados." Santa Fe: Congreso Argentino de Inmigración, 2005.

Couyoumdjian, Juan Ricardo. "El mate, el té y el café en Chile desde la independencia hasta 1930." *Boletín de la Academia Chilena de la Historia* 118, no. 1 (2009): 7–56.

Cosse, Isabella. *Mafalda: A Social and Political History of Latin America's Global Comic*. Durham: Duke University Press, 2019.

Cowan, Brian William. *The Social Life of Coffee: The Emergence of the British Coffeehouse*. New Haven, CT: Yale University Press, 2005.

Crotty, James. "Was Keynes a Corporatist? Keynes's Radical Views on Industrial Policy and Macro Policy in the 1920s." *Journal of Economic Issues* 33, no. 3 (1999): 555–77.

Cuestión-Misiones: Refutación del mensaje del presidente. Corrientes: La Verdad, 1881.

da Cunha, Antônio Geraldo. *Dicionário histórico das palavras portuguesas de origem tupi*. São Paulo: Companhia Melhoramentos, Universidade de Brasília, 1999.

Cunninghame Graham, Robert Bontine, and Gabriela Cunninghame Graham. *Father Archangel of Scotland and Other Essays*. London: Adam and Charles Black, 1896.

Daireaux, Godofredo. *La cría del ganado en la estancia moderna. Manual del estanciero.* Buenos Aires: F. Lajouane, 1887.

Daumas, Ernesto. "El problema de la yerba mate." *Revista de la Economía Argentina* 25 (1930): 15–66.

"Decreto del poder ejecutivo nacional prohibiendo la importación de palo de yerba y de congonilla sueltos." *Ministerio de Relaciones Exteriores y Culto—Circular Informativo Mensual* 80 (September 10, 1924): 555–56.

Delaney, Jeane. "Making Sense of Modernity: Changing Attitudes toward the Immigrant and the Gaucho in Turn-of-the-Century Argentina." *Comparative Studies in Society and History* 38, no. 3 (1996): 434–59.

Departamento de Hacienda. *Memoria presentada por el Ministro de Estado en el Departamento de Hacienda al Congreso Nacional de 1865.* Buenos Aires: Nación Argentina, 1865.

Departmento Nacional del Trabajo. *Boletín del Departamento Nacional del Trabajo, no. 5.* Buenos Aires: Coni Hermanos, 1908.

———. *Condiciones de vida de la familia obrero.* Buenos Aires, 1937.

———. *Costo de la vida. Presupuestos familiares. Precios de artículos de primera necesidad. índeces del costo de la vida.* Buenos Aires, 1935.

DeSoucey, Michaela. *Contested Tastes: Foie Gras and the Politics of Food.* Princeton, NJ: Princeton University Press, 2016.

Devoto, Fernando J. *Historia de la inmigración en la Argentina.* Buenos Aires: Editorial Sudamericana, 2003.

Dirección de Estadístisa Social. *Condiciones de vida de la familia obrera, 1943–1945.* Buenos Aires, 1946.

———. *Nivel de vida de la familia obrero. Evolución durante la segunda guerra mundial, 1939–1945.* Buenos Aires, 1945.

Dirección General de Agricultura y Defensa Agricola. *Debates de la conferencia de gobernadores de Territorios Nacionales.* 1913.

Dobrizhoffer, Martin. *Historia de Los Abipones.* Translated by Edmundo Wernicke. Resistencia: Universidad Nacional del Nordeste, 1967.

———. *An Account of the Abipones, an Equestrian People of Paraguay.* 3 vols. London: J. Murray, 1822.

Drago, Tito. *Dos en uno. Así nació, así se baila y así se canta el tango.* Madrid: Ediciones Comunica, 2009.

Dufour, Philippe Sylvestre. *The Manner of Making Coffee, Tea and Chocolate.* London: William Crook, 1685.

Duhau, Luis. *Censo nacional de yerba mate.* Buenos Aires: Ministerio de Agricultura, 1934.

Earle, Rebecca. *The Body of the Conquistador: Food, Race, and the Colonial Experience in Spanish America, 1492–1700.* New York: Cambridge University Press, 2012.

Ebelot, Alfredo. *La Pampa. Costumbres argentinas.* Buenos Aires: Librairie Française de Joseph Escary, 1890.

Economía doméstica al alcance de las niñas. Buenos Aires: Cabaut y Cía., 1914.

Eidt, Robert C. *Pioneer Settlement in Northeast Argentina.* Madison: University of Wisconsin Press, 1971.

Einzig, Paul. *Primitive Money: In Its Ethnological, Historical and Economic Aspects.* New York: Pergamon Press, 1966.

Elena, Eduardo. *Dignifying Argentina: Peronism, Citizenship, and Mass Consumption.* Pittsburgh: University of Pittsburgh Press, 2011.

Elliott, L. E. *The Argentina of To-Day.* London: Hurst and Blackett, 1926.

Elmore, Bartow J. *Citizen Coke: The Making of Coca-Cola Capitalism.* New York: W. W. Norton & Company, 2015.

Ennis, Huberto M. "Shortages of Small Change in Early Argentina." *Federal Reserve Bank of Richmond, Working Paper No. 03-12,* September 2003.

de Escalona y Agüero, Gaspar. *Gazofilacio real del Perú; Tratado financiero del coloniaje (1647).* La Paz: Editorial del Estado, 1941.

España, Claudio. "*Las Aguas Bajan Turbias:* Una denuncia contra toda esclavitud." In *Las aguas bajan turbias,* edited by Eduardo Borrás, 9–26. Buenos Aires: Editorial Biblos, 2006.

Ferm, Deane W. *Profiles in Liberation: 36 Portraits of Third World Theologians.* Eugene, OR: Wipf and Stock, 2004.

Fernández Ramos, Raimundo. *Misiones: A través del primer cincuentenario de su federalización, 1881-Diciembre 20–1931.* Posadas, Argentina: 1934.

Flynn, Dennis O., and Arturo Giráldez. "Born with a 'Silver Spoon': The Origin of World Trade in 1571." *Journal of World History* 6, no. 2 (1995): 201–21.

Folch, Christine. "Stimulating Consumption: Yerba Mate Myths, Markets, and Meanings from Conquest to Present." *Comparative Studies in Society and History* 52, no. 1 (2010): 6–36.

Fontanarrosa, Roberto. *20 años con Inodoro Pereyra.* Buenos Aires: Ediciones de la Flor, 1998.

Fox, Geoffrey. "Argentina: Putting the 'Perón' Back In." *NACLA: Report on the Americas* 23, no. 4 (1989): 4–7.

Fragueiro, Rafael, ed. "Lectura XXX: Te, chocolate, mate y café." In *La niña argentina,* 97–100. Buenos Aires: Cabaut y Cía., 1917.

Frézier, Amédée François. *A Voyage to the South-Sea and Along the Coasts of Chili and Peru in the Years 1712, 1713, and 1714.* London: J. Bowyer, 1718.

Fundación Tiempo Social. *17 de Octubre de 1945: 50 Aniversario.* Buenos Aires: Ediciones Historia Viva, 1995.

de la Fuente, Ariel. "'Civilización y barbarie': Fuentes para una nueva explicación del Facundo." *Boletín del Instituto de Historia Argentina y Americana "Doctor Emilio Ravignani"* 44 (2016): 135–79.

———. *Children of Facundo: Caudillo and Gaucho Insurgency.* Durham, NC: Duke University Press, 2000.

Furlong, Guillermo. *Misiones y sus pueblos de guaraníes.* Posadas: Lumicop y Cía., 1978.

———, ed. *José Cardiel, S.J., y su carta-relación (1747).* Buenos Aires: Librería del Plata, 1953.

Galarza, Juan B. "La yerba-mate." *Boletín del Ministerio de Agricultura* 18, no. 2 (1914): 44–101.

Galeano, Eduardo. "Mate." In *Genesis: Memory of Fire*, translated by Cedric Belfrage, 1:29–30. New York: Bold Type Books, 2010.

Galharretborde, Juan Omar. *Analisis de la demanda y oferta de yerba mate.* Pergamino: Instituto Nacional de Tecnología Agropecuaria, 1965.

Gallardo, Carlos R. *La industria yerbatera en Misiones.* Buenos Aires: Imprenta y Encuadernación "San Jorge," 1898.

Gallero, María Cecilia. *Querida Misiones hermosa! A través de las memorias de Alberto Roth.* Misiones: Araucaria Editora, 2014.

———. *Piporé: 80 años haciendo historia en yerba mate.* Buenos Aires: Su Impres, 2011.

———. *Con la patria a cuestas: La inmigración alemana-brasileña en la colonia Puerto Rico, Misiones.* Buenos Aires: Araucaria Editora, 2009.

———, ed. *El llamado del lro verde: Memorias de inmigrantes suizos en Misiones.* Buenos Aires: Araucaria Editora, 2008.

Gambini, Hugo. *Historia del peronismo: El poder total (1943–1951).* Buenos Aires: Planeta, 1999.

de Gandía, Enrique. *Indios y conquistadores en el Paraguay.* Buenos Aires: A. García Santos, 1932.

Garavaglia, Juan Carlos. *Mercado interno y economía colonial: Tres siglos de historia de la yerba mate.* México: Grijalbo, 1983.

García, Miguel Angel. *Peronismo: Desarrollo económico y lucha de clases en Argentina.* Barcelona: Mario Acosta, 1980.

García Mata, Carlos, and N. T. da Silva Carneiro. "Consideraciones sobre la exportación de yerba mate." *Revista de Economía Argentina* 35 (1936): 190–95.

Garguin, Enrique. "'Los Argentinos descendemos de los Barcos': The Racial Articulation of Middle Class Identity in Argentina (1920–1960)." *Latin American and Caribbean Ethnic Studies* 2, no. 2 (2007): 161–84.

Gaudio, Ricardo, and Jorge Pilone. "El desarrollo de la negociación colectiva durante la etapa de modernización industrial en la Argentina. 1935-1943." *Desarrollo Económico* 23, no. 90 (1983): 255–86.

Gay, Claudio. *Atlas de la historia físcia y política de Chile.* 2 vols. Paris: E. Thunot y Ca., 1854.

Gemelli Careri, John Francis. "A Voyage Round the World." In *A Collection of Voyages and Travels,* Vol. 4. London: Awnsham and John Churchill, 1704.

Gené, Marcela. *Un mundo feliz: Imágenes de los trabajadores en el primer peronismo, 1946–1955.* Buenos Aires: Fondo de Cultura Ecónomica, 2005.

Gerchunoff, Pablo. "Peronist Economic Policies, 1946–1955." In *The Political Economy of Argentina, 1946–1983,* edited by Guido di Tella and Rudiger Dornbusch, 59–85. Pittsburgh: University of Pittsburgh Press, 1989.

Gerchunoff, Pablo, and Damián Antúnez. "De la bonanza peronista a la crisis de desarrollo." In *Nueva historia argentina,* 125–206. Vol. 8, Los años peronistas (1943–1955). Buenos Aires: Editorial Sudamericana, 2002.

Gerchunoff, Pablo, and Lucas Llach. *El ciclo de la ilusión y el desencanto: Un siglo de políticas económicas argentinas.* Buenos Aires: Ariel, 1998.

Germani, Gino. "Mass Immigration and Modernization in Argentina." *Studies in Comparative International Development* 2, no. 11 (1966): 165–82.

Giberti, Gustavo C. *Flora del Paraguay: Aquifoliaceae.* Geneva: Conservatoire et Jardin botaniques, 1994.

———. "Maté (Ilex Paraguariensis)." In *Neglected Crops: 1492 from a Different Perspective,* edited by J. E. Hernándo Bermejo and J. León, 245–52. Rome: Food and Agriculture Organization of the United Nations, 1994.

Gillespie, Alexander. *Gleanings and Remarks: Collected During Many Months of Residence at Buenos Ayres, and Within the Upper Country . . .* Leeds: B. Dewhirst, 1818.

Girola, Carlos D. *Cultivo de la yerba mate en la República Argentina: estadística de las plantaciones: informaciones de los plantadores, quinta encuesta.* Buenos Aires: Gadola, 1929.

———. "Cultivo de la yerba mate: Formación de yerbales—gastos para la plantación—beneficios o utilidad. Costo de la yerba mate, Capítulo 11." In *Monografía sobre la yerba mate.* Buenos Aires: n.p., 1926.

———. *Cultivo de la yerba mate en la República Argentina (Ilex paraguariensis St. Hil): estadísticas de las plantaciones, informaciones de los plantadores, cuarta encuesta.* Buenos Aires: Gadola, 1925.

———. *Cultivo de la yerba mate (Ilex Paraguariensis St. Hil.): Consumo de la yerba mate.* Buenos Aires: Tall. Gráfs. "La lectura," 1923.

———. *Cultivo de la yerba mate (Ilex paraguariensis St. Hil.): Porvenir de la yerba mate en la República Argentina.* Buenos Aires: Imprenta Gadola, 1923.

———. *Cultivo de la yerba mate en Argentina (Ilex paraguariensis St. Hill): Estadística de las plantaciones, informaciones de los plantadores, 2nda encuesta.* Buenos Aires: Gadola, 1922.

———. "Cultivo de la yerba mate (Ilex paraguariensis St. Hil.): Comercio del producto." *Boletín del Ministerio de Agricultura de la Nación* 27, no. 3 (1922): 476–502.

———. *Yerba mate. . . una encuesta.* Buenos Aires, 1920.

Glusberg, Samuel. "Mate Amargo." In *La levita gris: Cuentos judíos de ambiente porteño,* edited by Enrique Espinoza, 53–80. Buenos Aires: Editorial Babel, 1924.

Gobernación de Misiones. *La tierra pública y su colonización. Yerbales.* Buenos Aires: Imprenta del Congreso, 1894.

———. *Memorias correspondientes a los años 1911, 1912, 1913, y 1914.* Talleres Gráficos de la Penitenciaría Nacional, 1915.

Gobierno de la Provincia de Misiones. *Evolución de la yerba mate: Producción, comercialización, mercado.* Posadas, Argentina, 1977.

———. *Posibilidades de la producción y comercialización de yerba mate en la Argentina. Proyecto.* Posadas, Argentina, 1976.

Goldman, Gustavo. *Lucamba, herencia africana en el tango (1870–1890).* Montevideo: Perro Andaluz Ediciones, 2008.

Gómez, Hernán F. *Corrientes y la república entrerriana, 1820–1821.* Corrientes: Impr. del Estado, 1929.

González Bernaldo de Quirós, Pilar. *Civility and Politics in the Origins of the Argentine Nation: Sociabilities in Buenos Aires, 1829–1862.* Translated by Daniel Philip Tunnard. Los Angeles: University of California Press, 2006.

González, Maximo P. *Recopilación de leyes nacionales sancionadas por el honorable congreso argentino.* Vols. 2 and 3. Buenos Aires: Imprenta Europea, 1888–1889.

Gootenberg, Paul. *Andean Cocaine: The Making of a Global Drug.* Chapel Hill: University of North Carolina Press, 2008.

Gori, Gastón. *Inmigración y colonización en la Argentina.* Buenos Aires: Editorial de la Universidad de Buenos Aires, 1983.

Gorman, Daniel. "Empire, Internationalism, and the Campaign against the Traffic in Women and Children in the 1920s." *Twentieth Century British History* 19, no. 2 (2008): 186–216.

Gorriti, Juana Manuela, ed. *Cocina ecléctica.* Buenos Aires: Félix Lajouane, 1890.

Grafe, Regina, and Alejandra Irigoin. "A Stakeholder Empire: The Political Economy of Spanish Imperial Rule in America." *The Economic History Review* 65, no. 2 (2012): 609–51.

Granada, Daniel. *Reseña histórico-descriptiva de antiguas y modernas supersticiones del Río de la Plata.* Montevideo: A. Barreiro y Ramos, 1896.

Griego, Viviana L. *The Politics of Giving in the Viceroyalty of Rio de La Plata: Donors, Lenders, Subjects, and Citizens.* Albuquerque: University of New Mexico, 2014.

Griffith, F. Ll. "A Drinking Siphon from Tell El-'Amarnah." *The Journal of Egyptian Archeology* 12, no. 3/4 (1926): 22–23.

Guibert, Rita. "Jorge Luis Borges, 1968." In *Seven Voices: Seven Latin American Writers Talk to Rita Guibert,* 75–117. New York: Alfred A. Knopf, 1973.

Gupta, Bishnupriya. "The History of the International Tea Market, 1850–1945." EH.Net Encyclopedia. Edited by Robert Whaples. March 16, 2008. URL http:// eh.net/encyclopedia/the-history-of-the-international-tea-market-1850–1945.

Gutiérrez, Eduardo. *The Gaucho Juan Moreira. True Crime in Nineteenth-Century Argentina.* Edited by William G. Acree. Translated by John Charles Chasteen. Indianapolis: Hackett Publishing, 2014.

———. *Historia de Juan Manuel de Rosas.* Buenos Aires: N. Tommasi, n.d.

Guy, Donna J. *Sex and Danger in Buenos Aires: Prostitution, Family and Nation in Argentina.* Lincoln: University of Nebraska Press, 1991.

———. "White Slavery, Public Health, and the Socialist Position on Legalized Prostitution in Argentina, 1913–1936." *Latin American Research Review* 23, no. 3 (1988): 60–80.

Guy, Kolleen M. *When Champagne became French: Wine and the Making of a National Identity.* Baltimore: Johns Hopkins University Press, 2003.

Haenke, Thaddáus. *Viaje por el Virreinato del Río de la Plata.* Buenos Aires: Emecé Editores, 1943.

Hale, Albert. "Yerba Mate—Paraguayan Tea." *Bulletin of the Pan American Union (Washington)* 32, no. 3 (1911): 469–87.

Halperín, Jorge. "¿Hay una cultura de la caída?" In *Cuesta abajo. Los nuevos pobres: Efectos de la crisis en la sociedad argentina,* edited by Alberto Minujin, 199–228. Buenos Aires: Editorial Losada, 1992.

Halperín Donghi, Tulio. *Historias de caudillos argentinos.* Buenos Aires: Extra Alfaguara, 1999.

———, ed. *Proyecto y construcción de una nación (Argentina 1846–1880).* Caracas: Biblioteca Ayacucho, 1980.

Hammerton, John Alexander. *The Real Argentina: Notes and Impressions of a Year in the Argentine and Uruguay.* New York: Dodd, Mead and Company, 1915.

Harrison, Cynthia. *On Account of Sex: The Politics of Women's Issues, 1945–1968.* Berkeley: University of California Press, 1989.

Heck, C. I., and E. G. de Mejia. "Yerba Mate Tea (Ilex Paraguariensis): A Comprehensive Review on Chemistry, Health Implications, and Technological Considerations." *Journal of Food Science* 72, no. 9 (2007): 138–51.

Hemy, D. E. T., ed. *Aimé Bonpland: Médecin et Naturaliste, Exporateur de l'Amérique du Sud.* Paris: E. Guilmoto, 1906.

Hernández, José. *El gaucho Martín Fierro; La vuelta de Martín Fierro.* Barcelona: Planeta, 1983.

———. *The Gaucho Martin Fierro.* Translated by Frank Gaetano Carrino, Alberto J. Carlos, and Norman Mangouni. Albany: State University of New York Press, 1974.

Hernández, Juan Jesús. "El Instituto Nacional de Vitivinicultura." *POSTData: Revista de Reflexión y Análisis Político* 19, no. 1 (2014): 71–103.

Hernández, Pablo. *Misiones del Paraguay.* 2 vols. Barcelona: G. Gili, 1913.

Hernández, Rafael. *Cartas misioneras [1883].* Buenos Aires: Eudeba, 1973.

Herzog, Tamar. *Frontiers of Possession: Spain and Portugal in Europe and the Americas.* Cambridge, MA: Harvard University Press, 2015.

Hicken, Cristobal M. "La yerba-mate." *Anales de la Sociedad Científica Argentina* 50 (1900): 56–66.

Hill, Kim, and A. Magdalena Hurtado. *Ache Life History: The Ecology and Demography of a Foraging People.* New York: Aldine de Gruyter, 1996.

Hinchliff, Thomas Woodbine. *South American Sketches; or, A Visit to Rio de Janeiro, the Organ Mountains, La Plata, and the Paraná.* London: Longman Green, 1863, 303–4.

Hobsbawm, Eric. "The American Cowboy: An International Myth?" In *Fractured Times: Culture and Society in the Twentieth Century,* 272–89. New York: The New Press, 2013.

Hochschild, Adam. *King Leopold's Ghost: A Story of Greed, Terror and Heroism in Colonial Africa.* Boston: HMH Books, 1999.

Holloway, Thomas W. *The Brazilian Coffee Valorization of 1906: Regional Politics and Economic Dependence.* Madison: The State Historical Society of Wisconsin, 1975.

Hora, Roy. *The Landowners of the Argentine Pampas: A Social and Political History, 1860–1945.* Oxford: Clarendon Press, 2001.

Huergo, Ricardo J. "La yerba mate (ilex Paraguayensis) su cultivo en Misiones." *Boletín de Agricultura y Ganadería* 2, no. 36 (1902): 633–43.

Huner, Michael. "How Pedro Quiñonez Lost His Soul: Suicide, Routine Violence, and State Formation in Nineteenth-Century Paraguay." *Journal of Social History* 54, no. 1 (2020): 237–59.

La industria yerbatera ante el gobierno argentino; hostilidad aduanera del gobierno brasilero. Buenos Aires: Imprenta de Coni hermanos, 1916.

"La industria yerbatera argentina. Informe del Gobernador de Misiones." *Revista de Economía Argentina* 117 (1928): 220–25.

Instituto Nacional de Estadistica y Censos. *Censo Nacional Agropecuario, 1988.* Provincia de Misiones, vol. 19. Buenos Aires: Hogares La Paz, 1991.

Instituto Nacional de la Yerba Mate. *Plan estratégico para el sector yerbatero argentino, 2013-2028,* 2013.

"Instrucciones para la siembra de la yerba mate." *Boletín de Agricultura y Ganadería* 1, no. 13 (1901).

Irigoin, Alejandra, and Regina Grafe. "Bargaining for Absolutism: A Spanish Path to Nation-State and Empire Building." *Hispanic American Historical Review* 88, no. 2 (2008): 173–209.

Irwin, Douglas A. *Trade Policy Disaster: Lessons from the 1930s.* Cambridge, MA: The MIT Press, 2012.

Isabelle, Arsenio. *Viaje a Argentina, Uruguay y Brasil, en 1830.* Edited by Ernesto Morales. Buenos Aires: Editorial Americana, 1943.

James, Daniel. *Doña María's Story: Life History, Memory, and Political Identity.* Duke University Press, 2000.

———. *Resistance and Integration: Peronism and the Argentine Working Class, 1946–1976.* Cambridge: Cambridge University Press, 1988.

Jarque, Francisco, ed. *Insignes missioneros de la compañía de Jesus en la Provincia del Paraguay.* Pampalona: Juan Micòn, 1687.

de Jaucourt, Louis. "Herbe du Paraguay." In *Encyclopédie ou Dictionnaire Raisonné des Sciences, des Arts et des Métiers, Par une Société de Gens de Lettres [1751–1772],* edited by Denis Diderot and Jean le Rond d'Alembert, Robert Morrisseey and Glenn Roe, 11:899–900. Chicago: University of Chicago, 2017. http://encyclopedie.uchicago.edu.

Johnson, Lyman L. *Workshop of Revolution: Plebeian Buenos Aires and the Atlantic World, 1776–1810.* Durham, NC: Duke University Press, 2011.

Joyce, T. A. "Yerba Mate: The Tea of South America." *The Pan-American Magazine* 33, no. 5–6 (1921): 306–28.

Kaerger, Karl. "La introducción de la yerba mate en Alemania, July 5, 1897." In *La agricultura y la colonización en Hispanoamérica: los estados del Plata,* 839–41. Buenos Aires: Academia Nacional de la Historia, 2004.

Karush, Matthew B. *Culture of Class: Radio and Cinema in the Making of a Divided Argentina, 1920–1946.* Durham, NC: Duke University Press, 2012.

———. "Populism, Melodrama, and the Market: The Mass Cultural Origins of Peronism." In *The New Cultural History of Peronism: Power and Identity in Mid-Twentieth-Century Argentina,* edited by Matthew B. Karush and Oscar Chamosa, 21–52. Durham, NC: Duke University Press, 2010.

———. *Workers or Citizens: Democracy and Identity in Rosario, Argentina (1912–1930)*. Albuquerque: University of New Mexico, 2002.

Karush, Matthew B., and Oscar Chamosa, eds. *The New Cultural History of Peronism: Power and Identity in Mid-Twentieth-Century Argentina*. Durham, NC: Duke University Press, 2010.

Kiguel, Miguel A. "Inflation in Argentina: Stop and Go Since the Austral Plan." *World Development* 19, no. 8 (1991): 969–86.

Koebel, W. H. *Argentina Past and Present*. New York: Dodd Mead and Company, 1911.

Korn, Guillermo, and Javier A. Trímboli. *Los ríos profundos. Hugo del Carril/Alfredo Varela: Un detalle en la historia del peronismo y la izquierda*. Buenos Aires: Eudeba, 2015.

Kriger, Clara. *Cine y peronismo: El estado en escena*. Buenos Aires: Siglo Veintiuno, 2009.

Kowaleski-Wallace, Beth. "Tea, Gender, and Domesticity in Eighteenth-Century England." *Studies in Eighteenth Century Culture* 23, no. 1 (1994): 131–45.

de Laferrére, Germán. *Aguas turbias*. Buenos Aires: Ediciones Huemel, 1943.

de Lafuente Machain, Ricardo. *Buenos Aires en el siglo XVII*. Buenos Aires: Emecé Editores, 1944.

Larguia, Alejandro. *Misiones—Itapúa y los pioneros del oro verde*. Buenos Aires: Ediciones Corregidor, 2006.

Larson, Carolyne R. *Our Indigenous Ancestors: A Cultural History of Museums, Science, and Identity in Argentina, 1877–1943*. University Park: Pennsylvania State University Press, 2015.

Lattuada, Mario J. *La política agraria peronista (1943–1983)*. 2 vols. Buenos Aires: Centro Editor de América Latina, 1986.

Lawson, Philip. *A Taste for Empire and Glory: Studies in British Overseas Expansion, 1660–1800*. Brookfield: Variorum, 1997.

Leguizamón, Honorio. "La yerba-mate: Cuestión económico social." *Anales de la Sociedad Científica Argentina* 76 (1913): 311–36.

———. *Yerba-mate: Observaciones sobre su cultivo y sus usos*. Buenos Aires: Minerva, 1877.

Lehman, Kathryn. "The Gaucho as Contested National Icon in Argentina." In *National Symbols, Fractured Identities: Contesting the National Narrative*, edited by Michael E. Geisler, 149–71. Middlebury, VT: Middlebury College Press, 2005.

Lenoble, Onésima. "La yerba mate." *Anales de la Sociedad Rural Argentina* 12 (1878): 501–2.

de León Pinelo, Antonio. *Question moral si el chocolate quebranta el ayuno eclesiastico . . .* Madrid, 1636.

Lesage, Julio. "Efectos fisiológicos del mate." *Anales de la Sociedad Rural Argentina* 43 (1908): 95–107.

Levene, Ricardo, ed. *Historia de la nación Argentina*. Vol. 7: Rosas y su época. Buenos Aires: Imprenta de la Universidad, 1850.

Linhares, Temístocles. *História econômica do mate*. Rio de Janeiro, Livraria José Olympio, 1969.

Lindblom, G. "Drinking-Tubes, especially in Africa." *Ethnos* 6, no. 1/2 (1941): 48–74.

Lindsay, Kenneth. *Eldorado: An Agricultural Settlement. A Brief History of Its Origin and Development.* London: The Kynoch Press, 1931.

López, Adalberto. "The Economics of Yerba Mate in Seventeenth-Century South America." *Agricultural History* 48, no. 4 (1974): 493–509.

López, Artemio, and Martín Romeo. *La declinación de la clase media Argentina. Transformaciones en la estructura social (1974–2004).* Buenos Aires: Libros de eQuis, 2005.

Love, George Thomas. *A Five Years' Residence in Buenos Ayres, During the Years 1820 to 1825.* London: G. Hebert, 1827.

Lozano, Pedro. *Historia de la conquista del Paraguay, Rio de la Plata y Tucuman.* Edited by Andres Lamas. Vol. 1. Lima: Casa Editora "Imprenta Popular," 1873.

———. *Historia de la compañía de Jesús de la provincia del Paraguay.* 2 vols. Madrid: Imprenta de la Viuda de Manuel Vernandez, 1755.

Ludmer, Josefina. *The Gaucho Genre: A Treatise on the Motherland.* Translated by Molly Weigel. Durham, NC: Duke University Press, 2002.

da Luz, Moisés. "Caruhis e barbaquás no Rio Grande do Sul: Resistência camponesa e conservação ambiental no âmbito da fabricação artesanal de erva-mate." PhD diss., Universidade Federal do Rio Grande do Sul, 2011.

Lvovich, Daniel. "Colgados de la Soga: La experiencia del tránsito desde la clase media a la nueva pobreza en la ciudad de Buenos Aires." In *Desde abajo: La transformación de las identidades sociales,* edited by Maristella Svampa, 51–79. Buenos Aires: Editorial Biblos, 2000.

Lynch, John. *Argentine Caudillo: Juan Manuel de Rosas.* Wilmington: SR Books, 2001.

———. *Massacre in the Pampas, 1872: Britain and Argentina in the Age of Migration.* Norman: University of Oklahoma Press, 1998.

MacCann, William. *Two Thousand Miles' Ride through the Argentine Provinces.* 2 vols. London: Smith, Elder & Co., 1853.

Machón, Jorge Francisco. *Misiones después de Andresito: Apuntes históricos.* Posadas, Argentina: Imprenta Creativa, 2003.

Madres de la Plaza de Mayo. *Memoria, verdad y justicia a los 30 años X los treinta mil:* 1:225–32. Buenos Aires: Baobab, 2006.

Madrid, Eduardo. "Argentina y Brasil: Economía y comercio en los años treinta." *Ciclos* 6, no. 11 (1996): 123–48.

Magalhães, Luiz Alfredo Marques. *Retratos de uma época: Os Mendes Gonçalves & a Cia. Matte Larangeira.* Campo Grande, Brazil: Gráfica e Editora Alvorada, 2013.

Magrassi, Alejandro. *La caá yarí. Novela de los yerbales misioneros.* Buenos Aires: Editorial Losada, 1945.

Maier, Charles S. "Between Taylorism and Technocracy: European Ideologies and the Vision of Industrial Productivity in the 1920s." *Journal of Contemporary History* 5, no. 2 (1970): 27–61.

Malisset, Jean Baptiste Antoine. *La Parfait Intelligence du Commerce...* Vol. 1. Paris, 1785.

Manzano, Valeria. *The Age of Youth in Argentina: Culture, Politics, & Sexuality from Perón to Videla.* Chapel Hill: University of North Carolina Press, 2014.

———. "The Blue Jean Generation: Youth, Gender, and Sexuality in Buenos Aires, 1958–1975." *Journal of Social History* 42, no. 3 (2009): 657–76.

Marcovich, Alejandro. *Vida y música de Alejandro Marcovich: Memorias de un genio del rock en Español.* Barcelona: Delbolsillo, 2018.

Markowicz Bastos, Deborah Helena, et al. "Yerba Maté: Pharmacological Properties, Research and Biotechnology." *Medicinal and Aromatic Plant Science and Biotechnology* 1, no. 1 (2007): 37–46.

Marrero, Andrea R., et. al. "Demographic and Evolutionary Trajectories of the Guarani and Kaingang Natives of Brazil." *American Journal of Physical Anthropology* 132, no. 2 (2007): 301–10.

Martín y Cía. *¿Qué la yerba mate?* Buenos Aires, 1942.

Martín & Compañía Limitada Sociedad Anónima. *Julio U. Martin y una empresa de tres siglos (historias sobre la yerba mate en la Argentina).* n.p., n.d.

Martínez Chas, María L. *Marcos Kanner: Militancia, símbolo y leyenda.* Posadas, Argentina: Editorial Universitaria, 2011.

Martínez Estrada, Ezequiel. *Radiografía de la Pampa [1933].* Edited by Leo Pollmann. Buenos Aires: Fondo de Cultura Ecónomica, 1993.

de Massiac, Barthélemy. *Plan francés de conquista de Buenos Aires, 1660–1693.* Edited by Alberto Casares. Buenos Aires: Emecé Editores, 1999.

Mateu, Ana María. "El modelo centenario de la vitivinicultura mendocina: Génesis, desarrollo y crisis (1870–1980)." In *Innovación y empleo en tramas productivas de Argentina,* edited by Marcelo Delfini et al., 19–42. Buenos Aires: Prometeo Libros, 2007.

Mateu, Cristina. "Encuentros y desencuentros entre dos grandes obras: *El Río Oscuro* y *Las Aguas Bajan Turbias* (Argentina, 1943/1952)." *Nuevo Mundo Mundos Nuevos,* 2012. https://doi.org/10.4000/nuevomundo.63148.

Maute, Jutta. *Hyperinflation, Currency Board, and Bust: The Case of Argentina.* Frankfurt: Peter Lang, 2006.

Meding, Holger. "Procesos de integración retardados en el marco de una colonización organizada. El caso de la migración germanohablante en Misiones." *Estudios Migratorios Latinoamericanos* 25, no. 70 (2011): 65–79.

Miers, John. "On the History of the 'Maté' Plant, and the Different Species of Ilex Employed in the Preparation of the 'Yerba de Maté,' or Paraguay Tea." In *Contributions to Botany, Iconographic and Descriptive, Detailing the Characters of Plants That Are Either New or Imperfectly Described,* 2: 90–111. Edinburgh: William and Norgate, 1860.

———. *Travels in Chile and La Plata.* 2 vols. London: Baldwin, Cradock and Joy, 1826.

Milanesio, Natalia. *Workers Go Shopping in Argentina: The Rise of Popular Consumer Culture.* Albuquerque: University of New Mexico Press, 2013.

———. "Food Politics and Consumption in Peronist Argentina." *Hispanic American Historical Review* 90, no. 1 (2010): 75–108.

———. "Peronists and Cabecitas: Stereotypes and Anxieties at the Peak of Social Change." In *The New Cultural History of Peronism: Power and Identity in Mid-Twentieth-Century Argentina,* edited by Matthew B. Karush and Oscar Chamosa, 53–84. Durham, NC: Duke University Press, 2010.

———. "'The Guardian Angels of the Domestic Economy:' Housewives' Responsible Consumption in Peronist Argentina." *Journal of Women's History* 18, no. 3 (2006): 91–117.

Milheira, Rafael Guedes, and Aluisio Gomes Alves. "O sítio guarani PS-03-totó: Uma abordagem cultural sistêmica." *Revista de Arqueologia* 22, no. 1 (2009): 15–41.

Miller, John. *Memoirs of General Miller, in the Service of the Republic of Peru.* 2 vols. London: Longman, Rees, Orme, Brown, and Green, 1829.

Ministerio de Agricultura. *Censo Nacional Agropecuario, Año 1937.* 2 parts. Buenos Aires: Guillermo Kraft Ltda., 1940.

———. *Memoria de la Dirección General de Tierras en el período administrativo de 1922–1928.* Buenos Aires: Casa Oucinde, 1928.

———. *Ley de bosques y yerbales.* Buenos Aires: Ministerio de Agricultura de la Nación, 1915.

Ministerio del Interior. *Censo general de los Territorios Nacionales, República Argentina.* 2 vols. Buenos Aires: Establecimiento Gráfico A. de Martino, 1923.

Ministerio de Salud Pública de la Nación. *Política alimentaria argentina: Conferencias pronunciadas en la campaña de educación sanitaria.* Buenos Aires: Departamento de Talleres Gráficos, 1951.

Mintz, Sidney W. "Eating Communities: The Mixed Appeals of Sodality." In *Eating Culture: The Poetics and Politics of Food,* edited by Tobias Döring, Markus Heide, and Susanne Mühleisen, 19–34. Heidelberg: Universitätsverlag, 2003.

———. *Sweetness and Power: The Place of Sugar in Modern History.* New York: Penguin Books, 1986.

Minujin, Alberto, and Gabriel Kessler. *La nueva pobreza en la Argentina.* Buenos Aires: Editorial Planeta, 1995.

Misemer, Sarah M. *Secular Saints: Performing Frida Kahlo, Carlos Gardel, Eva Perón, and Selena.* Rochester, NY: Tamesis, 2008.

Molfino, José F. "Carlos D. Girola (1867–1934)." *Revista de la Facultad de Agronomía* ser. 3, 20, no. 2 (1935): 103–7.

Molinero, Carlos, and Pablo Vila. "Atahualpa Yupanqui: The Latin American Precursor of the Militant Song Movement." In *The Militant Song Movement in Latin America: Chile, Uruguay, and Argentina,* edited by Pablo Vila, 163–92. Lexington Books, 2014.

Morales, Ernesto. *Leyendas guaraníes.* Buenos Aires: Editorial Futuro, 1960.

Moreno, Julio. "Marketing in Mexico: Sears, Roebuck Company, J. Walter Thompson, and the Culture of North American Commerce in Mexico City during the 1940s." *Enterprise & Society* 1, no. 4 (2000): 683–92.

Moya, Jose C. *Cousins and Strangers: Spanish Immigrants in Buenos Aires, 1850–1930.* Berkeley: University of California Press, 1998.

Muello, Alberto Carlos. *Yerba mate: su cultivo y explotación.* Buenos Aires: Editorial Sudamericana, 1946.

Mulhall, M. G., and E. T. Mulhall. *Handbook of the River Plate.* Vol. 1. Buenos Aires: Standard Printing Office, 1869.

Muriel, Domingo. *Historia del Paraguay desde 1747 hasta 1767.* Translated by Pablo Hernández. Madrid: Librería General de Victoriano Suárez, 1918.

Naboulet, L. R. *La justicia en Misiones.* Barcelona: Jean Valjean, 1917.

Nacuzzi, Lidia R., "Diarios, informes, cartas y relatos de las expediciones a las salinas Grandes, siglos XVIII-XIX." *Corpus: Archivos virtuales de la alteridad americana,* 3, no. 2 (2013), https://doi.org/10.4000/corpusarchivos.558.

Nállim, Jorge A. *Transformations and Crisis of Liberalism in Argentina, 1930–1955.* Pittsburgh: University of Pittsburgh Press, 2012.

———. "An Unbroken Loyalty in Turbulent Times: *La Prensa* and Liberalism in Argentina, 1930–1946." *Estudios Interdisciplinarios de América Latina y el Caribe* 20, no. 2 (2009): 35–62.

National Mortgage Bank. *National Territory of Misiones: Paraguayan Tea (Ilex Paraguayensis S. Hil.).* Buenos Aires: Compañía Impresora Argentina, 1927.

Navajas, Pau. *Caá porã: El espíritu de la yerba mate.* Gobernador Virasoro, Argentina: Establecimiento las Marías, 2013.

Navarro, Eduardo de Almeida. *Tupi antigo: A língua indígena clássica do Brasil.* São Paulo: Editora Global, 2013.

Newland, Carlos, and Eduardo Martín Cuesta. "Peronismo y salarios reales: Otra mirada al período 1939–1956." *Investigaciones y Ensayos* 64 (2017): 75–98.

Niederlein, Gustavo. *Mis exploraciones en el Territorio de Misiones.* Buenos Aires: Imprenta "La Universidad," 1891.

Niklison, José Elías. "Alto Paraná." *Boletín del Departamento Nacional del Trabajo* 26 (1914).

Nimmo, Evelyn R., and João Francisco Miró Medeiros Nogueira. "Creating Hybrid Scientific Knowledge and Practice: The Jesuit and Guaraní Cultivation of Yerba Mate." *Canadian Journal of Latin American and Caribbean Studies* 44, no. 3 (2019): 347–67.

Nohlen, Dieter. *Elections in the Americas: A Data Handbook.* Vol. II: South America. Oxford: Oxford University Press, 2005.

Nordland, Odd. *Brewing and Beer Traditions in Norway: The Social Anthropological Background of the Brewing Industry.* Oslo: Universitetsforlaget, 1969.

Norton, Marcy. "Subaltern Technologies and Early Modernity in the Atlantic World." *Colonial Latin American Review* 26, no. 1 (2017): 18–38.

———. *Sacred Gifts, Profane Pleasures: A History of Tobacco and Chocolate in the Atlantic World.* Ithaca, NY: Cornell University Press, 2008.

Notes on the Viceroyalty of La Plata, in South America. London: J. J. Stockdale, 1808.

Nouwen, Mollie Lewis. *Oy, My Buenos Aires: Jewish Immigrants and the Creation of Argentine National Identity.* Albuquerque: University of New Mexico Press, 2013.

Nouzeilles, Gabriela, and Graciela Montaldo, eds. *The Argentina Reader.* Durham, NC: Duke University Press, 2002.

Núñez Seixas, Xosé M., and Ruy Farías. "Las autobiografías de los inmigrantes gallegos en la Argentina (1860–2000): Testimonio, ficción y experiencia." *Migraciones y Exilios* 11 (2010): 57–80.

Oberti, Federico. *Historia y folklore del mate.* Buenos Aires: Fondo Nacional de las Artes, 1979.

Obligado, Pastor Servando. *Tradiciones argentinas.* Barcelona: Montaner y Simón, 1903.

Oestreich-Janzen, S. "Caffeine: Characterization and Properties." In *Encyclopedia of Food and Health,* edited by Benjamin Caballero, Paul M. Finglas, and Fidel Todrá, 1:556–72. Waltham, MA: Academic Press, 2016.

Oliveira, Arturo A. "Métodos prácticos para el cultivo de la yerba mate en el territorio de Misiones." Buenos Aires: Ministerio de Agricultura, 1922.

Orquera, Fabiola. "Paisaje social, trayectoria artística e identidad política: El caso de Ramón Ayala." *Estudios Interdisciplinarios de América Latina y el Caribe* 27, no. 1 (2016): 13–37.

Ostiguy, Pierre, and Warwick Armstrong. *La evolución del consumo alimenticio en la Argentina (1974–1984): Un estudio empírico.* Buenos Aires: Centro Editor de América Latina, 1987.

Page, Carlos A. *El colegio máximo de Córdoba (Argentina) según las cartas anuas de la compañía de Jesús.* Córdoba: Editorial BR Copias, 2004.

Palliere, León. *Albúm Palliere: Escenas Americanas.* Buenos Aires: Libreria L'Amateur, 1967.

Palma, Amelia. *El hogar modelo. Curso complete de economía doméstica.* Buenos Aires: Jacobo Peuser, 1902.

Palma, Frederico. "Un momento en la historia de Misiones, 1832–1882." *Boletín de la Academia Nacional de Historia* 38 (1965): 199–230.

Palma, Ricardo. "Un zapato acusador." In *Tradiciones Peruanas Completas,* 3rd ed., 840–42. Madrid: Aguilar, 1957.

della Paolera, Gerardo, and Alan M. Taylor, eds. *A New Economic History of Argentina.* Cambridge: Cambridge University Press, 2003.

Parish, Woodbine. *Buenos Ayres and the Provinces of the Rio de la Plata.* London: John Murray, 1839.

Pastore, Mario. "Trade Contraction and Economic Decline: The Paraguayan Economy under Francia, 1810–1840." *Journal of Latin American Studies* 26, no. 3 (1994): 539–95.

Paucke, Florián. *Hacia allá y para acá: (una estada entre los indios Mocobíes, 1749–1767).* Translated by Edmundo Wernicke. 3 vols. Buenos Aires: Editorial Nuevo Siglo, 1999.

Pavón Pereyra, Enrique. *Los últimos días de Perón: Un documento histórico*. Buenos Aires: La Campana, 1981.

Pellegrini, Carlos. "Mate." *Revista del Plata* 1 (1853): 54–55.

———. *Recuerdos del Rio de la Plata*. Buenos Aires: Litografia de las Artes, 1841.

Pernety, Antoine-Joseph. *The History of a Voyage to the Malouine (or Falkland) Islands*. 2nd ed. London: William Goldsmith and David Steel, 1773.

Perón, Juan Domingo. *La fuerza es el derecho de las bestias*. Montevideo: Ediciones Cicerón, 1958.

Persello, Ana Virginia. "Partidos políticos y corporaciones: Las juntas reguladoras de la producción, 1930–1943." *Boletín del Instituto de Historia Argentina y Americana "Doctor Emilio Ravignani"* 29 (2006): 85–118.

Peyret, Alejo. *Cartas sobre Misiones*. Buenos Aires: Imprenta "Tribuna Nacional," 1881.

Phipps, Elena, Johanna Hecht, and Cristina Esteras Martín. *The Colonial Andes: Tapestries and Silverwork, 1530–1830*. New York: Metropolitan Museum of Art, 2004.

Pickett, J. C. "Mate, or Tea of Paraguay." In *Letters and Dissertations upon Sundry Subjects*, 31–33. Washington, DC: William Greer, 1848.

Pilcher, Jeffrey M. "Eating á La Criolla: Global and Local Foods in Argentina, Cuba, and Mexico." *IdeAs [Online]* 3 (2012).

———. *¡Que Vivan los Tamales! Food and the Making of Mexican Identity*. Albuquerque: University of New Mexico Press, 1998.

de Pinedo, Agustin Fernando. "Informe del Goberrnador del Paraguay," June 22, 1778. *Revista del Instituto Paraguayo* 52 (1905): 3–31.

Pite, Rebekah E. "The Rural Woman Enters the Frame: A Visual History of Gender, Nation, and the Goodbye Mate in the Postcolonial Río de La Plata." *Journal of Social History* 54, no. 4 (2021): 1120–59.

———. *Creating a Common Table in Twentieth-Century Argentina: Doña Petrona, Women, & Food*. Chapel Hill: University of North Carolina Press, 2013.

Poenitz, Edgar, and Alfredo Poenitz. *Misiones, provincia guaranítica. Defensa y disolución [1768–1830]*. Posadas, Argentina: Editorial Universitaria, 1998.

Pohl-Valero, Stefan. "'La raza entra por la boca': Energy, Diet, and Eugenics in Colombia, 1890–1940." *Hispanic American Historical Review* 94, no. 3 (2014): 455–86.

Potthast-Jutkeit, Barbara. "The Creation of the 'Mestizo Family Model': The Example of Paraguay." *History of the Family* 2, no. 2 (1997): 123–39.

Powers, Nancy R. "The Politics of Poverty in Argentina in the 1990s." *Journal of Interamerican Studies and World Affairs* 37, no. 4 (1995): 89–137.

Presidencia de la Nación. *20 plan quinquenal*. Buenos Aires: Subsecretaria de Informaciones, 1953.

———. *IV censo general de la nación*. Vol. 1, Censo de Población. Buenos Aires: Dirección Nacional de Servicio Estadistica, 1948.

Prieto, Adolfo. *El discurso criollista en la formación de la Argentina moderna*. Buenos Aires: Siglo XXI, 2006.

———. *Los viajeros ingleses y la emergencia de la literatura argentina, 1820–1850*. Buenos Aires: Editorial Sudamericana, 1996.

A Proposal for Humbling Spain. Written in 1711. By a Person of Distinction. London: J. Roberts, 1739.

Prous, André. "Arqueologia tupiguarani no Paraguai: A pintura em ceramica—estudo das coleçoes dos museus de Assunção." *Cuadernos del Instituto Nacional de Antropología y Pensamiento Latinoamericano—Series Especiales* 1, no. 4 (2013): 161–72.

Provincia de Corrientes. *Recopilación completa de códigos, leyes y decretos reglamentarios vigentes de la Provincia de Corrientes.* Vol. 2. Corrientes: Teodoro Heinecke, 1904.

Provincia de Misiones: Secretaría de Planificación y Control. *Evolución de la yerba mate: Producción, comercialización, mercado.* Posadas, Argentina: Gobierno de la Provincia de Misiones, 1977.

———. *Planeamiento de la Provincia de Misiones.* 2 vols. Buenos Aires, 1961.

Pujol, Juan, ed. *Corrientes en la organización nacional.* 10 vols. Buenos Aires: G. Kraft, 1911.

Pulido, Justino. *Urbanidad y cortesía.* Buenos Aires: Cabaut y Cía., 1902.

Pusineri Scala, Carlos Alberto. *Historia de la moneda paraguaya siglos XVI al XIX.* Asunción: Imprenta Salesiana, 1992.

Queirel, Juan. *Misiones.* Buenos Aires: Tipográfica de la Penetenciaría Nacional, 1897.

Quesada, Vicente Galvez. *Memorias de un viejo: Escenas de costumbres de la República Argentina.* 3 vols. Buenos Aires: Jacobo Peuser, 1888.

Quino. *Todo Mafalda.* Buenos Aires: Ediciones de la Flor, 1993.

Quintana, Raquel, and Raúl Manrupe. *Afiches del peronismo, 1945–1955.* Buenos Aires: EDUNTREF, 2016.

Rábade Roque, Raquel. *The Cuban Kitchen.* New York: Alfred A. Knopf, 2011.

Raed, José Rosas. *Cartas confidenciales a su embajadora Josefa Gómez, 1853–1875.* Buenos Aires: Humus Editorial, 1972.

Ranis, Peter. *Argentine Workers: Peronism and Contemporary Class Consciousness.* Pittsburgh: University of Pittsburgh Press, 1992.

Rappaport, Erika. *A Thirst for Empire: How Tea Shaped the Modern World.* Princeton, NJ: Princeton University Press, 2017.

Rätsch, Christian. "Ilex Paraguariensis Saint-Hilaire: Maté Bush." In *The Encyclopedia of Psychoactive Plants: Ethnopharmacology and Its Applications,* translated by John R. Baker, 290–93. Rochester, NY: Park Street Press, 1998.

Rau, Víctor. *Cosechando yerba mate. Estructuras sociales de un mercado laboral agrario en el Nordeste Argentino.* Buenos Aires: Ediciones CICCUS, 2012.

Reber, Vera Blinn. "Commerce and Industry in Nineteenth Century Paraguay: The Example of Yerba Mate." *The Americas* 42, no. 1 (1985): 29–53.

Registro oficial de la República Argentina que comprende los documentos espedidos desde 1810 hasta 1873. Vol. 2: 1822–1852. Buenos Aires: La República, 1880.

Rengger, Johann Rudolph. *Viaje al Paraguay: En los años 1816 a 1826.* Translated by Alfredo Tomasini and José Braunstein. Asunción: Tiempo de Historia, 2010.

Repetto, Luis, Alberto Carlos Muello, and Aquiles D. Ygobone. "La yerba mate." *Revista de la Facultad de Ciencias Economicas* 4, no. 39 (November 1951): 1452–64.

República de Argentina. *Primer censo de la República Argentina, verificado en los días 15/16/17 de Septiembre de 1869.* Buenos Aires: Imprenta del Porvenir, 1872.

———. *Segundo censo de la República Argentina, Mayo 10 de 1895.* Vol. 2: Población. Buenos Aires: Taller Tipográfico de la Penitenciaría Nacional, 1898.

———. *Tercer censo nacional, levantado el 1 de Junio de 1914.* Vol. 2: Población. Buenos Aires: Talleres Gráficos de L.J. Rosso y Cía, 1916.

Ricca, Javier. *El mate. Historia, secretos y otras yerbas de una pasión rioplatense.* Buenos Aires: Sudamericana, 2012.

Richard, Analiese, and Arturo Giráldez. "An Appetite for Small Change: Cacao Beans and Pieces of Eight in New Spain." *Entremons. UPF Journal of World History* 9 (2017): 50–73.

Rivarola Paoli, Juan Bautista. *La economía colonial*, vol. 1. Asunción: Editora Litocolor, 1986.

Robertson, John Parish, and William Parish Robertson. *Francia's Reign of Terror: Being a Sequel to Letters on Paraguay.* 2 vols. Philadelphia: E. L. Carey & A. Hart, 1839.

———. *Letters on Paraguay Comprising an Account of a Four Years' Residence in That Republic.* 2 vols. London: William Clowes and Sons, 1839.

Rocchi, Fernando. "La americanización del consumo: Las batallas por el mercado argentino, 1920–11945." In *Estados Unidos y América Latina en el siglo XX. Transferencias económicas, tecnológicas y culturales*, 105–216. Buenos Aires: EDUNTREF, 2003.

Rock, David. *Argentina, 1516–1987: From Spanish Colonization to the Falklands War.* Berkeley: University of California Press, 1985.

Rodríguez, Lisandro R. "Estado y producción: La actividad yerbatero en el Territorio Nacional de Misiones (1926–1953)." *Folia Histórica del Nordeste* 23 (2015): 43–64.

Rodríguez, Laura Graciela. "Los radicalizados del sector rural. Los dirigentes del Movimiento Agrario Misionero y Montoneros (1971–1976)." *Mundo Agrario* 10, no. 19 (2009). https://www.mundoagrario.unlp.edu.ar/article/view/v10n19a03/610.

Roediger, David R. *The Wages of Whiteness: Race and the Making of the American Working Class.* New York: Verso, 1999.

Roger, León. "Cultivo de la yerba mate." *Anales de la Sociedad Rural Argentina* 41 (1906): 47–64.

Romero, Luis Alberto. *A History of Argentina in the Twentieth Century.* Translated by James P. Brennan. University Park: Pennsylvania State University, 2002.

Roulet, Florencia. *La resistencia de los guaraní del Paraguay a la conquista española [1537–1556].* Posadas, Argentina: Editorial Universitaria, 1993.

Ruffin, John N. "Yerba-Mate Cultivation in Paraguay," Asunción, June 7, 1900. *Consular Reports. Commerce, Manufactures, Etc.* 64, no. 242 (November 1900): 307–8.

Ruggiero, Kristin. *And Here the World Ends: The Life of an Argentine Village.* Stanford, CA: Stanford University Press, 1988.

Ruiz de Montoya, Antonio. *Arte, y bocabulario de la lengua guarani.* Madrid: Juan Sanchez, 1640.

———. *Tesoro de la lengua Guarani.* Madrid: Juan Sanchez, 1639.

———. *The Spiritual Conquest,* translated by C. J. McNaspy, John P. Leonard, and Martin E. Palmer St. Louis: Institute of Jesuit Sources, 1993.

de Saavedra, Hernandarias. "Carta al Rey," May 13, 1618. *Revista de la Biblioteca Nacional* 2, no. 5 (1938): 108–12.

Saguier, Eduardo R. "El mercado del cuero y su rol como fuente alternativa de empleo. El caso del trabajo a destajo en las vaquerías de la Banda Oriental durante el siglo XVIII." *Revista de Historia Económica* 9, no. 1 (1991): 103–26.

Saint-Hilaire, Auguste. "Note sur l'herbe du Paraguay (Ilex Paraguariensis, A.S.-Hil.)." *Annales des Sciences Naturelles. Botanique et Biologie Végétale* 1 (1833): 29–32.

———. *Histoire des Plantes les plus Remarquables du Brésil et du Paraguay . . .* vol. 1. Paris: A. Belin, 1824.

———. "Aperçu d'un voyage dans l'intérieur du Brésil, la Provincia Cisplatine et les Missions dites du Paraguay." *Mémoires du Muséum d'Histoire Naturelle* 9 (1822): 337–80.

Salinas Giménez, Osvaldo Emeterio. "18—Julián S. Bouvier, Santiago Misiones." In *Cien hombres y mujeres de Misiones que hicieron historia. Misiones ilustres,* edited by Camilo Cantero, 2:69–71. Asunción: Servilibro, 2012.

Salvatore, Ricardo D. "Yankee Advertising in Buenos Aires: Reflections on Americanization." *Interventions* 7, no. 2 (2005): 216–35.

Sánchez Labrador, José. *El Paraguay Católico.* Edited by Samuel A. Lafone Quevedo. 2 vols. Buenos Aires: Coni hermanos, 1910.

Sarlo, Beatriz. *Una modernidad periférica, Buenos Aires 1920 y 1930.* Buenos Aires: Ediciones Nueva Visión, 1988.

Sarmiento, Domingo Faustino. *Facundo: Civilization and Barbarism.* Berkeley: University of California Press, 2003.

Sarreal, Julia. "Jesuit Missions and Private Property, Commerce, and Guaraní Economic Initiative." In *Latin American History: Oxford Research Encyclopedia,* 2015. https://doi.org/10.1093/acrefore/9780199366439.013.313.

———. "Disorder, Wild Cattle, and a New Role for the Missions: The Banda Oriental, 1776–1786." *The Americas* 67, no. 4 (2011): 517–45.

———. *The Guaraní and Their Missions: A Socioeconomic History.* Stanford, CA: Stanford University Press, 2014.

Sastre, Marcos. *El tempe arjentino o el delta de los rios Uruguai, Paraná, y Plata.* Buenos Aires: Imprenta Arjentina, 1859.

Scala, Agusto. "Contribución al conocimiento histológico de la yerba-mate y sus falsificaciones." *Revista del Museo de la Plata* 26 (1922): 69–166.

Schamber, Pablo J. "Barajar y dar de nuevo. Consecuencias de la desregulación en el sector yerbatero." *Realidad Económica* 169 (2000): 125–48.

Schiffrin, Anya, ed. *Global Muckraking: 100 Years of Investigative Journalism from Around the World*. New York: The New Press, 2014.

Schivelbusch, Wolfgang. *Tastes of Paradise: A Social History of Spices, Stimulants, and Intoxicants*. Translated by David Jacobson. New York: Pantheon Books, 1992.

Schmidt, Ulrich. "Voyage of Ulrich Schmidt to the Rivers La Plata and Paraguai, from the Original German Edition, 1567." In *The Conquest of the River Plate (1535–1555)*, edited by Luis L. Dominguez, 1–94. London: Hakluyt Society, 1891.

Schmidtmeyer, Peter. *Travels into Chile, Over the Andes, in the Years 1820 and 1821*. London: S. McDowall, 1824.

Schulman, Sam. "The Colono System in Latin America." *Rural Sociology* 20, no. 1 (1955): 34–40.

Scobie, James R. *Revolution on the Pampas: A Social History of Argentine Wheat, 1860–1910*. Austin: University of Texas Press, 1964.

Sedgewick, Augustine. *Coffeeland: One Man's Dark Empire and the Making of Our Favorite Drug*. New York: Penguin Press, 2020.

Seeger, Eugene. "Agricultural and Industrial Conditions in Parana," Rio de Janeiro, Oct. 17, 1899. *Consular Reports: Commerce, Manufactures, Etc*, 62, no. 232 (January 1900): 41–46.

Segovia, Desiderio M. "Cultivo de la yerba mate." *Boletín del Departamento Nacional de Fomento* 6 (1914): 65–81.

Seibel, Beatriz. *Historia del circo*. Buenos Aires: Ediciones del Sol, 1993.

Seoane, Manuel. *Rumbo Argentino*. Santiago: Ed. Ercilla, 1935.

Serrano, Antonio. *Etnografía de la antigua provincia del Uruguay*. Paraná, Argentina: Talleres gráficos "Melchor," 1936.

Shell, Marc. *Wampum and the Origins of American Money*. Urbana-Champaign: University of Illinois Press, 2013.

Shua, Ana María, and Marta Prada. *La leyenda de la yerba mate*. Buenos Aires: Editorial Sudamericana, 2005.

Shumway, Jeffrey M. *A Woman. A Man. A Nation: Mariquita Sánchez, Juan Manuel de Rosas, and the Beginnings of Argentina*. Albuquerque: University of New Mexico Press, 2019.

Shumway, Nicolas. *The Invention of Argentina*. Berkeley: University of California Press, 1993.

Sidicaro, Ricardo. *La política mirada desde arriba: Las ideas del diario* La Nación, *1909–1989*. Buenos Aires: Editorial Sudamericana, 1993.

da Silva Mayer, Ricardo. "Bomba de chimarrão: Uma gênese a partir de missionários jesuítas e viajantes." *Revista Latino-Americana de História* 8, no. 22 (2019): 215–34.

Silva, Guillermo José. *Costumbres campestres de la república Argentina en las postales y fotos del siglo XIX y XX*. Buenos Aires: Editorial Dunken, 2016.

Slatta, Richard. *Gauchos and the Vanishing Frontier*. Lincoln: University of Nebraska Press, 1983.

Smith, Peter H. *Politics and Beef in Argentina: Patterns of Conflict and Change*. New York: Columbia University Press, 1969.

Smith, S. D. "Accounting for Taste: British Coffee Consumption in Historical Perspective." *Journal of Interdisciplinary History* 27, no. 2 (1996): 183–214.

Smith, Woodruff D. *Consumption and the Making of Respectability, 1600–1800.* New York: Routledge, 2002.

Solari, Juan A. "Trágicas son las condiciones de vida y de trabajo de los jornaleros de la yerba mate." *Finanzas: Revista Mensual de Economía* 5, no. 54–55 (1941): 11–12.

———. *Trabajadores del norte argentino. Debates e iniciativas en la Cámara de Diputados.* Buenos Aires, 1937.

Solt, George. *The Untold History of Ramen: How Political Crisis in Japan Spawned a Global Food Craze.* Berkeley: University of California Press, 2014.

Sorsby, Victoria Gardner. "British Trade with Spanish America under the Asiento, 1713–1740." PhD diss., University of London, 1975.

Southey, Robert. *History of Brazil.* 3 vols. London: Longman, Hurst, Rees, and Orme, 1810.

de Souza Pereira, Giovana, et. al. "Ecologia histórica guaraní: As plantas utilizadas no bioma mata atlântica do litoral sul de Santa Catarina, Brasil (Parte 1)." *Cadernos do LEPAARQ* 13, no. 26 (2016): 198–246.

Sprecher von Bernegg, Andreas. *Tropische und Subtropische Weltwirtschaftspflanzen: Ihre Geschichte, Kultur und Volkswirtschaftliche Bedeutung.* Vol. 3, Band: Der Teestrauch und der Tee Die Mate-oder Paraguayteepflanze. Stuttgart: Verlag von Ferdinand Enke, 1936.

Stanfield, Michael Edward. *Red Rubber, Bleeding Trees: Violence, Slavery, and Empire in Northwest Amazonia, 1850–1933.* Albuquerque: University of New Mexico, 1998.

Stephanis, Rebecca M. "From Resurrection to Recognition: Argentina's Misiones Province and the National Imaginary." Ph.D. dissertation, Princeton University, 2009.

Stillé, Alfred. *Therapeutics and Materia Medica: A Systematic Treatise on the Action and Uses of Medicinal Agents, Including Their Description and History.* 2 vols. Philadelphia: Blancard and Lea, 1860.

Stein, Stanley J. *Vassouras: A Brazilian Coffee County, 1850–1900.* Princeton, NJ: Princeton University Press, 1986.

Stein, Steve. "Essence and Identity: Transformations in Argentine Wine, 1880–2010." In *Alcohol in Latin America: A Social and Cultural History,* edited by Gretchen Pierce and Áurea Toxqui, 210–41. Tucson: University of Arizona Press, 2014.

A Summary Account of the Viceroyalty of Buenos-Ayres, or, La Plata. London: R. Dutton, 1806.

Svampa, Maristella, ed. *Desde abajo: La transformación de las identidades sociales.* Buenos Aires: Editorial Biblos, 2000.

Tamarin, David. *The Argentine Labor Movement, 1930–1945: A Study in the Origins of Peronism.* Albuquerque: University of New Mexico, 1985.

Taylor, Alan M. "Latifundia as Malefactor in Economic Development? Scale, Tenancy and Agriculture on the Pampas, 1880–1914." *Research in Economic History* 17 (1997): 261–300.

Telesca, Ignacio. "La colonia desde 1680 a 1780." In *Historia del Paraguay,* edited by Ignacio Telesca, 87–112. Asunción: Santillana, 2010.

Tempski, Edwino Donato. "Caingângues—Gente do Mato." *Boletim do Instituto Histórico, Geográfico e Etnográfico Paranaense* XLIV (1986): 1–383.

Torrado, Susana. "Estrategias de desarrollo, estructura social y movilidad." In *Población y bienestar en la Argentina del primero al segundo centenario,* edited by Susana Torrado, 1:31–68. Buenos Aires: Edhasa, 2007.

Torre, Juan Carlos, and Elisa Pastoriza. "La democratización del bienestar." In *Nueva historia argentina,* edited by Juan Carlos Torre, 8:257–312. Buenos Aires: Sudamericana, 2002.

Torrejón, Cipriano, *Lectura de economía doméstica.* Buenos Aires: Juan A. Alsina, 1887.

Tossounian, Cecilia. *La Joven Moderna in Interwar Argentina: Gender, Nation, and Popular Culture.* Gainesville: University of Florida Press, 2020.

Trages y costumbres de la Provincia de Buenos Aires. Buenos Aires: Viau, 1947.

Troncoso, Oscar. *El proceso de reorganización nacional: Cronología y documentación.* Vol. 5. Buenos Aires: Centro Editor de América Latina, 1994.

de Ulloa, Antonio. *A Voyage to South-America.* 2 vols. London: L. Davis and C. Reymers, 1758.

Uzal, Conrado Martín. "La yerba mate como bebida higiénica." *Anales de la Sociedad Rural Argentina,* no. 41 (1907): 64–65.

———. "La yerba-mate (ilex Paraguayensis)." *Revista de la Facultad de Agronomia y Veterinaria* 2, no. 6 (1906): 765–93.

Valenze, Deborah. *The Social Life of Money in the English Past.* Cambridge: Cambridge University Press, 2006.

Varela, Alfredo. *El río oscuro. La aventura de los yerbales vírgenes.* Buenos Aires: Capital Intelectual, 2008.

de Val Floriana, Mansueto Barbatta. "Diccionario Kaingang-Portuguez." *Revista do Museu Paulista* 12 (1920): 1–218.

de la Vega, Garcilaso. *Primera parte de los comentarios reales.* Libro 8. Lisbon: Oficina de Pedro Crasbeeck, 1609.

Veigel, Klaus Friedrich. *Dictatorship, Democracy, and Globalization: Argentina and the Cost of Paralysis, 1973–2001.* University Park: Pennsylvania State University, 2009.

Vidal, Emeric Essex. *Picturesque Illustrations of Buenos Ayres and Monte Video.* London: R. Ackerman, 1820.

Vidal de Battini, Berta Elena. "El léxico de los yerbateros." In *Antología Conmemorativa. Nueva Revista de Filolgía Hispánica,* edited by Alejandro Rivas and Yliana Rodríguez. Vol. 1. Mexico City: Colegio de Mexico, 2003.

Villanueva, Amaro. *Obras completas.* Edited by Sergio Delgado. Paraná: Universidad Nacional de Entre Ríos, 2010.

Villapol, Nitza, and Martha Martínez. *Cocina al minuto.* Havana: n.p., 1954.

Walker, Herbert J. "Yerba Mate." *The British Medical Journal* 1, no. 2250 (1904): 401.

Walsh, Rodolfo J. "La Argentina ya no toma mate." In *De la tierra sin mal al tractorazo. Hacia una economía política de la yerba mate,* edited by Javier Gortari, 155–61. Posadas, Argentina: Universidad Nacional de Misiones, 2007.

Walter, Richard J. "The Socialist Press in Turn-of-the-Century Argentina." *The Americas* 37, no. 1 (1980): 1–24.

Whigham, Thomas. *The Road to Armageddon: Paraguay Versus the Triple Alliance, 1866–70.* Calgary: University of Calgary Press, 2017.

———. *The Politics of River Trade: Tradition and Development in the Upper Plata, 1780–1870.* Albuquerque: University of New Mexico Press, 1991.

———. "Cattle Raising in the Argentine Northeast: Corrientes, c. 1750–1870." *Journal of Latin American Studies* 20, no. 2 (1988): 313–35.

Wilde, José Antonio. *Buenos Aires desde setenta años atrás.* Buenos Aires: La Nación, 1908.

Williamson, Peter J. *Varieties of Corporatism: A Conceptual Discussion.* Cambridge: Cambridge University Press, 1985.

Wilson, Jason. *Jorge Luis Borges.* London: Reaktion Books, 2006.

Wong, Samantha. "Materva: Un buchito de Cuba." *Food Writing* 4 (2014): 8.

"Yerba Mate." *Journal of Tropical Medicine Series* 2/Vol. 10 (1903): 303–4.

"Yerba Maté." *Monthly Consular and Trade Reports* 296 (May 1905): 252–68.

Yssouribehere, Pedro. "Investigación agrícola en el Territorio de Misiones." *Anales del Ministerio de Agricultura* 1, no. 9 (1904): 1–222.

Zago, Manrique, ed. *Pioneros de la Argentina, los inmigrantes judíos/Pioneers in Argentina, the Jewish Immigrants.* Buenos Aires: Manrique Zago, 1982.

Zahm, J. A. *Through South America's Southland.* New York: D. Appleton & Co., 1916.

Zamboni, Benito. *Escenas familiares campestres.* Posadas, Argentina: Universidad Nacional de Misiones, 1999.

Zapata, María Elisa, Alicia Rovirosa, and Esteban Carmuega. *La mesa argentina en las últimas dos décadas. Cambios en el patrón de consumo de alimentos (1996–2013).* Buenos Aires: Centro de Estudios sobre Nutrición Infantil, 2016.

Zavala, Silvio. "Apuntes históricos sobre la moneda del Paraguay." *El Trimestre Económico* 13, no. 49(1) (1946): 126–43.

Ziman, Ladislao, and Alfonso Scherer. *La selva vencida: Crónica del Departamento Igazú.* Buenos Aires: Ediciones Marymar, 1976.

Zlotchew, Clark M. "Tango from the Inside: Interview with Enrique Cadícamo." *The Journal of Popular Culture* 21, no. 3 (1987): 131–43.

INDEX

Note: figures and maps are indicated by page numbers followed by *fig.* and *map.*

and, 2–4, 14; yerba trade and, 77, 80, 84, 99. *See also* Paraná

Brazilian yerba: concerns about adulteration, 15–16, 138, 141; congonilla and, 15–17, 137–38, 167; cultivation and, 76; exports of, 80, 137, 164–65, 167–68, 170, 174, 178, 185, 313n41; health risks of, 15–16, 137–38, 167; inferiority claims, 14; production of, 14–15, 79, 92, 167–68, 281–82; taxation of, 84, 164–65, 167; wild yerbales and, 86, 167

Britain: coffee consumption in, 72–73, 244; importance of tea in, 3, 72; invasion of Buenos Aires, 70, 73; proposal to capture Buenos Aires, 48, 70; tea consumption in, 72–73, 119, 138, 244; yerba consumption in, 142, 145; yerba trade and, 69–70, 72, 296n117

Buenos Aires: botanical research in, 75; British invasion of, 70, 73; cafés and urban culture in, 108–9, 302n37; conflict with Paraguay, 77–80; cosmopolitanism and, 98–99, 221; deaths due to disease in, 110; defense expenditures in, 64; elite consumption of mate, 4, 6, 19, 122; European trade and, 48, 68, 74; independence movements and, 77–78; modernity and, 98, 109; superiority of elite in, 104, 301n19; *tertulias* and yerba consumption, 39–40, 100; yerba consumption in, 100, 105–10; yerba production and, 83–84; yerba trade and, 55, 59–60, 72, 84. *See also* Argentina

Bullrich, Silvina, 254

Bunge, Eduardo G., 169

Burmeister, Carlos, 135

caá (Guaraní), 10, 12, 17–18, 23, 26

Ca'a Yari (the goddess of yerba mate), 17, 22

caffeinated beverages: Europeans and, 30–31, 36; habit-forming, 37; middle class and, 266; purported health benefits of, 36–37; yerba mate as, 8–9, 30, 145–46, 162, 283

Caldcleugh, Alexander, 79–80

Campo, Luzán del, 242

canchada. See dried yerba (*canchada*)

Cantero, Marcelo, 277

Cárcano, Miguel Ángel, 184–85

Cardiel, José, 40, 50, 53

Carril, Hugo del, 191, 215–17

Casal, Pedro del, 37, 290n78

Catholicism, 23, 25, 30, 32–33, 36. *See also* Jesuit missionaries

Cavallo, Domingo, 271

Cawy Bottling Company, 147

Ceballos, Mariano, 180

Charrúas, 52–53

Chile: botanical expeditions to, 71; New Song Movement in, 253; sugar trade and, 66; tea and coffee consumption in, 108; yerba consumption in, 29, 39, 42, 108; yerba shortages in, 79; yerba taxation in, 64–67; yerba trade and, 70, 72, 80, 108. *See also* Potosí; Santiago

chocolate: European trade and, 8, 30, 48–49, 67, 74; Indigenous cultivation of, 43, 61; Indigenous peoples and, 8, 21; Spanish suspicion of, 30, 33; *tecomate* and, 286n20

Cithaalin, 50, 52

Clavigero, Francesco Saverio, 13

Clemenceau, Georges, 108

Cleveland, Grover, 85

Club-Mate, 20, 147, 282

coca, 11, 42–43, 61, 285n13

cocido (yerba mate as tea): families and, 263, 266, 274; immigrants and, 125; laborers and, 127, 139, 232; marketed as te-mate, 223, 322n54; military and, 144; Perón and, 243, 263, 323n81; youth culture and, 254

coffee: Argentine consumption of, 230–31, 247, 255, 264, 266, 274, 277; associations with upward mobility, 247, 264, 266; Brazilian valorization program, 172–73, 179; British consumption of, 72–73, 244; colonial economy and, 4; elite consumption of, 108, 274, 277; European consumption of, 6, 8, 12, 30, 48, 74, 289n45; taxation of, 73; working class and, 231; yerba mate as substitute for, 148, 247, 250–51, 266, 277

côgôi (Kaingang), 10, 17–18, 23, 26

Colatastinés people, 52

colonization: ban on yerbales in, 89; European immigrants and, 19, 132; Misiones region and, 89–91, 96, 134–35, 154–55, 157; yerba cultivation and, 151, 155; yerba production and, 96

colonos, 134, 157–58, 279, 306n10

Comercio Libre (Free Trade), 71

Comisión Reguladora de la Yerba Mate (CRYM): government intervention and, 220, 258–59; impact on workers, 208; ineffectiveness of, 261–62, 267; large processors and, 257; liquidation of, 271–72, 277; Misiones intervention in, 258–61; reform of, 256–58; regulation of yerba sector by, 160, 187, 231, 260, 266; small and medium sized growers and, 187, 256–57; Socialist opposition to, 206

Communism: capitalist exploitation of yerba workers and, 19, 212, 216, 282; deregulation and, 271; labor rights and, 190, 207, 214–15; mythologizing of yerba workers, 191

Companhia Matte Larangeia, 164

Compañía Eldorado Colonización y Explotación de Bosques Ltda., 151, 155, 310n142

Compañía Larangeira Mendes y Cia, 92

Confederación General de Trabajo, 233

congonha, 16–17, 287n43

congonilla, 15–17, 137–38, 167

Conquest of the Desert, 22, 119

Convertibility Plan, 270, 273

Corrado, Alberto, 148

Corrientes: agriculture in, 77, 87–88; civil war in, 82; *colonos* in, 134; economic policy and, 85; latifundia system in, 88; Misiones and, 297n25; yerba cultivation in, 149; yerbales in, 81–82, 89, 299n67; yerba production and, 6–7, 84, 297n32; yerba trade and, 78–79, 84. *See also* northeast borderlands

Costa, Lysimaco Ferreira da, 168–69

Council of Indies, 35, 44, 56, 60, 68

Cresser, Luke, 79

criollo identity: Argentina and, 22; beef and wheat products, 8; cuisine and, 6, 116–17, 242; culture and, 116, 119, 121, 123, 125, 129, 174, 211, 228, 237, 243;

folklore movement and, 241–42; *gauchos* (cowboys) and, 114, 116–17, 129, 214, 229, 242; immigrants and, 123, 125–26; mixed race and, 211; modernity and, 248; nationalism and, 123, 126, 219, 229, 231, 237, 241–42; nostalgia and, 116; rural associations of, 112, 211, 229; tango songs and, 229; theater and, 116, 305n116; yerba consumption and, 6, 36, 39, 43, 112, 116–17, 125, 129, 229, 242–44, 247; yerba marketing and, 228–29, 237; yerba workers and, 212, 218

Crist, 268–69

Cruz de Malta, 92

CRYM. *See* Comisión Reguladora de la Yerba Mate (CRYM)

Cuaraçí, Juan, 25

Cuba, 146–47, 197, 217, 282

Cunha, Luis da, 72

Cunninghame Graham, R. B., 117

Customs Law of 1835, 84

Daireaux, Godofredo, 112–13

De la Madrid, Alonso, 31–32

Demarchi, Verónica Capurro de, 126

Descalzi, Cayetano, 105

Dhers, Cinthia Solange, 1–3

Díaz Usandivaras, Julio, 123–25

Diderot, Denis, 69

Dobal, 267, 267*fig.*, 268, 268*fig.*, 269

Dobrizhoffer, Martin, 37, 40, 52, 64, 72–73

dried yerba (*canchada*): Argentine imports of, 181, 313n41; corporatism and, 179; pricing for, 167, 261–62, 280; tariffs and, 162–66, 169, 312n8; yerba production and, 162, 181

Duarte, Eva. *See* Perón, Evita

Duhau, Luis, 178, 180

East India Company (EIC), 72–73

Ebelot, Afredo, 110, 113

economic policy: Argentine newspapers on, 185–86; *canasta familiar,* 262; corporatism and, 179–80; deregulation and, 270–73; free market reforms and, 250–51, 262, 267, 280; free trade and, 173, 175, 177; government intervention and, 178–79, 184–87, 232–33, 256–61,

International Commercial Congress, 143–44
International Monetary Fund (IMF), 260,
    272
International Tea Market Expansion
    Board, 224
International Treaty for the Suppression of
    the White Slave Trade, 195
Irala, Martínez de, 53
Isabelle, Arsène, 100

Jara, Victor, 253–54
Jê-speaking people, 22
Jesuit missionaries: aversion to yerba mate,
    23, 27, 31–32, 287n7; criticism of Indian
    yerbales labor, 44–45; discovery of
    yerba attributed to, 22, 304n110; expul-
    sion of, 81; gifting yerba to converts,
    51–52; Indigenous peoples and, 23;
    prohibition on yerba consumption, 35;
    provisioning of yerba for Indigenous,
    49–52; Spanish empire and, 49–52;
    substitution of yerba for alcohol, 50;
    written sources on yerba, 12, 23–24,
    29–30, 49; yerba cultivation and, 51, 81,
    134; yerba production and, 35, 42–43;
    yerba trade and, 51
Jewish immigrants, 126, 128–29
Junta Nacional de Carnes, 179
Justicialista Party, 257–58, 260
Justo, Agustín P., 179–80, 182
Justo, Juan B., 203, 205
J. Walter Thompson, 222, 228

Kaingang: ceremonial use of yerba, 24;
    côgôî (yerba), 10, 12, 17–18, 23, 26; dis-
    covery of yerba by, 22, 282; identifica-
    tion of, 287n6; Jesuit missionaries and,
    23–25; Misiones region and, 86; yerba
    labor and, 46; yerba mate consumption
    and, 5, 10, 22–24, 281; yerba production
    and, 86. See also Indigenous peoples
Kanner, Markos, 204, 207
Keynes, John Maynard, 173
Kichwa people, 18, 287n50
Kirchner, Cristina, 280
Kirchner, Néstor, 280
Koebel, W. H., 126
Kordon, Bernardo, 254

laborers: beneficios and, 46; European
    immigrants as, 87, 114; exploitation
    of, 190–91, 196; importance of yerba
    mate to, 37–39; Indigenous peoples as,
    43–44; Indigenous women as, 34;
    mita labor draft and, 46, 291n116;
    muckraking journalism and, 190–91;
    rural conditions and, 205–6, 210,
    214–15; tobacco rations and, 38–39;
    union organizing and, 210, 214, 216,
    232–33; yerba rations and, 38–39, 53,
    127. See also working class; yerba
    workers
Labor Party (Partido Laborista), 219, 232
Lagier, Eugenio, 151, 155
Lahitte, Emilio, 15–16, 137–38
La Industrial Paraguaya, 92–93, 164
Lanusse, Juan José, 90
Larangeira, Mendes, & Cia., 164
Larangeira, Tomás, 92, 164
La Rubia del Camino, 244
Las aguas bajan turbias, 215–17, 319n109
Ledesma Valderrama, Martín de, 53
Leguizamón, Honorio, 139–40
Leiva, Luciano, 151
León Pinelo, Antonio de, 68, 295n96
Lesage, Julio, 139
Liebig colony, 310n139
Lindsay, Kenneth, 158
Llamas, Antonio de, 136
López, Carlos Antonio, 78–79
López, José M., 202
Love, George Thomas, 100
Lozano, Pedro, 24, 53

MacCann, William, 105
Machoni, Antonio, 35
Mackinnon y Coelho, 171–72, 221
Mafalda, 247
Maidana, Bonifacio, 86
Mansilla, Lucio, 162
Manuel Belgrano, 150
Maracayú, 44–45
Marcovich, Alejandro, 254
Martín, Julio Ulises, 131, 133, 136, 157, 212
Martínez de Irala, Domingo, 34
Martínez de Salazar, Joseph, 64
Martínez Estrada, Ezequiel, 244

Martín y Cía.: yerba labor and, 212–13; yerba marketing and, 163, 223–24; yerba plantations and, 131–32, 135–36, 153, 157, 306n24

Masseta, Simón, 25–26

Massiac, Barthélemy de, 69

Mastrillo Duran, Nicolas, 39

mate, 12–13, 16, 40, 41fig.. See also yerba mate

"Mate Amargo" (Glusberg), 128

Materva Soft Drink Company, 146–47, 282

Matiaúda, Vicente, 211–13

Matte Larangeira, 92

Mattè Non-Alcoholic Beverage Syndicate, 146

Medrano, Luis J., 234–35, 235fig.

Mendes, Francisco, 92

Mendes, Ricardo Antonio, 92

Mendoza, Pedro de, 30

Menem, Carlos: cronyism and, 275; deregulation and, 270–72; as governor of La Rioja, 249, 270; mate consumption and, 249–51, 270, 276; populist campaign and, 249–51, 269

"El Mensú" (Ayala), 217, 320n115

Mercado Consignatario (MC), 259–60, 325n34

Mexico, 68, 236, 260

middle class: caffeinated beverages and, 266; consumer culture and, 220–22, 273; as "new poor", 265–66, 269; rejection of yerba mate by, 4, 6, 120–21, 246–47; standard of living and, 3, 273; threat of working class to, 246–47; as threat to elites, 114; yerba consumption and, 266–68, 277; yerba marketing and, 227, 235–36. See also social class

Miers, John, 14

Mígiuez Bonino, Jose, 253

Misiones: agriculture in, 77, 88–91; colonization of, 89–91, 96, 134–35, 154–55, 157; colonos in, 134, 158; contested territory in, 85–86; debt peonage and, 198–201; development of, 86–88, 91; ethnic diversity in, 133, 154; European immigrants and, 90–91; federalization of, 88–89, 93; immigrants and, 87–91, 133, 135, 153–55, 157, 159; Indigenous control

of, 86; isolation in, 93, 198, 216; land ownership in, 133–34, 158; latifundia system in, 88, 133, 149–50, 158; as part of Corrientes, 82, 297n25; population loss in, 87, 298n53; white slavery rhetoric and, 198–99, 202, 204; yerba cultivation in, 19, 95–96, 132–36, 149–51, 153–55, 157, 183, 210fig.; yerba grower strike in, 183; yerbales in, 81–82, 91, 93–97; yerba mate marketing and, 274–76; yerba production in, 6–7, 16, 86, 91, 168–69, 275, 297n32; yerba sector refrm and, 258–61; yerba worker exploitation in, 189, 195–96, 198–202, 206–8, 216–17, 320n114. See also northeast borderlands; Posadas

Mitre, Bartolomé, 104

mixed-race people (mestizaje): cultural practices and, 34; growth in numbers of, 34; immigrants as role models for, 87; whiteness and, 197; white slavery rhetoric and, 20, 190, 193, 196; yerba consumption and, 21, 34, 166; yerba labor and, 151, 189–90, 193, 196–97, 211, 218

modernity: consumer culture and, 220–22; mate associations with poverty and, 20, 220; yerba marketing and, 222–23, 225, 227, 229, 235–36, 239, 241, 244, 248, 320n5

molida. See processed yerba (molida)

Montana Brewing Company, 146

Montenegro, Pedro, 25

Monvoisin, Raymond, 105, 106fig.

Morel, E.D., 191

Moreyra brothers, 213–14

naming of yerba mate: centrality of gourds in, 13–14; Guaraní people and, 10, 12–13, 17, 286n20; Kaingang people and, 10, 12, 17; as paraguariensis, 13–14; as Paraguayan yerba (yerba del Paraguay), 12; Spanish conflation with coca, 11, 285n13; Spanish replacement of Indigenous terminology, 10–14, 18, 286n20, 287n44

Ñande Yerba, 259–60

Ñanduty yerba mate, 124, 124fig., 125

Napoleon I, 75–76

nation-state, 19, 49, 76, 82, 86

Sekt-Bronte, 147
Seoane, Manuel, 127
Simón Padrós, Juan, 176–77
Sití, Francisco Javier, 83
"Slacker" (Aulino), 246
slavery, 93, 189, 193, 196. *See also* white
  slavery rhetoric
social class: Argentine identity and, 176;
  blurring of, 246; foodstuffs and, 273–
  74; labor rights and, 205; popular class
  threat to elites, 3, 246; sharing mate
  and, 110–11; threat of middle class and,
  114; yerba as status symbol, 25, 31; yerba
  consumption and, 1–6, 9, 12, 19, 40–42,
  99, 119–21, 128, 176, 281; yerba paraphernalia and, 40. *See also* elites; middle
  class; working class
Socialist Party: anti-prostitution and,
  195–96; on capitalist exploitation of
  yerba workers, 189–90, 202–3, 205–7,
  215, 282; free trade and, 166, 175, 177–
  78; internationalism and, 166, 183;
  mythologizing of yerba workers, 191;
  opposition to yerba regulatory board,
  183–84, 186–87, 206; urban labor and,
  183, 206; on yerba consumption, 176
Sociedad Rural, 179, 181
Solari, Juan A., 189, 205–7
Solari, Justino, 202–3
Soldado de la guardia de Rosas (Monvoisin),
  105, 106*fig.*
South America: botanical expeditions to,
  71, 75; European writers on, 41–42;
  independence movements and, 49,
  76–77; map of, 7*map*; Spanish conquest
  of, 29–30; Spanish empire in, 14, 49,
  52–53, 100; taxation of yerba, 60–67;
  Wars of Independence in, 76; yerba
  consumption in, 2, 4–5, 8, 10, 18–19, 21,
  29, 36, 39–43; yerba trade and, 48, 52–55
Southey, Robert, 69
Spaniards: adoption of Guaraní practices,
  30–31; advocacy for yerba production,
  33–34; aversion to yerba mate, 29–32, 35;
  caffeinated beverages and, 30; compar-
  ing yerba to Chinese tea, 12; marriage
  with Guaraní women, 34; naming of
  yerba mate, 10–12; yerba as taxable

commodity, 4, 37–38, 290n77; yerba
  consumption and, 39, 291n86
Spanish Crown: *Comercio Libre* (Free Trade)
  and, 71; commercial policies of, 4, 57;
  expulsion of Jesuits, 81; inspection of
  Indian labor, 44, 46; payments in yerba
  mate, 51, 58–59; silver trade and, 57; South
  American conquest and, 29–30; taxation
  of yerba, 61–64, 67; trade policies and, 8,
  48, 67–72, 74, 101; use of yerba as diplomatic tool, 52; yerba production and, 36,
  55; yerba trade and, 67–68
Spanish empire: alternate currencies in,
  57–59; *asiento* licenses and, 69; geographic expansion of yerba consumption and, 53–54; independence movements and, 76; Jesuit missionaries and,
  49–52; use of yerba mate as diplomatic
  tool, 52–53; yerba mate and, 4, 18,
  48–49; yerba mate monopoly and, 63;
  yerba trade and, 54–56, 60–61
Spinetto, Alfredo, 166
Szychowski, Juan, 262

TabacanVi, 26
tango songs, 229, 244–45, 321n23
Taragüi, 17, 255
tea: adulteration concerns, 138; Argentine
  consumption of, 255; associations with
  upward mobility, 223, 247; British
  consumption of, 3, 72–73, 244; colonial
  economy and, 4; competition with
  yerba, 73; educational texts and, 111;
  European consumption of, 6, 8, 12, 30,
  48, 74, 289n45; Indian cultural practices and, 4; promotion of, 111; taxation
  of, 73; yerba mate as substitute for, 148,
  247, 250–51, 266, 277
Temple, William, 70
tereré, 5
Thays, Carlos, 135
Saint Thomas, 17, 22, 36
Tierra y Yerbales S. A., 212
tobacco: Indigenous cultivation of, 43;
  Jesuit gifts of, 51–53; rations for Indian
  labor, 32, 38–39; Spanish use of, 21, 30;
  as threat to Catholicism, 33; trade in, 8,
  49, 57–58

Toledo, Francisco de, 291n116
Torin, Samuel, 69
Torre, Juan Carlos, 234
Torre, Lisandro de la, 167
Torre, Manuel Antonio de la, 59–60
Torrejón, Cipriano, 111
Torres Bollo, Diego de, 32–33, 44
Tractor Protest (*Tractorazo*), 279
trade: *Comercio Libre* (Free Trade), 71;
economic policy and, 83–84; foreign
foodstuffs and, 30, 289n43; livestock
exports and, 84; Paraguay and, 289n42;
Río de la Plata region and, 8, 64; Span-
ish restrictions on, 8, 48, 67–72, 74, 101;
taxation of Paraguayan, 78; tobacco
and, 8, 49, 57–58; yerba tariffs and, 84.
See also yerba trade
Triple Alliance War, 85, 92–93
Tupi, 22–23, 287n44

Ulloa, Antonio de, 43, 71
United States: coffee-wheat trade agree-
ment, 175; European immigrants and,
114; Great Depression in, 173; market-
ing of yerba mate in, 17–18, 143, 143*fig.*,
144, 146–47; yerba mate and, 142–44;
yerba mate consumption in, 8, 10
upper class. *See* elites
Uribe S. A., 92
Uriburu, José Félix, 173–74, 179
Urquiza, Justo José de, 85
Urquiza Anchorena family, 212
Uruguay, 4, 85, 116, 124–25, 129, 145, 278
Uzal, Conrado Martín, 137, 144

Valle, Gonzalo del, 63, 288n30
Varela, Alfredo: *El río oscuro,* 213–14, 216;
ethnic stereotyping of exploiters, 212;
on exploitation of yerba workers, 191,
207–8, 210–15; on labor organizing,
208, 210, 214, 216; muckraking exposés
and, 191, 207; novel adaptation and,
215–16; racialized language and,
210–12
Vargas, Getúlio, 180
Vega, Garcilaso de la, 13
Villanueva, Amaro, 242
Volcker, Paul, 272

Walsh, Rodolfo, 217–18
Weinberg, Gregorio, 254
wheat: Argentine-Brazil trade accord,
180–81; Argentine exports of, 132, 161,
174–75, 185; Argentine production of, 8,
19; Brazil-U.S. trade, 175
whiteness: Argentine identity and, 190, 197,
204, 211, 239; European immigrants
and, 204; mate traditions and, 5; mixed
race and, 190, 197; white slavery rhetoric
and, 93, 193–200, 202, 204, 211
white slavery rhetoric: labor activists and,
195; mixed-race people (*mestizaje*) and,
20, 190, 193, 196; social reformers and,
195; yerba workers and, 20, 190, 193–97
Wilde, José Antonio, 39, 107
Workers of the Argentine North (Solari), 205
working class: coffee consumption and, 231;
consumer culture and, 219–20, 234–36;
criollo nationalism and, 126, 207;
foodstuffs and, 273–74; gaucho myth
and, 103; hunger and, 262–65; immigrants and, 126–27; labor rights and,
214–15, 232–34; Peronism and, 219,
232–35, 283; rural lifestyle and, 141, 230;
standard of living and, 182, 230–32, 234,
248, 273; upward mobility and, 245–46,
323n100; wage increases under Perón,
233–34; yerba consumption and, 19, 42,
99, 120, 127, 174, 182, 230–31, 234–35,
235*fig.,* 244, 246, 274; yerba marketing
and, 235–36. *See also* laborers

X-Ray of the Pampa (Martínez Estrada),
244

Yachack, 18
Yaguariguay, Rodrigo, 25
Yaro people, 53
Ychoalay, 52
yerba *caamini,* 42, 51
yerba consumption: in Argentina, 99–100,
119–20, 129–30, 152; Argentine efforts
against, 105–13; associations with poverty, 20, 219–21, 244–48, 253, 263–66;
bombilla and, 2, 6, 9–10, 14, 29, 99, 147,
255; centrality of gourds in, 13; clandestine, 19, 99, 120–22, 129; class-based,

1–6, 9, 99, 176–77, 281; criollo identity and, 3, 29, 36, 42, 174, 229, 242–43, 247; cultural importance of, 251; decline in, 20, 108, 113, 219–20, 241, 243–44, 246–48, 250, 254–55; elite paraphernalia and, 40, 41*fig.*, 42; elites and, 4, 19, 40–42, 99, 107–9; Europeans and, 8, 21, 31; flavorings and, 40; *gauchos* (cowboys) and, 5–6, 19, 99, 103; geographic expansion of, 53–54, 141–48; habit-forming, 37, 39, 65–66; health concerns and, 15–16, 33, 137–38; hygiene concerns and, 109–12, 123, 129, 222–23, 302n43, 320n6; immigrants and, 6, 99, 125–29; increased productivity and, 140, 307n43; Indigenous techniques for, 28–29, 31, 99, 282; laborers and, 38–39, 53, 127; leftists and social reformers, 253–54; middle class and, 266–68, 277; military and, 144–45; outside South America, 8, 10; perceptions of, 107–8; preparation of infusion and, 27–28, 144, 147, 223; prohibitions on police and, 302n39; racial mixing and, 21, 34, 39; regional identity and, 39; resurgence in, 250–51, 262, 266–67, 272–78, 280–81, 328n5; in the Río de la Plata region, 5, 8, 12, 38, 41–42, 100–101; rural associations of, 102–5, 109, 112–13; as shared social activity, 1–2, 6, 9–10, 37, 42, 109–12, 117, 123, 248, 274, 278, 282; Spanish adoption of, 21, 31–32; Spanish elites aversion to, 29–33; as substitute for alcohol, 50, 145–47, 225–26; as substitute for tea and coffee, 148, 247, 250–51, 266, 277; symbolic meaning and, 127–29; tango songs and, 229, 244–45, 321n23; *tertulias* (social gatherings) and, 39–40, 100, 101*fig.*, 108; transnational, 124, 124*fig.*, 125, 281; universality of, 39–41; as a waste of time, 105, 113, 122–23, 176, 246; working class and, 19, 42, 99, 120, 127, 174, 182, 230–31, 234–35, 244, 246, 274. *See also* Indigenous yerba consumption

yerba cultivation: in Argentina, 14–17, 76, 81–82, 85, 95–96, 131–33, 148–55, 157–59; Bonpland and, 75–76, 81–82, 84–85, 131;

in Brazil, 14–15; congonilla and, 15–16; corporatist regulatory boards and, 179–80; economic growth and, 130; European immigrants and, 149–50, 150*fig.*, 151, 153, 155, 157–59, 282, 309n111; expansion of, 95–96; federally-supported colonies for, 150, 309n111; germination and, 134–36; government intervention and, 178–79, 184–87, 256–61; Guaraní-Jesuit missions and, 51, 81, 134; Indigenous labor and, 151–52; initial investment in, 157–58; mechanized harvesting and, 316n4; in Misiones, 19, 95–96, 132–36, 149–51, 153, 155, 157–58, 183, 210*fig.*; nationalist rhetoric and, 135–41, 161–62, 169; northeast borderlands and, 19, 76–77, 80–81, 136, 149; profitability of, 131–33, 135–37, 148, 151–53, 161–62; protectionism and, 166–67, 170–71, 174, 177; regulatory commission and, 182–85; sales of unprocessed yerba, 261; tariffs and, 160–62, 311n3; transportation costs and, 148; tree species and, 14–16, 286n30. *See also* yerba growers

yerba *de palos,* 42, 51

yerba growers: agricultural workers and, 158–59, 177, 205; Brazilian competition and, 160, 167–68, 178; CRYM and, 161, 187, 256–58, 266, 272; economic policies and, 161; general strike and, 182–83; government intervention and, 163, 170–71, 173, 177–79, 181, 184, 186, 257–59, 261, 272, 279–80, 282; military dictatorship and, 254; protectionism and, 166, 177–78; small and medium sized, 158, 169, 182–84, 186–87, 256–58, 272, 279–80; Tractor Protest (*Tractorazo*) and, 279; Yerba Mate Growers Association and, 169–70; yerba prices and, 167–68, 179, 181–82, 256, 261, 272, 279–80. *See also* yerba cultivation

yerbales: attempts to protect, 94–97; government investigations and, 202–3; government ownership of, 89, 94–97; Indian labor in, 32, 34–35, 43–46, 56, 91, 93; Indigenous claims to, 83; Indigenous harvesting of, 4, 27, 43, 51, 81; as mines,

yerbales *(continued)*
62, 76, 89; in the northeast borderlands, 77, 91–97, 134; overharvesting and, 93–96, 200, 205; privatization of, 96; prohibition on Indian labor in, 32–35, 44, 46; smuggling and, 163; taxation of, 149, 312n8; worker exploitation in, 191–99, 213–14, 216; workers in, 209*fig.;* yerba tree, 11*fig.*

yerba marketing: affordability and, 226–27, 320n13; bombilla and, 147; as coffee, 255; consumer culture and, 220–21, 227, 229, 235–36; forms of drinking mate in, 223–25; *gauchos* and, 237, 239; health benefits and, 144, 281; Indigenous roots of mate in, 17–18, 287n50; as an infusion, 144, 147, 223; Misiones region and, 274–76; modernity and, 222–23, 227, 229, 235–36, 239, 241, 244, 248, 320n5; nationalism and, 172, 212, 228–29, 236–37; Paraguayan yerba and, 163–64, 171; paternalism and, 241; Peronist identity and, 234; as personal drink, 222–23, 282; political campaigns and, 249–50; as a South American drink, 281; as a temperance drink, 146–47, 225–26; in the United States, 17–18, 143, 143*fig.*, 144, 146–47; upper- and middle-class lifestyle and, 227, 229, 231, 236–37; to upper income levels, 276–77; whiteness and, 237; working class and, 235–36; yerba mate as energy drink, 20; youth culture and, 252–53, 276–78. *See also* Salus

yerba mate: Argentine identity and, 5–8, 20, 99, 104, 118, 120, 123–29, 132, 243, 255, 278, 280–83, 328n5; associations with *gauchos,* 5–6, 105, 115–22, 129, 281; as a basic necessity, 36, 38–39, 95, 120, 152, 162, 171, 230, 262, 264–65, 304; as caffeinated stimulant, 8–9, 30, 145–46, 162, 283; as commodity money, 56–59; compared to Chinese tea, 12; consumer prices for, 152–53, 162, 165, 171, 182, 184, 186, 261–62, 266–69, 272, 280; cultural authenticity and, 5–6, 20, 118, 251, 281, 283; as diplomatic tool, 52–53; economic importance of, 48, 60–61; educational

texts and, 111; energizing properties of, 25, 50; European scholarship and, 141–42; European trade and, 30, 289n42; festivals and, 242, 323n72; as foodstuff, 30, 38–39, 230, 264–65; health benefits of, 10, 21, 25–26, 36–37, 42, 139–40, 281; Indigenous discovery of, 22, 282, 304n110; as inferior good, 247, 255; nationalist rhetoric and, 15–16, 137–41; natural habitat of, 7*map;* origin stories of, 17, 22, 36; popular culture and, 242, 244–47, 253–54, 267, 267*fig.*, 268–69, 324n108; rural associations of, 102–5, 220; scientific study of effects, 139; sources of, 13–17; Spanish negotiations with Indigenous and, 51–54; taxation of, 182, 185–86. *See also Ilex paraguariensis*

Yerba Mate AG, 157

Yerba Mate Gardel, 229

Yerba Maté Tea Co., 143, 143*fig.*, 144, 146

yerba production: *beneficios* and, 46, 295n82; caudillos competition for, 83; colonization and, 96; deregulation and, 272; dried yerba and, 162, 181; economic policy and, 3, 9, 267; exploitation of Indigenous workers, 86; Guaraní and, 27–28, 43; immigrants and, 133; Indigenous technologies for, 27–28, 28*fig.*, 43–44; industrialization and, 161–62; Jesuit missions and, 35, 42–43; Kaingang and, 86; laborer draft and, 46, 292n116; nationalist rhetoric and, 171–72; overproduction and, 262; royal approval of, 35–36, 45; Spanish advocacy for, 33–34; Spanish prohibitions on, 31–35, 289n50; transnational, 125, 164; wild yerbales and, 162. *See also* Argentinian yerba; Brazilian yerba; dried yerba *(canchada)*; processed yerba *(molida)*

yerba trade: Argentine-Brazilian relations, 164–71, 174, 178, 180; Argentinian restrictions on, 78–80; Brazil and, 77, 80, 84, 99; British merchants and, 69; British prohibitions on, 73, 296n117; Buenos Aires and, 55, 59–60; commercial potential of, 48–49, 71–72; compe-

CALIFORNIA STUDIES IN FOOD AND CULTURE

Darra Goldstein, Editor

Founded in 1893,
UNIVERSITY OF CALIFORNIA PRESS
publishes bold, progressive books and journals
on topics in the arts, humanities, social sciences,
and natural sciences—with a focus on social
justice issues—that inspire thought and action
among readers worldwide.

The UC PRESS FOUNDATION
raises funds to uphold the press's vital role
as an independent, nonprofit publisher, and
receives philanthropic support from a wide
range of individuals and institutions—and from
committed readers like you. To learn more, visit
ucpress.edu/supportus.

www.ingramcontent.com/pod-product-compliance
Lightning Source LLC
Chambersburg PA
CBHW020817270326
41928CB00006B/381